the BISHOP, *the* MULLAH, *&* *the* SMARTPHONE

the **BISHOP**, the **MULLAH**,
& the **SMARTPHONE**

*The Journey of Two Religions
into the Digital Age*

Bryan Winters

RESOURCE *Publications* • Eugene, Oregon

THE BISHOP, THE MULLAH, AND THE SMARTPHONE
The Journey of Two Religions into the Digital Age

Resource Publications
An Imprint of Wipf and Stock Publishers
199 W. 8th Ave., Suite 3
Eugene, OR 97401

www.wipfandstock.com

ISBN 13: 978-1-4982-1792-7

Manufactured in the U.S.A.   04/28/2015

Unless indicated otherwise all verses quoted from the Qu'ran are from the Saheeh International version, The Qu'ran: Arabic Text with Corresponding English Meanings.

Unless indicated otherwise, all verses quoted from the Bible are from the North American Standard Bible (NASB), from the Lockman Foundation.

CONTENTS

ACKNOWLEDGMENTS

IT SEEMS FITTING IN a book about unknown outcomes that I should thank the digital world. Beginning for me in 1982, IBM drenched me in computer knowledge, and not much soaked in, but perhaps more than I thought. They dominated that business and looked after their own, a memory I still cherish. Inadvertently, like in all commerce, young entrants transition from gratitude for a salary, to perceiving the smoke and mirrors pervading the information technology sector. For all this, I am grateful for my exposure to many levels and nations within this sometimes mystical realm.

Perhaps the church should have been first in this list, a collective that will outlast any I.T. company despite mixed reviews since its inception. Their intended outcomes were not always explicit, but I couldn't have written this book without a background in one faith.

Which brings me to the third component—it's difficult getting inside the heads of believers in a competitive religion, and still harder to grasp their hearts. Neither atheists nor agnostics have an advantage either. By definition they don't feel the pull of any theistic belief, and if that hasn't happened, it's awkward explaining how billions of others do. I got lucky, or the universe led to Safwan Mason. He painstakingly corrected spelling and grammatical errors whilst schooling me on Islam, a once chosen belief of his. Since I have one foot in the church and the other out, he was the best person for the job because he mirrored that.

Of course my lovely wife should have come at the top, my best friend who encourages my niche interests. But then we share intended outcomes, a benefit of face to face communication in a digitally imaged globe.

1

THE PRIEST AND THE PRINTER

FIVE HUNDRED YEARS AGO Europe experienced a foretaste of the digital revolution: the industrial printer replicated handwriting. It was the first time Westerners duplicated knowledge with a machine—and it split European Christianity.

It all started when Martin Luther nailed his 'Ninety Five Theses on the Power and Efficacy of Indulgences' on a church door in Wittenberg, Germany, on October, 31st, 1517. However, when Protestants celebrate five hundred years of existence, which they will in 2017, the printer might not get much mention.

In fact I'm not sure what they will commemorate because so many stories have altered over those five centuries. For at least the first four, Protestants were quite vehement about Roman Catholics, even referring to the Pope as the Whore from Babylon, mentioned in the Bible in the book of Revelation. In our twenty–first century ecumenical world of inter–denominational dialogue, those phrases are unlikely to be recalled into official memory—especially if Roman Catholics and Orthodox priests are invited. Some blend of truth and fiction will emerge, although it won't sound like mythology during the speeches.

We might see lines of clerics from different corners of the globe, dressed in symbolic garb, amiably chatting. Watching this mimicry of dress, much of the world will recognize them as clergy, but the commentators will need to inform viewers that the clues to telling them apart are in the headgear. Catholic Cardinals wear pointed red galeros, whereas the hatless men in beige suits are televangelists.

In these beginning paragraphs we've already encountered four themes that will run through this book;

- Memory

- Mythology

- Media

- Mimicry

These themes are there because the journey of Christianity and Islam into the digital age is driven by a matrix of factors, just as the birth of Protestantism was five centuries ago. These four Ms are not categories. They are different views on religions. Not only that, but the Ms enable us to compare events and circumstances between these two faiths. Parallel views help us understand both of their pasts, and give clues to their present states.

Let's dig a little deeper into the printer story.

Mythologies about the sixteenth century break from the Pope exist amongst Protestants and Catholics to this day. Many Protestants think Catholics worship Mary, the mother of Jesus, and that Catholics added books to the Bible. Catholics endlessly refute these, and Protestants endlessly repeat them.

In recent times, historians have entered the fray, and exposed this connection with the printing press. It all started around a church fund raising drive, not an uncommon event in any community. True, selling tickets to avoid perdition was a little off beam, but if Hell Pizza ever picked the idea back up today, it'd probably be a best seller. Buying an Indulgence enabled believers to earn divine credit, perhaps even ahead of spending it on a sin. I realize there is a whole genre of humor here, and the reader can search the Monty Python film archives if they like.

However, matters were more serious five hundred years back. Being burnt at the stake, or disemboweled after you've been nearly hung was still in vogue—that's right, you choke until the last second, then they lower you down for phase two. Luther was taking a serious risk. Nobody denies that.

It was the explosive expansion of the sale of Indulgences that drove him to complain. Prior to the printing press, such documents were handwritten by priests. There was no cramped industrial complex full of men of the cloth, working around the clock writing out Indulgences. Production was quite limited in fact.

Enter the printing press, and the replication problem was solved. Gutenberg himself printed thousands of Indulgences in one of the few profitable ventures he undertook, but only about 180 Bibles. As it happened, the Roman Catholic Church never formally approved the sale of Indulgences.[1] Had it been restricted to the domain of hand printing, the issue might not have generated the foment it did.

Technological advances produce unplanned outcomes. Who would have thought a printer could lead to a new worldwide religion? Ironically it annoyed at least one priest enough with its ability to multiply iniquity, then provided the means to avoid an ordained leader on earth. The very mantra of Protestantism informs us—sola scriptura—which means a sole reliance on scripture. And how do you get scripture out to the masses? You need a printing press.

It posed a challenge elsewhere too.

The first Qu'ran was printed by Venetians in 1537 coveting that huge Muslim market to the east, in the Ottoman Empire. After all, they were people of the book too. Unfortunately the Venetians didn't judge buyer demand correctly. This center of Islamic power prohibited printing in Arabic. The language was that of Allah according to Muslims, and was therefore due more respect than a mechanical device. Islamic legal scholars outlawed printing of the Qu'ran up until 1726, initially on pain of death. It took the obvious and growing power of Europe to convince the Grand Mufti, and the Muslim clergy, on the efficiency of the printing press.

My own copy of the Qu'ran was produced in collaboration with Saheeh International in Saudi Arabia, who perform "Professional Editing and Typesetting of Islamic Literature." This Qu'ran, with Arabic neatly alongside an English version, was given to me. It is careful to point out that it is not a translation. It is "The Qu'ran: Arabic Text with Corresponding English Meanings" because "The words of Allah can never be translated literally."

Let's not speculate why these disclaimers and definitions are in there yet. The point is that this printed Qu'ran exists. It also boldly states on the cover that it is a "Gift Not For Sale." I wonder if Saheeh International mimicked The Gideons International who since their inception in 1899 have given away 1.8 billion Bibles around the world.

More mythology, media and mimicry.

1. "Does the Catholic Church still sell indulgences," para. 1.

And the weaving of these two religions together like that is only possible due to everything we've remembered. We humans think that transmitted memories are the sole domain of humans. Elephants and dolphins may have recall too, but mankind grew clever at storing memory through media devices including books, the Internet, and television.

MEMORY

Memory is the building block on which the religions of man began, and yet religious leaders don't refer much to the tools of memory we all use. Goldfish, whose recall of events extends to only six seconds according to urban myth, do not form religions. Man used language and human memory to pass on knowledge before the book came, that most marvelous memory storage device. Much of this book you are now reading refers to the storing and sharing of memory through the media of books. The term 'book' can be subdivided into specific media including the hand written book, the industrially printed book, and the digitally printed book.

Categories of memory exist too. We have personal memory and cultural memory, besides many forms of stored memory. Computer memory is a step forward over books or scrolls because it does more than store memory—it processes, or reorganizes memories too. Processing of data requires programs; storing of data is simply that—putting data, audio, video and imagery in a box where we can retrieve it again. The very logo of Dropbox, one of the most well known consumer cloud storage options, portrays this as it looks like a cardboard box we might leave books in. Much, much, more 'memory' is stored this way than was ever achieved with books. As Google's Eric Schmidt tells us; "From the dawn of civilization until 2003, humankind generated five exabytes of data. Now we produce five exabytes every two days, and the pace is accelerating."[2]

Due to this the rules on memory are changing for the first time in human history. Our problem is no longer the challenge of remembering—from now on we face the problem of forgetting.

Let's put some context around cultural memory and personal memory. You can have a lot of fun with the concept of cultural memories, and it's a great phrase to drop into a dinner party conversation. Our group, or collective memories, resonate with it. In fact, they are it. All of us as individuals have forgotten more than we've remembered. Well, surprise, surprise, so

2. "Google CEO Eric Schmidt," para. 1.

have all cultures. The further back you go, the more they've forgotten. And somehow, the further back you go, the bigger were the victories, the nobler were the rulers, and the grander was the culture.

Remembering and forgetting both subdivide into active and passive. Both our religions practice 'active remembering' around their holy texts. These stored memory devices, whether in book or iPad form are endlessly recalled and reinterpreted to make sense of the world their followers live in. The holy texts are in fact past as present. They are actively remembered.

Items stored in museums are 'passively remembered.' Pots and spears sit in their glass cases, and we recall them when visiting, but they are past as past. They aren't woven into the meaning of our lives any more.

'Active forgetting' is the deliberate destruction of memory, an example of which was the burning of heretical books and their authors long ago. Early Christians nearly wiped out the gospel of Thomas seventeen centuries ago. Somehow, one copy survived until 1946, a time when it would be valued. The gospel of Thomas has moved from being actively forgotten to actively remembered. Politicians practice active forgetting as well as religions. After Chief of Soviet Security, Lavrentiy Beria, was purged in 1953 in the USSR, subscribers to the Great Soviet Encyclopedia around the world were instructed to tear out the article on Beria and replace it with one sent to them on the Bering Strait.

'Passive forgetting' is an important category. Passively forgotten items that are later rediscovered have no motive attached to them. Like the shard of a clay tablet with the price of corn on it, these traces, as cultural historian Jakob Burckhardt[3] calls them, might be date stamped information. That price of corn enables archaeologists to verify other writings claiming to be from the same era. If they have the price wrong, then maybe they were written later. Combined with archeology, a discipline called literary criticism can wreak havoc with religious beliefs using such techniques.

These concepts are not new, although they have been polished since Nietzsche mentioned the benefit of a bad memory in the nineteenth century; "Blessed are the forgetful: for they get the better even of their blunders."[4] He didn't foresee an age when that was more difficult—and neither did our two religions.

---

3. Erll et al., *Media and Cultural Memory*, 98.
4. "Friedrich Nietzsche Quotes," line 1.

MYTHOLOGY

Many Christians don't like the word mythology being applied to the Bible. Yet Jesus continually taught people using myths, only they're called parables. Despite his example many Christians treat all Old Testament stories as fact. Mythology gets mixed up with memory here because religious people often hold core beliefs that they think are fixed to historical data. A comment from a Rabbi sums up the emotional impact when deep core beliefs come into question; "When I heard for the first time that the exodus might not have happened, I did want to weep . . . then I thought, what does this matter? You have to distinguish between truth and historicity."[5] Her pain is shared, or rejected, across many faiths. It's not easy uncovering myths in your own religion. It's not so difficult finding them in another. This Rabbi reached a valid conclusion—she saw what truth really was, and it wasn't necessarily historical fact.

Another angle on mythology is illustrated by the difference between truth and reality in World War 2. After the battles of Stalingrad and El Alamein in 1942 to 1943, the General Staffs of both the Allied and German armies knew the decisive battles had been fought, and the truth was that the war was decided. Similarly, the Japanese Generals knew they were defeated after the Battle of Midway in 1942. This truth was not conveyed to the public, who needed to be inspired to further efforts. So the reality was three more years of battle with losses and gains, before the Japanese and Germans finally surrendered.

Both our religions understand this. Hardcore believers are firmly convinced their faith will triumph eventually, and indeed has already won a cosmic battle, which we will understand at some future time. Theologians in either faith see any current troubles as just the reality of the world, but certainly not the final truth.

Rather than get into debates over where facts end and myths begin, let's look at myths another way then. Myths do not claim to represent reality or truth, although they can do both. Insightful truths are often presented via fables, or in Jesus' case, through parables. Hinduism's holy book, the Bhagavad Gita, is a classic example, as two men converse about morality and war. The book of Job in the Bible is a debate where a once wealthy man ponders his demise with his friends. These two discussions may be the most famous ever recorded. Are the books of Job and the Gita factual

5. "Man versus myth," para. 2.

stories? Did Job and Hinduism's Krishna actually live? Perhaps a more appropriate question is, are the books of Job and the Gita stories of truth? Both books yield timeless insights about good and evil—much more so than any modern television documentary could.

Sometimes mythology is obvious unreality, as in the Hindu depictions of the struggle between right and wrong engraved on the walls of Angkor Wat. Of course good and evil wasn't created by men struggling with snakes, although it's interesting that Adam and Eve wrestled, metaphorically, with a serpent at the start of the Bible too. Sometimes they are not obvious unreality, as in the story of the exodus, which yet remains to be proven fact or fiction.

That's the good news.

Myths can simplify good and evil nicely sorted out between a wicked person and a righteous one, or an evil crowd and a good one. These types of myths have been indispensable in motivating armies, and starting wars by "fighting for freedom." Myths can reconfigure bygone events, turning defeat into victory, or at least a stalemate. Golden pasts can be created by those living in a blighted present. Political leaders frequently rouse their peoples with mythical heroics from bygone days. This reinvention of history has always gone on, which is why it's good to read books written fifty years ago as well as current perspectives. Opinions on Islam and Christianity have drastically shifted in just that time–frame, and we shouldn't be so naïve as to think we are beyond mythology today. If views have changed previously, they will alter again.

Sometimes we see efforts in the opposite direction, as people strive to take a past incident and shift it into a mythical category. As social tastes change, an historic event can become embarrassing, and too hurtful to acknowledge. We will track an example of this throughout this book. Active remembering and active forgetting are basic instruments in the formation of mythology. One of our broad themes is the re–mythologization of both faiths. A turbulent re–mythologization of Islam towards peace is being attempted in the world today, using the tools of active remembering and active forgetting. Muslims cannot call it re–mythologization as that would concede items are being moved out of the factual category, and into the mythical. In the long run this doesn't matter. The world just wants a successful migration to peace, and if that means forgetting a few things, then so be it.

Christianity too, has undergone various re–mythologizations during its two thousand year history, so adherents can hardly complain if another religion manages to re–engineer some ugly incidents. Yet many Christians criticize Muslims for this, not recognizing hearts and identities are torn by this globally disorderly process.

MEDIA

'The medium is the message'[6] is a phrase that reached fifty years of age in 2014, ever since Marshall McLuhan first used it in his book, Understanding Media, in 1964. Despite its vintage, it was not understood at a church gathering I attended in 2008 in Palmerston North, a university town in New Zealand. A speaker from India named Ken addressed us. Although he was genuinely Indian, Ken dressed and spoke like a Westerner. He worked for an organization spreading the gospel in India via television and radio, but they weren't making much progress. Ken said one of their problems was that Christianity was perceived in India as a modern Western religion, not suited to Indian traditional ways. Question time came. I asked Ken whether the fact he used television as his medium did not prove to the local Indian communities that indeed, yes, Christianity was such a modern Western religion. He didn't need to respond. The whole audience shouted, "no!" When it subsided, Ken asked me whether my question had been answered. Obviously outnumbered, I shrank into my seat.

That church audience thought of media as information content. When we say the media tells us this or that, we are generally referring to the story told, say about a cat stuck up a tree beside a motorway. The cat's predicament may be related by a newspaper, or a TV crew. This is still the most common use of the word media. I use the word media here after the definition coined back in the 1960s by McLuhan, who is regarded as the father of media studies. His main point was that the nature of the media alters how it is received. For example people reading the cat up the tree story in the newspaper will gain a different impression than those seeing it on TV. The media itself altered how the content would be grasped.

Not only that, but media alters other sectors of life as well, as we learnt from the industrial printer which enabled a book centric religion to evolve out of a clerical centered one. It wasn't the content, or the message conveyed—that didn't change. The words of a handwritten Bible are the

6. McLuhan, *Understanding Media*, 15.

same as those in a printed version. It was the actual media device itself, the printer, that was crucial for the Bible to spread so widely and become the mainstay of Protestantism. To be pedantic, we could argue that Protestantism might not have emerged without the printer.

McLuhan used the phrase 'The Extensions of Man' as the subtitle to Understanding Media.[7] It's still the best way to understand media. Let's take the book again. The book is an extension of our memory. Long ago people memorized scriptures or cultural traditions or family lineages in order to preserve them. Then along came writing. The book gave us a convenient extension to our memory—a transportable extension that was carried to other cultures that had no concept of the media. Then, long after writing emerged, industrial printing arrived.

McLuhan rolls his media phrase out through numbers, automobiles, clocks, telephones, and even weaponry. And if you think about it, a sword is an extension of man. It gives him an edge—pun intended—in battle. Economics and financial models are other extensions of man, enhancing his abilities to create wealth. These extensions of man arrive randomly, upsetting, or disrupting, existing social fabrics. Sometimes they are planned at state level, as envious nations attempt to mimic others. This is problematic because you can't simply introduce or alter an existing layer of society without ramifications. Rahman showed how difficult it was to change the economic layer in Islamic society;

> Whereas (The rulers of modern Muslim states) saw the necessity of economic development, they generally did not admit the desirability of change in institutions in the socio–moral sphere. Since the Muslim community was sound spiritually, morally, and socially, and was weak only economically, it must borrow from the West only its economic techniques and must guard itself generally from the socio–moral evil of the modern West, with the exception of modern education—more particularly technicological education—and the West's attitude to work.[8]

Trying to change that economic layer disrupted all the others in Muslim society. Looking back, it seems hard to believe economists thought they could just alter a single layer of life a hundred years ago when Turkey tried to modernize its way out of its Ottoman Empire past. Simply put, it was a learning curve about the complex weaving of extensions of men.

7. Ibid., 11.
8. Rahman, "Islamic Modernism," 319.

Historians have mooted that industrial printing also expanded in Europe because the accounting and commercial professions needed it. Good point. One media layers upon another to shape social change, as had to happen before printing was accepted in the Ottoman Empire. It was originally accused of using pig bristles, and up to 90,000 copyists of the Qu'ran in Istanbul might have thought their livelihoods were threatened by the printing press. Alone however, these may not have been enough to stop it. Nasr adds another reason it didn't catch on for a further 200 years; "The traditional Muslim education system, and the established manuscript tradition simply did not give rise to needs that could be fulfilled by typographic printing. That is, there was no glaring problem that the typographic press could solve."[9] If the commercial development of the Ottoman Empire had been at another stage, Nasr is suggesting printing would have been established earlier. And indeed, when the economic conditions demanded it, industrial printing was adopted in the Islamic world.

Media also starts with M, and our other choice was the multisyllabic duo of technological advances. The French philosopher Jacques Ellul studied the impact of technique in his books from 1954 through to 1988. Ellul complemented McLuhan (and McLuhan complimented Ellul) by exposing the psyche we have inherited from modern media or technological advances. He introduced the theory of technique in the 1950s in France, later to be popularized in English speaking societies after his seminal work, 'The Technological Society,' was translated in 1964.

Ellul basically said that as Westerners entered the technical age, the technical age entered Westerners. Efficiency, production, and rationality, permeated our thinking. Without being aware of it, these same factors became the matrix by which we judged the world. We criticize nations and races that we deem inefficient, or irrational. Ellul suggests, by the very title of another book, that we have been bluffed by technology[10] into believing it solves all our problems and moves us forward. The very concept of progress, unknown only a millennia or so ago, but unquestioned today, demonstrates this. We describe those who do not think along efficient, productive, and rational lines as backwards.

Ellul defined technique as follows;

---

9. Nasr, "The Reasons behind the delay of adopting the early printing," 13.
10. Ellul, *The Technological Bluff*, title.

The totality of methods rationally arrived at and having absolute efficiency (for a given stage of development) in every field of human activity.[11]

We might think of distribution techniques, marketing techniques, psychological techniques and more. In a religious sense, the North American decision to move from tent revivalist meetings to radio in the 1930s was rationally arrived at and having absolute efficiency (for a given stage of development), considering you could reach more listeners for less effort.

At the heart of it, that decision was based on technique. The radio pioneers didn't consider that the process of listening to the radio preach at you imparted different human responses than listening to a human being preach to you. The easiest analogy to make is the difference between attending the football game, and watching it on TV.

These communications mediums have become so influential in our lives that an old political term has been given new life—mediatization—which means; "In communication studies or media studies, mediatization is a theory that argues that the media shapes and frames the processes and discourse of political communication as well as the society in which that communication takes place."[12]

The concept isn't new. Thirty years ago Neil Postman told us, "... television has gradually become our culture. We rarely talk about television, only about what is on television. . . . it is taken for granted, accepted as natural."[13] Postman couldn't have known how the Internet would integrate into the mix. In the early twenty–first century, debates are still going on about the impact of the Internet on our lives. It may be, like Postman's discussions on television fifty years ago, that they will recede into the background once the Internet is taken for granted and becomes natural.

Some technological advances or media alter the religious equation catastrophically and blatantly. And we can't blame the inventors. Gutenberg did not plan to start a new religion. Nor did the designers of the jet plane write a list of pros and cons including, 'ability to fly full passenger load into densely occupied office buildings as a religious protest,' in their submission to head office. Other devices have huge impacts, but in a subtle, apparently harmless manner. Amplified sound is an example. Where would either Christianity or Islam be without the microphone and loudspeaker?

11. Ellul, *The Technological Society*, 25.

12. "*Mediatization (media,.*" para. 1.

13. Postman, *Amusing Ourselves to Death*, 79.

In the 1950s and 60s Billy Graham became a household name preaching his evangelical message to 200 million people worldwide during his Crusades. None of Graham's work would have been possible without a combination of electrification, sound amplification, and the sports stadium. Some Christians claim those Crusades[14] expanded the Kingdom of God, while others fret that Graham exported a cut down, homogenized, message.

Of course it's not too hard to find derogatory comments about noise. Ask travelers to the Middle East when the mosque next door to their hotel winds up its call to prayer—or elderly church members arriving on Sunday morning to the screams of an electric band shrieking out the chapel doors. Amplified noise has transformed Christianity, as we shall see when we look at music.

Not everyone agrees that social or religious change is determined by technology, which is interesting because those Qu'ran hand copyists in Istanbul long ago could probably see the industrial printer would affect them. However, one can be tempted to see the end of mankind in these machines or fields of inquiry invented by mankind. This is the extremist argument, and not a good trap to fall into. We've been involved in media, myth, mimicry and memory a long time, and we're still here. Martin makes three points against apocalyptic views;

> A major problem with notions like the "technological revolution" and the "information society" is that they are powerful metaphors with a misleading message. The message is misleading in three ways.
>
> First, these terms create the impression that social change is determined by technology. . . Even the most spectacular inventions are rooted in a social order that enabled them to happen and then identified them as important. We have made the "Information Society" and the "Digital Age" for ourselves.
>
> Second, the attribution of events to a technological origin is also a moral statement, since the blaming of human actions on technology allows humans to escape responsibility for actions which were the results of their own choices.
>
> Third, ideas like "technological revolution" and "information society" suggest that social change is characterized by revolutions, i.e., sudden, unexpected, and simple shifts from one mode of activity to another; whereas in reality change displays more

14. I'm sure others have explored why the Billy Graham Evangelistic Association still uses the word 'Crusades,' as did Dabiq, the online magazine of the Islamic State, so we won't here.

embeddedness in what came before, and all inventions have an ancestry.[15]

Let's proceed with caution then, remembering that the relationship is non–simple, and that change displays more embeddedness in what came before. Another way of expressing embeddedness is the concept of standing on our forebears shoulders, of gaining the advantage of their breakthroughs. It took centuries of thinking to create the decimal numbering system. Now that it exists, children can learn it in a year or so. Media or technologies have this layering effect that enables us to stand on our forebears shoulders. There is enough layering just in writing words—how it came about, all the way from clay tablets to Samsung ones. Now insert the video revolution, from television to smartphone. All these layers accumulate within our social conditioning, but not as layers we can peel off like clothing when the weather warms up. It's too simplistic to start blaming human actions on any of the layers of technology or media. And it's just as simplistic to think we can extract ourselves from participating in a society or religion dressed in them.

And when Martin mentioned above that we made the "Information Society" and the "Digital Age" for ourselves, he probably wasn't considering other factors in the matrix, such as memory or mythology, and especially not our fourth M, which is often based on envy.

MIMICRY

Yes, nations get jealous about the success of others, occasionally even admitting it. After World War 2, the Japanese copied their way to success, becoming the second wealthiest nation on the planet until China dropped the economic principles of Socialism and mimicked Western ones instead. The same elements can be detected between religions, the spokesmen for which can never admit such sins. And mimicry frequently gets leveled at religions from outside, starting with the phrase, all religions are the same. This is followed by claims like all religions are violent, which is far too general. That's like saying, all fruits are the same, followed by all fruits are sweet.

Mimicry crops up in the biological arena. Plants and insects often mimic successful competitors, or make themselves look like they are powerful to scare off predators, when actually it's all show. Plenty of businesses

15. Lankshear et al. "Digital literacy," 152–153.

do exactly those two things too. A pioneering company might exhaust itself just getting started. A mimic doesn't need to waste effort replicating the pioneer's failures. A failing company might take showy action to bluff its shareholders or the press that they're still powerful.

Our approach in the religious sphere is on specific instances of mimicry, or copying of ideas, although it's not easy to accuse religions of that. For example, several religions give hard–copy versions of their holy texts away. Perhaps they all print Not for resale on them. One could say, as I am sure Saheeh International would, that their giving away of the Qu'ran is purely coincidental with the Bible gift giving of the Gideons. The simple solution is to say there is conscious and unconscious mimicry.

Predicting possible mimicry is permissible. It's interesting that 98 percent of US Roman Catholics think birth control is okay despite admonitions from the very top of their vast denomination. Will European immigrant Islamic women bear smaller families despite encouragement in their faith not to? Good question. The point is that mimicry gives us clues about what might happen, although this borders on a risky field called futurism.

INNOCENCE AND OUTCOMES

Futurists have long been aware of the consequences of technology. As far back as 1849 Henry David Thoreau foresaw how long distance communications would alter what sort of information was delivered. North American Indians used smoke signals to convey information at distance, but smoke is not a very eloquent medium. Indians were generally restricted to one to three puffs, and they chose important data to send including 'all well' or 'danger.' Informed of the boundless potential of telegraph, Thoreau wasn't convinced it would help significant news arrive faster. Instead he mused that unimportant knowledge would be shared; "... perchance the first news that will leak through into the broad, flapping American ear will be that the Princess Adelaide has the whooping cough."[16] It sounds like he's talking about Facebook.

He was not the first to speculate about the real outcomes of introducing new extensions of men. We will later find Plato did. By the time we reached the late twentieth century, two and a half millennia after him, writers realized the pace of introduction had quickened. People started to worry. Closer to our era, Don Fabun wrote in 1971;

16. "Henry David Thoreau Quotes," para. 1.

> Since, in the over populated highly urbanised world, the introduction of technological innovations assumes immediate and monstrous proportions, would it not seem reasonable to establish an International Council for Technological Review, made up of the best minds of dozens of disciplines, to consider whether the introduction of an innovation can be absorbed by the human society and the ecosystem? Such a device would, to be sure, slow down "progress." Slowing down a little may not hurt.[17]

Even forty years ago, he was not alone. Famous authors including Herbert Marcuse in One Dimensional Man, Theodore Roszak in The Making of a Counter Culture, and Alvin Toffler in Future Shock, were all talking about the same concepts between 1964 and 1970.

Now, here's the nub. While those luminaries wrote to worldwide readerships, none of them gave any credence to an experiment to slow down progress that had been under way for a thousand years in the Middle East. It appeared as if it was dying anyway, and indeed it was when faced with the power of the West. Serious students of Islam, such as Timur Khan, acknowledge its aim however;

> In early Islam, scholars and theologians more or less freely developed answers to problems that scripture and tradition left unresolved. However, between the 9th and 11th centuries, freedom of innovation ended when it was declared that independent judgment was no longer permissible. This closure meant that all answers were already available: thenceforth, one needed only to follow and obey. In treating Islamic learning as having attained perfection and the Islamic world as self–sufficient, it gave legitimacy to values, attitudes, and practices that promoted stability and discouraged inquisitiveness. Helping to legitimize an educational system that emphasized rote learning and memorization, it also fueled a culture that limited curiosity about the outside world.[18]

Westerners readily find fault with Muslim ability to slow things down, and indeed such values contributed to the economic backwardness of the Middle East North Africa (MENA) region compared to the modern West. Islamic stability also entrenched values that certain demographics, such as women, complain about. Nevertheless it was, and still is, the world's most widespread effort to put society on pause. It is not seen that way, nor do most of its own adherents think of Islam like that. Muslims think of their

17. Fabun, *Dimensions of Change*, 33.

18. Kuran, "Economic Underdevelopment in the Middle East," 9.

faith along the lines of how many times to pray daily, how to be part of their community, how to get to Mecca once in their lifetime, and how to dissociate themselves from their violent brethren. They did not traditionally brand their religion as a means of achieving income equality, although some of their commentators do that today. Neither did early Muslims construct theories of economic development, but nobody else knew how to do that in the eleventh century either. Some outcomes in Muslim–majority nations today were foreseen by Muslims, including laws based on religious precepts, but that was common elsewhere back then too. Many outcomes were unforeseen however, as Kuran refers to above. An education system based on rote learning doesn't breed inquisitive minds because all major questions have been answered. And neither did Muhammad or his closest circle want to see Muslim-majority nations at the corrupt end of any of the scales we shall later encounter.

Unforeseen outcomes have always been with us of course, and especially today when change is faster than ever. Time Magazine gave a modern day example when they told us; "The story of the deep web is a fable of technology and its unintended consequences."[19] Time was referring to the exposure of the Silk Road illegal drug purchasing website which was almost untraceable. Outcomes from some inventions are easier to judge, such as the 3D plastic gun you can print. Download the plans from the Internet, purchase a 3D printer from eBay, and you've got a gun that the authorities have already banned. In the first days after the public heard about it in May 2013, kindly thanks to the press who told us all, some 100,000 downloads occurred. Most were to English speaking nations by the way, not the Middle East.

This is an apparent hazard, and we should be well past the naivety of Hiram Stevens Maxim, the inventor of the famous rotating barrel gun that revolutionized warfare. When asked if his machine gun would be catastrophic in battle, he exclaimed, "no, it will make war impossible!" One could argue we didn't learn from his mistake as the Mutually Assured Destruction (MAD) concept of equal nuclear stacks between the United States and the Soviet Union almost illustrated during the Cuban missile crisis in 1962.

Once we get past the obvious end of the moral continuum, we reach the questionable section. Questionable in that it doesn't take much to see how a device could be iniquitous. We can hardly expect inventors, or more

19. "The Secret Web," para. 7.

precisely, their mythology builders (branding agencies), to inform the public of possible wicked outcomes. The inventors are too enamored their device will enhance mankind, and the brand builders too ecstatic over the fees they'll charge.

In 2013 we learned about, "The insect of the future . . . the Robobee." This electronic fly, the size of a fly, can be directed into places hard to get to, like high–rise buildings that have fallen down in an earthquake, trapping victims. Sounds like a great idea, locating people still alive down there. According to the journal Science, "(the Robobee) could be used for everything from environmental monitoring, search and rescue operations, to helping with crop rotation."[20]

Come on. A simple search of the Internet reveals how it will sell. Smart individuals who can't be tracked will have these things flying in corporate boardrooms, and sell the video captured to competitive corporate boardrooms—let alone the military who will use them to ensure terrorists like Al–Awlaki are actually in the target building before the drone missile is dispatched.

Morality gets blurred in this section, and inventors are innocent because 'anything can be employed for good or evil.' And the truth is that you cannot introduce a moral matrix at the beginning of a products life cycle because you don't know what the market will tell you, or how it will be employed. This is Sales 101, and the reason prototypes are thrust into public as soon as possible. The mantra of finding how the market will react sits behind every blasé statement like those about the Robobee. Every technological advance has impacts beyond their initial intent except one: if it sells, it's on target. That's a relatively new criteria in historical terms. Up until at least five hundred years ago, people and nations could make decisions outside market demand, as our mullahs did about printing in the sixteenth century Ottoman Empire.

Further down the moral spectrum are those that spring surprises on us. This is the majority category actually. A mobile phone app called Firechat fits here. It was not designed to help the forces of the Islamic State (ISIS) communicate with each other as they butchered their way through Iraq in mid 2014. It was designed for people who are in the near vicinity to communicate using a technology called mesh networking rather than the Internet via a cellular network. Firechat is a good idea for finding your wife in an expensive department store whose multi–floor infrastructure blocks

20. "The insect of the future," para. 4.

cell coverage. It is a great method for spreading a rave party date around the campus for anyone close by who has the app installed. Unfortunately Firechat is also perfect for a team of militants to stay in touch with each other after the government has blocked Internet access.[21]

In a way every technical advance springs surprises on us though. A car is not just a faster horse. The car changed society much more than shrinking the horseshoe market. Television is not a continuation of books. When I read a headline such as an Internet founder telling the government to stop snooping,[22] it tells me they don't understand Postman's concept that; "Each technology has an agenda of its own."[23] Even money does, that marvelous extension of man that allows us to trade anything by agreeing on the concept of price. Thomas Piketty, author of the acclaimed book, Capital in the Twenty-First Century, told us what happens to money if you leave it long enough; "Capital is never quiet: it is always risk-oriented and entrepreneurial, at least at its inception, yet it always tends to transform itself into rents as it accumulates in large enough amounts—that is its vocation, its logical destination."[24]

That Internet founder didn't help build the world wide web for evil reasons, but he could not grasp its own agenda. It opened a highly lucrative avenue for Silk Road drug marketers, money launderers, and of course the mafia, by its very structure. The Internet was designed not to be centrally controlled, and it isn't. So anyone can access it. Nobody can stop Al-Qaeda or the ISIS from posting videos because the Internet has no authorized control centre to stop that. The very term—world wide web—with its spider like ramifications, may be a more appropriate indication of its vocation. This extension of man allows experts to cripple commercial websites from thousands of kilometers away. It's also useful in tracking the movements of people who might plant bombs in subways, who, metaphorically speaking, might send a shiver down an internet spider strand. No government who wants to stay in power can ignore those signals.

Nor is only technological media culpable in social and religious change. Psychology has drastically altered perspectives. Victorious Roman legions were faithfully etched on stone walls leading manacled victims home, along with the loot they stole from other civilizations. Politicians

---

21. "Iraqis use Firechat messaging"
22. "Tim Berners-Lee urges government to stop the snooping bill," line 1.
23. Postman, *Amusing ourselves to death*, 84.
24. Piketty, *Capital*, 85.

and religious leaders have learnt not to do that anymore. Starting some centuries ago, engravings are more like the one in today's tourist attraction, the former Hanoi Hilton in Vietnam. It displays bestial prison guards beating up peace loving socialist comrades, (who probably sang each other to sleep from a Lenin's greatest hits album).

Is psychology an extension of man? In that it leads us to understand how other men will react, yes it is. Psychology has taught us we'll get far more mileage from portrayals of suffering, or even defeat. Why do you think press photographers are welcomed into the overcrowded hospitals of Gaza to photograph the wounded? Does psychology have unexpected outcomes? It extends further than analyzing personal problems—it's utilized in advertising and political campaigns to sway hearts and minds.

Many other disciplines have evolved in the past century with interesting outcomes for religion. We will learn of Orientalism, and how it attempts to get us looking at Eastern societies without prejudice. It will be up to the reader whether they think it is an enlightening discipline, or one that deflects guilt.

SETTING THE SCENE

To the joy of the Western world, communism crumbled, publicly starting on November 9th, 1989, with the fall of the Berlin wall. Then to the amazement of the same Western world, the threat of Marx was replaced by what appeared to be the threat of Islam. Like the jet planes, this global challenge came out of the blue, also seeming to arrive on a single day—September 9th, 2001. The communist versus West conflict turned into what many think is a war between East and West. A plethora of YouTube videos warn us about the Islamization of Europe, that Germany will be a Muslim state in the year 2050 if current demographic trends continue. Conspiracy theories abound, refilling the bookstore thriller shelves after the KGB downsized. Negative forecasters almost lead us to believe Muslim women of the world obediently fall pregnant to the commands of shadowy figures lodged in some mountain fastness in Pakistan. Western Christians are angry that immigrant Muslims not only "take their jobs" but are allowed to build mosques while Christians are forbidden from building churches or evangelizing Muslim–majority nations.

At the same time Islam emerged onto the world stage, Christianity was, and still is, re-engineering itself. The pace of new extensions of man didn't slow down after either the fall of the Berlin wall or the twin towers. The world is much more connected now than the sixteenth century, yet even with the level then, the media impact was big. Today, we have a connected planet, where the trends, pressures, inventions, ideas, and science quickly proliferate around the world. It is no surprise that on about the same day in May 2013, Samsung released its S4 smartphone in most nations of the world. Within a week, anyone on earth who wanted one, and had the money, could have bought one.

When you think about it, that's amazing. A business firm developed a technical product, coordinating manufacturing, advertising, partner training, warehousing, pricing, shipping, news releases, rumors, websites, movies, and mythologies on how impressive you'll look holding one, resulting in the availability of their smartphone across the entire world on the same day—leading, by the way, to ten million sales of the S4 within the first month.

Only it's not amazing any more. It's ho hum. It's the norm. If you can't do that, you're not in the league of important players. Apple superseded it a year later by reaching the ten million mark in three days with their iPhone 6. We are all accustomed to the connected world.

Compare this to seventeenth century Britain, less than four hundred years ago, during the English Civil War in the 1640s. On either side of a fog filled valley, well after this conflict had begun, the Royalist and Roundhead armies waited for the valley to clear so they could commence battle. As the mist lifted, one side could make out a man plowing a field below, on the very ground that would soon be soaked in blood. A rider was sent down who shouted, "don't you know there's a battle about to be fought here!?" The nonplussed response from the plowman was, "no! Who is fighting?"

Can we learn from past impacts and do some forecasts? Unfortunately futurism doesn't have a good track record. Statistically speaking, most predictions don't come true. Nevertheless, here and there, we have a question to ask over a fog filled valley today: if the same technologies provoked changes in both Christianity and Islam in the past, could it be that today, given parallel pressures in a connected world, we will find parallel outcomes?

Life in the Muslim–majority nations is behind the West in terms of life–spans, Internet penetration, literacy levels, and infrastructure. The bulk of those ten million S4s and iPhones went to Western and Asian buyers, and not to the Middle East. Will the smartphone media change Western society, and as usual drag Western Christianity along with it? If it does then it's reasonable to posit that parallel changes might emerge in Islam once the prices drop and smartphones become a ubiquitous item. Certainly this cellular extension of man is spreading much faster than fixed line telephone communication in the Third World. Let's not fix on the smartphone as the only game changer though. The reason I've included the word in the title is as an example, a metaphor if you will, of many trends that are upon us. While we will examine some specific effects, it is by no means alone, nor will the smartphone remain in its current form. All we will glimpse are possible parallel trends, and we don't know the time–frame.

Is this arrogance to suggest the West is ahead of the Middle East? It's all subjective isn't it? More than that, perhaps the idea of suggesting Islam is behind Christianity is an insult. However, I didn't say one religion was be-hind the other—but we do know that literacy levels, Internet penetration, employment demographics, and incomes, lag in Muslim–majority nations. In fact this is evidence of the slow down strategy alluded to earlier.

Do parallels exist between these two religions? Most pastors, mullahs, bishops and emirs highlight their faith's unique selling points. Put Christi-anity and Islam side by side though and we find:

1. They are huge, with two billion something adherents apiece.

2. They are both monotheistic.

3. They both adhere to a fixed set of holy texts.

4. Both have exclusive claims.

5. Various sexual phobias are parallel.

6. Both have battlegrounds past and present.

7. Denominational divisions exist within their own ranks.

8. Their religious leaders command followings beyond national borders.

9. They recite the same stories, and revere the same founders.

10. And finally in this list you could add to, both are religions. We're not finding trends from Microsoft that the Pope adopts.

There's fertile ground for mimicry in that list, albeit often separated by hundreds of years as we shall see.

In 1995 Benjamin Barber analyzed American cultural dominance in his book, Jihad vs McWorld.[25] He showed us that while the world loved

25. Barber, Jihad vs McWorld, title.

Big Macs and Hollywood movies, rebellions were afoot. Much of the world did not want McWorld. (Get back to me however if you see a global chain of Halal butchers moving into your neighborhood.) A serious amount of Islamic disquiet is about this 'invasion' of their cultural turf. It is viewed as the assault of secularism. Barber used the word Jihad to refer to all movements opposed to McWorld. His definition of Jihad grouped Islam along with the environmental movement, the peace protesters, and native rights lobbyists. No such inclusive use can be made of the word today, and he would probably have had to rename his book had it been published post 2001.

Barber's work was heavily populated with statistics, and aimed to show us how the world was divided into a series of camps. Mine is more specific, getting to two religions that tent in these camps. Many members of one camp have moved and settled comfortably, or uncomfortably, in the campsite of the other. While there is an East versus West tension, much of the East wants to live in the West, which is in turn the invasion of turf many Westerners are afraid of.

Ellul differed from Barber in one vital perspective. Ellul wrote that Islam was the one unitary force capable of challenging the excesses and faults of Western civilization fifteen years before those jets flew into the World Trade Center.[26] Communism was a Western idea, transplanted to the Far East by exposure to the West. It had not entered deeply into the hearts and minds of the Third World. Don't be surprised that this export from Western writers such as Marx and Lenin is being abandoned by both China and Vietnam. Islam is a Third World creation. It was not born from Western thinking, which is why Westerners do not grasp it in the way they do socialism. Many hated Marx, but at least they understood his economic and social concepts, which have impacted Western politics to this day. Islam does not attempt to sort its precepts into a matrix that the average Westerner understands.

This is a conundrum to many. Climate change, deforestation, poverty, and the banking system, are all recognizable worldwide problems that the world generally tries to blame the West for. None of those global issues has the collective aggressive power to confront the secular Western world that Islam musters though. Possibly the green movement wish they could summon the level of outrage that Muslims can. Muslims are certainly aware today of the extent of their group clout since they read about it every day.

26. Ellul, *The Technological Bluff*, 234.

They are front page news for the first time in centuries. Hundreds if not thousands of Islamic writers have climbed on to the Internet, a Western invention, to add to their rising chorus of dissent, and they're not necessarily openly militant either. www.khilafah.com is one of many websites firmly telling us that Islam is the only answer;

> We assert, without compromise, that it is only by the establishment of the Khilafah (Caliphate) State, that the practical solutions of Islam can once again provide a real alternative for the entire world. The 'Clash of Civilisations' first discussed by Samuel Huntington is real and inevitable. We endorse the notion that there is a civilisational difference between Islam and the West and that the problem for the West is Islam and the problem for Islam is the West. By arguing this, we also maintain Islam, as a universal ideology, came for all of humankind, Muslim and Non–Muslims, and as such it is only Islam that serves as a Rahma (mercy) for all mankind. As the western ideology dominates the world today, the only challenge to it must come from Islam.[27]

While this is meaningless or anathema to a Western mind, it is not to both militant and non–militant sectors of Islam. To add to the mix, many, many, Westerners agree their own civilization is not headed along the right path. Move from the front to the editorial page of your newspaper to read about that.

Having formulated our thrust, we need some trend data, some opinions, and some statistics. Who should we ask? Do we march around the religious bosses? In fact we will get some of their thoughts, and we don't need to go far for those. Invariably though, people who run large institutions have a filtering layer around them who prepare their speeches, press releases, book contributions, and articles. And unfortunately, due to these pressures, chief clerics do not always tell us their true thoughts. Tariq Ramadan is possibly the most respected Muslim intellectual in the Western world, yet he admitted this about discussions he had with Middle Eastern Muslim leaders; "In private meetings, we agree. Publicly, we don't."[28] Christian leaders must have thoughts behind closed doors too. How did the Roman Catholics and Anglicans manage to keep straight faces about their orphanages, their boy's schools, and those wayward priests, over all those years?

27. "About Khilafah.com," para. 2.
28. "A Conversation With Tariq Ramadan," para. 70.

To cap it all off, significant change in religion does not generally come from rulings from the top. It comes from the bottom, the sides, or outside the box. Of course all religions start outside boxes, and end up creating their own. From the boxes we deal with, neither bishops nor mullahs have great roles in the modern history of religious change by edict. Some have great roles in political change, but not on the tone or nature of a religion.

Another angle on this comes from a quote by the CEO of Microsoft, Satya Nadella, in February 2014;

"our industry does not respect tradition—it only respects innovation."[29]

You might already be thinking;

"religion does not respect innovation—it only respects tradition."

At best, people might think religions are only capable of trivial change. Here's two examples to add into that dinner party conversation;

One of the great leaps forward from Vatican II, the most recent worldwide council for change (which ran from 1962 to 1965 by the way—these councils are rare) was this: the priest was authorized to optionally face his congregation during Mass, instead of it being compulsory to face away.

Secondly I was watching lectures from a conference organized in England in 2010 entitled Rethinking Islamic reform.[30] Shaykh Hamza Yusuf, a Muslim intellectual from the USA, relayed to the audience how people misinterpret either tradition or the Qu'ran. With an obvious flourish of pride, he exclaimed how if you truly examine their holy texts, you will find that women can lead prayer in the mosque from the front, rather than the back.

The point is not the near mimicry again, although that is interesting. Rather, it is the minor tweaking offered as radical insights while religious worlds convulse around them. I side with someone hallowed by both Christians and Muslims here. Jesus notoriously didn't trust religious leaders. Sustaining readership numbers, or church attendance, or college enrollments, or donations, or keeping suicide volunteer streams up, often means compromising your public utterances, or delivering proclamations like the two above—so niche they're worthless. Perhaps these religious leaders have risen so high in their institutions that, according to a friend of mine, they know all the reasons why nothing can be done.

You will note I used the phrase "religious change by edict." Religious change by example is another matter. Pope Francis gains more mileage with the poor from owning that twenty year old Renault, (another pun), rather

---

29. "Meet the CEO," para. 2.
30. "Rethinking Islamic Reform," film.

than saying he feels sorry for them. The Dalai Lama may be the best example of leading by example in our era.

Can the academic realm help us?

Pew Research is a good start. This American based fact tank interviews 35,000 people at a time around the world. They have an impeccable survey process, where they test the very testing. This method ensures accurate results but narrows what you can actually ask. They don't survey schoolchildren in Tajikistan about how the smartphone will alter their religious behavior. They can't ask that, and the kids don't know anyway. Don't even have a smartphone. Yet.

Pew's objectivity is above question, and they would correctly call this book subjective. Statistics are not the only way of getting to the bottom of things though. An old saying used to rank evils in this order—there are lies, damned lies, then statistics. So we need to be careful how we use them. I am reminded of a joke thirty years ago about the statistics of car ownership in the United States. It goes like this: twenty years ago there were four people per car in America. Ten years ago that had fallen to two people per car. If things go on like this, soon every third car driving by will be empty.

To complicate matters, Google may yet cause this wisecrack to be true. Driver-less cars are now a fact. We don't know how many already clutter our highways, perhaps sent by test group mums to pick up kids from play centers. No, they wouldn't do that, surely not.

How about the non-academic realm?

We will visit cathedrals, churches, and mosques, throughout this book. They inform us about past and present Christianity and Islam through their floors, their artwork (or lack of it), their crypts, their gift shops, and their visitor segmentation studies. So do statues, movies, poems, and the thickness of protective city walls. More people encounter history this way than read detailed books on the topic.

Visiting the forest with one natively schooled in it was an eye opener for me to compare urban man with. A discussion with a vicar in the center of St Paul's in London uncovered the dilemma of working for peace in a building crowded with memories of war heroes. The inner soul that shone at me through the smile of a Muslim Mandingo lady I chatted with outside a back country mosque made of corrugated zinc and mud brick in West Africa proved again that enlightenment does not obey religious boundaries.

In addition to scholarly articles and approved traditional research we will deliberately refer to Internet data. The main reason, as per climbing mountains, is because it is there, and increasingly there in voluminous quantities. It is now possible for anyone to publish anything on the web, and the most outlandish opinions may be read more widely than thoroughly academic articles. To dismiss that sector is to ignore the means that the average person uses to find answers, and will do so more in the future.

Not only that, but search engines automatically track what people read, and what they search to read. These statistics are compiled without our knowing or asking, and are in many cases freely available. We will find some shocking variances between data formally collected, and that unknowingly gathered. The Internet itself is a challenge as to how anyone, including the academic community, will conduct research.

It also presents authors with opportunities to direct readers straight to Internet sources. Throughout this book you will come across QR or Quick Response codes. Lots of free QR code apps are available for your smartphone or tablet. Download and install one, and you can be transported straight to an Internet site when you aim your mobile device at a QR code.

While these two religions have a list of parallels, we acknowledge some significant differences. In general, the lives of ordinary Pakistanis and Egyptians are much more entangled with Islam than the lives of average Australians and Spaniards are tied up with Christianity. By many accounts the West is actually post–Christian, to the misguided delight of atheists. Surveys in Europe reveal that while church attendance is dropping, belief in the divine is not decaying as fast. It is commonplace to find people with some sort of Christian faith who never attend church. Surprisingly perhaps to Christians, it is also easy to encounter Muslims who don't attend mosque.

The scenario is further complicated, but well illustrated by this comparison a Muslim joked about the West: "The difference between us is that we pray in public and have sex in private. You Westerners pray in private and have sex in public." It's a good line, but Westerners do not pray—at least not until their share portfolio is facing sudden ruin. Muslims do though, five times a day. While the average Muslim may accept we are not as religious as they are, many still judge us through the lenses of their own society. We hear flashes of this now and again. During some marches against a Western film deriding Muhammad, I heard a distraught Pakistani protester shout despairingly at a news camera. His words were to the effect of, "how can they ridicule our prophet like this? How would they like it if we ridiculed their prophet?!"

If only he knew. Western billboards or books, or films, or even adverts mocking Jesus, or Joseph and Mary, or other Bible characters, are commonplace in the Western world. Woe betide the straight laced pastor who complains. His lament will end up on the comic pages of the morning paper.

Where do the boundaries of Christianity begin and end? And where do the boundaries of Islam start and finish? There are many answers, but we will only offer one viewpoint here. Let's reformat the question by asking how much Christian there is in any of us Westerners. What proportion of us, as an individual, is Christian?

The answer is unlikely to be zero, and never one hundred percent. Not even the Pope would claim that. Most Westerners know about Christmas and Easter. Even the most hedonistic have remnants of this 2000 year old cultural memory residing somewhere, or a personal background, or friends, relatives, and other connections. Richard Dawkins, the world's most famous atheist in the early twenty–first century, describes himself as a cultural Anglican and a secular Christian.[31]

It's the same with Muslims. I once had an African Islamic employee who was very devout about observing the Ramadan fast, and would give away copies of the Qu'ran. He moonlighted as a bouncer for a public bar, consuming far more whiskey and beer than the average denizen of our land. While one of the world's nicest guys, he was not pure Muslim.

Islam is made up of flawed people with families, cultures, memories, and sports teams. They laugh, they weep, they work, they love, and they die.

Just like Christians.

31. "Richard Dawkins," line 1.

2

PEOPLES OF THE BOOKS

THE INCA KING AND THE BIBLE

ON NOVEMBER 16TH 1532, an illuminating media misunderstanding took place between two civilizations meeting for the first time. Fransisco Pizzaro, accompanied by 160 battle hardened Spanish troops, met Atahualpa, the Inca king, high in the mountains of Peru. Atahualpa had come with 80,000 supporters, mostly unarmed.

Among the items on display that day were several the Incas had never seen. One can hardly call a wild horse media. Put an armed man on a trained one however, and the animal definitely extends his abilities. Add in armor, steel swords, and cannon, all of which enhance the power of warriors, and you have some interesting discoveries if you're an opponent.

There was another present, one more easily understood as media by modern man.

A book. The Bible to be precise. Incas had never seen a book, and did not even understand the concept of writing, pages, binding, or paper. Yet this stored memory device had reached divine status in the Western and Middle Eastern hemispheres by then.

The Spanish records tell us their priest approached Atahualpa bearing the Bible, a hand printed one that had carefully been brought thousands of miles across two oceans and up this mountain trail. He read from it, commanding the Inca to accept the Catholic faith and Charles V of Europe as sovereign. Spanish religious duty had been performed. Atahualpa then struck the book from the hands of the friar. Such an outrage was enough provocation for the Spaniards to spring out of hiding and attack the group guarding the Inca monarch. They captured him alive, going on to slay two thousand of the gathered Inca without loss to themselves. And South America was shortly thereafter plundered for centuries by the Spanish and Portuguese.

An Inca later recollected the clash with interesting additions and omissions compared to the Spanish version. Faced with all those extensions of man, in undoubtedly the most eye opening day of his life, Atahualpa coveted the Spanish weaponry. Military hardware is always the first category to break through any media acceptance problems. Warriors have this knack of noticing when a particular device kills enemies more effectively than others.

Understandably the slapping away of the Bible was not mentioned by the Inca. The Inca reporter cannot have grasped its significance, or even what it was. How could they know, amidst all those items on show, that the pen was mightier than the sword? And more specifically, this particular written article was believed by the Spanish to come from God.

Fast forward to March 2013. The mere rumor that a Christian had burnt a Qu'ran enraged Pakistani Muslims so much they torched and ransacked 200 homes in Lahore. Hardly an isolated incident, the West now has to tread carefully in dealing with its own Christian right wingers hoping to provoke Muslim wrath by burning Qu'rans in the USA, probably beside the Statue of Liberty if they could get their own way. It wasn't always like this. A long historical sequence of media developments brought humanity to both the Spanish and the Lahore incidents.

Linguistics has enlightened us for some time now about speech, clearly a precursor to writing. A little as 1 percent of total information is conveyed by conversation between people present with each other. Other signs include physical wellbeing, dress, emotions, and distractedness. These all convey data to the listener.

There's even more fun when you climb into the words of any particular language. e.g Arabic has dozens of words describing camels, including a single word to describe this particular camel; A female camel that doesn't drink from the watering hole when it's busy, but waits and observes.

Imagine that. It took seventeen English words to translate one Arabic word. On the other hand, Arabic only has one word for snow. As you'd expect, Eskimos have no word for camel. When it comes to snow, they have dozens.

Men drew pictures on cave walls for thousands of years. One day, someone marked a rock or piece of clay, and carried it with them, transporting a memory. People swapped goods, and trading began. Writing was actually birthed as part of accounting more than 5000 years ago. Trading of goods in Mesopotamia was based around different shaped clay tokens.[1] Over time these different shaped tokens were flattened and inscribed on clay tablets. They went from 3D to 2D. People could bypass the tokens simply by inscribing them on a tablet with a stylus.

From that came written language, converting human speech to symbols you could store on a flat surface. Interestingly, as we mention elsewhere, the ancient Hebrew language of the Old Testament reflects this because it is a language that combines numerals with language. We think that is clever, looking back. The really smart move was separating numbers out from symbols conveying speech.

At the time of the Roman Empire, books didn't exist. A Roman graveyard statue unearthed near their famous hot water pool in Bath, Great Britain, shows the deceased holding a scroll. This was to show that the buried man was educated and knowledgeable.

Scrolls were certainly an upgrade over stone or clay tablets. Papyrus changed the rules, and obviously allowed simpler transportation. Papyrus would roll up too. Ah, the marvels of technology.

It didn't stop there. Between the first and third centuries the codex slowly emerged, which looks like our paper book of today. Scribes were tired of winding all the way through those scrolls to get to where page forty nine later was. Opening and closing a scroll takes time. Not so the pages of a codex, or book. Nevertheless it took a few hundred years for that innovation to disrupt the scroll trade.

No paper to start with though. They used vellum or even animal skins as pages. Producing the hardware of the book was time consuming and expensive. It's small wonder that books were deemed valuable, especially after all that handmade ink, bindings, and covers, were made, and all that work writing it out in the absence of a printer. Destroying a book would have been outrageous. Or deliberate.

Alongside the developments of this stored memory device, the church also began formalizing its content. Deciding which texts were sacred was

1. Schmandt-Besserat, "How Writing Came About," 2–6.

very important. Many individual books didn't make the cut. Only a select number were agreed to be 'inspired' and therefore to be included in the compilation known as the Bible. In an age that didn't read McLuhan, the medium was indeed the message however. In other words, this particular book, as a stored memory device, was divinized along with its content—which is why it is still termed The Holy Bible.

Think about that. We've traced a short path about how mankind started drawing on cave walls, which eventually led to books. Thousands of years later, this device began to shape the very memories it contained.

By definition, the Bible in book form has a fixed sequence within it. That is a significant shift from a cupboard full of scrolls, any one of which can be pulled out at random. The book with pages created its own linear nature, assumed by modern readers to be time sequenced, which it is not. The letters by Paul are sequenced according to size, not timeframe. The later letters were not necessarily written later in time. Marcus Borg published a New Testament with all the books in historical sequence. Among other things, Borg says this method shows how the New Testament evolved over time, one example being; "Seeing John separated from the other gospels and relatively late in the New Testament makes it clear how different from them John's gospel is."[2]

It also created issues with definitions the Bible itself contained. An earnest friend of mine, worried about chatter concerning which books were in the Bible canon, and which might be removed, quoted to me from a closing verse of the Bible itself;

- . . . and if anyone takes away from the words of the book of this prophecy, God shall take away his part from the tree of life and from the holy city, which are written in this book.[3]

"Just be careful," he warned. "Look at that promise."

I explained to him there was no Bible as a book when Revelation was written. There were only separate scrolls. The warning must be meant for people taking words away from the book of Revelation, not the Bible as a book, since that didn't yet exist.

He was visibly startled when this dawned on him. "I never thought of that!" he exclaimed.

2. Borg, *Evolution of the Word*, 4.

3. Revelation 22:19

As part of the selection process of which works actually made it into the Bible, some titles were declared heretical. These books, often accompanied by their authors, were burnt in public. Incinerating books was deliberately symbolic of destroying ideas, of eradicating a stored memory. In other words, these works were actively forgotten. Christians were remarkably good at this. Hence only one copy of the heretical gospel of Thomas has ever been found.

In 640 AD, legend has it that the largest library in the world, in Alexandria in Egypt, was burned by the victorious Muslim conquerors. Claiming that all the works had been superseded by the Qu'ran, the library contents were used to fuel bath houses for six months. That was serious active forgetting at work.[4]

Bible content was sorted at about the same time book technology supplanted scrolls at the end of the fourth century. Statues of church fathers then held books. A further two hundred years passed, enough time for the new stored memory device to attain sanctified status, and we find many famous sixth century icons of Christ from Byzantium showing him holding a book. Neither the Bible nor any books existed when he walked this earth, but mythology had fused Jesus to it before Muhammad arrived one hundred years later.

Byzantine artwork

Ironically Jesus is only recorded as writing once. He stooped down while a crowd ranted about stoning a woman, and wrote in the dust. When they finished their accusations, he stood up and famously said, "He who is without sin among you, let him be the first to cast a stone at her."[5] I like to think he was actually doodling, waiting out their rave. Whatever, it was very Buddhist of him. There is not a hint that Jesus intended writing a book, even though he could have. He was literate.

Muhammad began receiving his revelations in the year 610 AD. Clearly he knew about the Bible, since many of his characters came out of that. He also grasped the book as a media device because he intended that his revelations be written down. Generally Muslims claim he was illiterate, using this as part of the miracle of Allah, that the angel Gabriel (who appeared in the Bible too), transmitted orally to him. The Qu'ran is some

---

4. The reader may care to investigate the Alexandria story themselves, as it has come under dispute from various parties.

5. John 8:7

77,000 words long, while the Bible is ten times that size. Yet the Qu'ran lists the word book 193 times against the Bible's 156.

We might say that the Qu'ran is an example of layers of media, or the concept of standing on our forebear's shoulders. It had taken thousands of years for the idea of written words to evolve off cave walls, onto portable devices, out of trading symbols, and on to folding pages. Scribes knew how to bind books, and include multiple titles into one volume. Muslims didn't need to reinvent any of that. While it took centuries for the Bible to find its way into book form, Muslims started compiling the Qu'ran only ten years after Muhammad passed away. It has been suggested the process was hastened in order to provide a uniform holy text across their young, enormous empire.[6]

And so those words of Allah were frozen onto the written page. Muslims also realized the difficulty of reproducing it, and severe penalties were introduced for destroying a copy. They backed this up by fusing the written word with Allah: to burn the book was to torch the words of Allah. Their immediate jump into the textual book was not without ramifications. No pictures were allowed. They got fixated on written language as their chosen media.

Understandable. History had brought them to that point. The religious book had already been divinized by their most powerful neighbor, and the iPad was not available. We might laugh at that, but at least one religion has emerged in the post–book, digital era. Since the 1977 launch of the Star Wars movie series, Jedi master Obi–Wan Kenobi and protege Luke Skywalker have captured imaginations. 390,127 residents of the UK wrote Jedi as religion of choice in their 2001 census. The Jedi Church movement claimed 200,000 members worldwide in 2014. Even New Zealand, with a population of only 4.5 million, saw 20,000 write Jedi in their 2006 census. This is over half the 36,072 who ticked the Islam box. Like any new religion starting out, Jedi should not of course receive official state recognition by getting its own tick box in the census papers—as neither Christianity or Islam would have if census forms been printed in the time of Jesus or Muhammad.

All that aside, Jedi is a religion which could truly claim, "In the beginning was the movie." The point of this digression is not to belittle any religion, including Jedi, but to highlight the media comparison. You might laugh, "don't be ridiculous, you can't make a religion based on a movie."

6. "What Is the Koran?" page 2, para. 12.

Is that so? In the fifth century BC, Plato quoted Socrates on the wisdom of trusting in that extension of men known as the writing of books, well before they became divinized. He spoke out of a culture that valued the spoken word, and the meeting of minds that might change when an opposing argument was voiced;

> Theuth said, "Here O King, is a branch of learning that will make the people of Egypt wiser and improve their memories: my discovery provides a recipe for memory and wisdom."
>
> But the king answered and said, "O man of arts, to one is it given to create the things of art, and to another to judge what measure of harm or profit they have for those that shall employ them. And so it is that you, by reason of your tender regard for the writing that is your offspring, have declared the very opposite of its true effect. If men learn this, it will implant forgetfulness in their souls; they will cease to exercise memory because they rely on that which is written, calling things to remembrance no longer from within themselves, but by means of external marks. What you have discovered is a recipe not for memory, but for reminder. And it is no true wisdom that you offer your disciples, but only its semblance, for by telling them of many things without teaching them you will make them seem to know much, while for the most part they know nothing, and as men filled, not with wisdom, but with the conceit of wisdom, they will be a burden to their fellows.[7]

Plato may well have exclaimed, "are you telling me you're creating a religion based around books!?" Learning spirituality from the movie theatre is happening anyway as we shall learn in the next chapter on imagery.

This distrust of text lasted a long time. Vasiliu points out that as late as the thirteenth century; "writing was thought to bring about the death of memory and deterioration of human mind."[8] Jesus is portrayed in the Bible as the Word of God made flesh. St. Paul himself wrote;

- for the letter kills, but the Spirit gives life[9]

The Qu'ran has been described as the Word of God made text. And Muslims surely restricted themselves to text, in fact, to only one language—Arabic. The oral transmission was received in Arabic, the language of Allah, and it was written in Arabic. Muslims can print the sayings of Allah or

7. Martin, *History and Power of Writing*, 91.

8. Vasiliu, "The road to the Cathedral," 13.

9. 2 Corinthians 3:6

Muhammad all over their buildings, which is the artwork they have developed. Untutored Westerners think all those curvy designs and mosaics are clever and beautiful. Well, they are too, but they are also sections out of the Arabic Qu'ran. The calligraphy sometimes overlaps, shadowing words or phrases behind others. A Muslim literate in Arabic can read his way around the mosque.

Christians can read their way around cathedrals and churches too, but they are allowed art work. Roman Catholic ones contain the fourteen stations of the cross. St Giles Church in Bruges, Belgium, has the most intricate 3D wall engravings of these I have seen. Belgian churches love artwork. It's the budget way of viewing sixteenth and seventeenth century art in Bruges because there are no entry fees. As for stained glass windows, cathedrals have the premium franchise. To a non–literate population, such as the twelfth to nineteenth centuries mostly were, these stained glass windows were the most attractive and economical way of educating the masses.

Viewing the multi paneled series about Adam and Eve in a cathedral window in St. Florentin, France, one comes to the conclusion these were the original educational comic strips. Others illustrate the stories of the disciples, or Jesus, or saints, or even local heroes. Who needs printers when you have a flow of generations past the same windows over time? Very cost effective training aid. Stained glass windows last hundreds of years, and you need to be inside the church to see them. Perfect strategy for retaining the faithful. And like magazines today, those centuries old colorful windows also carried adverts about the local butcher or baker, and the glass–makers name.

A glitch occurred with Christian graphics in Byzantium during the eighth and ninth centuries. The Byzantine Empire was wary of Islamic armies for seven hundred years before finally falling to them in 1453. That legendary historian, Arnold Toynbee, mooted that Byzantium may have been impressed with Islamic victories and emulated some of their religious practices to copy their success.[10] These included outlawing images of God in churches, thereby overturning traditional Western church practices of painting and statues. In fact the issue heated up so much it became part of the general disillusionment between the Eastern and Western churches. It was one reason the West declined help to Byzantium in the fifteenth century, and the subsequent fall of the Byzantine Empire. In another of the

10. Toynbee, *Study of History*, 259.

strange twists of history then, if Toynbee was right, Byzantium's mimicry of Islam was a factor in their defeat by it.

One advantage Islam has in keeping the pictures away is retaining the sequential coherence of their holy book, whereas Christians pepper their new Bibles with pictures, panels, notes and diagrams, confusing the mind. Not too many decades ago Christian children were encouraged to memorize Bible verses, in fact whole chapters. It was not unknown for some wizards to commit a whole book out of the Bible into their brain. Introducing pictures and maps on every page dilutes the memorizing process, and few churches today award certificates for reciting Bible verses by heart anymore.

Such a decline fits well with our Internet world. Sergey Bryn, founder of Google, claimed; "We want Google to be the third half of your brain."[11]

It's another way of saying we'll lose our memories because we won't need them. The church, with its endless videos, graphics, TV media and Internet competing with the Bible, is well on the way to this paradigm. Over the last thirty years, many Pastors and Vicars have noticed a decline in Bible knowledge and awareness amongst Christians. Don't tell me that has nothing to do with the growth of visual media.

Muslims might be better off than Christians as memorizing the Qu'ran is not such an earth shaking feat among them. Since they are denied graphics, the book of words retains its essential form and structure. Oodles of young and old Muslims have committed the entire book to memory, and continue to do so to this day. Those who have memorized it are called hafiz. Such an exercise undoubtedly strengthens that part of their cranium for other memory uses as well. I guess I'm saying hire a Muslim youth as a waiter in your cafe: when he walks back to the barrista, he can still remember what was ordered.

Before I forget, let me return to the Bible. It took the Irish to introduce spaces between words in the Bible in the seventh century, explaining to us how those earlier manuscripts have all the words running together. The Irish figured out gaps might help the less gifted recognize where a word began and ended. To cap it all off, the Bible didn't originally come neatly separated into chapters and verses either. That move occurred in the thirteenth century as a way of helping readers quickly find a certain section. The Jews liked it so much they copied the chapter and verse system across to their Bible too, which is of course the Christian Old Testament. We could

---

11. "Sergey Brin," line 1.

assume with some safety that the saying "quotes it chapter and verse'" came after that innovation.

Today's Qu'ran with "Corresponding English Meanings" comes with verse numbering, but not the Arabian versions, apparently because it would upset the rhythm and sound of the Qu'ran.

As for language, the Old Testament was written in Hebrew, which had evolved from ancient Hebrew. We speak modern English, which has evolved from ancient English. If you don't know the difference, you can easily find text and audio on the Internet, as Chaucer wrote and spoke English for The Canterbury Tales six hundred years ago. It's barely understandable to the modern English speaker.

The New Testament was composed in Greek, which was developed from the Hebrew language, so there's some commonality. However Jesus spoke in Aramaic, which is a street level version of Hebrew. Some modern scholars have tried to reverse engineer Greek into Hebrew into Aramaic illustrating the fun linguists have with the Bible. Rome translated it again into Latin, losing various meanings, and under King James I, the historic 1611 Authorized Version bearing his name appeared in the English of his day—which you might also find unreadable.

Many Protestants ended up thinking their Bible canon was the only true one. Remember that myth that the Catholics added books to the Bible? In fact those extra books, known as the Apocrypha, were included in the Protestant King James Authorized Version up until 1885. With their much longer history, Catholics are more aware that other Christian titles didn't make it into the Canon, and are therefore more relaxed about recent discoveries such as the gospel of Thomas. These archaeological finds are both a boon and a threat to Protestants. They love the fact the book of Isaiah found amidst the Dead Sea Scrolls corresponds perfectly with the current day version of Isaiah. However they don't mention that the Dead Sea version of Jeremiah is substantially different from modern translations.

Nor are Muslims immune from this problem. Since the Qu'ran cannot be burnt, very old copies should still exist. Up until a few years ago most had vanished however. Then a trove was discovered in Sanaa in Yemen in 1972 comprised of fragments dating back to the seventh century. Differences between the Sanaa Qu'ran and current versions have been noted, which raise difficult questions for those maintaining it is the pure word of Allah. As the Sanaa project, still administered in Yemen, is accused of tardiness by some, others want to see it move ahead, including some Muslims.

Archeology is an interesting media, or extension of man. Archaeological tools enable us to get a more accurate picture of our past, and that is a challenge for both faiths. Their findings have raised up opponents determined to prove them wrong, such as the fellow who photographed chariot wheels from the Exodus story of Moses destroying the Egyptian Pharaoh's army. Moses commanded the Red Sea to flood over them, wonderfully portrayed in the old Charlton Heston movie shot before CGI days, and spruced up in the 2015 film, Exodus. Sure enough, the blurred underwater photos in the recent documentary looked like barnacle encrusted wheels.

However the team ran into problems. Somehow the Red Sea photo shoot site couldn't be found again, or there were legal problems of access, or the expedition ran out of money to dredge a wheel up—all excuses that raise suspicion. Funnily enough none of those impediments to proof stopped a worldwide showing of the movie to enthralled church youth though.

Christians may seize on Muslim conspiracy theories to silence Sanaa, but one can easily find the same opposing ends of the spectrum within Christendom. Conservative Christians may like archaeologists digging up something that appears to discredit the Qu'ran, but they hate it when a find casts questions on the Bible.

ATTENTION DEFICIT

Newspapers appeared a few hundred years back, then television in the 1950s, quickly followed by the glossy magazine revolution. These three between them presented multichannel information streams competing with the single theme book. You just need to divert your eyes on the newspaper to change topics, a factor seriously shifting journalism from dry facts to passion in order to retain your attention. Glossy magazines have taken this further, placing adverts where the eye naturally rests. Such multi-paneled pages have been accused of creating Attention Deficit Disorder (ADD) in all of us. Our gaze flickers across pages without retaining anything, or we change TV channels via the remote without moving from our chair.

Modern Bibles have picked this up and are now cluttered with photographs or colored explanatory note panels as we mentioned previously. Such Bibles are marketed as appealing to the young distracted mind, thereby proving the ADD theory. Christianity has clearly come a long way since the Gregorian Monastic age with its focus on meditation and reflection. Their timeless routines, every day the same with seven prayer breaks more or less repeating the same mantras and hymns, seem out of place in a hectic, time squeezed consumerist church offering a smorgasbord of instant spiritual fixes or remedies.

With every action there is a reaction however. I asked a sample group of friends whether they thought Monasticism was declining. Their quizzical looks required an explanation on what Monasticism was, a telling factor in itself. Without much thought they all agreed it would be declining.

Wrong. The Cistercian and Gregorian Monastic movements are alive and well, with compound growth rates around the world. They attract tired bankers, I.T. Professionals, and farmers into their midst, but sorry, no ladies yet. Nunneries for them.

What about the digital media world? Bibles and Qu'rans are available on computers, tablets and mobile phones. Debate has emerged in blogs on what to do with PC hard disks when the computer has reached its use by date. Theologically, what is the difference between burning a Qu'ran and deleting it from your computer? Islam could have quietly dropped their fury at the burning of Qu'rans once they adopted the printing press. The condemnation was embedded too deeply however, hence the Lahore torching of two hundred homes in 2013.

So if you have a Qu'ran on an aging computer disk, what do you do? Advice given includes; go into hiding after you've destroyed it, or have the right mental attitude when you do the act. I could not find an official ruling, and in any case the ground has moved—anyone can download a copy onto their smartphone, tablet, or ereader. When your download a Qu'ran to your smartphone, chances are you agree that the supplier can track your phone numbers and other information about you.

A further quandary is introduced if there is a version update. This is unlikely to be a revision of the actual text of the Qu'ran. Instead it will be an update to the software it is encased in. However, downloading version 1.1 overlays, i.e. destroys, burns, the entire version 1.0, including the text. And they know who you are. More than that, if GPS is enabled, they know where you live. To complicate matters, the producer of the app is as culpable as the recipient by encouraging the download replacement.

I've also seen an online debate on whether you can go to the toilet carrying a smartphone that has a Qu'ran installed on it. It doesn't take too much reflection to figure out why Muslims forbid reading the Qu'ran in the loo. Maybe there's a business opportunity here, building little boxes just outside. I digress.

It's hard to visualize any militant organization having the clout to track the millions of tablets and smartphones that will spread through the Middle East in the next several years. Another decision, or in actuality, non–decision, is to ignore it and go quiet, just as we shall learn the churches did over charging interest on money.

Christians however have blithely learnt, with only minor resistance, that computers and the Internet are okay. Back in the early 1980s, as a budding I.T. professional, I was frequently warned there was a gigantic computer in Brussels of all places, presumably an EEC plot back then. It knew everything, and was numbered 666—the mark of the beast.

The church swung over in the mid 1980s and now a plethora of Bible computer programs compete with each other. It's even gone Open Source, which mostly means free download, and is a sign of how trendy the industry is. Immune to further anti–computer bursts, the smartphone was welcomed by players such as Youversion. Free of charge, this app offers multiple translations along with all sorts of plans to get you reading the Bible. In an ADD world, I suspect the suggestions and updates are there to remind us we actually have the app installed among the other 136 we've downloaded since.

HOLY MIMICRY

There's a heading in the page to indicate we're shifting topics.

This is another universal book media habit among the many we are barely conscious of. The Inca King would not have picked this up. Whether you realize it or not, every time you read anything, your long cultural memory has conditioned you to automatically recognize these patterns. Followers of either faith frequently miss the whole point about media, believing content is the only thing worth examining. I deliberately placed those previous sections ahead of what the holy books actually say for this reason.

Well, here we are.

At content.

What do these two holy books say? Don't expect a full answer in this restricted volume. The world is full of such works. Both religions have an enormous heritage of active remembering. We'll look at recent disciplines that are upsetting traditional ways of viewing scriptures.

Muslims believe they were delivered the final, summarizing message of God via Muhammad. Using the word "final" means they accept other books written before the Qu'ran, especially from the Jews and Christians. Jews and Christians share the Old Testament, and disagree completely over the New Testament.

Islam holds that both were tampered with anyway, and only put right when Muhammad got the last word. Anyone with Biblical knowledge reading the Qu'ran discovers that it refers to the same characters as the Bible, but gets events mixed up. Mixed up according to Christians or Jews that is. e.g. there is a part in the Qu'ran where King Saul has his army drinking from the cups of their hands.[12] The Bible tale of drinking from cupped hands is about Gideon,[13] hundreds of years earlier than King Saul. Elsewhere in the Qu'ran Moses speaks about the Samaritan.[14] Samaritans come from the town of Samaria, neither founded nor occupied by Israelites until they were well established in the promised land.[15] Moses died before Israel even entered the promised land according to the Bible.

Many Christians then dismiss the Qu'ran as a hodgepodge, confusing different stories with each other. Not so, claim the Muslims. They say the Bible was wrong all along as it got reworked through the ages. Muhammad's version is correct according to Muslims, right back to his narrations about Adam and Eve. The angel Gabriel straightened everything out by relaying the Qu'ran directly.

From one point of view it's a clean cut argument. God gets annoyed with people getting his message mixed up, so he makes one focused effort to deliver his final word to one person. Muslims have arguments in their favor—even in the first two chapters, the Bible contains two differing accounts of creation.

Either way, there's not going to be much agreement between Biblical and Quranic students. By definition, one side has got these stories wrong, if not both. Archeology is not kind to either as it happens. Proof that Moses even existed is still lacking. However Egyptian Pharaohs did not write up failures, and losing Israel was a serious loss, if it did occur. As was famously once said, "Absence of proof is not proof of absence." Let's remind ourselves of our focus however: what happened amongst Christians with their book, and are the same things happening in Islam? And, significantly, what will it mean for Islam?

12. Sura 2:249
13. Judges 7:4–8
14. Sura 85–95
15. 1 Kings 16:24

One of the first things that happened to the Bible was the transition to Greek thinking from Jewish, or Hebrew thinking. Hebrews, (an early name for Jews), thought in narrative stories: Greeks thought in logical concepts. The Old Testament was written in Hebrew, the New Testament in Greek. Even though the New Testament was written about Jews mainly, it was not written in their tongue.

This is important because Western Christians think more like Greeks. They love logic and concepts. Christianity inherited books of law, a collection of narrative stories, and poetic and futurist books, in the Old Testament. The New Testament has narrative and church concept material, plus some futurist texts, especially in the Revelation to John. Christians have been sorting all this into formulas, or creeds, ever since.

Let me give an example.

The book of Job is a narrative story relating how God is provoked by Satan to deliver bad news to the most righteous man on earth. At the beginning of Job are some verses where Satan talks with God. That part is told quickly, in order to get to the main part of the book which is the discussion Job has with his friends about his woes. Here are the verses;

- And the Lord said to Satan, "From where do you come?" Then Satan answered the Lord, and said, "From roaming about on the earth and walking around on it."[16]

Christians can build a whole theology about this, explaining how Satan can't be in every place at once. Sometimes he is present, and sometimes absent. That can be imputed from those lines in Job. The narrative story teller looks across at the theologian with bewilderment, wondering why he doesn't get onto the important part, which is the human dialogue between men under stress. In turn the theologian thinks the narrative story teller has missed the wider lesson; mankind is afflicted by Satan sporadically, whereas the love of God is permanently available everywhere.

Who's right? There is no right or wrong here, there are simply different perspectives, and different eras. Christians have spent two thousand years converting these stories into concepts, creeds, or church dogma. These have changed over time, and will again. They have been actively remembered.

You see, there are no bullet points in the Bible, and no subsections explaining concepts like the Four Spiritual Laws, a gospel tract printed one hundred million times. If you look in the Bible, you won't find the Four

---

16. Job 1:6–7

Spiritual Laws. They were extracted from it by people thinking like Greeks, looking for conceptual keys.

In a way, same with Islam. There are no bullet points in the Qu'ran either. Muslim scholars have pored over it for thirteen hundred years, drawing concepts and laws out of it. They have their own theories about Satan for example, formed by examining stories about him in the Qu'ran. In that sense, they think like Greeks. Like Westerners.

Now of course this is a generalized view, but you can see how we're not going to get far bringing these two faiths together with the clash of logic, using conceptual models. However, even from this brief analysis, we can see active remembering at work on those texts, presenting them both to us as "past as present."

Now, since both Christians and Muslims insist their respective books are consistent and logical, how come there is still no internal agreement on the body of logic inside each faith? How come after two thousand years Christians still don't have definitive agreement on just what those concepts are? Why there are 35,000 different denominations worldwide, many with differing theories? Same thing with Islam. Thirteen hundred years is a long time. Surely they could have worked out their body of logic by now, and all agreed on exactly what Islamic law is.

The answer from both sides is that these are living religions, and have adapted to the times. Laws need constant review to keep them relevant. i.e. active remembering. This is not a good argument for a society that adopts and discards new media as fast as today, but I'm jumping ahead, so let's leave that a while.

These issues get complicated on the Christian side by another factor, disagreed over between Protestants and Roman Catholics: Protestants hold the Bible to be the final word on matters, and concepts and creeds: Roman Catholics claim church authority and tradition also has a role. This explains why the Pope can come out with a statement and claim it is infallible. He very rarely does this by the way, but he's been allowed to for about 150 years.

This significant difference aligns Protestants with Muslims, in that they each claim their book is infallible. The Bible is infallible. And to Muslims, the Qu'ran is infallible.

Gridlock?

Maybe not.

A shift is in the wind in Christianity, aided by the Internet. In the days when you could eradicate different theological opinions by burning books and authors, the church had an advantage in enforcing dogma. After his conversion and legitimization of the faith, the first Christian Roman emperor, Constantine, realized what a hornet's nest of opinions existed within Christianity. He somewhat let church leaders fight it out among themselves, and they began formalizing belief. The Nicene Creed emerged in 325 AD and the Apostle's Creed in 390 AD. To this day these creeds are read by far more people than read the Bible. Every Sunday, congregations around the world recite them. They were an early attempt to formalize the concepts of the faith, a major one of which was who goes to heaven and who goes to hell.

Other Christian ideas disagreeing with the prevailing theories got trod on long ago, one such being Universal Reconciliation, which claims everyone goes to heaven, no matter which belief or religion you adhere to. Universal Reconciliation isn't exactly a power statement requiring adherence to a church. If anything it's a theory freeing you from church, or indeed mosque authority, because it doesn't matter what they say, you're going through the pearly gates anyway.

Universal Reconciliation never quite died. It was strong enough not to be termed a heresy, and always maintained a following among thinkers who couldn't conceive of a loving God throwing the vast majority of humans into an eternal fire. Along came the Internet, and followers of Universal Reconciliation began to discover each other around the world, and lots of them wrote up websites. Google returned 38,500 hits on the phrase "universal reconciliation" in January 2015. However, while Universal Reconciliation is growing once more, it is nevertheless still a Greek theory of logic. It finds scriptural proofs for a formula of salvation. But at least it includes Muslims, by definition.

Islam has followed similar paths, in a case of unconscious mimicry. Similar to the Christian Councils and Creeds, Islam tried to formalize their theories in its early years. Classical Sunni Islam punished unbelievers in unending Fire, supported by many verses from the Qu'ran.[17] Muhammad Ali gave us the shortest reason about becoming a Muslim when he said, "It means a ticket to heaven."[18] That concept sat there a long time, until, again, modern communications permitted discussion. The title of a conference presentation by Asma Barlas says it all; "Reviving Islamic Universalism."[19]

17. E.g. Sura 4:56

18. "Text Illustration Search Results for Ali," line 2.

19. Barlas, "Reviving Islamic Universalism," line 1.

It turns out that the narrative school of thinking is being revived. Some theologians are getting back to Hebrew thinking and focusing on the importance of each Bible story or parable of Jesus, and its application to life today. Rather than build complicated theories, this new, (or old) school, doesn't bother so much with creeds and formulas. Narrative works with the morals of the tales.

In fact some recent theologians have conceded, like Stephen Hawking has for science, that it's not that simple finding a grand theory that explains everything,[20] and that Christians have spent too long looking for one. That the New Testament for example, contains "a plurality of theologies."[21] Pick one. Your choice doesn't matter, the narrative people say. What matters is how you will act tomorrow in a stressful situation at work. A hint of narrative is creeping into Islam as well.[22]

Now be careful about this narrative theory. Mullahs, Imams, Pastors, and Bishops, all over the world use narrative many times when they preach sermons. They tell stories, metaphors or parables. That's how they get ideas across. At first hearing, it sounds like narrative has always been around, and it certainly appears in the stained glass windows of St. Florentin. The listener needs to dig deeper.

In Christianity for example, those formulas are still deep down in the psyche of preachers. Pastors will tell stories, show movies, and sing songs in our modern world, but they rarely mention hell any more. It's not so popular. Sometimes you have to ask them point blank. Frequently the narrative tale covers up a concept door. Those entertaining stories mostly lead back to the prevailing theology formula called Penal Substitution, which is the widespread concept that you have to accept Jesus to avoid perdition. On the other hand, a true narrative speaker will not have a theological formula waiting in the wings—he or she will just have the story itself.

If these debates are hard to follow, that is understandable. It may seem like arguing over how many angels can fit on a pinhead, which was a medieval discussion. Surely everyone would be better off just changing channels to Britain's got Talent. It's worse than that though. These arcane questions provoke more fire than hell can possibly produce. For example, accepting the Universalist theories or the narrative schools means both Christians and Muslims end in up in heaven with each other, or that neither side has

20. Hawkings and Mlodinov, *The Grand Design*, 180–181.

21. McDonald, *Formation of the Christian Biblical Canon*, 236.

22. See Bodman, "Poetics of Iblis,"

any say in it. It's not belief that is at risk here—it's power. Both narrative and Universalist theories challenge power structures that are based on the logic of various theological concepts and formulas. For all that we might castigate the Internet then, perhaps it is impacting those power structures.

For Christians, understanding how Muslims handle the Qu'ran is further complicated by the existence of the hadith, which is the collection of traditions from early days. As Nabeel Qureshi, a former Muslim, explained;

> The Qur'an comprises only a small part of a Muslim's worldview. Far from "sola scriptura," the Islamic way of life mostly comes from traditions, called "hadith." How many times to pray, rules for ceremonial washing and rituals, details on fasting and commerce laws. . . almost everything comes from hadith. Some hadith even render Qu'ranic verses "abrogated," or repealed, depending on which imam interprets them. Thus, a complex system of time-honored traditions, authoritative leaders, and theological branches interact with the Qur'an to form Islam. As Muslims, we did not learn Islam directly through the Qur'an. We absorbed it by being immersed among other Muslims.[23]

Faced with these varying similarities, differences and approaches, Western researchers began poking their their nose into the Bible about two hundred years ago using a relatively new extension of men. It is a contentious field called textual or "literary criticism." I have chosen this bland phrase to describe it. Alternatives such as "higher criticism" can provoke ire from Bible teachers. Take the two words at face value though—it is the analysis of literature, practiced on many other books, including the works of Shakespeare.

Among other things literary criticism means examining the text of any document to see when it was written, by comparing it to other texts whose date is known. e.g. if an undated article talked about any topic, not just religion, but in passing the author bought a brand new Model T Ford for $440, you then have a clue when the article was written. The price of a Model T was $850 in 1909, $440 in 1915, and $260 in 1920. So the article was written in 1915.

Go back hundreds or thousands of years, and you might find a shard of clay with the price of corn tallied on it. Comparing that to other finds gives you clues. One shard might mention a meteor shower alongside the cost of a cow. Scientists narrow down meteor showers to windows of time,

23. Qureshi, "Should Christians read the Qu'ran?" para. 6.

and then calculate cow prices in that era. This is the beauty and power of those articles that were passively forgotten. These passively forgotten traces of the past assist literary analysts.

A challenge arises when say, a holy text purportedly written by a significant religious figure has the price of the cow wrong for the time he lived in. If you take the analysis at face value, it is saying that important figure didn't write that—that it might have been written several hundred years after they died. At that point, active remembering or forgetting pops up. Believers pinning their credibility on the factuality of a specific holy text do not like to be told it was written by another author in a later era.

Another branch of literary criticism examines different textual styles. We all express things differently, and we all have habits or clichés in our writing. Imagine if you wrote several chapters of a story, and someone else wrote other chapters. The story could well be logical and have a plot, only you did chapters 1,2 4 and 7. Your friend wrote chapters 3, 5 and 6. An expert would able to go through and find patterns unique to those sections. Even if it was all typed up. We're not talking about handwriting styles. With enough study time, that expert could sort it out. And experts pore over and study the holy texts for decades. They examine every word, every phrase.

Challenges emerge when they get to the Torah, the first five books of the Bible. Jews and conservative Christians believe the Torah was written by Moses. Okay, Moses wrote about how he died. Christians can generally accept a little humor there, but that's about it. Literary critics meanwhile have found up to ten different styles, i.e. ten author sources in the Torah.[24] These sources were put together by someone called a Redactor, long ago. It was the original cut and paste, but thousands of years back. Some authorities think it might even have been Ezra, an actual Bible character as it happens.[25] This is how commentators explain those two creation stories in the first two chapters of the Bible—they were written by different authors and patched together.

The findings of the literary critics contradict the fervent beliefs of some religious groups. The scientific method of the critics is powerful and rigorous. So is the vehement denial of some branches of Christendom. Don't even go there with the Orthodox Jews. Despite some two hundred years of such research, books by literary critics about the Bible are still on the periphery. They are not talked about by pastors, and you would be hard

---

24. Friedman, *The Bible with Sources Revealed*, 32.
25. Friedman, *Who Wrote the Bible*, 223–225.

pressed to hear positive lectures at a church leadership gathering. You have to go to a secular conference on literary criticism. Indeed many Christian groups fund alternative research to establish that Moses did indeed write the Torah. There is still a widespread belief that the Bible is inerrant, was virtually dictated by God, and is completely error free.

Not all church groups reject these findings. A growing movement accepts that say, Moses didn't write the Torah. The Emergent Church movement, (which is so disorganized it shouldn't have a label like Emergent), generally accepts literary criticism.

It doesn't stop with Moses. Critics have examined the New Testament as well, the part of the Bible containing the words of Jesus. Using their bag of tools, they tell us that Jesus probably didn't say many of things he is reputed to have said. The Gospel of John is a central document to Christians, yet many analysts tell us it is unlikely Jesus said anything recorded by the author.

Now the Gospel of John contains the verse most widely quoted in the whole world attributed to Jesus;

- For God so loved the world, that he gave his only begotten Son, that whoever believes in Him should not perish, but have eternal life.[26]

Literary critics feel Jesus didn't say this, and they have strong arguments for their claim. It's a biggie, because if accepted, it alters an entire Christian formula and belief structure. Numerous smaller beliefs, attitudes and values sit, domino like, waiting to be knocked over if this one falls. What trail of evidence do the analysts have to question the gospel of John? Several other works in the New Testament were also written by the same John. John wrote that Revelation to John, and it lists several unique churches in Asia Minor that are not listed elsewhere, especially not listed in the main history book in the New Testament, which is the Acts of the Apostles. This omission from an associated work leads analysts to the reasonable possibility that these churches grew later than the ones in Acts.

Moreover, John writes to them in Revelation on the basis of them having problems. In other words, some time has passed—firstly for these unknown churches to have been founded, secondly for them to have developed problems, and thirdly to have the author know about them. After all, he lists seven churches. That's a lot of research and time given high speed broadband access wasn't available then. Therefore John must have written

26. John 3:16

them much later; therefore he could not have lived side by side with Jesus unless he started writing at the age of eighty or ninety. Borg dates all the books written by John somewhere between 90 AD and 110 AD.[27] Two options remain: sixty or seventy years is a long time to remember any lengthy verbal address, either word for word, or indeed the general gist of what was said. John's gospel contains several lengthy passages of Jesus talking: or John probably wasn't alive when Jesus was, and can't be quoting him firsthand.

Now the above is a list of therefores. Although it does make sense, denying Jesus actually said John 3:16 causes pastors and priests worldwide to hit the roof. Literary critics are condemned as devilish. I have even heard a preacher relate the fact the literary criticism movement sprang out of Germany in the nineteenth century is linked to the emergence of Nazism there in the twentieth.

The analysts also compare the Gospel of John with claims from other gospels in the New Testament. The oldest one is the Gospel of Mark. Don't get confused again by the sequential order, it's not the Gospel of Matthew. Mark tells us;

- and He (Jesus) did not speak to them without a parable;[28]

There are no parables in the Gospel of John.

All these literary analytical debates get the opposite reaction from Jews, who part company with Christians over the New Testament. Jews love bad news about Jesus. An ancient author named Josephus wrote a huge history book around the time of Jesus. Josephus mentions Jesus. Some authorities claim a redactor planted that sentence in the works of Josephus later on.[29] I heard one entertaining Jewish Rabbi tell his audience excitedly about the Josephus redaction, but when I emailed a question about whether he agreed the Torah was also redacted, he didn't write back. We're seeing deep core memory challenges here. It's easy to criticize, or find mythology, in another religion, but not so simple with your own.

There was a time when such beliefs could do more than challenge your core thinking—they might cost you your life. Literary critics would have been charged with blasphemy. In 1697 young Thomas Aikenhead was hung in Edinburgh after being found guilty of questioning the origins of the Bible. He was the last to be executed, although the odd blasphemer was

27. Borg, *Evolution of the Word*, 32.

28. Mark 4:34

29. "The Jesus Forgery," para. 5.

jailed up until less than a hundred years ago. Since then scientific inquiry has proceeded to the point where at least public debates on the issue are run.

What can we say for certain about literary criticism of Christianity's holy texts?

- It exists. It's not illegal and has a big following in the West, albeit mainly outside the church.

- It has not gone away despite a two hundred year history. Indeed it has expanded as a field of academic inquiry. The Flat Earth Society also continues to exist, but no longer in University curricula.

- It deeply affects the faith decisions of individuals, to the point of controversy and angry personal attacks.

- Some Christian groups (rather than academic groups) are taking on the ramifications of grappling with a new emerging faith which accepts the findings of literary criticism.

Two astounding troves of ancient texts were found in caves shortly after World War 2—the Dead Sea scrolls in Israel, and the Nag Hammadi scrolls in Egypt. The first finding was welcomed by Christians by and large, because it proved translation efforts of Bible books like Isaiah were accurate. Nag Hammadi was a different kettle of fish because it uncovered some books that had been deemed heretical nearly two thousand years ago—especially the Gospel of Thomas. Comprised of 114 sayings of Jesus, it is completely unlike any of the other gospels. It looks more like Buddha wrote it, which is the point of contention. Authors of such texts were condemned as Gnostics, which fundamentally had more in common with Buddhism. Just to add to the woes of those fighting the literary critics, pressure exists to include the Gospel of Thomas within the Bible. Not much as yet, but it's there.[30]

Why is this a big deal? Many Protestants think their holy text, the Bible, is closed. Nothing more can be added to it, and certainly not taken away. Those same Protestant conservatives don't realize that Martin Luther himself, the founder of Protestantism, wanted to remove four New Testament books, but could only get them assigned to the back of his Lutheran Bible.

Other books have also been discovered or made public in recent years, including the Gospel of Judas. This was purported to lay open what really

30. See http://www.westarinstitute.org for more.

happened in Christianity, but it proved to have been written long after the lives of either Jesus or Judas. However, at least it got out into the public arena and was examined by the scientific community.

Where do Muslims stand over literary criticism of their holy text?

In comparison to Christianity, Qu'ranic literary criticism is barely off the starting block. Islam is too big not to have scholars delve into it. However, they're mostly Westerners. Similar to those probing the New Testament sayings of Jesus, literary analysts risk criticizing Muhammad himself. This is bigger than a suspicion of Bible authorship. The Bible has multiple authors, but with the Qu'ran it all comes from one man. And that one man has it directly linked to Allah.

Muslims believe this transmission was so exact you can't experience the Qu'ran fully unless you read it in Arabic. To some extent, there's a parallel with the church. To this day many Roman Catholics prefer the Mass to be read in Latin. Maybe that ancient tongue sounds more holy. Many in the Middle East, using Islamic logic therefore, say Arabic must be the language of God since he dictated the Qu'ran that way. And if you convert to Islam, you generally get an Arab name too. They take this so seriously that many Muslim services and sermons in the West are given in Arabic. Second generation, English speaking believers, might not understand a word that is said.

It's a major point because linguists and Muslims scholars remind us that this single original language has a lot more going for it than seventeen ways to describe a camel. It has a style best heard and appreciated in Arabic, like poetry almost. That's understandable. Translating poetry from one language to another will lose some of the rhythmical timing, and the rhyme endings on sentences, if they happen to be there. The rhyming nature undoubtedly assists Muslims to memorize the Qu'ran and become hafiz. This is a significant difference. Simplistically speaking, the Bible is studied, and the Qu'ran is recited. Of course it's not that general, except that you are unlikely to hear the Bible recited at length.

From their particular background, Western linguists begin their literary criticism of the Qu'ran the way they have been trained. To begin, what sort of Arabic existed back then? After all, English has markedly changed, even since the first officially printed Bible in 1611. The letter J didn't exist back then, so Jesus was spelled Iesus. And the letter S looks like today's letter F. Has the same language evolution affected Arabic? Turns out there are hints of that. Awkward words are inserted here and there in the Qu'ran, betraying possible redaction work. When we found all those 193 references to the word book in the Qu'ran, they were not technically book—the word was codex, which was the first term for a folded page book.

The critics also widen the scope of their questions to include other nearby historical documents. The Qu'ran doesn't like the Trinity. In Christianity the Trinity refers to Father (God), Son (Jesus) and Holy Spirit (The Comforter). The Qu'ran disparages this, pouring cold water on the idea that God has taken a son.[31] The Qu'ran then gets the Trinity mixed up, intimating it is comprised of Father, Mary and Son.[32] We are on argumentative ground here by the way; the Arabic Qu'ran doesn't use the word Trinity, as eager Muslims will point out. It uses a word that can be translated as polytheist. (Polytheism is not belief in a supreme parrot, no more than monotheism reveres a black and white god).

Christians believe in a single God, with three personalities in one. It is an imputed doctrine though, one worked out a few hundred years after Jesus. It is a formula again. The word Trinity does not appear in the Bible either. Muslims were not the first, nor certainly the last to have trouble with the doctrine of the Trinity. Plenty of Christians dispute it too, to this day. Now, hypothetically speaking, say you were God, trying to correct the error of this mistaken dogma. One might think you, God, would outline the nature of the problem clearly to the one tasked with rectifying it. i.e. Muhammad. But it didn't happen like this. So where did the Father, Mary, Son idea come from?

Nearby discoveries tell researchers the answer. Muhammad closely associated with Jews and Christians, spending time in the marketplaces listening to, and talking with them. Some of these Middle Eastern Christians had odd theories about the Trinity. One such strange, minor Christian theology from a region near Muhammad had Father, Mary and Son.[33] Muhammad had no way of knowing this was not the major Trinitarian belief, but this fringe idea that never got anywhere in mainstream Christian belief was much closer to him than Rome.

Another Qu'ranic passage refers to the Companions of the cave[34] which has some interesting political and spiritual encounters between youths and rulers. Stories about sleeping for three hundred years for example. It doesn't

31. Sura 18:4
32. "Islamic view of the Trinity," para. 12.
33. Reynolds, *The Qur'an in its Historical Context*, 112.
34. Sura 18:9–37

make sense until one investigates nearby Syrian Christian tales.[35] A parallel story had floated around the region for about two hundred years, with all sorts of miracles attached to it. It must have been a commonplace tale back then, because in the Qu'ran Allah actually asks Muhammad his opinion on those miracles, or signs.[36] Yet this tale is a side event, unknown by mainstream Western Christianity, and certainly not listed in the Bible.

These Western literary critics are trying to tell us Muhammad's version of Christianity might have been picked up from local chatter. Since he could not read, he could not pore over books that he did not own, nor write comparative lists on paper he did not possess. So he challenged Christian ideas he heard locally, which were never widespread anyway. And at this point, currently, Qu'ranic scholars draw a serious bold line—the Qu'ran came from God, and that is all there is to it. How could this immense rhyming work in Arabic of 77,000 words that they love being recited, arrive any other way? That's not a question the West understands. Cardinal Jean–Louis Tauran, a Vatican official, noted, in response to a request by Muslim world leaders for more dialogue between the faiths; "Muslims do not accept that one can discuss the Qu'ran in depth, because they say it was written by dictation from God. With such an absolute interpretation, it is difficult to discuss the contents of faith."[37]

Cardinal Tauran has a point. He's got used to different media approaches to analyzing the Bible. Don't forget literary criticism was forced on him by the universities. So you have to take your hat off to him. Far from moaning there aren't enough executions of Thomas Aikenhead's who question the Bible's origins, he accepts that as today's norm—and finds Muslims lacking because they won't go there. Which, unfortunately, is true. In 1989 author Salman Rushdie wrote a book entitled The Satanic Verses. The then ruler of Iran, the Ayatollah Khomeini, issued a fatwa, in this case a death sentence, against Rushdie, for purportedly questioning the Qu'ran in his book. Despite at least one assassination attempt, Rushdie is alive and well, but apparently receives a card every year from Iran warning him the fatwa is still valid.

However, literary criticism of the Qu'ran is too big a research field to go away. As mentioned earlier, in 1972 a team discovered a trove of ancient scripts in Yemen, eventually persuading a German team to fund restoration

35. Reynolds, *The Qur'an in its Historical Context*, 116–122.

36. Sura 18:9

37. "Vatican rebuffs Muslim outreach," para. 4.

efforts. A lot of microfilm was shot and taken back to Europe, and is still being organized—forty years later. These texts are some of the oldest of the Qu'ran ever found, and evidently some discrepancies occur, although not a great amount. The researchers don't want to upset accessibility by saying anything too radical in case the Yemeni door swings shut on the manuscripts.

The Western researchers come complete with Western reasoning, convinced they can convince others;

> "So many Muslims have this belief that everything between the two covers of the Qur'an is Allah's unaltered word. They like to quote the textual work that shows that the Bible has a history and did not fall straight out of the sky, but until now the Qur'an has been out of this discussion. The only way to break through this wall is to prove that the Qur'an has a history too. The Sana'a fragments will help us accomplish this."[38]

This issue is not a matter of logic, that apparatus of academia. Nobody will break through this wall by proving anything academically. It is deeper than that. Muslim scholars respond, but appeal to a different form of logic than Western researchers proffer.

> The Qur'anic challenge was addressed not to the believers but to the unbelievers, and was not simply denunciation of the unbelievers, but constituted an invitation to them to carefully examine the Qur'an and see if it could have been, as they claimed it was, the product of the mind of a man possessed. Irrespective of what conclusion one reaches on the question of the Qur'an's origins, one must agree that the underlying assumption of the challenge was that the merit and beauty of the Qur'an could be appreciated even by those outside the fold of the faith.[39]

This writer has reworded the Islamic assumption we put before, namely that this immense rhyming work could not have come from a man. And if we think about it, that is a reasonable claim, depending on where you stand.

Before we go any further, we ought to look into our brains to understand what we think is logic. If you are a Westerner, there's a reasonable chance you grasped the logic of how literary critics go about their work in our universities. Their method makes sense to the way Westerners are

38. "What is the Koran?" para. 7.
39. "The Qur'ān As Literature," para. 4.

trained to think. Westerners may not be so persuaded by the logic of the Muslim scholar above who starts from a different premise. His logic is that the Qu'ran is beautifully put together, and therefore anyone would see that it must have had the mind of God behind it to construct it. It is simply too much for an individual to compile. The scholar could go further and say that if any individual didn't see that, then he is cursed. As it happens he didn't, but the Qu'ran itself does.[40] Remember that we are not dealing with Socialism, a construct from the West. Islam is a genuine Third World invention. It was not designed from a Western world–view of logic.

Step two for the Muslim scholars is easy. They have now proved the Qu'ran is the word of God by its rhyming structure at the least. So belief in the book is established. Now the mind is clear to ferret out what Allah is actually saying between the lines. In other words what are the theologies, the formulas, and the laws that wait to be revealed? There is a logic to that, especially when everyone in the university theology staffroom thinks the same. East and West can lock academic horns here, when actually the real issue is they both defend differing views of logic. These are deep core beliefs, which prefer to remain undisturbed by memory and mythology studies.

Literary criticism of the Qu'ran doesn't stop by trying to see whether Muhammad wrote it or copied some from Christian and Jewish sources. The Qu'ran is sequenced from longest Suras to shortest, although apparently that was ordered by Muhammad and Allah.[41] Another movement has rearranged the books of the Qu'ran into the historical order they were written in. We've already noted Marcus Borg tried that with the New Testament.

A school of thought holds that if you read the Qu'ran that way you will see the unfolding nature of Muhammad's political platform. In fact the Qu'ran has a verse indicating that Allah was allowed to change his mind;

- We do not abrogate a verse or cause it to be forgotten except that We bring forth (one) better than it or similar to it. Do you not know that Allah is over all things competent?[42]

While this may raise a question about infallibility of the work, that's not our point here. Muhammad went through several phases of his own career. Starting with hope, he suffered disappointment before he conquered. Accordingly, this school claims the books get more violent and more condemnatory if read chronologically, as Muhammad seems to lose patience

40. Sura 2:161
41. Sura 75:17
42. Sura 2:106

with unbelievers. This view is often adopted by ex–Muslims who have "seen the light." More than one book has been written by an ex–Muslim explaining how he was able to re–read the Qu'ran after exiting the faith, and what a shock it was to discover its real agenda.

To throw the cat among the pigeons, Muslim scholars today claim Islam was way ahead of the West in their own method of literary criticism. Scholars such as Bukhari wanted to know every person in a chain of transmission of stories right back to Muhammad. After publishing their findings, they were scrutinized by a process Westerners would equate to peer review. Western literary criticism was late off the mark by Muslim standards, because this construction of the hadiths about Muhammad began over a thousand years ago.

Hadith science is very important to Muslims. One could think of the hadith as being the history of the man from whom it came, which is parallel to the history of the men figuring in the Bible. However, the hadiths did not come from Muhammad. They were written about him. Stories that were told or remembered about Muhammad, and passed a proof test were included in the hadith. The key to understanding the role of the hadiths is to think of Muhammad as the perfect man. Many books and essays with the phrase "perfect man" relating to Muhammad can be found. If he did or said anything then, it must be the correct thing to do or say.

The next step for Muslims was to figure out laws based on the actions and words of this perfect man that we can all live by. Sometimes there were contradictions to clear up. e.g. the Qu'ran allows a man to marry only four wives, whereas Muhammad had eleven in total. Such discrepancies invite criticism of Islam.

The Qu'ran mentions the mercy of Allah continually, and we are told by commentators today that the religion is one of peace. So when an episode like the beheadings of six hundred Jews in the presence of Muhammad in 627 AD found its way into the hadiths,[43] it needed to be explained, and formed into a legal statute. Imam al–Shafi'i, 767—820 AD , one of the four great imams of juridical matters after whom the Shafi'i school of Islamic Jurisprudence thinking is named, set his mind to working out a legal framework around it.[44]

The Jews of Banu Qurayza tried to double cross Muhammad prior to a battle, despite the fact they had an earlier treaty with him. Muhammad

43. "Translation of Sahih Bukhari," para. 26.

44. Kister, "Massacre of the Banu Qurayza," 66–68.

outfoxed them, and their chance to muster overwhelming force against Muhammad's army melted away. So they surrendered, and awaited the verdict of the Muslims. The grown men were lined up along a trench, possibly dug in the marketplace, and beheaded in groups. Imam al-Shafi'i outlined all the conditions in which this seeming aberration from other Qu'ranic texts on mercy occurred. It takes exhaustive reading, but basically he lists a series of conditions whereby the guilty party set up a treaty, then broke it. He formulates his statute under the legal heading 'Violation of a treaty.' He is thorough, as one in his place should be, realizing that not every man among the Jews decided on this reneging. Nevertheless in the circumstances he carefully analyses, he comes to the decision that it is okay to kill all the men, but not the women or children—they can be taken as booty though. It is not compulsory, al-Shafi'i carefully says, but it must be allowed because Muhammad approved it. Imam al-Shafi'i wasn't alone. Another early eminent Muslim jurist, al-Mawardi, agreed with him. He said;

> If it is argued: "He struck the heads of the Banii Qurayza deliberately during one day, their number being about seven hundred, so where is his disposition to forgive and pardon? After all he retaliated like a man who was not inclined towards them by mercy, nor had in his soul softness for them," the answer would be: "He merely did it in order to carry out the rules of God (incumbent upon him)"[45]

In other words, since Muhammad was ordered by Allah to conduct this multiple beheading, then so be it. These are examples of how Sharia law is constructed. If you examine the deeds of this perfect man you can come up with guidance and legal precedents.

Given that we are focused on media, let's finish this chapter with a little exercise illustrating the emergence and effect of media on a Qu'ranic passage over the centuries. We will look at two verses in the Qu'ran, and at the following observations;

- The works of Al-Tabari, an ancient Muslim historian.
- A nineteenth century English writer.
- A voice from islamtoday.
- The application of a Western literary critical tool.
- Twenty-first century Wikipedia.

45. Ibid., 69.

An adopted son of Muhammad's named Zayd had a beautiful wife named Zaynab bint Jahsh. Here is the story as related by Al-Tabari, a renowned Muslim scholar and historian who died in 923 AD;

> Tabari 8:1 "In this year the Messenger married Zaynab bt. Jahsh (a first cousin): Allah's Messenger came to the house of Zayd bin (son of) Muhammad. Perhaps the Messenger missed him at that moment. Zaynab, Zayd's wife, rose to meet him. She was dressed only in a shift. . . She jumped up eagerly and excited the admiration of Allah's Messenger, so that he turned away murmuring something that could scarcely be understood. However, he did say overtly, 'Glory be to Allah Almighty, who causes hearts to turn!'
>
> So Zayd went to Muhammad. 'Prophet, I have heard that you came to my house. Why didn't you go in? Perhaps Zaynab has excited your admiration, so I will leave her.'"
>
> Tabari 8:3 "Zayd left her, and she became free. While the Messenger of Allah was talking with Aisha, a fainting overcame him. When he was released from it, he smiled and said, 'Who will go to Zaynab to tell her the good news? Allah has married her to me.'
>
> Then the Prophet recited (Qu'ran 33) to the end of the passage. Aisha said, 'I became very uneasy because of what we heard about her beauty and another thing, the loftiest of matters, what Allah had done for her by personally giving her to him in marriage. I said that she would boast of it over us.'"
>
> Tabari 8:4 "One day Muhammad went out looking for Zayd. Now there was a covering of haircloth over the doorway, but the wind had lifted the covering so that the doorway was uncovered. Zaynab was in her chamber, undressed, and admiration for her entered the heart of the Prophet. After that Allah made her unattractive to Zayd.'"[46]

Al-Tabari's version of history slumbered for over a thousand years, seemingly without dispute. It was not outlawed in early Islam, nor were his works burnt. Indeed he is still regarded as reputable, much as the historian Josephus of Rome, from the first century AD, is by Christians and non-Christians today.

Muhammad received his divine revelation, which was inserted into the Qu'ran, sanctioning this marriage.

> It is not for a believing man or a believing woman, when Allah and His Messenger have decided a matter, that they should (thereafter) have any choice about their affair. And whoever disobeys Allah

46. Al-Tabari, *History of al-Tabari*, Vol. 1–8

and His Messenger has certainly strayed into clear error. And (remember, O Muhammad), when you said to the one on whom Allah bestowed favor and you bestowed favor, "Keep your wife and fear Allah," while you concealed within yourself that which Allah is to disclose. And you feared the people, while Allah has more right that you fear Him. So when Zayd had no longer any need for her, We married her to you in order that there not be upon the believers any discomfort concerning the wives of their adopted sons when they no longer have need of them. And ever is the command of Allah accomplished.[47]

You may have noticed something already. The Qu'ran says wives might be discarded, but not to worry about it—"that there not be upon the believers any discomfort concerning the wives of their adopted sons when they no longer have need of them." However, that part doesn't seem to raise debate yet, so let's push on.

We roll forward to the nineteenth century, to an esteemed British author of the time, Sir William Muir. Muir governed the North Western Provinces of India in the nineteenth century. Amongst other achievements he established a school which eventually became Allahabad University, once termed the Oxford of the East. Muir was a leading political and educative figure in his day. He commented on these very verses;

"The scandal of the marriage was removed by this extraordinary revelation, and Zeid (Zayd) was thenceforward called not the son of Mahomet, as heretofore, but by his proper name, Zeid, the son of Harith. Our only matter of wonder is, that the Revelations of Mahomet continued after this to be regarded by his people as inspired communications from the Almighty, when they were so palpably formed to secure his own objects, and pander even to his evil desires. We hear of no doubts or questionings; and we can only attribute the confiding and credulous spirit of his followers to the absolute ascendancy of his powerful mind over all who came within its influence."[48]

With twenty–first century hindsight, Muir has been termed an Orientalist. Orientalism is defined as; "the representation of Asia in a stereotyped way that is regarded as embodying a colonialist attitude."[49]

---

47. Sura 33:36–37
48. Muir, *Life of Mahomet*, Vol. 3, p. 231.
49. "Orientalism," line 1.

In other words, Muir should not have had opinions about that extraordinary coincidence of the divine revelation with the availability of this beautiful girl. Orientalists would hold that Muir's views are those of the outsider, judging the incident from an invalid, external, moral framework. Here is a twenty-first century rebuke from a Muslim about Al–Tabari's story;

> This story is a favorite of the Orientalists and is patently false. Please understand that many people concocted false stories and false hadith for various reasons. That is the reason why the science of hadith came about. Hadith are graded as authentic (sahih), good (hasan), weak (da'if), rejected (munkar), and fabricated (mawdu). This grading is not arbitrary and not according to anyone's desires. A hadith is graded based on a study of the chain of transmission by way of which it reached us. If a chain of transmission has gaps in it or contradictions or contains people who were known liars, then the hadith is not acceptable.
>
> This story is baseless. It does not come to us with any chain of transmission worth mentioning. If we wish to believe this story, we might as well believe anything that people tell us.[50]

He is correct in that it appears Al–Tabari's works are not hadiths. They are history books, containing both fact and mythology.

Western literary criticism would likely declare the story of Al–Tabari as probably true. They have another tool in their literary criticism kit. It's called the embarrassment factor, well illustrated by its Wikipedia definition;

> The criterion of embarrassment, also known as the "criterion of dissimilarity," is an analytical tool that biblical scholars use in assessing whether the New Testament accounts of Jesus' actions and words are historically accurate. Simply put, trust the embarrassing material. If something is awkward for an author to say and he does anyway, it is more likely to be true.[51]

Since this episode about Muhammad tends to embarrass him, one must explain how it remained in texts whose prime purpose was adulation of the prophet. The embarrassment tool has yet to be adopted within Islam.

Various other media have made their impact since Orientalism, as displayed by our final explanatory passage from Wikipedia;

50. "The Prophet's Marriage to Zaynab Bint Jahsh," para. 18.
51. "Biblical criticism," section 4.3, para. 1.

Muhammad, fearing public opinion, was initially reluctant to marry Zaynab. The marriage would seem incestuous to their contemporaries because she was the former wife of his adopted son, and adopted sons were considered the same as biological sons. According to Watt, this "conception of incest was bound up with old practices belonging to a lower, communalistic level of familial institutions where a child's paternity was not definitely known; and this lower level was in process being eliminated by Islam." Muhammad's decision to marry Zaynab was an attempt to break the hold of pre-Islamic ideas over men's conduct in society. The Qur'an, 33:37 however, indicated that this marriage was a duty imposed upon him by God. It implied that treating adopted sons as real sons was objectionable and that there should now be a complete break with the past. Thus Muhammad, confident that he was strong enough to face public opinion, proceeded to reject these taboos. When Zaynab's waiting period was complete, Muhammad married her.[52]

So there. We have the 2015 version of the matter. Muhammad was challenging traditional social mores by marrying his adopted son's beautiful ex-wife. When he was "confident that he was strong enough to face public opinion, (he) proceeded to reject these taboos."

Let's leave it at that because we're not interested in moral opinions here. We're interested in the media that shaped those opinions from the very start, until today. At least three or four major extensions of man influenced those views.

In our particular era we can see the influence of Ethnography and Social Anthropology. These are both relatively modern, starting in the nineteenth century according to some commentators. These extensions of man enable us to get out of our own moral judgment zone and examine cultural incidents from within their own framework. They're parallel to Orientalism. In other words, let's not judge events, let's just tell the story.

There is another media that plays havoc with both Islam and Christianity, and doesn't like obeying rules of hadiths, history, ethnography, or anthropology, and that is the tabloid press. In 2014 the Harvard Press published an article about a papyrus fragment that had these words on them; "Jesus said to them, 'My wife . . .'"[53]

---

52. "Muhammad's wives," section 2.4.1, para. 3.
53. Allen, "Wife of Jesus Tale," para. 2.

The tabloid press picked this up and turned an otherwise bland conference that the author of the Harvard article attended in 2012 upside down; "King's Coptic–conference bombshell and the New York Times article unleashed a rhino herd of news reporters onto the Rome conference and also a torrent of talking–head commentary stateside, mostly directed to the question of whether Jesus had actually been married and what that meant for the future of Christianity."[54]

Christians are getting used to this sort of thing, what with the worldwide sales of the Gospel of Judas telling us all the underground reasons why Jesus died, let alone the verse in the Gospel of Phillip that has Jesus kissing Mary on the mouth to the puzzlement of his disciples. In an earlier era, the authoress of the Jesus wife article may well have joined Aikenhead on the Edinburgh scaffold, since she was challenging core elements of the Jesus story. Now she gets her picture in the paper, and perhaps more importantly, research funding.

It has been observed that citizens in some Muslim–majority nations react to tabloid or popular press, sometimes with flag burnings, protest marches, and fury. Westerners possibly wonder why all the rage flares up, but expect that either Uncle Sam or Britain or France will be blamed. In between the flames and the marches and the shouting on TV, Westerners may well see adverts on Anger Management courses. And that's the problem with our final extension of man—international television. It broadcasts footage without respect for the literary analytical, ethnographic, orientalist, or anthropological awareness of its viewers.

54. Ibid., para. 4.

3

THE POWER OF SOUND AND IMAGE

In the context of media, Isidore of Seville earned the title given him as the last scholar of the ancient world with a single sentence. Sometime during his thirty year tenure as Archbishop in Spain in the early seventh century, he wrote, "Unless sounds are held by the memory of man, they perish, for they cannot be written down."[1] He was well acquainted with the book as a memory device, since he wrote a twenty volume Etymologiae on everything. An obvious challenge existed with music—how do you capture sound?

Modern music is the result of solutions to that question, but it took a long time to arrive. We could begin with King David who danced before the Israelites,[2] or Miriam the sister of Moses, who led a tambourine flash mob.[3] All those Old Testament characters contributed to the vast library of Christian music, but we will start within the era of Christianity itself. Towards the end of the Roman Empire Constantine moved the capital eastwards to a site called Byzantium. The famed city of Constantinople was built there, and the Roman Empire morphed into the Byzantine Empire. There they built the tallest, most famous cathedral in the world in the sixth century.

The Hagia Sophia was, and still is, one of the most amazing buildings employing sunlight, sound, and stone, ever constructed. It was the world's

1. "Musical notation," section 1.5, para. 1.

2. 2 Samuel 6:14

3. Exodus 15:20

first mega-church, pre–dating St. Peters in Rome by nine hundred years. Hagia Sophia had a full time clerical staff of six hundred, which is huge, even for today. Byzantine liturgy and chanting portrayed mixed up material life, ascending to higher spiritual unity. A visiting Russian delegation in 988 AD felt that, "we did not know where we were, on heaven or on earth,"[4] and after reporting this back to Vladimir the Great, all of Russia converted to Orthodox Christianity.

To this day, Hagia Sophia has the highest church ceiling in the world at 48.5 meters. St. Peters, in third place, is 46 meters. Hagia Sophia has a dome top, not a spire, the width of which is 31 meters. Descriptions of services conducted there read like they are from another planet. Visitors spoke of the shimmering nature of the floor evoking thoughts of the ocean, the sound of wind rushing through like a spirit, and white surfaces appearing as sheep's wool. Somehow they enabled inanimate materials to appear animated. At certain angles, the sunlight rippled across the green marble floor transforming it into a sea. Such a metaphor of movement and change was deliberate, illustrating their understanding of transience amidst permanence. A quote from Paul the Silentiary, a Byzantine palace official, tells of the sensual movement and ritual;

> And as an island rises amid the waves of the sea, so in the midst of the boundless temple rises upright the tower–like ambo of stone. Here the priest who brings the good tidings passes along on his return from the ambo, holding aloft the golden book; and while the crowd strives in honour of the immaculate God to touch the sacred book with their lips and hands, the countless waves of people surging break around.[5]

A variant on Gregorian chanting developed in Constantinople. Choir boys and adults learnt chants, and sang during services. The congregation didn't sing hymns like we might think people do in church, because there were no hymn books scattered along the pews. It was well before factory printing. There were no pews either. The congregants couldn't even sit down. Today we cover church floors with pews, which is a shame in buildings like Chartres cathedral which has a wonderful labyrinth in the middle to stroll around on and meditate. Seating didn't start until the thirteenth century, and picked up later in Protestant circles so that people could concentrate

4. Graves, "We did not know where we were," para. 1.

5. Pentcheva, "Hagia Sophia and Multisensory Aesthetics," 99.

on listening to those sermons with morals that you need to concentrate on after you'd read from a Bible that came from a printing press. Sermons in Hagia Sophia were chanted or sung.

All of this came to a sudden halt in 1453 when the Ottomans captured Constantinople, eventually renaming it Istanbul. The Hagia Sophia was converted into a mosque until the early twentieth century when it became a museum by state decree. More on that later.

Christian music as demonstrated in Hagia Sophia is a lesson in the media of the times. With a thousand years of the Roman Empire behind them, the Byzantines had accumulated a serious amount of experience working with stone. Electricity for lighting or sound systems did not exist. There was only mother nature. This one difference explains nearly every difference with today. Since widespread electrification has only been with us about a hundred years, many existing buildings still display a non–electric architecture. St. Georges Church in Singapore was built in 1913. The sides are not solid, but have porticoes allowing people to walk in late, partly shielded by an inner row of pillars. It wasn't designed strictly for the tardy, but to allow air to circulate in an age predating air conditioning, yet while keeping tropical downpours at bay. No artificial lighting is required for its day time services. Visit a modern, glassed in wonder like the Singapore Life Church, recipient of several design awards, and you are a world away from St Georges which barely falters if the power goes off.

So Hagia Sophia ran entirely on sunlight and candles throughout its eight hundred year Christian history. Electricity is one of the most significant extensions of man if you try to think of life without it. Electric lighting, and electric sound, have changed the game everywhere, not just in churches. Apparently Britain uses more electric lighting at night, and it shines under doors and through windows leading to fitful sleep. They can even find a correlation between too much lighting and obesity.[6]

How ironic. Stronger street lighting has been introduced as a security measure, and it interrupts our rest. Perhaps it's not strange though. The Romans and the Byzantines worked with natural light and stone for a thousand years. We've only been electrifying buildings for less than one hundred. We are still at the outset of this extension of men, and don't even know whether it is part of any global warming problem.

Neither did Hagia Sophia have electric noise. Sounds bounced around naturally several times inside the building resulting in an

6. "Light bedrooms," line 1.

echoing reverberation lasting up to ten seconds. Listening to the chanting is impressive if this Youtube version is true to form. If church services were ever allowed there today, a full house would be guaranteed.

Now, although the actual services must have been visually and aurally amazing, let's imagine if we were able to time travel like some alien spaceman. Imagine if this time traveler had been able to walk around Israel with Jesus for a few days, hearing him disparage religious paradigms, then was fast forwarded eight hundred years to a service in Hagia Sophia. Might the spaceman have thought he was experiencing two unrelated stories? What had that wandering Jew in common with this vast stone building, an earlier version of which, in Jerusalem, he predicted the end of?[7]

Hagia Sophia virtual chanting

Over those eight hundred years, the Orthodox Church created its own mythologies, strongly shaped by the political, architectural, and musical media, it had available. This is not to say the men who designed and built Hagia Sophia and the stone textures, acoustics, and use of natural sunlight, were not devout, sincere followers. Hagia Sophia however, is a Christian output shaped by Byzantine extensions of men. Did the nature of chanting lead the church designers to their stone creation, or did the echoing qualities of stone enclosures enable chanting? There is more to it of course, including the social power of repetition and rhyming amongst masses who didn't possess those printed Bibles.

These influences lasted a long time. We can feel some of what impacted the Russian delegation when we enter medieval European cathedrals, especially minimalist ones. Gaudy buildings like St Peters in Rome are garish works of art, but rough stone structures such as Chartres silence you. I have seen tough men deeply moved by simply walking into the almost bare Abbey–de–Fontenay in Burgundy. Pacing slowly through the soft light towards a lone thirteenth century Madonna standing beside the sarcophagus of a mail clad Crusader with arms folded, and weeping cherubs perched on the lid, one is stripped of any worldly worries one might have had before entering.

Nor was this medium of stone lost on Muslims. To the contrary, their architecture displays divine oneness by its symmetry. Great mosques are perfectly proportional. The Taj Mahal, which is not a mosque but was

---

7. Matthew 24:1–2

created using Islamic design principles, illustrates this. It is deceivingly flawless, with its four outer pillars slanting slightly outwards, bringing more balance to the eye at ground level than if they were absolutely upright. Ayatollah Khamenei explained that the mosque displays "the objectivity of creation, a planned and computed order in the world."[8]

Great mosques invoke awe as well when you go inside. After you've walked up the bustling Meena Bazar street in Delhi, India, through the army of deformed beggars, past the flowers, the curry stands, the cigarette sellers, and the lads with large kettles of hot sweet tea, the average tourist is fairly hot, not to say bothered. At the top of the stairs you walk through the gates into the famed Jama Masjid (mosque), suddenly and amazingly free of the human debris below. The wide open pavement imparts something, even to the foreigner, at least while prayers are not underway. It feels solid, flat, connected to an energy somewhere, perhaps something a Muslim might term numinous.

By the thirteenth century Europe was busy building spired cathedrals in the Gothic style, quite different from the domed Hagia Sophia. The then Christian worldview, with its hierarchy of commoners at the bottom, rising to monarchs, bishops, the apostles, then Jesus at the top, frequently lines the outer walls for all to see. Somehow various extensions of men including politics, finance, and the principles of feudal society, had caused medieval Christians to forget the quote from their founder that; "the one who is the greatest among you must become like the youngest, and the leader like the servant."[9]

Our instant society cannot create buildings that took twenty years, like the Taj Mahal, or two hundred years, like many European cathedrals. New Zealand lost its most famous stone cathedral to an earthquake in 2011. It was replaced by a cardboard one, which may not evoke the same feelings of awe. Busy Westerners can transform an empty warehouse into a digital church in a few months though, even based on volunteer labor. C3 in Auckland, New Zealand, complete with a budget array of data projectors, LED screens, boom boxes, and about forty strobe lights hanging from the ceiling, is typical of many electric churches. Song lyrics overlain onto an appropriate video clip appear on the vast screen behind the eight strong rock band including a drummer in a glass cubicle. If the congregation is singing about moving forward, a fast car journey taken through the front

8. Longhurst, "Theology of a Mosque," 5.

9. Luke 22:26

window might appear. As for climbing past the cloud layer to sunshine on the mountain top, well, there must be plenty of footage one could download from the other cloud. Even smoke appears, mimicking that incense burning of Hagia Sophia. I'm told there's a way of replicating the aroma coming soon in digital form.

Can you imagine swapping the congregations of Hagia Sophia and C3 with each other using that time machine? It might not work because Hagia Sophia didn't have a barrista making coffee takeaways at the door.

In the eleventh century, Guido of Arezzo invented musical notation, and the forerunner of the doh–re–mi scale that has come through to us today. He solved the problem described by Isidore of Seville. From then on, music could be stored. Naturally his methods have been improved upon over the centuries but it wasn't until the nineteenth century that another device was invented to save sound.

After the printing press, hymn books eventually ended up in pews, along with an organist who learnt the tunes to accompany the congregation singing. Two or three hundred years of this resulted in a common set of hymns, at least in the English speaking world. Globalization took those hymn books to nearly every church in the British Commonwealth. From Malaysia to Africa, they were a common bond, with well known tunes assisting them to lodge in ones memory. None of those lyrics had copyright applied to them by the way. They were given away by personalities such as John Newton, the ex–slaving ship's captain, who penned the words to Amazing Grace in 1779. To this day, numerous elderly people, even with Alzheimer's, can burst into song for all seven—or was it eight—verses. In the nineteenth century a new device disrupted this scenario—the gramophone. This gave mankind the ability to store sound. And listen to it again. And again. And again.

You see, reading music off those notated lines, with the bars, and the semi quavers and all that signage is still exacting. We meet people every day who can read a book. Well, you used to be able to anyway. However you will not meet many people in your life who can sit at a piano and flawlessly play a piece they didn't previously know from a sheet of music. The church organist had to practice a lot in previous centuries because actual sound could not be exported or carried anywhere. But with the gramophone it could. Ask any musician and they will tell you the best way to learn music is to play alongside others. This is not limited to humans. Isolated song birds are not as accomplished as those in flocks. Following the invention that captured sound, human musicians didn't need to read music—they could mimic other performers by listening to them. Music became much easier to learn.

Electric amplification appeared, a wonderful breakthrough enabling mankind to make live or stored sound louder. By and large mankind promptly lost most of the natural audio skills he had built up over several millennia, and we now have microphones and loudspeakers everywhere. It is hard to imagine music without these enhancements. It is true that you can still hear church choirs gathered to sing Handel's Messiah occasionally. At enormous local effort, performances like these are still created. However they are dwarfed in comparison to global tours of iconic bands, Youtube sensations, and the itunes store.

Neither were mosques free of electronics, even if they didn't do music. Mosques did not mimic those church bells summoning the faithful, and which still peal today. But Umayyad caliph Muawiyah did encourage the construction of minarets to bring mosques on par with Christian church bell towers only eighty years after the passing of the prophet.[10] Along came the microphone, and in what Singapore claimed in 1936 was a world first, loudspeakers were installed in the Masjid Sultan Mosque. Some difficulties were experienced "from excessive reverberation,"[11] telling us those mosques were designed for natural noise as well. In what the reporter paradoxically terms, "Muslim's gift" it goes on to explain that, "In the early morning, the summons to prayer will carry more than a mile." A few of those 1930s Singaporean worshipers were dubious about installing an electric amplifying system, but the majority believed that the noises of a modern city demand an accompanying increase in the "power of the muezzin's voice."[12]

From its invention in the 1860s, waiting until 1936 pales in comparison to the acceptance of printing by Islam, a point we shall come back to. And by 2013, loudspeakers in mosques were a global issue. Complaints surfaced in Kandy about the din from this Sri Lankan minority religion; "Even in the citadel of Buddhism, the regular worship in Kandy is disturbed by the loudspeakers of the mosques showing a flagrant example of lack of respect for the predominant religion of Sri Lanka."[13] The complainant mentions some English people are annoyed with mosque noise in Britain too,

10. "Sacred architecture," section 6, para. 5.

11. "Loudspeakers in Singapore Mosque," para. 6.

12. Ibid., para. 15.

13. Waduge, *Mosques and loudspeakers*, para. 1.

mixing it up with stories of attacks on mosques. By listing them together he intimates attempts at arson are provoked by locals fed up with the daily din—which is a believable lunacy. He claims mosques in New York turn the volume up to 130 decibels, equivalent to a jet engine and audible four miles away.[14] I don't think he's been to a Christian rock concert, or a head–banger Muslim hip hop one, but we're visiting both soon.

Fortunes were made by radio stations, recording studios, record labels, MTV, global bands, and CD stores. More noise filled the world than it had ever known. It is said that the biggest difference we would notice if we were transported (in the alien space travel machine) back to 1000 AD, would be the silence. No cars, no industrial machinery, but most of all, in 99.99 percent of homes in the world, there were no bands playing music. The 0.01 percent were the kings who could afford their own retinues. Of course people sang together back then, but the point is that bands, via electronic music, now invade our homes, our automobiles, our shopping malls, and our smartphones. If Paul the Silentiary was employed to maintain silence in the Byzantine palace, I'm sure he'd be employable today by lovers of quiet who are forced to purchase sound cancelling headphones.

In the late twentieth century the Internet came along to disrupt further not only the old world of Gregorian chanting, but also the very recent one of recording contracts and CD stores. All of this technology enabled religious music outside church buildings. The average believer now listens to much more Christian music at home or in the car, than they do at church.

Shift over to Islam, and the history is just as complicated, and is being altered just as much. Islamic music has always had a legacy, especially among the Sufis with their mystical inclinations. However, it is outlawed or frowned on in many Muslim–majority societies. Since electric songs were banned inside the mosque, they emerged outside it.

Let's introduce a few personalities before we go there.

CAT AND BOB CONVERT

On the 23rd of December 1977, a famous English musician converted to Islam. He later admitted, "I never knew that Muslims believed in God."[15]

14. Ibid., para. 4.

15. "Cat Stevens," para. 15.

Cat Stevens was not a complex youth during the formative 1960s era of music, only wanting to be popular and make money at it. A serious brush with tuberculosis moved him to investigate religions other than Christianity. He had been brought up in a mixed Orthodox/Roman Catholic setting, and only retained impressions of the Devil with two horns, the temptation of Adam and Eve, and Jesus on the cross, representing salvation.

After experimenting with Buddhism and a few other beliefs, some coincidences lined up for him. A near drowning experience was followed by his brother presenting him with a Qu'ran. It seemed to indicate a road to Islam, and that is what happened. After renaming himself Yusuf Islam, he disappeared from view into the Muslim world for over twenty years, emerging into the spotlight again to make a stand for Muslims following the 9/11 twin tower catastrophe.

In 1978 another famous musician converted to Christianity. Bob Dylan went on to record some strictly Christian albums including "Slow Train Coming." The Christian world was delighted, as they always are when a celebrity joins their ranks. They couldn't wait to tell the world, or buy his records. His old music friends reacted against his conversion, John Lennon even writing a parody about one of Dylan's songs. About two years into what is termed his "Christian period," Dylan appeared to drop out of the faith. In 1983 he recorded the album "Infidels," hardly a Christian title.

If there are lessons to be learnt about religion from the above two tales, one is this—don't release converts into the world too soon. They need to be toughened by the years. This lesson is very much lost on the youth oriented globe we live in because it is the young who largely produce the new media. And our celebrity culture craves fame prior to experience. And this is a good time to introduce Sufi musical philosophy.

Sufism, the contemplative branch of Islam, brings mysticism to music, or music to mysticism. Nasr quotes Ruzbahan Baqli from the twelfth century telling us the circumstances in which Islam frowns on music, and yet brings direction to it;

> If they were to listen to music with these means they would become veiled from God. And if they were to listen to it with the carnal soul they would become impious. And if they were to listen with the power of reason they would become creditable. And if they would hear with the heart they would become contemplative.

And if they were to listen with the spirit they would become totally present.[16]

He has a point—which might not be understood in a music industry driven by sales and talent shows, but which some Christians find common ground with—that modern music appeals to the carnal nature, not the spiritual one. Nasr argues that;

> Islamic civilization has not preserved and developed several great musical traditions in spite of Islam but because of it. It has prevented the creation of a music, like the post–classical music of the West, in which an "expansion" takes place without the previous "contraction" which must of necessity precede expansion in the process of spiritual realization.[17]

Religions are very present in the playground of music because the hearts and minds of youth are more available then, and they have money to spend. Our Sufi mystic hoped people would go through a philosophical "contraction" in order to be enlightened by music. Try telling that to the next teenager you find connected to an iPod.

A volatile mixture of rapidly changing musical tastes and digitization has struck Christianity. New Zealand ran a successful Christian musical festival for more than a dozen years. Pulling 20,000 youngsters together out of nation of less than five million, 80 percent of whom never attend church, makes good stats. Walking over the breast of the hill into the Parachute festival, the sea of tents resembling an upmarket refugee camp, was equally impressive. It survived on entry tickets, music sales and rents from the hot-dog stands. After a shaky season or two, it closed permanently in 2014 before it could fall deeply into the red. It was a casualty of the digitization of the music industry, another disappointment to the crowds of followers who maybe didn't loyally buy CDs, but obtained them from elsewhere.

Digitization ruined a lot more careers than a few earnest Christian bands from the bottom of the world producing serious titles like "the worship project." It's a global shakeup. In fact the whole nature of church changed from its previous hymn book era as the music industry popularized by the Beatles of all people, reinvigorated the faith. "All you need is love" was an affront, or wakeup call, to the religion that thought it had a franchise on the word. At first there was plenty of denial. Leading Christian figures

16. Nasr, "Islam and Music," 5.

17. Ibid., 8.

advised that rock music was of the Devil, but they were mainly American. They probably confused Elvis swiveling his hips around the microphone with those clean cut Beatles from Liverpool who charmed the USA in 1967. Early into the Christian action was an entertaining, long haired, blond guitarist, wrapped in a stars and stripes suit, named Larry Norman. He cheekily published titles in the 1970s like 'Why Should the Devil have all the Good Music?' and sang about the role of CBS in the Vietnam war in 'The six o'clock news.' Thirty years after the Christian music industry had adopted rock concerts, auditoriums, drummers, and commerce, it was disrupted by the Internet—and the Parachute festival fell over.

WE WILL, WE WILL, ROCK YOU

Hillsong in Australia sells music to a multitude of churches around the world. Imagine if John Newton had done that. I wonder how many copies of Amazing Grace his family trust could have grown wealthy on? A constant array of new material issues forth from Hillsong, with an interesting outcome—church congregations have difficulty learning the new numbers. There is an answer to this problem—shift the main thrust of the music back where it used to be, which is with the choir. Only now it's not called a choir, it's a band. The C3 Church has a slick group running a rock show every Sunday morning with behind–the–back sign language from the worship leader to repeat the number if the audience is in full swing. As the lyrics pop up, in perfect timing with the singing, the crowd joins in to the extent they can with a new number. The Hillsong model could not exist without the data projector or the LED screen, as it would be too time consuming and expensive printing out those new song sheets every Sunday.

Hold that thought: churches are losing the hymn book to the data projector. What will those old ladies in rest homes remember singing in fifty years time? Wait till we focus on the business of disruption. The Hillsong business model must, by definition, keep producing new numbers. Undoubtedly it will be justified on the basis of satisfying their clientele's changing tastes, which are equally undoubtedly synchronized with those ever shortening cycles of fashion, even in church circles.

Let's meet a few more artists from both the Christian and Muslim camps. Many Muslim commentators don't like music—to this day. In 2010 Iran banned private schools from teaching music. Ali Bagherzadeh, head of the private schools office in the Education Ministry said, "The use of musical instruments is against the principles of our value system."[18] I don't think he's visited www.muslimhiphop.com, which is registered in Arizona, not Tehran. Artists like Imam Jihad, Jabbar and Ali, Halal Productionz and belikeMuhammad compete for your attention. I randomly clicked on Manifest ONE, to read his profile;

> Fueled by the fire of napalm on his brothers and sisters across the globe, he writes with a passion that keeps the victims of injustice in his mind and heart. He is known to openly release his views through his music. Endless messages can be heard dealing with topics from the corruption of Hip Hop to hidden philosophies on life. In his efforts, he attempts to spread a message of Islam in a universal understanding of it. Manifest stresses, more than anything, conscious thinking that could free the masses from mental enslavement into a world of flowing thought and reflection on Allah and His creation.[19]

Manifest ONE starts with fire and passion and it doesn't look like that passion is love. Midstream, he switches to universal and conscious thinking inserting some Lenin speak in 'free the masses from mental enslavement.' It hints at the Sufi contemplative model, and I bet he claims he's 'totally present.'

I turned to www.todayschristianmusic.com which had many, many, more budding artists than muslimhiphop, and again randomly selected Karyn Williams. She is a young American singer, with her own website, but her profile was on the group site as well;

> I stepped out on a huge leap of faith and moved to Nashville. I prayed, 'Lord, I promise to walk through every door that You open no matter what.' I have kept that promise and He has been faithful in providing opportunities to share His name. You just never know how God is going to use your songs. All we can do as songwriters is pour out our hearts and leave it up to Him—let go of it and then trust God with the results. Christian music is the music that has always moved my heart and made me want to use my voice to draw people closer to the Lord.[20]

It would be unfair to leave the comparison there, because there is another genre of Muslim music that parallels Christian music, and that is

18. "Iran Bars Music," para. 2.

19. "Manifest ONE," para. 1.

20. "Karyn Williams," para. 2.

worship. Muslims may take exception to the following list, but a cursory search reveals an extraordinary mimicry between how Christians perceive Jesus, and Muslims see Muhammad. Both are referred to as;

- the perfect man[21][22]
- the reason the heavens and earth were created[23][24]
- intercessors with God[25][26]
- the supreme example of love[27][28]

These themes are found embedded into both Islamic and Christian lyrics. A Muslim Pakistani group called the Sabri brothers, still going strong since 1956, sing this;

> O Muhammad
> Embodied light
> My Beloved
> My Master
> You are:
> The image of the perfection of love
> The illumination of God's beauty[29]

Compare their lines with these by Chris Tomlin, a Christian artist.

> You came down from heaven's throne
> This earth you formed was not your home
> A love like this the world had never known
> On the altar of our praise let there be no higher name
> Jesus son of God
> You laid down your perfect life.[30]

Let's do the basics again, and emerge wide–eyed and wondering from the alien spaceship. Both Manifest ONE and Karyn Williams are trying to

21. "The Doctrine of the Perfect Man," para. 9.
22. "The Perfect Man," line 1.
23. "Hadith: "If not for you I would not have created creation,"" para. 1–4.
24. Colossians 1:16
25. "Intercession in the Hereafter," para. 6.
26. Romans 8:34
27. "Compassion in Islam," para. 8.
28. "Jesus Christ Is a Model of Perfect Love," line 76.
29. "Sabri brothers "Embodied light.""
30. "Jesus Son Of God," para. 2–3.

break into a tough business that is changing by the day, but we from another galaxy wouldn't know those challenges. We would instead see they're using the same mediums of electrified music, website promotion, the same sample tune players embedded in the pages, profiles, photographs, bios etc, and from all that we would make some common assumptions about them. Slightly stumped by the word Allah, we could find out it means God in another language, so we could safely make a bet they're talking about the same divine being.

Hearing of Jesus and Muhammad, we would learn about two Middle Eastern men who lived over a thousand years ago. A quick search would confirm they are both seen as supreme examples of men, and the lyrics about either certainly seem similar. Including the older musicians into the equation, we would find both faiths have music adoring these historic figures, as well as political messages for their times.

Neither of our young artists are going to admit, like Cat Stevens did, that he was there to be famous and make money. No, they are both out to change the world. Behind their mimicry are Public Relations polishing, and that celebrity culture. A sensitive alien visitor might feel that one of our youthful singers seems angrier than the other though.

Why is traditional Islam supposedly against music? It's an interesting question because when Westerners hear the Qu'ran being recited, it can sound like music. It does have melody. It turns out there are no verses directly prohibiting it although the Qu'ran warns about having fun;

- Then at this statement do you wonder?
  And you laugh and do not weep
  While you are proudly sporting?
  So prostrate to Allah and worship Him.[31]

  Another translation rephrases the first line to a more musical nuance;
- Do ye then wonder at this recital?[32]

Yahoo publish questions and then chooses the best email answer. This street level method, rather than consulting a mullah or a university, does have credibility in that it canvases popular opinion. The question posed was;

31. Sura 53:59–62
32. *The Holy Qu'ran*, Sura 53:59

Where in the Holy Qu'ran does it say that Music is forbidden?[33]

The chosen best answer contained this revealing paragraph;

> Insha'Allah, in Islam, we are taught that our deeds will be judged
> by the intentions of the same. This might refer to both the inten-
> tion of the person or persons who composed the music you are
> listening to as well as to your intentions is listening to the music.
> Is it to praise and glorify Allah, and call your mind to remember-
> ing Him or is it to idle your time away? Does it lead you to care
> and concern for others that will lead you to correct actions so as
> to assist them or does it simply make you feel like the world is a
> horrible place and that you don't want to be there? Does it glorify
> improper sexual expressions, degrade others, especially women or
> does it promote chastity and purity? Insha'Allah, I would opine
> that listening to music by Yusuf Islam might well be very different
> from listening to music by a heavy metal headbanger band or most
> rap music.[34]

The respondent is certainly Islamic, and our first insight is that, just
like Christianity, it would seem Muslims like name dropping their converts
too. They're not immune from celebrity status either which is more a carnal sign than a spiritual one. Neither the Bible nor the Qu'ran recommend
celebrities. In fact there are many verses promoting humility. That's enough
preaching. It also prompts the question of why Islam's most famous modern music convert put his guitar away for twenty years, then pulled it out
again. What happened during that period, and is there anything behind the
given reasons. What did Cat Stevens say? In 1980, soon after his conversion, he commented;

> "I have suspended my activities in music for fear that they may
> divert me from the true path, but I will not be dogmatic in saying
> that I will never make music again. You can't say that without add-
> ing, Insha Allah (if God Wishes)."[35]

Twenty five years later, he added;

> "There were many Muslims offering me advice and telling me
> their opinions about all sorts of issues, some were very convincing.
> Nevertheless, legitimate variant opinions exist on all sides dealing

33. "Where in the Holy Quran," line 1.
34. Ibid., para. 4.
35. Islam, "Floating on a Cloud of Mercy," para. 5.

with the subject of music. When closely studying the details of Prophetic evidences, there are many which point to the possibility of wide-ranging conclusions. Now, after having studied the subject for more than a quarter of a century, I can say that it is certainly not as black and white as some have tried to make it out to be.

In Islam, as with religion and life generally, there always will be room for cultural and artistic expression. Some of the most beautiful works of art in human history have been lovingly dedicated in praise of the Divine. Their enjoyments are part of the gifts given to mankind by the Creator.

Music is part of God's universe. We need all sorts of nourishment and music fulfils and satisfies the hunger we all experience and the need for harmony and aesthetic beauty to decorate our daily lives, particularly when times are hard.

Sometimes songs are vital in keeping people's spirits high in times of trial and hardship."[36]

So, in his words, he picked up music again, despite debate within Muslim circles. He sounds a genuine man, and I don't think there is a conspiracy here. A cynic might think that the mullahs suggested he become an icon to prop up slippage with the Islam brand by "keeping people's spirits high." Let's not speculate. The only point we can state with confidence is that he did return to musical tours, and it has not aroused ire from Islam in general. Muslims approve of him. In other words, there's an element of unconscious mimicry with the Christian church. Disapproval of music existed, but has gradually dropped. At least in the West it has.

On the other hand, do not forget that the Qu'ran is recited much more than the Bible. Whereas Christians love investigating every word in the Bible, and seeking different Hebrew or Greek interpretations, Muslims love repeating the Qu'ran. Many forms of recitation exist, which either border on, or are plainly musical. And again, this is all very well, but it's time to visit another Muslim genre which seems diametrically opposed to Sufi enlightenment or Qu'ranic recitation. Muslim head-banger concerts are alive and well in the MENA region.

Running rock shows is not possible without electricity, loudspeakers, buses, stadiums, and refrigerators to store the hot-dog beef. Remove all those and opportunities for large crowds of youth to congregate diminish. Coincidentally those elements were sparse in the Middle East until recent

36. "Didn't he say music is forbidden?" para. 7.

years. Now they're all in place, except rising incomes. Given the media infrastructure is there though, that one significant omission becomes a passionate force for the gigs to take place anyway. Attending a head–banger concert in the Middle East is a protest statement. The title of one book by Mark LeVine tells us this—Heavy Metal Islam: Rock, Resistance and the Struggle for the Soul of Islam.

While many forms of Islamic music exist, it is interesting to find heavy rock inside the faith. The title to LeVine's book suggests, as does our earlier Yahoo respondent, that heavy metal has not yet registered the approval of the mullahs. But if the authorities banning music in Iran think they've crushed their challenge, events elsewhere might inform them otherwise. Morocco has a thriving plethora of heavy metal bands, and Dubai Desert Rock, the only formal concert in the MENA region, ran every year between 2004 and 2009. Facebook claims they'll be back.

Now, while Muslim rockers find their governments repressive, they do draw strength from their faith. The musicians know all the Qu'ranic verses and hadith quotations they need to question traditional assumptions. As we saw from the Qu'ranic injunctions, it's quite simple finding other interpretations. Of course the MENA region is heavier with conservative clerics than with heavy metal singers. The latter have never been known for their grace in telling clergy that they've got it wrong. That's how rock musicians speak to priests in the West, so we're definitely talking mimicry here. Prison stays are commonplace for Muslim head–bangers, but not for abusing the prophet—rather for insulting the king, or a government department. They are political therefore, as every metal rocker probably claims they are political, fighting for justice through their music.

However, Middle Eastern governments have a blind spot right now. While following Western trends, their musical young also believe America is the root of all evil. Muslim–majority leaders could exploit that. As Hollywood turned the hippy revolution into movies, don't be surprised if corporations help Muslim–majority governments give more ear to musical demands, especially if the lyrics are pro–Islamic. It is true that at least one 2000s era Middle Eastern concert had a Nokia phone displayed on the biggest banner on stage.

COMIC HISTORIES

Youth swarm through other modern media besides music. Graphics is another world, from art to graffiti to digital expression. Christianity likes art, as illustrated for centuries in churches and cathedrals. Modern art is everywhere as well. Realism for example is readily seen in the roughly hewn wooden crosses you can come across, a far cry from the ornate medieval structures that no Roman soldier could ever have fashioned from the stunted trees surrounding Jerusalem.

Church buildings themselves have changed in response to art forms. Gaudi's unfinished cathedral in Barcelona is probably the most famous example, with its Batman like Gothic appearance. New Zealand built its cardboard cathedral. European artwork has evolved through so many styles and there must be hundreds of books written about the various epochs. Occasionally artists paint questions, as with Francis Bacon's series (the twentieth century Francis Bacon) of screaming popes, the best of which has a pontiff sitting on a chair inside a transparent cube. His head is dissolving upwards while he is shrieking. The painting is not about a pope being tortured, but it is surely trying to query the nature of Christianity. Yet it is a popular piece of work that Christians will readily discuss. I cannot imagine a series of screaming prophets being sought as collector's items in Baghdad or Cairo. Even so, would Bacon's works have received acclaim in sixteenth to seventeenth century Italy? Maybe not. Not in the era that condemned Galileo.

Francis Bacon's
Screaming Pope

One game has never changed, and that is portraiture. Monarchs, Dukes, Baronesses and the otherwise rich and powerful have posed for centuries. The very phrase "cost an arm and a leg" came from this art trade several hundred years ago. Entry level fees were charged for merely a head portrait, but adding other parts of the anatomy resulted in a sliding scale of charges. One must imagine that displaying the full self, with a background of one's castle, was prominently placed in the grand hall when visitors came. So we can hardly blame youth today for the selfie craze. Entire websites are devoted to this, untold gigabytes being uploaded every hour of every day. The word selfie had found its way into the online Oxford Dictionary. That's old news, because belfie, the image of one's rear end, wasn't there at the start of 2015.

It hasn't stopped with stills. Go Pro video cameras are now mounted on trail bikes, skiers heads, surfboards, and otherwise hand carried by parachutists and more, all recording some extreme event that the photographer felt they were undertaking. Is the selfie fetish a sign of increasing narcissism? Not if you visit all those castles and manors and see the artwork. The nobility back then just had the means to indulge their egos. We have no way of gauging humility amongst the masses. Today's deluge is merely a reflection that youth have that means as well now.

Newer art like comics and digital games are an eye opener. 500,000 visits to a website followed the creation of Qahera in Egypt—the hijab-wearing comic–book character battling against crime and prejudice. Her creator wanted to fight against the Islamophobia of the West;

> "Look, it is a Muslim woman," says one of the characters in a story featuring Western feminists. "Sister, take off your oppression!"
> But the superheroine reacts angrily to their call.
> "You have constantly undermined women. You seem unable to understand we do not need your help!"
> Qahera dons her long black hijab and carries a sword as she chases down male abusers, and flies to fight wherever a woman is mistreated.
> "Never bother another woman again!" Qahera warns a beaten–up culprit.[37]

She sounds worked up. Manifest ONE should meet her.

In one of the greatest coincidental mimics ever, Marvel Comics began a series at the same time whose lead character, Kamala Khan, is a teenage Muslim girl living in Jersey City. Kamala has a mask, and a decidedly un–Egyptian short skirt with boots. She has inner struggles, and verbal ones with her conservative brother and mother, who are frightened she will touch a boy and get pregnant. Kamala's creator says the series is, "about the universal experience of all American teenagers, feeling kind of isolated and finding what they are—through the lens of being a Muslim–American with superpowers."[38]

Pakistan climbed aboard the wagon with Burka Avenger which is highly Internet based. Colorful professional video playbacks are available at the click of a mouse from www.burkaavenger.com. The series even won an International Gender Equity Prize in Munich in 2014. All these ventures are well targeted. Qaehera may fulfill Egyptian longings to beat up Orientalist Westerners. Marvel comics probably did some of the market

37. "Egypt's new hijab-clad superheroine," para. 21.
38. "Mighty, Muslim and Leaping," para. 15.

survey work we will later learn about, and picked up on the inner struggles of Muslims living in the West. I wonder when the Muslim male superhero will appear though. 2014 only saw superheroines.

Media in the form of movies, news, and imagery has taken over much of the traditional Christian sphere, diluting their message. Long ago the only graphics in your French or British village were in the nearest church— if you were lucky. All information about spiritual matters certainly resided there, as no library or broadband existed, and you probably couldn't read anyway. If you did, you most certainly encountered the Bible because the school was run by the church as well.

Fast forward to today, and you can get spiritual content from a variety of changing sources. Studies done in Denmark[39] inform us that the Lord of the Rings movie series prompted more Danes to think about spirituality in the early 2000s than traditional religious sources. I wouldn't mind betting if they had done the questionnaire in the 1970s, the answer would have been Star Wars. "May the force be with you" has lasted nearly forty years now, as illustrated by the ongoing existence of the Jedi Church.

If we look back, we can see early trends in what we might call the triumph of the image over words. The great spiritual discussions in Job and the Bhagavad Gita do not work well in either movies or wall engravings. Eight hundred year old intricate art on Angkor Wat walls does not have men discussing good and evil, which is the real point of the Bhagavad Gita. Instead they show the full pitched battle that took place after the discussion. Star Wars and Lord of the Rings movies are action packed because action is the agenda of the movie.

Then there are fragments, such as images of a cemetery under lightning, a black cat, or a devil in tights, which impart messages that Hjarvard terms 'banal religion.'[40] Banal religion shouldn't be taken seriously, but it is. Churches fight a losing battle attempting to counter Harry Potter and World of Warcraft, both of which provided spiritual content to the masses while they were popular. The Bible has fallen from the top of the reference list for spiritual or religious nourishment to the bottom according to the Danes. People learnt more about Christian rituals and concepts out of Dan Brown's Da Vinci Code, because this particular book mimicked the dominant culture of action imagery by telling a spell binding tale. All of this is why Hjarvard uses the phrase 'Mediatization of Religion' which he

39. Hjarvard, "*Mediatization of Religion*," 9.
40. Ibid., 5–7.

explains as follows; "By this, religious imaginations and practices become increasingly dependent upon the media. As a channel of communication the media have become the primary source of religious ideas, and as a language the media mould religious imagination in accordance with the genres of popular culture."[41]

On this basis, Muslims have a point about imagery. They attempt to prohibit banal religion by focusing on the text from Allah, rather than pictures, and they particularly don't like cartoons of Muhammad. Cartoons disparaging religion are not new. Martin Luther himself oversaw the printing of some that make so called anti–Islamic ones tepid. In one the Pope was represented as Satan, in a donkey body masked by a woman's corset. Christendom probably reached a zenith of religious cartooning in his time, and The Economist even claims Luther used them as part of his 'social media' campaign.[42]

Anti–Christian cartoons were created well prior to then. The earliest known was a piece of graffiti scrawled on a Roman wall in 225 AD. It is a cartoon of a boy raising his hand in reverence to a donkey on a cross. The inscription in Greek reads, 'Alexamenos worships his god.' Possibly that would still be offensive today, who knows. We can safely bet it didn't result in street demonstrations as Christianity was still illegal, but it does prove the faith was alive and growing in 225 AD. At best, (or worst, depending on your viewpoint), it may have resulted in some local laughter or embarrassment.

Cartoon from Luther era

Danish cartoons of the prophet Muhammad created an international controversy in 2005. Faced with difficulties getting any cartoonist to illustrate a children's book on Muhammad, some journalists created a contest. An evolving idea to test journalistic freedoms had arisen from the original idea, as the cartoonists were afraid of an Islamic backlash. In the words of Fleming Rose, the culture director of The Jutland Post who arranged the subsequent contest;

> The cartoonists treated Islam the same way they treat Christianity, Buddhism, Hinduism and other religions. And by treating Muslims in Denmark as equals they made a point: We are integrating you into the Danish tradition of satire because you are part of our

---

41. Ibid., 13.

42. Economist, "How Luther went viral," para. 1–4.

society, not strangers. The cartoons are including, rather than ex-
cluding, Muslims.[43]

He's saying cartoonists in Northern Europe have been lampooning
religion ever since Luther, and that Christians, among others, have got used
to it over the past five hundred years. So, Muslim community, what's your
problem?

That concept didn't get across. The Islamic world erupted over the
cartoons. Eleven ambassadors from Muslim–majority countries asked for a
meeting with the Danish Prime Minister. They wanted to discuss what they
perceived as an "ongoing smearing campaign in Danish public circles and
media against Islam and Muslims."[44]

Danish Muslims tried to bring the newspaper to court, but the charges
were dismissed as Danish case law extends editorial freedom to journalists regarding subjects of public interest. Protests overseas led to some two
hundred deaths in the Middle East, and calls for bans on Danish products.
Minority Muslim populations protested worldwide, and Al–Qaeda urged
Muslim–majority nations to boycott not only Denmark, but also Norway,
France, Germany and any others who insulted the prophet. While bans on
Danish exports to the Middle East fell by 15 percent, a counter movement
sprang up promoting 'buy Danish' in the USA. Exports increased by about
the same amount, with an overall negligible effect on Denmark's economy.

The incident was a serious convergence of media. None of it would
have happened without Tele–communications, digital imaging, news reporting and global politics. Westerners were amazed over the reactions
from the MENA region, and various explanations with occasional apologies were given. Were the Danish cartoons really a test of journalistic freedom, or were they a test of the powers of technology?

The answer got complicated, or the question changed, by another test
in 2010. Throughout late 2004 Facebook had only spread through educational institutes, expanding by October 2005 to include twenty one British
Universities. By 2010 however, Facebook had 500 million users. Molly Norris began a Facebook page, 'Everybody Draw Mohammed Day' aiming to
announce winning artists on May 20, 2010. Her movement grew rapidly,
but she pulled out of it prior to the day due to mounting Islamic protest.

43. Rose, "Why I published those cartoons," para. 10.

44. "Jyllands-Posten Muhammad cartoons," section 1.4, para. 3.

Norris acknowledged, "I said that I wanted to counter fear and then I got afraid."[45]

The event took on a life of its own however, attracting some 11,000 Facebook followers and 460 cartoons by May 3rd, 2010. A counter Facebook site sprang up, and numbers of supporters and opponents skyrocketed. On May 19th, 2010, Pakistan shut down access to Facebook after Islamic Pakistani lawyers took action against the 'Everybody Draw Mohammed Day' as blasphemous, therefore illegal. On May 20th, they extended their ban to Youtube, Flickr and parts of Wikipedia. On May 20, 2010, the actual day of the event, the Toronto Sun reported that the 'Everybody Draw Mohammed Day' group was up to 101,870, and the 'Against Everybody Draw Mohammed Day' site had 106,000 members. True to Norris's fears, in July, the Yemeni cleric Al–Awlaki said, in the Al–Qaeda magazine (Inspire); "The medicine prescribed by the Messenger of Allah is the execution of those involved,"[46]

Up sprang a legion of Westerners either condemning the 'Everybody Draw Mohammed Day' crowd or the Muslim reaction against it. One of the more illuminating, from our focus, was an article by The Times on May 30, 2010, headlined with, and containing the following;

> This is a poor way to draw attention to intolerance
> If a cartoonist wants to satirise Islam by drawing Mohammed, I'm on his side all the way. But among the 13,000 pictures on the EDMD Facebook page, you have Mohammed as a dog in a veil, Mohammed as a pig and Mohammed as a monkey. That's not resistance, but picking a fight. Issuing a death threat against somebody who drew a picture isn't my thing, but this isn't either.[47]

I am not sure on what basis the reporter judged that it was 'a poor way to draw attention to intolerance.' He could not complain on the basis of coverage as it reached the globe. Did he expect Molly Norris had the means to organize a warm conference on intolerance in Iceland? The Times wasn't alone. A number of respectable writers had opinions along the line that, 'we all need to be more reasonable, both Western writers and Middle Eastern readers.' Such suggestions are meaningless in an age of unfettered digital publishing, and digital access.

45. "Everybody Draw Mohammed Day," section 1.4, para. 2.

46. Ibid., section 2.4, para. 1.

47. Ibid., section 2.2, para. 2.

Actual outcomes were predictable. The number of websites parodying Islam ballooned since those incidents, ranging from hate websites to humor to debate. It was no longer possible for al–Qaeda or IS to issue fatwas against them because there were too many.

By mid 2014, blaming social media for blasphemous content had seemingly lost its dazzle. On May 18th, Twitter blocked content in Pakistan, by Pakistan government request, relating to anti–Islamic sentiments, images depicting the Prophet Muhammad, the burning of the Qu'ran, and American pornography actresses. Compared to the 2005 Danish cartoons, this news item got nowhere. So nowhere in fact that Pakistan failed to follow up with details requested by Twitter. Accordingly Twitter announced its own move on June 18th, stating, "We have re–examined the requests and, in the absence of additional clarifying information from Pakistani authorities, have determined that restoration of the previously withheld content is warranted,"[48]

If anything, these Western driven moves may have encouraged those in Muslim–majority nations to mimic them. In July 2014 the BBC reported the contents of a speech by Turkey's Deputy Prime Minister Bulent Arinc. He was concerned about, . . ."moral corruption" in Turkey. "Chastity is so important," he said. "She (meaning women in general) will not laugh in public."[49] Within days 300,000 Turkish women had posted Instagram and Twitter images telling about or showing themselves laughing.

Now religions do not about face in response to Facebook likes. They thrive on persecution (the Christian word) or resisting the 'enemies of Islam.' It is not the purpose of this book to moralize on whether religious stands are right or wrong, although I am personally interested in reflection. Occasionally an individual in the wars of words and images does ponder their actions. One such is Ahmed Akkari. One of the foremost protesters against the Danish cartoons, Akkari backtracked in 2013 and apologized. "At that time, I was so fascinated with this logical force in the Islamic mindset that I could not see the greater picture. I was convinced it was a fight for my faith, Islam. I was shocked. I realized what an oppressive mentality they have."[50] Other Muslims wrote off Akkari as seeking attention.

Islamic anti–cartoon fury was not down and out however. On January 7th, 2015, two masked Islamist gunmen burst into the offices of Charlie

48. "Twitter unblocks 'blasphemous' tweets," para. 8.

49. "#BBCtrending: The women having a laugh in Turkey," para. 2.

50. "Ahmad Akkari, Danish Muslim," para. 6.

Hebdo in Paris, shooting ten of the staff involved in making cartoons, and two policemen, then attacked a Jewish synagogue, in the worst terror atrocity yet in France. At first glimpse, their timing was either brilliant, or horrible. Days earlier many Germans had counter protested against marches by right wingers afraid of the Islamization of their nation; the same day in France saw the release of a novel satirizing the political takeover of France by a Muslim political party: during the same week the Islamist Boko Haram army slaughtered 2000 people in West Africa. The Parisian terrorists did everything they could to vindicate any right wing worries Northern Europe had. The Internet was almost brought to its knees by bloggers disparaging Islam, many deriding an earlier statement by President Obama to the United Nations; "The future must not belong to those who slander the prophet of Islam."[51] One reporting site summed up the blogging opinions with the headline; "The Future Should Belong To Those Who Can Slander The Prophet of Islam. Radical Islam doesn't like being mocked. Truth is, it's not mocked enough"[52] The Internet allows this, and the bloggers are now too many to assassinate. Nevertheless a near clone Islamist assault on a cartoonist gathering and a synagogue in Denmark occurred a month later.

Time will tell whether the actual intent of the perpetrators was to find an issue Europe will not back down over, and that Muslims cannot condone. The West enshrines freedom of speech, and Muslims find it difficult to align themselves with parties printing Muhammad cartoons. The only thing we can be sure about is the variety of digital and psychological weaponry utilized by all sides. Anything and everything in the realm of social media, Youtube videos, and blogging sites will be used.

IN FRONT OF THE STORY

If Muslims are tired of seeing themselves in the media, the Irish Catholics are over it. Movies such as 'The Magdalene Sisters' in 2002 depicting the brutality handed out to unmarried mothers in Irish convents, were but one in a series of global hits the Roman Catholic Church has had to endure. As people felt freer to testify about shocking upbringings in Catholic schools and convents around the Western world, the Vatican initially hoped it would blow over.

---

51. "Remarks by the President," para. 43
52. "The Future Should Belong," line 1.

Lacking the political power they had long ago to silence dissent, an inevitable penny dropped after years of bad press. The Catholics could no longer go on reassigning pedophile priests to back-room duties. They had to do something. And if the announcement by Archbishop Diarmuid Martin in June 2014 was anything to go by, they have realized proactive openness works better. Time Magazine term this strategy as, "getting out in front of the story."[53]

Eight hundred dead babies bodies were discovered in a mass grave at a convent run mother and child home in Ireland, dating to the twentieth century rather than the nineteenth as was originally thought. Before the press could crucify someone, the Archbishop said; "The truth must come out (and) a full investigation was needed. The indications are that if something happened in Tuam, it probably happened in other mother and baby homes around the country. That's why I believe we need a full-bodied investigation."[54]

Is he genuine? In my opinion he probably is, but we're interested in the impact of media. And the real point is the Catholic Church could no longer hope for silence, their only option once they lost the power to enforce it. A combination of church under state law, with the camera, sensationalist press, and worldwide exposure through television and the Internet, was enough media pressure for the Catholics to embrace publicity before it squeezed the dignity out of them.

In the same week in June 2014, the rumors of Islamic extremists infiltrating British schools rose another notch with the publication of an official report by Britain's Office for Standards in Education, Children's Services and Skills, or Ofsted; "A report (Ofsted) released on Monday concluded that pressure from fundamentalist Islamic school board governors had created a culture of "fear and intimidation" among senior staff members in a number of British schools said to have been the targets of a campaign to impose Islamist views on parts of the educational system."[55]

No mimicking of the Archbishop occurred. Nobody got out in front of the tale. The report findings were criticized by the Muslim Council of Britain (MCB), which argued that, "Extremism will not be confronted if Muslims, and their religious practices are considered as, at best, contrary to the values of this country and at worst, seen as 'the swamp' that feeds

53. "Myth of Inevitability," para. 2.
54. "Tuam babies," para. 6.
55. "In Britain, School Report Cites Division Over Islam," para. 1.

extremism. There is scant evidence that the education system or the Muslim community are the reasons for why people turn to terrorism."[56]

News reporters are relentless today. Will the MCB beat the journalists to it one day, and release their briefing to the press about the proactive investigative work they are doing in schools? That way, they can type it up themselves. Reporters are reputed to be lazy, preferring prepared copy to writing their own. Then again, they might not. Perhaps the MCB could ask Lance Armstrong, who after years of denial against growing evidence, finally admitted, and apologized for, using drugs to win seven Tour de France cycling victories.

Compare his stand to that of Sachin Tendulkar. Cricket is a worldwide sport, although not grasped by Americans. The slightest nick of a ball by the bat means you're out—if the ball is caught before hitting the ground. Prior to the Television Umpire, many a batsman bluffed his way past this error because the human umpire didn't hear or see it despite the protestations of the opposing team. The legendary Tendulkar would famously not wait for the umpire's call. He strode off the field prior to it because he knew he had nicked the ball. Crowds loved his honesty. Other batsmen foolishly stood their ground until the TV Umpire zoomed in, slowed down, and after some audio enhancement, told them to walk. Such batsmen do not receive accolades from the waiting press corps. Armstrong clung to denial too long. At the end of years of pressure, the world did not then forgive, corporations clamoring to retrieve their sponsorship fees from him.

I hope the analogy is obvious. Whether it comes down to openness or honesty is almost no longer the point. There is too much media around to dodge bullets. Centuries ago you could silence ideas and people by burning both, or just being plain quiet about them. At some point in the mediatized twentieth century, that changed. Public relations companies have emerged to guide you through organized denial and obfuscation. Reporters have caught up with all that, and we now celebrate the open world. Whether we like it or not, media compels us to give credence to it. And a good spin doctor can mentor you on how and when to do the apology.

There's another problem too—the way the Internet collects and displays data. It's extremely unfair because it reports on volume. Wouldn't you know it, apologies are measurable too. If you enter a phrase enclosed in quote marks, Google searches for the exact phrase, not the separate words.

56. Ibid., para. 12.

In January 2015, Google informed me, 'No results found for "mullah apologises."'

In deference to US spelling I tried "mullah apologizes." Still 'No results.'

I tried another phrase; "bishop apologises" About 9,770 results. And "bishop apologizes" About 10,700 results.

These searches are compromised by definitions and names. Many people have Bishop as a surname for example, although that did not appear to represent the majority of hits. Muslims might argue mullah is not equivalent to bishop, just as Christians may say there are more mullahs than bishops. References do occur with the name of the mullah inserted, but that's the same for bishops too.

It gets worse. I tried; "imam apologizes" About 5,610 results.

That sounds fine—except that the first pages were about an imam apologizing to the Islamic State, or for comparing various persons to holocaust victims. This is obviously a snapshot in time, and next months results may well be different, (although I did not find a mullah apologizing over a six month stretch.) There are two media points here; Google, or another search engine of the future, will be used because it's the easiest way to find anything; secondly, it reports on volume, another word for which is gossip. And gossip creates your brand. Digital gossip is just a fact. There's no point complaining because we all welcome that new Internet driven world, including Muslim–majority nations. However, while it does make getting out in the front of the story more strategic, it can become harder for leaders, which explains the reticence of Tariq Ramadan and Pope Francis to say something unexpected.

ATTENTION DEFICIT DISORDER

Al–Qaeda used the Internet too, and anyone can find and download a copy of their photoshop produced online magazine, 'Inspire.' Inspire is the title of a multitude of periodicals, but the top half dozen search results referred to the Al–Qaeda one in mid 2014. The others must not have realized the brand name had been hijacked.

Inspire Magazine was actually a very successful venture into the Internet since it achieved top ranking without any Google search fees changing hands. Drop the word 'magazine,' and 'Inspire' on its own still brought the magazine to the first Google page of 63,800,000 results in 2014. Corporations would give their right arm for such exposure (bad taste analogy).

Clearly Al–Qaeda's cleric, Al–Awlaki, prior to his demise by a drone, only had to issue that fatwa against Molly Norris onto the web and it found its way to anyone that mattered.

One of the most obvious influences of the pictorial nature of the Internet, is that Islam has got pictorial. Despite that Islamic penchant for words, Inspire is replete with imagery. Somehow, Al–Qaeda, the most famous militant group until the Islamic State usurped pole position, had pictures, photos and diagrams, all the way through its premiere publication. We might ask why, but the first two requirements are photoshop, and faster broadband. If we still ran 33.6K Internet speeds, as we did in the 1990s, Inspire would have been a flop. It takes too long to download.

A third major reason is the decline of reading. It is said that Americans were better readers two hundred years ago than they are today. In 2004, the National Education Association conducted its largest study of literature participation, and concluded, "The percentage of adult Americans reading literature has dropped dramatically over the past 20 years."[57]

A follow–up NEA report to the 2004 Reading at Risk study found similar declines in reading by adults. The 2004 NEA report also suggests that persons who read literature are three times more likely to be involved in civic activities.[58] Postman warned us about this thirty years ago; "Pictures have little difficulty in overwhelming words, and short–circuiting introspection."[59]

Some critics do not believe that reading has declined as much as is indicated by the NEA studies. These critics believe that researchers should also measure comic book, graphic novel, and Internet reading as legitimate substitutes for book reading.

Comic books, you say? Anything to get the stats up when they go for increased funding, I suppose. Anyway, they agree that people look at moving and still pictures now. And Inspire Magazine has lots of imagery despite admonitions in the history of Islam not to utilize those.

Al Qaeda and IS can therefore publish videos to the Internet, which is turning into the mother of all television stations, with limitless channel availability. IS don't have the PR skills to win Western hearts and minds, but they're not after those anyway. They too, developed their own magazine called Dabiq, which is a town in Syria mentioned in an Islamic hadith on

57. Bradshaw and Nichols. "Reading At Risk," 9.

58. Ibid., 12.

59. Postman, *Amusing ourselves to death*, 103.

the final Armageddon battle. Westerners get bored quickly however, another by product of switching between available TV channels or infinite websites. From a relatively high figure with issue no. 1, downloads of subsequent Inspire Magazine issues have 'tanked,' as The Atlantic put it in June 2012.[60] Google had tired of Inspire magazine by early 2015, and it had disappeared from the first search page.

Attention Deficit Disorder (ADD) may ultimately be the enemy of militant Islamists. The world wide web itself isn't. Social media experts had given up trying to deny them Internet access by mid 2014. It was too complicated. Nobody, not even governments, the United Nations, or Internet experts, can stop anyone, no matter how wicked they are, from displaying their gruesome workings to the world. Therefore, anyone who wants to, can watch them. Surges in views will occur.

We can be assured however that fascination of the horrible palls, and attention drifts back to American Idol. One supposes, after you're read one, it's 'same old, same old.' Science has not yet confirmed the idea the Internet is at fault, but at least one researcher has quipped we might be shrinking back to grasping only 140 characters at a time,[61] (the length of a twitter tweet). The ultimate contradiction is that even Al–Qaeda and IS were forced to play in an arena virtually defined by ADD. They had to though, because the Internet has wrecked everything else.

TELEVANGELISM

Perhaps Islam could try television. Guess what? Muslims do already. Another mimic, I'm afraid.

The tale starts with nineteenth century American evangelists who traveled around the nation doing tent revivalist meetings, which often gathered thousands together out on the prairie. When radio appeared in the 1930s, both Protestant and Roman Catholic preachers saw its potential. 1920s broadcasts by S. Parkes Cadman reached a listening audience of five million.

Television is brilliant in that it is radio with pictures. Imagine visiting your neighbors long ago in their castle to see the new painting that cost them an arm and a leg. What might you have thought back then if the picture moved? And then spoke to you? Wow. We've forgotten this was a

60. "It's Not Just Newspapers: Circulation Tanks," line 1.

61. "Attention loss feared," para. 3.

technical wonder. Later you could watch films at home, on this box in the corner called a television, rather than driving into town. More wow. In 1952 Time Magazine first called Fulton Sheen a televangelist, which shows how quick the church invaded that media, or that media invaded the church. By 1957 Oral Roberts was preaching to 80 percent of the possible US television audience. And Christianity was in television to stay.

Or was television in Christianity to stay? The most obvious signs of mimicry with television celebrities were evident in the personal lives of the preachers themselves. Jimmy Swaggart, whose reach extended to 260 stations by 1983, was found twice in the company of prostitutes, and that went down with his viewers as fast as his ratings did. Jim Bakker fell for the same vice, was divorced from his charismatic wife Tammy, and did prison time before returning to the trade.

Of course much more copying than that went on. The stage sets, the choreographed music, the wow factor, and the beige suits all came from somewhere, and you won't find them in the Bible. It is true, as Jay Newman points out, that, "what is the slickness of an Oral Roberts compared to that of a typical talk show host? The style and content of the typical televangelical program strikes most people, including most Christian believers, as rather crude and rather silly."[62]

He hits the very point, which is that since the televangelists engage with that media, they will be judged within it. They are compared with slicker presenters, as if that were their point. And to the viewer it is. Newman stresses some televangelists are earnest and well meaning. I would hazard most, if not all are, even if they deceive themselves. The issue is not a moral one, it is that television is the chosen medium. They are attempting to get a spiritual message across, but the remote audience will notice, subliminally perhaps, that the podium wasn't as colorful as the CNN one they just saw, and the adverts have changed.

Discovering what communication is like in a non–television society is an eye–opener. In 1979 I lived in one of those—the villages in the West African forest of Liberia. Even a cassette player was a rare, envied item. A young African church worker was given a truck full of books and tasked with driving around these villages. One day I was with him. He stopped his vehicle in the main street, and rolled up the side of the truck. Inside he had a small loudspeaker and microphone. He just started talking. He was

62. Newman, *Religion vs. Television*, 96.

neither showman nor dunce, yet immediately drew a crowd who listened avidly.

I was blown away. Such a tactic would never work in the West. You would be ignored, even shunned as some sort of crank. It took me a while to recognize that almost nothing happened in these villages. The paucity of any media or entertainment guaranteed an audience when anyone appeared. That's how the tent revivalist preachers drew those thousands out on the prairies. That's how preachers anywhere used to be able to work, and now in Western Christianity, it's gone because we've all got too much media distracting us elsewhere.

We might have the impression from historians that medieval peasants were forced to go to church and sit there listening to dull priests. Maybe it was actually the best show in town simply because it was the only live channel. The question is whether Islam may suffer the same decline today, and we're going to see some interesting mosque attendance stats in the Netherlands, Iran and America later on.

Nevertheless it was inevitable that Muslim televangelists arrived. Amr Khaled, an Egyptian one-time accountant turned televangelist star, burst onto screens in 2001 with his show 'Words from the Heart.' The Western suit dressed (black as well as beige) Mr Khaled and his audience (of men and women) discussed the concerns of young Muslims, such as whether Islam forbids cinema-going.

He was emulated elsewhere in the Islamic world. In Indonesia, Abdullah Gymnastiar, known as 'Elder Brother Gym,' attracted millions of viewers to his television shows and seminars—until his decision to take a second wife in 2006 outraged his many female fans.

4

HISTORIES OF VIOLENCE

"Of the three great world–religions, Islam is the only one which was born militant. The victory of Islam in Arabia was largely accomplished by the sword, and circumstances induced the Prophet's heirs to employ the armies of tribesmen at their disposal in the propagation of the new faith in the world beyond."[1]

So wrote historian J. J. Saunders, a specialist in the Crusades, in 1968. Several hundred years had passed since large scale Muslim–inspired violent outbreaks had occurred anywhere against Western powers. Indeed, by the nineteenth century, apart from some obscure battles in the middle of Africa, many Westerners felt the faith was well past its use by date, as illustrated in this 1878 newspaper article;

For more than a thousand years the political power of Mohammedanism dominated a large part of Asia, Africa and a considerable portion of Europe. This power was exercised by the Turkish Empire and many independent kingdoms scattered throughout Asia and Africa, and for ages these Mohammedan powers commanded the respectful consideration of other powers. During the last 200 years the Christian nations have been gradually capturing the political strongholds of Mohammedanism, and now but little remains. The utter extinction of Mohammedanism as a political power is then an assured fact; Mohammedanism, as a religion,

1. Saunders, *Aspects of the Crusades,* 21.

may continue to exist, but it will be shorn of all political significance; it will be a sect among sects and ism among philosophers.[2]

Saunders was not alone. Prior to the 1980s, both Western and Muslim historians freely told us Islam had a militant beginning, if not nature.
Ibn Khaldun, "one of the greatest philosophers to come out of the Muslim
world"[3] had this to say in 1336;

> "In the Muslim community, the holy war is a religious duty, be-
> cause of the universalism of the (Muslim) mission and (the obli-
> gation to) convert everybody to Islam either by persuasion or by
> force. Therefore, caliphate and royal authority are united in (Is-
> lam), so that the person in charge can devote the available strength
> to both of them at the same time. The other religious groups did
> not have a universal mission, and the holy war was not a religious
> duty to them, save only for purposes of defense."[4]

Nevertheless United Kingdom Prime Minister David Cameron on
May 23rd, 2013, immediately following the open air murder of a British
soldier by an Islamist youth, and over a decade of the most explosive violent
acts worldwide in the name of Islam, claimed the following; "This was not
just an attack on Britain and on our British way of life. It was also a betrayal
of Islam and of the Muslim communities who give so much to our country.
There is nothing in Islam that justifies this truly dreadful act."[5] A year
later, on September 29th, 2014, after the horrendous beheading of a British
aid worker by the Islamic State, Mr Cameron described the IS: "They are
not Muslims. They are murderers."[6]

He was not alone. On September 10th, 2014, after unbelievable atrocities in Iraq had been committed by IS (Islamic State, also known as ISIS or
ISIL) President Obama addressed the US nation on his military plan to defeat them. He stated, "ISIL is not Islamic. No religion condones the killing
of innocents. And the vast majority of ISILs victims have been Muslim."[7]

Other Western and Muslim commentators have written Islam up as a
peaceful religion since terror burst onto the world stage under the Islamic

2. "The Decline of Mohammedanism," 2.

3. "Ibn Khaldun," para. 2.

4. "Remarks on the words "Pope" and "Patriarch" in the Christian religion," para. 2–3.

5. "Terror attack," para. 19.

6. "Political Correctness," para. 1.

7. "Statement," para. 4.

banner on September 11th, 2001. This is an utter change from the past fourteen hundred years.

If you think there might be some contradictions above, look at these two from Christendom. The first quote is from Jesus himself;

> "But I say to you, do not resist an evil person; but whoever slaps you on your right cheek, turn the other to him also. If anyone wants to sue you and take your shirt, let him have your coat also. Whoever forces you to go one mile, go with him two. Give to him who asks of you, and do not turn away from him who wants to borrow from you. "You have heard that it was said, 'You shall love your neighbor and hate your enemy.' But I say to you, love your enemies and pray for those who persecute you,"[8]

One thousand years later, in 1095, Pope Urban II urged Christians to take the sword against the Turks and the Arabs.

> "For, as the most of you have heard, the Turks and Arabs have attacked them and have conquered the territory of Romania as far west as the shore of the Mediterranean and the Hellespont, which is called the Arm of St. George. They have occupied more and more of the lands of those Christians, and have overcome them in seven battles. They have killed and captured many, and have destroyed the churches and devastated the empire. If you permit them to continue thus for awhile with impunity, the faithful of God will be much more widely attacked by them. On this account I, or rather the Lord, beseech you as Christ's heralds to publish this everywhere and to persuade all people of whatever rank, foot-soldiers and knights, poor and rich, to carry aid promptly to those Christians and to destroy that vile race from the lands of our friends. I say this to those who are present, it is meant also for those who are absent. Moreover, Christ commands it.
>
> All who die by the way, whether by land or by sea, or in battle against the pagans, shall have immediate remission of sins. This I grant them through the power of God with which I am invested."[9]

We have some problems here. Somehow today's Islam is associated with almost daily suicide bombings somewhere on the globe. Yet for the first time in their long history of contact with the faith, Western leaders tell us the religion is one of peace. On the other hand a medieval ruler of Western Christendom called for a military response against a Muslim-majority

8. Matthew 5:39-44
9. "Speech at Council of Clermont," para. 4-5.

region despite a founder of Christianity telling followers to love their enemies. How did this shift happen over the first thousand years of Christianity? And, what has happened over the past fifty years in Islam?

In the midst of much media, mythology and mimicry, we will examine why Mr Cameron and Mr Obama issued those statements, and surprisingly perhaps, why they were the proper, and only things they could say. Histories of our two religions abound, and this is not the place to replicate them. But we do need to begin with beginnings.

CHRISTIANITY BEGINS

There are two major founders of the faith—Jesus and the Apostle Paul—and a few minor ones including John and James, depending on which viewpoint you adopt. Jesus didn't claim to start a new religion, and many feel he thought of himself as Jewish. They already had a faith.

Neither did Jesus start Christianity when he was born, which was sometime between 4 BC and 4 AD. The historical clock known as year numbering wasn't standing in Bethlehem behind the shepherds at the manger waiting to be switched on. Paul began writing letters to Christians around the year 50 AD. Jesus didn't write a thing, apart from those words in the dust one day—but he could read.

No violent encounter initiated by Jesus is recorded, except one: he famously fashioned a whip and drove the moneychangers out of the Jewish temple in Jerusalem. Paul did approvingly observe the stoning of a Christian, but that was prior to his conversion. Paul may never have met Jesus, and was not one of the twelve disciples, yet he was the most formative mover in the early years of the faith.

Israelis sum this all up poetically.

Roses are red, violets are blue,
If they didn't have Paul, they'd all be Jews.

About three hundred years later, the Roman emperor Constantine converted to the faith. He purportedly had a vision of the cross, and committed that if he won a pending battle, he would convert. And he did. Was Constantine really moved by the vision to elevate the faith from a household affair of a few dozen churches to the empires state religion? Historians have difficulty swallowing such zeal. They're more scientific now. Rodney Stark paints a comprehensive picture showing how this small, Jewish dominated sect, rose to claim the allegiance of half the Roman Empire in three centuries. Stark outlines a modern day parallel of how numbers can grow—the Mormon Church. Demographics show that the Mormon Church has expanded 40 percent, on average, in every decade since its inception.[10] In the first decade that doesn't mean much. After ten years, your original 1000 faithful has only reached 1400. However we all know the power of logarithmic growth. Mormonism today is approaching the threshold of being a global religion. There is only one definition for joining the club of global faiths, and it is nothing about how good, bad or ugly that belief is—it's plain numbers.

If Christianity had grown by the same proven, possible growth rate, it would have commanded the hearts of over half the Roman Empire by the time Constantine came along. Did this religion get to that size without military backing? In fact it was a persecuted belief right up until it was legitimized. Crucifixion was not outlawed until 313 AD. We can say, with strong historical backing, that in its first three hundred years, Christianity was not a religion of violence. In the fourth century St Basil recommended that even the soldier who killed an enemy in war should abstain from holy communion for three years. The faith reached legitimacy (attracted numbers, that is) via peaceful means. This is one reason why Christians of the twenty–first century refer longingly back to the early church.

Practically coincident with Constantine, Christianity entered its long political power phase, and peaceful theories started to alter. It didn't take long. St Augustine, (354–430 AD), regarded by many as the greatest theologian of them all, opened the discussion of a just war; "But, say they, the wise man will wage just wars. As if he would not all the rather lament the necessity of just wars, if he remembers that he is a man; for if they were not just he would not wage them, and would therefore be delivered from all wars."[11]

It took another nine hundred years for this thought to be formalized by another theologian, St. Thomas Aquinas. (1225–1274 AD) Among other points he concluded; "war must occur for a good and just purpose rather than for self-gain."[12]

Prior to Aquinas though, Pope Urban II called for that holy war in 1095 against those who had "occupied more and more of the lands of those

---

10. Stark, *Rise of Christianity*, 4–13.

11. Augustine, *The City of God*, chapter 7, para. 1.

12. "Just war theory," section 1.2, para. 3.

Christians." He assured the faithful that any slain during this enterprise would receive immediate forgiveness, and therefore, entry to heaven.

ISLAM BEGINS

The prophet Muhammad was born in the year 570 AD in Arabia. He fought in at least three battles during his lifetime, and he either participated in, or agreed with, the beheading of those six hundred Jewish men at Banu Qurayza. After he passed away, Muslim armies immediately went on the offensive for a few hundred years, informing opposing Persian forces in approximately the year 630 AD as told by Bukhari, the most reputable re-corder of all Muslim writers;

> "Our Prophet, the Messenger of our Lord, has ordered us to fight you till you worship Allah Alone or give Jizya (i.e. tribute); and our Prophet has informed us that our Lord says: "Whoever amongst us is killed (i.e. martyred), shall go to Paradise to lead such a luxu-rious life as he has never seen, and whoever amongst us remain alive, shall become your master."[13]

Only one hundred years after Muhammad's death, Muslim warriors had swept across North Africa, through Spain, and had reached Tours, near Paris. They were finally turned back there. Historians have long marveled at the speed in which that first Muslim empire was created. Some feel it was well timed. Powers to the east and west (Persia and Byzantium) had exhausted themselves fighting each other. Islam expanded militarily in the Western hemisphere then rather than through the process of peaceful con-version as with the early Christian model. Malaysia and Indonesia became Islamic through more peaceful engagements, picking up in the thirteenth century after a slow start.

Debate does not exist over whether Islam conquered peoples from India to Morocco, but it does over whether those nations were coerced into the new belief. It is indeed maintained that Muslims respected religious freedom in those early days. They even employed a Jew to the highest level in the kingdom they created in Spain, and allowed Christians to continue as they were. It is worth noting however, the options offered the Persians, which include paying a tax (Jizya), rather than convert.

---

13. Sahih Bukhari, "Volume 4, Book 53, Number 386," para. 1.

Muslim armies reached the stout walls of Constantinople and laid siege to it for two years in 717–718 AD after years of attack and preparation. They were defeated by winter, famine, disease, and the Byzantine's military advantage—Greek fire against the Arab navy. Buttressed by the Pyrenees mountain range in northern Spain, and the Byzantine Empire to the east, Europe was safe for a while. It had time to regroup, although this took over eight hundred years. This is the standard opinion of many historians, although differing interpretations are now emerging.

Let's stray into mimicry. Did Muhammad copy the militarist nature of Christendom that was in vogue by the time he arrived?

Clearly he was influenced by Christianity and Judaism. After all, he didn't try to correct the words of Buddha or Confucius. Given that his exposure to Christianity must have also included the then existent political nature of Christianity, we see either unconscious or conscious mimicry. Powerful seventh century nations to the west of Muhammad had integrated religion with the state. It is not unreasonable to suggest the militaristic nature of Islam, and its cohesion of politics with religion, may have been influenced by forerunners in nearby precincts who revered the same ancients.

Secondly, as we found earlier, if we accept Muslim authorities that Muhammad was illiterate, he would have been less able to distinguish between the actual texts of Christianity, and its then political form. Both would have been relayed to him via conversation.

Let's briefly compare the holy texts and their stances on violence.

SANCTIFIED VIOLENCE

It's not too difficult to find passages condoning violence in the Qu'ran;

- "And kill them wherever you overtake them and expel them from wherever they have expelled you, and fitnah is worse than killing. And do not fight them at al–Masjid al–Haram until they fight you there. But if they fight you, then kill them. Such is the recompense of the disbelievers."[14]

- "Fighting has been enjoined upon you while it is hateful to you. But perhaps you hate a thing and it is good for you; and perhaps you love a thing and it is bad for you. And Allah Knows, while you know not."[15]

14. Sura 2:191
15. Sura 2:216

- "And fight in the cause of Allah and know that Allah is Hearing and Knowing."[16]

- "So let those fight in the cause of Allah who sell the life of this world for the Hereafter. And he who fights in the cause of Allah and is killed or achieves victory—We will bestow upon him a great reward."[17]

Neither does the Bible lack violent approvals;

- Only in the cities of these peoples that the Lord your God is giving you as an inheritance, you shall not leave alive anything that breathes. But you shall utterly destroy them, the Hittite and the Amorite, the Canaanite and the Perizzite, the Hivite and the Jebusite, as the Lord your God has commanded you,[18]

- O daughter of Babylon, you devastated one, how blessed will be the one who repays you with the recompense with which you have repaid us. How blessed will be the one who seizes and dashes your little ones against the rock.[19]

- "Behold, I am against you," declares the Lord of hosts. "I will burn up her chariots in smoke, a sword will devour your young lions; I will cut off your prey from the land, and no longer will the voice of your messengers be heard."[20]

Although both President Obama and Thomas Aquinas agreed that religionists should not attack innocents, Psalm 137 clearly approves of he who "dashes your (Babylonian) little ones against the rock" whether Bible believing Christians like it or not. In fact, it is argued that the Bible contains more violent verses than the Qu'ran—but then it is ten times longer.

Christianity has a New Testament however, expressing an almost complete absence of retaliation apart from a few verses condemning Jews. Some New Testament verses refer to hell, but perdition is an after–life violence. Hell is not consistent in the New Testament as it turns out. Sometimes it means Gehenna, the burning rubbish pit outside Jerusalem, and the word hell is never used by Paul, one of the major founders of the faith. Christians also disagree over whether the Bible is downloaded straight from God,

16. Sura 2:244
17. Sura 4:74
18. Deuteronomy 20:16–17
19. Psalm 137:8–9
20. Nahum 2:13

whereas virtually all Muslims claim the Qu'ran is a direct transmission of the words of Allah. In other words, plenty of preachers, bishops, and pastors, have no problem telling their congregations to ignore those violent Biblical passages. It's a little harder for imams or mullahs to go there with the Qu'ran.

However, many writers don't examine differences between religions—as we noted earlier—and oodles believe "all religions are the same." For example the author of this next comment has not examined the Baha'i faith which has an extraordinary record of non–violence; "It may be that Islam is violent, indeed, by its very nature. But then, so, too, might Judaism and Christianity. Religion itself may be inherently violent."[21] That aside, many Christians agree the history of Christianity has been violent, and readily concede that believers justified their warrior behavior in previous eras. One might ask whether an equivalent number of Muslims concede the historic violence of their faith. It would be an interesting survey to run.

Actually a prior question could be asked of both religions—do people read their own history? Are Christians by and large aware that their ancestors fought and killed Muslims in both offensive and defensive battles? Are Muslims by and large aware their ancestors fought and killed Westerners in both offensive and defensive battles?

History is an extension of man, well put by the philosopher George Santayana: "Those who cannot remember the past are condemned to repeat it."[22] Being a media, it continues to be modified. There is in fact a study of the history of history, called historiography. History was originally written to celebrate victories, not relay bare facts, and certainly not defeats. We've already noted there is no story about Moses amongst the hieroglyphics of Egyptian Pharaohs. Perhaps Moses didn't exist. Then again, Moses defeated the Egyptians in the Bible story.

Wartime mythology exists to this very day. It takes decades, sometimes centuries, occasionally millennia, for passions to subside. It is well known that Japan has not been an accurate teacher of its young. When I lived in Singapore in the 1990s, young Japanese visitors would go through the Sentosa Island multimedia show of the invasion of Singapore by Japan in 1942. Many would emerge weeping and wailing. They had no idea that their country inflicted such barbarity on another. It wasn't taught at their schools.

21. Qureshi, *New Crusades,* 4.

22. Santayana, "Quotes," section 1.2.1, line 5.

In 1996 I drove my family through Scotland and Ireland, following the Jacobite trail. Fundamentally this was a long clash in the seventeenth and eighteenth centuries between the forces of Protestants and Roman Catholics, which morphed into an ongoing conflict of the English against the Scots and the Irish. We visited the battleground of Culloden, part of Britain to this day, where the English General Cumberland pulverized the Scots in 1745. The exact final stand of each highland clan is marked with its own plaque.

Crossing over into Northern Ireland, part of the UK, the trail continued through the Londonderry museum, which was replete with displays of sieges and battles. Then we headed south into Ireland itself, which gained its independence from Britain in 1916. I promised the kids we were getting near the famous Battle of the Boyne site, memorialized by the old Irish independence cry, "Remember 1690!" We turned up alongside the Boyne river, only to find a hill covered in weeds, with a lonely rusty sign informing us we had reached the place.

I was baffled. Later that evening, parked up in a camping ground, I chatted to an Irishman. "You people need to spruce up your history," I told him. "Build a memorial or a museum there."

"Ah, to be sure, to be sure," he agreed. "But you have to remember—we lost that one."

We can learn a lot from the English however. They were in the colonization game for about a thousand years. Roughly speaking, they got better at it. There are many differences between Wales, their first colony, and New Zealand, their last. The first peoples of their various dominions around the globe may disagree with this, but the fact that the British Commonwealth still exists, and those independent nations play each other at cricket is a good sign the English did a few things right.

Some insights have been recorded over the years into the manner they attempted to solve religious quarrels between Protestants and Catholics in Ireland. On Bloody Sunday in January 30th, 1972, British soldiers shot dead thirteen Catholic civilians in Derry, Ireland. Conway relays how different memories of that act were perpetuated by different parties. The official side differed markedly from the Catholic side:

> . . . the mediums through which this unofficial memory has been established and maintained, the meanings associated with it, and how and why these have changed over time. Traditionally, it has been invested with a negative meaning associated with

sectarianism, colonialism, and victimization. In recent times, the folk memory has been framed within a broader global context with a focus on its healing and reconciliation potential.[23]

This broader context means looking at the woes of the world and concluding that actively remembering your particular sour past doesn't get you anywhere. Conway points out the British government recognized this at the highest level, and aimed at healing and reconciliation between the parties. Religious animosity is much quieter in Northern Ireland these days, so again, the British must have done something right. This is an example of a modern government that has discovered peace is better than war. Although this sounds basic, it took a long time to learn, and the impact of various media and myths were crucial in that dawning realization.

Historiography is also revealing interesting features about Islam's historians. Andersson had this to say about the halcyon years of Muslim territorial expansion shortly after Muhammad died;

> In the historical thinking of the time, Muslim scholars tended to attribute the events, whether good or bad, to the Muslims themselves, including leaders and subjects. They primarily focused on internal rather than external factors for historical development, although based on the underlying recognition of Allah as the All–Powerful and direct causer of events. Thereby, the roles of individuals were emphasized and larger societal developments were often discoursed in terms of individual decisions, responsibilities and characteristics.[24]

We can imagine the enthusiastic success of those early warriors, thinking that Muhammad was right after all. This thing is working, they might have told themselves as nation after nation fell. Andersson tells us they were wise enough to look at themselves and accept responsibility when something didn't go that well, like any smart business would. No wonder Umar, the central character Andersson wrote about, is regarded as one of only four rightly guided caliphs in the entire history of Islam. What a contrast with today, when most Muslim commentators endlessly castigate external events, mostly blaming the US and allies for any woes they suffer.

23. Conway, "Active Remembering," 2.
24. Andersson, "Governance and Economics in Early Islamic Historiography," 26.

THE 800 YEAR WAR

Pivotal events, conceptual mimicry, and emerging technologies came into play for eight centuries. We will trace it from 710 AD to 1571 AD. Spanning the Middle Ages and the Crusades, this long era saw the rise of the West and the eventual humbling of the armies of Islam, but not after gains, losses and infighting on both sides. The epoch is crammed with mythology, much of which remains to this day, cluttering and confusing the actual truth, which may never be fully known. Historians have to make a living, and reinventing the Crusades has always been a good earner. Tourist shops selling model Crusader or Templar knights are sited outside nearly every major cathedral in France and Britain to this day. Not one sells a Muslim Saracen warrior.

One such mythological tale, from the school of romantic poets, is the Song of Roland. At the heart of Paris, the geography of the spot marked by a pin in the ground beside the cathedral of Notre Dame, stands a bronze statue of three men. About fifty percent bigger than human size, and a fitting tribute for the actual larger than life king Charlemagne, he is mounted, with two characters leading his horse by the bridle. It represents a victory long ago against the forces of Islam.

In the year 778 AD, Charlemagne was the ruler of the Holy Roman Empire, encompassing about the same territory as the six original nations of the European Economic Community (France, Germany, Italy, Belgium, Netherlands and Luxembourg). He was returning from warring against the Saracens occupying Spain, having extracted a promise they would convert to Christianity if he withdrew. Charlemagne was thirty leagues ahead of Roland's crew who were bringing up the rear with the baggage. A force of treacherous Muslim warriors fell on them as they made their way through Roncevaux pass, and although Roland carried the huge horn proudly hanging from his side on the bronze, for reasons of honor he did not blow it and summon his king for assistance.

Eventually, as they began to lose the battle, his friend Oliver, portrayed on the other side of Charlemagne's bronze horse, persuaded Roland to put the horn to his lips. Charlemagne heard the clarion call, and immediately returned to put the Saracens to flight, but too late to save Roland. Such was the significance of this fight that the Song of Roland was written about it, running to 32,000 words. Condensed versions were told to schoolchildren as recently as forty years ago.

It's a perfect medieval story—except most of it isn't true.

Right from the start in fact. As wags put it, the Holy Roman Empire was neither Holy, nor Roman, nor an Empire. Charlemagne was in fact scurrying back through the Pyrenees with his tail between his legs after an abortive attempt against the Islamic kingdom in Spain. Roland probably existed, but even the most naïve of us may have trouble accepting that the sound of a blown horn will rise above the noise of battle, and wind thirty leagues through a mountain chain. No such disclaimers have been posted on the statue, which sees thousands of tourists a day ignore it as they hurry past hoping to gain uncrowded entry into Notre Dame itself. Many of these visitors are Muslim, and even though I didn't survey any, I somehow doubt they would know who Roland or Charlemagne were.

This is a classic example of the mythology making of history. Among others, three thoughts are worth pointing out;

Firstly, the main character certainly existed. You need to start with some facts. Charlemagne did weld Europe together in his lifetime, although his kingdom fell apart shortly after he passed on. In 2005, a modern day version of this type of mixing facts with myth was produced as a movie called 'Kingdom of Heaven,' starring Orlando Bloom. While not claiming to represent medieval Crusader reality, it contains a hodge podge of actual events, sewn together to sell seats to crowds.

Secondly, the West loves displaying statues of its military heroes on plinths bearing their names. Many thousands more see these visual representations than read history. Displayed either in parks, or cathedrals, or art galleries, statues and paintings are gloriously visual means of presenting the past to the masses. Today that artwork includes movies, like The Kingdom of Heaven.

And thirdly, if mankind was able to develop wartime mythologies using history, statues, movies, paintings, and cathedrals, then surely he is able to create myths of peace.

Frequently, commentators betray a lack of basic historical awareness in our world. By this I mean dates of battles, who fought whom, and who lost what. English speaking Westerners find it difficult to believe that other nations would fudge the facts about victories and losses. Perhaps it is understandable. Perhaps the British concede defeats in their past because they won more often than they lost. Perhaps this psychology becomes political. Perhaps leaders of cultures that have had a hard time, historically speaking, generate enthusiasm by referring back to a Golden era or a Glorious past.

That's four 'perhaps' there—excuse my speculation.

However, as if to illustrate my point, in mid 2014 the BBC told us;

> Ancient landmarks like Mar Behnam show how deeply embedded Christianity is in the culture and history of Iraq. Just as in many other Arab countries, churches and monasteries are a timeless part of the landscape. For years, though, Christians have been warning that their hold in parts of the Middle East is weakening. Iraq is home to one of the world's most ancient Christian communities but its population has dwindled amid growing sectarian violence since the US–led invasion in 2003.[25]

The article intimates that Christians have been in trouble in Iraq since 2003, but it's been much longer than that. Possibly the writer was schooled at the same university as the British Labour parliamentarians whom Archbishop Rowan Williams petitioned about the persecution of Iraqi Christians—they had no idea there were any, or that their existence predated Islam.[26] Those Christians have survived in a Muslim–majority land for about 1300 years. Historian Philip Jenkins puts it quite simply; "Much of what we today call the Islamic world was once Christian."[27]

In 1581 Heinrich Bunting drew a clover leaf map of that earlier Christian world. Besides Europe, two equal sized leaves covered Asia and Africa. Basically Islam overran those two. Faced with the seeming ruin of Christianity by attack from outside, and endless infighting in Europe, Pope Urban aimed the European knights back at their common foe. That's a tried and true formula throughout the ages. There's nothing like a common external enemy to unite squabbling locals.

Heinrich Bunting's map

Muslim historians seem to give little credence to the fact they had overrun much of the known world and possibly provoked a day of reckoning. Those invading Crusaders were a surprise to them. Three hundred years had passed admittedly, which is enough time for a new normal to descend. What right had those Crusaders to remember that far back? And yet much of the Islamic world today continually refers to the Crusades, which happened nine hundred years ago. Very few Muslim writers ask such questions, although we will meet some later on.

25. "Isis militants 'seize Iraq monastery," para. 8.
26. "When foreign policy was closer to heaven," para. 5.
27. Jenkins, *Lost History of Christianity*, 4.

And I have read about a little old lady in Baghdad who has. On the previous day to the BBC article cited above, the New York Times ran one quoting, in my opinion, the wisest reporter of them all—an elderly Iraqi Muslim woman attending church in Baghdad in support of displaced Iraqi Christians. She reached out and touched a Christian mother of three little girls, saying; "You are the true original people here, and we are sorry for what has been done to you in the name of Islam."[28]

That single sentence contains more historical insight and compassion than any news reporter I have come across.

Faced with such passion, and so many agendas and views regarding history, let's simply list dates and events here. The significant milestones over this eight hundred year period are as follows;

- 710 AD. Islamic forces enter Spain.

- 732 AD. Charles Martel turns an Islamic force back from Poitiers in France

- 778 AD. Charlemagne crosses into Spain and is repulsed by Islamic forces.

- 1054 AD. The Eastern Orthodox Church splits from Rome.

- 1095 AD. Pope Urban calls for a Crusade against Muslim forces in the Holy land.

- 1099 AD. The first Crusade succeeds in capturing Jerusalem and other strategic cities.

- 1204 AD. Fourth Crusade sacks Constantinople instead of attacking Egypt.

- 1258 AD. Baghdad falls to the Mongols.

- 1291 AD. Removal of last Crusader strongholds from the Holy land.

- 1453 AD. Constantinople falls to the Turks, and the Byzantine Empire is no more.

- 1492 AD. The last Muslims are expelled from Spain.

- 1571 AD. The Turkish navy is defeated at the Battle of Lepanto.

This brief outline is enough for us to unravel various media, myths and mimicries, some of which survive to this day. Speaking of Ms though, you might first be asking how the Mongols crept in there. Actually, the

---

28. "Concern and Support for Iraqi Christians," para. 3.

Mongols never crept anywhere. They butchered and destroyed their way. Their influence was decisive, because they were possibly a bigger threat to Islam than Christianity. More on that soon.

Given the early church disapproval of armies and bloodshed, no wonder it took a thousand years to turn this prohibition around to a divine sanction—but it happened. It wasn't the only factor behind the success of the first Crusade, although we know there was a lot of prayer and fasting before battles with the Saracens commenced.

Once this heavenly bound concept of the armored knight caught hold in Christendom, it lasted a long time. French and British cathedrals show the long link between the church and the powers of this world. Westminster Cathedral is hardly a place of worship. It is a cemetery of nobility, their plaques or flagstones lining the walls and the floor. Walk on down to St Paul's, the only truly Protestant cathedral in London, built after the reformation, and the linkage is yet more powerful. Central place in the crypt is given to Lord Nelson, and other warrior luminaries.

I mentioned this to a young priest, whose duties include conversing with any of the tourists who might approach him. "There's a lot of military heroes buried down here, aren't there?"

He laughed politely. "Oh, that's to do with all the regiments that used to be stationed around the district."

I pressed deeper. "I mean, it's interesting about the obvious linkage between military and church. How do you guys deal with that in this day and age?'

He laughed again, nervously I felt, but didn't reply.

He knew what I meant though. He earns a living via contradiction. The website 'Vision of the Cathedral Church of St Paul in London' stated the following in 2015;

- St Paul's Cathedral seeks to enable people in all their diversity to encounter the transforming presence of God in Jesus Christ.

- As a community of worshippers, staff and volunteers we work with care and imagination to be a centre for welcome, worship and learning which inspires successive generations to engage with the richness of the Christian faith and its heritage.[29]

In fact St Paul's is a tourist monument, charging entry fees of US$23.00 per adult and US$13.00 per child. It tells all who walk around inside that

29. "Who We Are," para. 1.

the British won wars left, right, and center, and gloried in that. Nearly two million visitors swarm in each year, ticking off Nelson's tomb and the whispering gallery.

However, good on the clergy for trying to shift the goalposts. Poor blighters, I can imagine those young vicars are overjoyed to get a placement at St Paul's, and possibly learn to ignore the fact it is a building dedicated to armed conquest. I imagine they wholeheartedly swing in behind the relatively new Christianity that seeks peace despite the obvious memorabilia they walk amongst every day.

St Paul's is not alone. Even the much humbler Abbey de Fontenay in Burgundy, founded by the renowned Bernard of Clairvaux in the twelfth century, contains funerary of soldier knights. They are clad in armor and bear swords, while delightful cherubs perch on the side of their sarcophagi reading a book that is not Harry Potter.

It took Christendom over nine hundred years to begin to discard this tactic. A local family commissioned a stained glass window in their church in the Welsh town of Tenby in the 1920s, one of the last of its kind. It portrays, in brilliant colors, a World War 1 soldier kneeling at the feet of Jesus just before he enters heaven. This son of the family, slain in that conflict, is dressed in the shining armor of an eleventh century Frankish Crusader, not the khaki uniform of a corporal in the Somme. Jesus is blessing his work and sacrifice, welcoming him to heaven.

Such stained glass windows, or memorials to the slain, didn't disappear. Those windows were well made, and they last for hundreds of years, but I don't think any will be put up welcoming a British soldier slain in the Iraq war through the pearly gates.

Welsh stained glass window

In a cold blooded sense, blessing the death of warriors was an interesting tactical move. Alexander the Great commanded such allegiance from his followers that he could order them to die. He did it once to impress an opposing city on the obedience of his troops to die fighting if they didn't submit. He lined up ten men and ordered them to march over a sheer drop. The watching city drew its breath, then opened its gates to Alexander as the ten voluntarily pitched over.

Did Muhammad originate the fast track to heaven theory of dying in battle as his followers told the Persians about? Perhaps not. Dead Norwegian Vikings went to Valhalla, for example. More to our point, did Pope

Urban II know of this idea prior to endorsing it himself in 1095? From its inception, the Christian church honored martyrs who gave their lives, but not military ones. Christian martyrs were forbidden to strike back, or to call for revenge. Their deaths were not in the same league as suicidal soldiers.

There is no way of proving Urban mimicked it, which is why historians can only allude to it as a possibility. Urban certainly knew about Islam however, and since he was the Pope, it's not unreasonable to assume he understood the Islamic connection between battle and paradise.

Let's bring re-mythologizing in at this juncture because that's what is happening in Christianity. It started peacefully, went warlike, and is now midway through dismantling that.

Clearly this particular form of warrior sacrifice is still condoned in many Islamic scenarios. You might see where we are headed, so let's lay out two rather obvious questions;

- What factors caused Christianity to retreat from the warlike image it built up since at least 1095?

- Will those same factors shift Islam back from violence?

Both these questions are of course in dispute. At varying points along a vast spectrum of opinion you can encounter responses including;

- Both Christianity and Islam will always be violent religions.

- Islam is a religion of peace and does not have an anger problem. There are only misguided individuals acting under the auspices of Islam.

- That violent Islamic history listed above is wrong, and the West is at fault.

This third alternative is alive and well, believed by more people than just former President of Iran, Ahmadinejad, who claimed the Jewish Holocaust in World War 2 was a fabrication. Channel 4 in Britain ran a TV series in 2009 called Christianity—a history. The series was accompanied by a PDF guide, still available from the Channel 4 website. Episode 4 was about the Crusades, and was fronted by Rageh Omaar, a reknowned BBC reporter. Omaar writes as follows;

> I was brought up as a Muslim and I've reported on different jihad-ist movements in the Middle East over the last eight years but, speaking to different experts for this programme, it was clear that much of what we understand today as jihad came out of the

Muslim world's reaction to the First Crusades. The Qur'an talks about jihad but that means 'struggle', an inward struggle, a bit like what Holy War meant for Christianity before the First Crusades— fighting the devil in prayer. But the Crusades made fighting and killing an act of worship.

When Pope Urban declared that Christian lands in the Middle East had to be freed from the 'pollution' of Islam, and Christians went to fight a Holy War, Muslims who had been divided amongst different kingdoms realised that they had to fall back on something akin to what the Christians were doing in order to fend off these foreigners. The legacy that left for Muslims is the idea that jihad should actually mean Holy War, struggling for your religion against invaders.[30]

Omaar is claiming Islam copied Christianity's deployment of the suicide warrior, or holy war. At least he agrees with the concept of mimicry. It's an intriguing conclusion. If Muslims did pick it up off Christians, it got well and truly embedded in their faith, lasting until today, and justified by references to the Qu'ran, not the Bible. On the other hand, if Christians invented the concept, they've shrugged it off. Omaar has some interesting history to remodel, but that's re–mythologization in action.

Besides mimicry, the Crusades yield interesting lessons in both mythology and the extensions of men. The surprising thing about the first Crusade is that it succeeded. Thousands of miles from their own country, climate, and kinsmen, with diminishing resources and larger enemy forces, the Crusaders won three crucial battles. One was fought at Antioch, up in modern day Turkey. Having tricked their way into Antioch, at least the battle wearied, outnumbered Crusaders had a wall around them. A new, much larger, Turkish army then arrived to reclaim the city. Imagine the Crusaders' despair.

However a creative priest found a holy relic: the lance that pierced Jesus' side as he hung on the cross. Let's not get into how they proved that. Holy relics became a big thing as the Crusaders found so many when they plundered the Middle East. I have personally looked the head of John the Baptist in the face through a special window in Amiens Cathedral. Sure, there is another head of John the Baptist in the Church of San Silvestro in Capite, and a third in the Umayyad Mosque in Damascus. Those don't stop pilgrims crossing themselves and praying in front of the Amiens one to this day .

30. "Christianity: A History," 14.

The discovery of the lance inspired the Crusaders to march out the next morning and rout the larger Muslim forces. If you had asked any of the victorious knights whether God had a hand in their win, they would have agreed, to a man. Place that myth in front of a modern clergyman and he will chuckle, shift in his seat, and muse how beliefs change.

As for Islamic mimicry, when the Ottoman Empire was besieging Constantinople in 1453, progress was not as fast as hoped for. An enterprising Muslim discovered the tomb of one of the Prophet Muhammad's standard bearers, a tremendously inspiring find for the disheartened troops.

We've already learnt the mounted horse was an extension of man, but the Muslims had them too. Over several centuries the feudal system in Europe had nurtured the emergence of the mounted knight. He had obligations to protect serfs, and was in turn required to support his monarch. By the time the Crusades came around, a reasonable knight was trained in mounted combat, and covered with chain mail or armor. One of the greatest inventions was the stirrup, which enabled knights to literally stand on their horses while they fought. Some theorists maintain that little stirrup was the key advance.

Another useful factor in winning wars is good provisioning of your forces. A starving army won't last long. The first Crusade had the best supply chains of all Crusades. When your supply chain falls apart, soldiers can go wild. This is fundamentally what happened during the fourth Crusade that ended up sacking the wrong city. They had intended to regain Jerusalem by invading Egypt from the sea, which was a smart idea. Egypt was the Muslim superpower at that stage, and to break it would have made regaining nearby Palestine that much easier.

Only they ran out of money, and got diverted to Constantinople instead. In 1204 they ransacked the place, in lieu of arrears. A previous religious division between Eastern and Western churches didn't help matters. In 1054 Constantinople had fallen out with Rome. Pope Urban hoped the crusades would mend that rift. Entertaining thousands of ruffian knights didn't exactly cement the two branches of Christendom back together in the first Crusade, especially considering the Eastern Church didn't contribute fighters. Western armies had to do it on their own.

To complicate matters, Mongol forces were on the move, threatening both East and West. They had their sights on everyone, although more so on Islam than the West. Indeed various Frankish Knights fought alongside them. In 1258 the Mongols sacked Baghdad, the center of Islamic civilization, slaughtering well between 200,000 and 1,000,000 inhabitants. This single death toll exceeded all fatalities resulting from all nine of the Western medieval Crusades in the Middle East. By then, the Mongols had successfully created their own mythology of invincibility. One year later the Mongol Khan Mangku died in China however. Internal quarrels between various Mongol factions diluted their drive. In 1260 they were beaten by Egyptian Islamic forces at the battle of Ain Jalut. Saunders declared, "Ain Jalut deserves to be ranked among the world's decisive battles."[31]

A new mythology was created, and a much more conservative Islamic order. Allah saved the day for Islam at Ain Jalut, and there is a school of thought that had they lost, Islam might have been swept away. Central rule moved from Baghdad to Cairo, the Christians who had supported the Mongols suffered severely, and the so called Golden Age of Islamic tolerance came to an end. Memories are selective however, and the Mongols have been either actively or passively forgotten. If China arises as a threat, will the Mongols be recalled? Memories of the West have not been misplaced, especially since it has dominated the Middle East for a century or more.

Neither were Eastern and Western Christian divisions forgotten, so when the last emperor of Constantinople asked the West for assistance again in the 1450s, Rome turned a deaf ear. No Pope Urban arose to heed the request this time and tour Europe building up support. On the contrary, the Turks hired the services of another Urban, this time a talented Hungarian engineer. He crafted the cannon that enabled the Turks to blast their way into the city that had withstood more sieges than any other.

The last Byzantine emperor, also named Constantine, returned to face overwhelming Turkish forces threatening his city that had lasted a thousand years. Constantinople fell to Muslim forces in 1453. The subsequent sacking of the city, raping, looting and auctioning of the defeated as slaves, equaled or surpassed the savagery of the Crusaders when they took Jerusalem three hundred and fifty years prior to that. Most Westerners wouldn't know Istanbul has much more of a Christian history than an Islamic one, only being renamed from Constantinople in 1930. The Hagia Sophia still stands there, a silent witness to a previous life.

This victory in 1453, which had taken some seven hundred years to accomplish, reignited Turkish ambitions. A century later Turkey had designs on Rome itself. The Mediterranean states were in fear of their existence, fueled by stories of Turkish savagery against those who resisted them in

---

31. Saunders, *Aspects of the Crusades*, 76.

Cyprus and Malta. Another visionary Pope, Pius V, managed to bring some cohesion to the normally squabbling powers of Italy, Austria and Venice. Technological superiority, in terms of firepower, enabled the smaller Western fleet to defeat the Ottoman navy in 1571 at Lepanto, a battle that many claim saved Europe from Islam. The Ottoman Empire began a long era of decline until the West defeated it in World War 1. And ever since 1571, financial and technological advantage has favored the West, as outlined in the next chapter.

Far from being a threat, since the Middle East was rediscovered during World War 1, Arab nations have been playthings of the West, or of Russia. And as such, our Western viewpoint has moved from paranoid to paternal. We have extracted their oil, redrawn their national boundaries, and sent aircraft carriers to remind them who is boss. Small wonder that Muslims look back upon their Golden Age when they were once a heavyweight.

In 1937 Henri Pirenne published a widely acclaimed explanation of the decline of Rome and the rise of Islam.[32] Northern European tribes often made murderous assaults on the Mediterranean, which contributed to the decline of Rome as a political force. However those northerners never upset the flow of commerce on what the Romans once called Mare Nostrum (our sea). The Mediterranean Sea was the motorway of the time, the fastest way to trade anything, and the reason that economic power was centered in southern Europe. This trading advantage didn't change when the political power center shifted from Rome to Constantinople in 330 AD.

Islamic warriors burst upon the entire Mediterranean in the eighth century, eastwards into Persia, and south into Africa. Not only did they take those two clover leaves of Christendom from Bunting's map, they entirely disrupted seafaring Mediterranean trade. As the Muslim historian Ibn Khaldun subsequently boasted in the 1300s of that earlier time, "the Christians could no longer float a plank upon the sea."[33]

Two enormous outcomes resulted;

Firstly, Byzantium's trade connection with Europe was hampered, and Eastern and Western Christianity started to grow apart, eventually separating in 1054 AD.

Secondly, Northern European states emerged, who learnt not to be reliant on the Mediterranean motorway. The very name of Charlemagne's kingdom illustrates this. It was termed the Holy Roman Empire. Yet the

---

32. Pirenne, *Mohammed*

33. Scambray, "Islam: Victors Vanquishing Victims," para. 6.

Roman Empire had been ruled from Constantinople since 330 AD, and to a great extent still existed, although in Byzantine form. When Charlemagne was crowned by a Pope from Rome in 800 AD, it was the first time anyone outside Constantinople had used the term Emperor in nearly five hundred years.

It was a grand statement that the game had changed. European power was no longer based on the traffic of the Mediterranean because it had been disrupted. The economic engine of Europe moved from southern Europe to northern, where is has remained to this day. New seafaring powers such as Holland and England emerged, who didn't need the Mediterranean Sea.

Three hundred years after Charlemagne, the Crusades were launched, not from a weakened southern Europe, but from present day France and Germany. Although no Muslim authors to my knowledge consider that the Crusades were a sort of counter attack, plenty of Westerners do. However, none of this changes the fact that Christianity endorsed military action in 1095 despite their founder's commands.

So, just how did Christianity retreat from its own mythology of violence after adopting it for a thousand year period?

Media perception is a start, and we've seen hints of this already. The book, as media, was divinized. The iPad won't be. Neither will the Thompson submachine gun. The sword, listed in the Bible, indeed handled by angels, is a divine weapon. Add in the romantic era of chivalrous knights like the mythical Ivanhoe, and in fact the Crusades themselves until they became discredited, and you have a weapon virtually sanctioned by God. Small wonder Joan of Arc's vision contained a sword. Why do you think that World War 1 Welsh soldier in Tenby was clad in armor rather than khaki, holding a sword instead of a Lee Enfield rifle? A stained glass window of a machine gun nest just wouldn't look right.

Battles with swords didn't result in many deaths compared to machine guns either. Close, person to person combat, led to far less slain than twentieth century battles saw. The Mongol Tamerlane was probably the worst killer prior to repeating rifles with a toll of 17 million amassed over 35 years in the fourteenth century. Even so, that number is swollen with civilian deaths as he was fond of slaughtering them after battles were over. He was vastly exceeded in the twentieth by Hitler and Stalin with some thirty million each, and Mao tse tung who was responsible for up to twice that number, all within Chinese national borders.

Furthermore the visuals of these sword fights, or chariot dashes, or naval engagements, were displayed, to the victors, in still life paintings. Artwork commemorating defeats was not sponsored, so you are unlikely to see the sea battle of Lepanto in Turkey. It's in a Belgian church in Bruges though. It is said that the greatest carnage prior to World War 1 was that very clash, during which the Western navy slew 30,000 Turks in the last naval battle using galleys. It was the first navy to use firepower, a military technological advance, giving forewarning that technology was able to up the ante. That is not apparent in paintings of Lepanto. All you see is a myriad of bobbing vessels. No anguished bodies hacked apart, or still smoldering from Greek fire, are apparent in the panorama portrait.

Battle of Lepanto 1571

From a slow start during the American Civil War, then picking up in World War 1, that all changed. The Great War was the first conflict in which tens of millions died rather than thousands. The factors are well known, and they all include technology, or extensions of man, such as railways, machine guns, tanks, and submarines. Mankind had no idea such horror was about to be released by mechanization. Front line photographs appeared showing the atrocious living conditions, the mud, the explosions, and the priests blessing the troops. War looked nothing like those romantic paintings any more. Even though both sides had priests praying for victory, as visual and numeric news of losses seeped back, a shift in perception began. The nobility of battle faded.

Those photographic stills, and movies, brought the war at close range to those at home, publicized through newspapers. Incredibly, twenty years after World War 1, another world conflict erupted, and that sealed it. More films were taken, more movies rolled, and more soldiers returned home, never to attend church again. For the second time in thirty years the nations of the world agreed war was not a good thing. With all its faults, the United Nations was the outcome of that discussion. From a small start in the nineteenth century, international law got underway with the UN. Is international law an extension of men? Think about the alternative of no international law before deciding.

Combine the UN with CNN and its cohorts, and the end of divinely sanctioned wars is obvious. Real life news footage beamed straight to our TVs, PCs, or smartphones, brings the horror and blood of battle to everyone. Photographs of the dead trump newspaper articles hands down.

Movies of the dying in crowded Third World hospitals are more effective in sickening the masses than a dozen written reports—especially to Western populations who are ceasing reading.

And the result? Look at the numbers. The Vietnam war lasted about a dozen years, involving multiple nations. The USA lost 58,193 men, and South Korea 5,099. 426 Australians were killed, and 55 New Zealanders. Thailand had 351 killed in action, and the Philippines 7, in a conflict that listed about a dozen years. South Vietnam lost 266,000, and North Vietnamese military losses exceeded 1,100,000.

Let's compare that to a recent conflict—the war in Afghanistan. Out of the 28 nations in the Coalition forces over approximately a dozen years, the USA death toll reached nearly 2,200 by mid 2014, from a Coalition total of some 3,300. Included in that figure is the UK loss of 447 military personnel, Canada 158, Australia 41, and New Zealand 11. Afghani civilian fatality statistics are hard to gather but commentators agree on numbers in the 25,000 region.

Modern wars are less costly in terms of human life, but more footage is shot. It is in fact the newsworthiness that helps 'keep our boys safe.' The US military understands very well the public impact of even a few coffins draped with the stars and stripes. A famous 1968 photograph of a South Vietnamese police chief shooting a Viet Cong prisoner at point blank range with a pistol practically changed public opinion overnight. It was later called the photo that helped America lose the war.

The nature of battle has changed markedly in the War on Terror. Nations don't fight nations formally anymore. New forms of war termed Hybrid Wars, which includes Fourth Generation Warfare, Compound Wars and Unrestricted Warfare, have completely new rationale, strategies and outcomes.

Conveniently the church has been able to distance itself from its approval of World War 1 to a disapproval of modern wars. Priests now lead anti-war protests and write to their parliamentary members. This is what we can term a mythological shift. Only angry commentators refer back to the Crusades as if such behavior is still exhibited by the church. Foreign armed incursions are not arranged by the Pope these days. The straight talking one time Prime Minister of Australia, John Howard, when defending Pope Benedict's right to put violence and Islam into the same sentence, said that; "Muslims should move on. I don't, at the moment, note terrorist groups killing people and invoking the authority of the Catholic Church."[34]

The question of what happened in Christianity is also answered by asking what didn't happen inside Christianity. It did not undergo its own shift through internal moral decision making. It required carnage brought to our living rooms by visual media. It took many shifts including the peace movement being taken over by Hollywood and turned into movies, plus lots of active remembering of those peaceful exhortations in the Bible.

Do we have any parallels with Islam?

We have world leaders, reporters, authors and blogs out there, in either their blissful or purposeful statements, such as Prime Minister Cameron, re-mythologizing Islam. Naive as this may sound, all that work recreating Islamic mythology, coupled with today's psychologies and media environment, is bearing fruit. Immigrant Muslim groups are readily joining those world leaders such as Mr Cameron who already claim violence is not part of Islam.

The West started buying into this over a hundred years ago when the press stopped using the term Mohammedanism and began using Islam. Winston Churchill used Mohammedanism, but he's been called an Orientalist. Westerners had variously used Moors, Musselmen, Moslems and Mohammedans. Informed that the term was insulting, the press almost exclusively uses the word Islam today, which, as we are taught by the press, means religion of peace or submission. It was a wonderful public relations re-branding exercise, and I'd give credit to the agency or group who started it if only I could identify them. Only opponents use Mohammedanism today.

We also know that CNN or BBC television is beamed nightly into hundreds of thousands of Muslim households in the West, and, as we shall find, through illegal satellite dishes into Iran. The population of Pakistan is not a monolithic entity blindly reacting en-masse to someone burning a Qu'ran in New Jersey. While I'm told some do tell their wide eyed children that the footage is engineered in a Disney studio, many, probably the majority, won't. Don't tell me intelligent Muslims, not their religious leaders, but ordinary thinking people, all refuse to ponder about the worldwide atrocities that contain the brand word Islam. Our wise old lady in Baghdad certainly did.

34. "Pope row in past," para. 13.

As with Christianity, a religion under stress will produce new denominations, followings, or offshoots. Sufism is the longest established example. Formalized as an Islamic order in the twelfth century, Sufis generally believe the jihad verses in the Qu'ran need to be read allegorically. The verses are actively remembered, not to mean to fight physically, but rather to struggle against inner spiritual forces.

This is parallel to Christianity and Hinduism. The Bhagavad Gita takes place before a huge battle. It is not a historically verifiable battle, nor do Hindus concern themselves about that. It's a myth that you draw innermost truths out of. The story of Moses in the Bible can be read like this. As we learnt earlier, there is no evidence Moses even existed. Perhaps the exodus story is a myth, a way of telling us how to battle spiritual or inner bondage.

Sufism is growing around the world and plainly presents itself as an alternative view of Islam. Stephen Schwartz 's book 'The Other Islam: Sufism and the Road to Global Harmony ', says it in the title[35]. Al–Ghazali (1058–1111), sometimes referred to as the single most influential Muslim after the prophet Muhammad, became a Sufi. Sufism is not modern therefore, but its adherents span the globe, with growth sectors in the West. Sufism is a simpler step for Muslims to take than say, converting to Christianity or Buddhism.

Excising the Qu'ran is another option. Given the Qu'ran is the direct transmission of God it seems hard to believe Muslims would consider publishing abridged or shortened versions. That would mean choosing the words of God they happen to like. Yet they do. 'The Essential Qu'ran' is an English example. The Essential Qu'ran simply leaves out the most violent suras.[36]

This is not a new idea. Retired President Jefferson famously took a pair of scissors to the New Testament of the Bible, removing passages that he didn't like, (possibly looking out the window at his two hundred toiling African slaves, it must be pointed out!). Retired Bishop John Shelby Spong has made a career in our age of disparaging sections of the Bible that don't fit with modern thinking. Indeed some Christians from the earliest centuries wanted to discard the Old Testament with all its violent passages. Do not expect this to happen overnight with the Qu'ran. While plenty of Christians ignore the violent texts, major denominations will not cross them out of the

---

35. Schwartz, *The Other Islam*, title.

36. Cleary, *The Essential Koran*

Bible. It's much more problematic with the Qu'ran, since Muslims believe it is all that direct transmission from God.

Governments have known since the Vietnam war that the way to contain religious or political restlessness is to give people jobs that pay money. Malaysian communists quite readily traded their guns for factory work, stemming the domino theory of communist expansion from ultimately threatening the shores of Australia. People don't move from Pakistan to London so they'll be nearer to a mosque. They move for a new life, with a house, and a car.

Which neatly brings us to Western Muslim organizations. Besides assisting Muslims in business by teaching 'Effective negotiation skills' and 'Business models and Governance,' The Muslim Council of Britain (MCB) deserves our admiration for the remodeling PR work they are doing on Islam. Their website carries numerous admonitions against Islamist violence. On a single page in late 2014 I found headings of the following statements and articles;

- Not in our Name: British Muslims Condemn the Barbarity of ISIS
- Muslim Council of Britain Condemns Yet Another Murder in Iraq
- Alan Henning's Murder a Despicable Act, Offensive to Muslims
- British Muslims Condemn Murder of Fellow Briton David Haines
- Terrorist attacks in Kenya, Pakistan and Iraq: Muslim Council of Britain Decries a Weekend of Carnage

Concerning the Kenyan atrocities, Farooq Murad, Secretary General of the MCB said: "The utter carnage we have witnessed is sad and shocks us all. These are acts that have no basis in our faith, and no cause should condone the slaughter of innocents. These people who perpetuate these murders have no regard for the sanctity for human life. We must stand together within faith and from across faiths and not allow them to divide us. I can only reiterate the words of the Grand Mufti of Bosnia, which he made a few days ago on the occasion of the International Day of Peace, "God did not create people to fight one another and shed blood. . ."[37]

My, how we have moved from the hadith of Bukhari. Long ago, Jubair bin Haiya narrated, 'Umar sent the Muslims to the great countries to fight the pagans. When Al-Hurmuzan embraced Islam, 'Umar said to him. "I would like to consult you regarding these countries which I intend to

37. "Tag Archive"

invade."[38] Obviously he made this statement prior to the formation of the United Nations, or the reporting capability of Al Jazeera. There is no question the MCB are distancing themselves from historically earlier expressions of their faith, just as Christian priests today distance themselves from medieval expressions of theirs.

Let's see how the shift in mythology is appearing in Muslim commentaries over time. Our first quote is from a time when the Ottomans still considered themselves a world power. Thomas Jefferson and John Adams called on the London Ambassador of the Ottoman Empire in 1786 to organize the Treaty of Tripoli. US merchants were tired of attacks by Barbary Pirates in the Mediterranean and Jefferson and Adams took 30,000 Guineas to persuade the Ottoman Empire to call them off. The Ottoman Ambassador had no problem accepting the money, and later informed them about Ottoman expansionist theories;

> The Ambassador answered us that it was founded on the Laws of their Prophet, that it was written in their Koran, that all nations who should not have acknowledged their authority were sinners, that it was their right and duty to make war upon them wherever they could be found, and to make slaves of all they could take as Prisoners, and that every Musselman who should be slain in battle was sure to go to Paradise.[39]

For over one thousand years, from that warning to the Persian forces to the one given to Jefferson, Muslim–majority governments had little problem explaining their intent. Our next quote is a much more recent one. See what it doesn't tell us;

> Muslims populated Spain for nearly 700 years. As you'll see, it was their civilization that enlightened Europe and brought it out of the dark ages to usher in the renaissance. Many of their cultural and intellectual influences still live with us today.
>
> Way back during the eighth century, Europe was still knee-deep in the medieval period. Medieval Europe was a miserable lot, which ran high in illiteracy, superstition, barbarism and filth.
>
> During this same time, Muslims entered Europe from the South.[40]

38. Sahih Bukhari, "Volume 4, Book 53, Number 386," para. 1.

39. "American Commissioners," para. 6.

40. "Islam in Spain," para. 1–5.

Ignore the opinions of the misery of Europe and enlightenment of Islam portrayed here. This is a blog writer when all said and done, but we've quoted him as an example of an earnest young person trying to make sense of his supposedly threatened worldview. The mythology to focus on is what is missing. The writer says when 'Muslims entered Europe.' They do not say when Muslims reached the shores of Spain, they burnt their boats as a statement there was no return. Nor do they mention the Muslims fought numerous battles defeating local armies before they took over southern Spain, even though both these things happened.

This is more than political correctness. It may well be part of our earlier question that the writer simply doesn't know the Muslims fought their way into Spain. Whatever his circumstances, the absence of that history is an example of active forgetting. However he probably knows that the IS issued a statement to Christians in Mosul, Iraq, when they took it in mid 2014.

> Earlier this month, ISIS issued an ultimatum in Mosul, citing a historic contract known as "dhimma," under which non–Muslims in Islamic societies who refuse to convert are offered protection if they pay a fee, called a "jizya." "We offer them three choices: Islam; the dhimma contract—involving payment of jizya; if they refuse this they will have nothing but the sword."[41]

This was, after all, worldwide news. Does our same writer realize the IS claim is a clone of that decreed by Umar, one those four rightly guided Caliphs of the original Muslim empire, who was a companion of Muhammad himself?

We might expect such an omission from a blog writer, since the world is open to anyone publishing anything to a worldwide audience. However it creeps into scholarly articles from Islamic writers. Abushouk from the International Islamic University of Kuala Lumpur skirts past the fact that Islamic armies took most territory by the sword; "Following the rapid territorial expansion of the Islamic state and the spread of Islam as a global religion, Islamic civilization entered a new phase of "globalism," based on interaction with other civilizations."[42]

Further along he informs us that the conquered peoples later willingly converted to Islam. ". . .refutes the allegation propagated by Orientalists, such as Oliver of Paderborn, that "Islam began by the sword, was

41. "Iraqi Christians flee," para. 6.
42. Abushouk, "Globalization and Muslim Identity," 4.

maintained by the sword, and by the sword would be ended," and indicates that the mass conversion took place when Islam became as a way of life and a guidance for all Muslims."[43]

He'd come to a conclusion predicted by Pirenne back in the 1930s: "What they proposed was not, as many have thought, their conversion, but their subjection, and this subjection they enforced wherever they went."[44]

Let's not debate forcible conversions, because it's speculative. The same could be said of the Spanish conquering South America. Today the continent is overwhelmingly Roman Catholic, even though it achieved independence from Spain long ago. If all the South Americans were unwilling converts, they would have dropped the faith when they defeated Spain. However the point is that Abushouk forgets to mention the Islamic wars of aggression to conquer the territories in the first place. He is not alone. We have much active forgetting and active remembering, even in the academic community.

The major difference across the ages is that taking over nations by violent means used to be mainstream, but it's not any more. It cannot be any more since the United Nations outlawed that type of takeover. The IS is not supported by the majority of Muslims. Western Islam is, roughly speaking, moving towards a more peaceful version today. Signs of that flicker in the Muslim–majority nations too, and certainly their leaders did not flock to join the IS. The writers in islamcan.com and The Muslim World may be from either end of the educated spectrum, but both are participating in the re–mythologization of Islam. Most modern Muslim writers bring benign intent to the page. That was not historically the case. They wrote up victories, discussed who they would take over, and formed battle plans. Now most don't. Up to 40 percent of American Muslims,[45] and a minority ranging from 9 to 28 percent in a range of Muslim-majority nations,[46] don't believe Arabs brought down the World Trade Center. It is too shocking to contemplate. This is as good an indicator as we will see that Islam is changing. A recently as only two hundred years ago, we could reasonably suggest that the Ottoman ambassador speaking with the Americans would have boasted about such an achievement as 9/11, rather than deny or be ashamed of it.

43. Ibid., 4.
44. Pirenne, *Mohammed*, 150.
45. "Muslim Americans," page 32.
46. "Muslim-Western Tensions Persist," chapter 3, para. 14.

Unfortunately, life isn't so clean cut. Various organizations and web-sites point out practices of Islam such as taqqiya. Wikipedia's definition is backed up by other Islamic sources, who feel awkward about the term in today's world. They also use the word dissimulation. So I'm printing the Wikipedia definition as it appears neutral;

> taqqiya is a form of religious dissimulation, or a legal dispensa-tion whereby a believing individual can deny his faith or commit otherwise illegal or blasphemous acts while they are at risk of sig-nificant persecution.[47]

Sources not so kind towards Islam tell us taqqiya allows Muslims to lie to get out of trouble. So when the public reads an article like that in The New York Times, April 24th, 2014, entitled 'Film at 9/11 Museum Sets Off Clash Over Reference to Islam,' they will have varying opinions about it. Indeed the characters in the true plot of the story did.

> "The screening of this film in its present state would greatly offend our local Muslim believers as well as any foreign Muslim visitor to the museum," Sheikh Mostafa Elazabawy, the imam of Masjid Manhattan, wrote in a letter to the museum's director.
> "Don't tell me this is an Islamist or an Islamic group; that means they are part of," he said in an interview. "We are all of us against that."[48]

Mr. Daniels, the president of the museum foundation, added;

> "I believe that the average visitor who comes through this museum will in no way leave this museum with the belief that the religion of Islam is responsible for what happened on 9/11. We have gone out of the way to tell the truth."[49]

Mr. Daniels had to say he was telling the truth. It is one thing to bring up mythology in a book like this—it is another to run a museum remem-bering the destruction of the World Trade Center, a potentially divisive institution from the start. His problem is whether the heartland of America

---

47. "Taqiyya," para. 1.

48. "Film at 9/11 Museum Sets Off Clash Over Reference to Islam," para. 5 and para. 24.

49. Ibid., para. 28.

will believe him. In the short term, they probably won't. Less than a quarter of Americans believe the news anyway.[50]

Time Magazine swung in behind the re–mythologization going on with this museum and reported; "An interfaith panel of clergy assembled by the museum says the film doesn't do enough to make clear the distinction between Al–Qaeda inspired terrorism and the beliefs of the great majority of Muslims."[51]

They didn't go deeper and point out that in 2011 Pew Research found majorities of over 50 percent in Turkey, Egypt, Lebanon, Israel, Palestinian Territories, Indonesia, Pakistan and Jordan didn't believe the twin tower attack was undertaken by Arabs.[52] If these are the 'beliefs of the great majority of Muslims,' they can be read in at least two ways;

- That Islam is as violent as it has always been, and its leaders are liars trying to lull Westerners into believing them—this is the remembering the past option, and backs up the taqqiya proponents.

- That whatever Islam's past, many Muslims are trying to shift to a peaceful version, and they are doing that by actively forgetting violent involvement instead of being proud of it.

We have already read the apology option from the wise old lady of Baghdad, but we also know Muslims leaders can't publicly open up their past like that.

Clocked time, as averse to Time Magazine, was not on the side of Sheikh Mostafa Elazabawy. Less than two months passed before the IS blasted onto the world scene front pages with atrocities matching 9/11, and a rapid military advance on Baghdad. As IS stands for 'Islamic State,' and is an offshoot of Al–Qaeda, the Sheikh's point about naming conventions was unfortunate.

We are less than two decades from 9/11, and time in religious circles runs slowly. Sheikh Mostafa Elazabawy had to resign from the panel approving the seven minute movie, (which is only a small part of the museum), because he too, is a public figure. We don't know what the Sheikh privately thought, nor does that matter.

This re–mythologization won't take place via another conference or worldwide announcement. Many may want a press statement like, say,

50. "Majority of Americans Don't Trust Newspapers," para. 1.

51. "Remains of the day," 55.

52. "Opinions About September 11," para. 24.

'Muslims now realize they have a history of military aggression and suicidal warriors, and regret that. However we are turning a new page. From now on we will . . . '

No, it won't happen like that, no more than a Pope or Archbishop could ever make such a global announcement, or that Vladimir Putin could close the mausoleum housing Lenin, who virtually became a divinity for founding the USSR. Such a move would backfire in the most extreme way as adherents to beliefs would be outraged that the church, or the state, or Islamic leaders, could denigrate the sacrifices made by the many who lost loved ones in battle.

Australian Archbishop Pell meant well when he said; "the nation's Muslim clerics should address the links between Islam and violence instead of sweeping them under the carpet."[53] Unfortunately it's very difficult to make a man understand something when his core beliefs depend on him not understanding it. Australian Muslim leader, Dr. Ali, responded to the Archbishop as best as he could; "Why continue this controversy? I don't understand," he said. "It is a charged environment we live in. We don't need another thing to cause more division."[54]

We have suggested that the church has altered its mythology twice over the past two thousand years, from peace, to war, and back towards peace. It would be interesting to gauge responses. I suspect most people would, at least grudgingly, admit the church is less supportive of military action than it was prior to World War 1. Moreover most would not view the churches shift as a plot to outfox Islam, or trick Muslims or indeed anyone into complacency. Conspiracy theory websites run by protestants do exist warning us the Catholic church is in cahoots with sometimes the CIA, and sometimes the Mafia, but they do not receive serious attention.

However others think the re–mythologization of Islam as a peaceful religion is a ploy. Islam is often portrayed as an underground conspiracy lulling the West into silence while it gradually takes over. Even though both religions have been engaged in disarmament moves, Muslims are more distrusted than the church. The point is not that there are still Islamic terrorists out there; the point is that most Muslims aren't militant, and they're not fooling us. At least one prominent Muslim lost his life standing up against other violent Muslims still in the grip of the earlier version of their faith;

53. "Pope row in past," para. 8.
54. Ibid., para. 10.

Professor Mahmoud Al 'Asali, a law professor who lectures on pedagogy at the University of Mosul, had the courage to make a stand against this brutal duress which he believes go against the Muslim commandments. But he paid for this gesture with his life: he was killed by ISIS militants in Mosul yesterday.[55]

They are reinventing their beliefs, and if that involves a blind spot about their past, so be it. The transition is clearly not without tumult. Some Muslims don't want a peaceful version. This doesn't invalidate the process. It's the outcome that's important. In the best scenario, the one Mr Cameron hoped for, new members will fill vacant seats in influential religious committees, different Public Relations personnel will be engaged, scriptural re-interpretations will become mainstream, and as we shall see, the population dynamics of the world will not see the Islamization of Europe.

A relatively peaceful gap of several hundred years transpired after 1571 between Europe and the Middle East. Conflict between Muslim–majority and Western states returned in World War 1. Today only Turkey out of the MENA region is in the top ten military powers, ranking beneath the USA, Russia, China, India, United Kingdom, France and Germany.[56] The modern fight of militant Muslims against various Satans is the work of terrorist groups who mostly slay their fellows. In order to fit the media puzzle together with wars between the faiths, there is one major question to ask; how were the armed conflicts between the West and the Middle East somewhat equal up until the end of that eight hundred year era, but are militarily so one sided today?

In the next chapter we switch to two different media to explain the ascendancy of Western power after 1571; the ability to use numbers and the propensity to change laws.

55. "The Muslim who gave up his life," para. 1.
56. "Countries Ranked by Military Strength," para. 4.

5

AN INTEREST IN NUMBERS

NOTHING IS IMPORTANT

When God commanded mankind to be fruitful and multiply,[1] he didn't mean mathematics. Another theory accords that breakthrough to a Hindu god named Zero. It wasn't until 1000 AD, well after the starts of both Christianity and Islam, that mankind in general could multiply numbers. Many numbering systems were developed earlier than that, the most commonly remembered today being Roman.

As an exercise, try multiplying a couple of Roman numerals together, say XVI by VII, and supply the answer in Roman again—without converting them in your mind into decimal. Only the highly trained could do it. Neither is it straightforward with Hebrew characters, that wonderful Old Testament language that is both numbers and words. Although mathematical geniuses can somehow extract the age of the universe, and other computations from an Old Testament rendered into numbers, Hebrew is just as difficult to multiply. It has numerous different signs, such as one for 4, another for 40, and yet a third for 400, whereas I've expressed those three numbers using only two different digits.

Today we only need to learn ten numerals, 0 through to 9. Yet we perform wizardry to any number possible, including percentages. Our brains are so permeated with decimal, it's impossible to think without it. Every day

1. Genesis 1:27–28

we perform dozens of calculations based on percentages, or multiplication or division. None of that was possible before zero.

Even if the rumor is untrue, it is fitting that zero should be Hindu, that religion that can contemplate nothingness. Transferring the concept of the void, or emptiness, over from meditation to a number, or non–number, was a huge leap. It had, after all, taken millennia for mankind to appreciate the common thread between a pair of rabbits and the two days just past.

Accurate counting was a long time coming, as is seen by the growing reality of numbers slain in battles when one reads through the Old Testament. Early on, warriors falling in a single day often exceeded the entire population of the nation fighting. After Solomon it gets more real, illustrating he may well have scattered wisdom around.

Let's not forget the other half of the inventors of the Hindu–Arabic system that we know as decimal. Were they Islamic? History is unsure, but whatever the answer, I am willing to speculate they did not conceive that the system they were about to give to the world, free of copyright constraints, would enable all cultures, including their own, to calculate usury easily. Such are the unplanned outcomes of media, and decimal fits into that category. It was the biggest breakthrough ever in mathematics, and beats the theory of relativity hands down. By definition Einstein couldn't have worked out the algebraic $e=mc2$ without a numeric system.

Christianity and Islam alike prohibited charging usury, or interest. The Old Testament of the Bible outlaws it on pain of death:

- he lends money on interest and takes increase; will he live? He will not live! He has committed all these abominations, he will surely be put to death; his blood will be on his own head.[2]

The Qu'ran promises a nasty afterlife:

- Those who consume interest cannot stand (on the Day of Resurrection) except as one stands who is being beaten by Satan into insanity. That is because they say, "Trade is (just) like interest." But Allah has permitted trade and has forbidden interest. So whoever has received an admonition from his Lord and desists may have what is past, and his affair rests with Allah. But whoever returns to (dealing in interest or usury)—those are the companions of the Fire; they will abide eternally therein.[3]

2. Ezekiel 18:13
3. Sura 2:275

That great theologian, St Augustine, had this to say about numbers. "The good Christian should beware of mathematicians. The danger already exists that mathematicians have made a covenant with the devil to darken the spirit and confine man in the bonds of Hell."[4]

Makes me wonder if he'd seen the terms of my thirty year house mortgage. I'm jumping ahead though, because it was a long time before money became synchronized with numbers. Let's get back to our historical trail to see how that happened.

The West had a convenient way around their interest charging problem—the Jewish moneylender, who was not subject to Christian law. Whether Jews were forced into this trade or chose it is a point argued often, but it let the Barons off the hook, especially as there is another verse earlier in the Bible:

- You may charge interest to a foreigner, but to your countrymen you shall not charge interest,[5]

That was jolly handy as the medieval Jews were hardly seen as brethren, and they were permitted to lend to foreigners, i.e. Christians. Complicated procedures were worked out so the Baron could loan the moneylender cash, which the Jew would in turn let out at interest. The moneylender had to repay the Baron, but this was a pre-calculated figure, not computed in terms of mathematical interest. Both sides were happy if the Jew and the Baron clipped the profit ticket. If the money disappeared, the Baron might call on the moneylender with a sword, so one could say the Jew's life was his collateral. This was rarer than the movies might suggest, otherwise the Jews would have gone out of business faster than a mortgagee waterfront sale.

THE MONETIZATION OF DECIMAL

And so developed the rudiments of finance. Nearly every kingdom in Europe ended up with a Court Jew, as this race gathered knowledge and expertise in calculating how much money floated about the nation, or what value Venetian ducats could be exchanged for in Austria. Court Jews were the precursors of Finance Ministers, or Secretaries of the Treasury, invaluable for guidance on how much taxation revenue might be extracted from the populace.

4. "Augustine of Hippo," section 1.8, line 3.
5. Deuteronomy 23:20

Decimal spelled the end of exclusivity for the Jews however, although it took several centuries, and they tended to remain at the forefront of this trade due to long experience. The Rothschild family of financiers came from a Court Jew background. Decimal enabled a broader merchant class to participate in what was purported to be an enviable activity. Jews may have felt they were persecuted and forced into this trade, but the rest of the world thirsted after their perceived wealth. Despite church teaching to the contrary, prohibitions against levying interest gradually fell away, especially as it was now so easy to learn with the new numbering system.

It did not end in a climactic encounter, or a global religious decision where everyone had to change their minds. There was no international bankers conference on the needs of Small and Medium Enterprises, nothing like that. The prohibitions and stigma simply faded away over time to the point where we look back in amusement at the fact they were ever there.

Remember this point. We've already mentioned it. This is a classic example of how social norms alter religious ones. If you swamp them enough, some prohibitions sink. The question needs to be put therefore, how did it get swamped in the West, but remain in Islam, a core part of the team that invented modern numbering?

To segue briefly before answering that question, and to show how everything is interconnected again, the first recorded foreign exchange transaction was by a Crusader traveling from Western Europe through Constantinople. When those Frankish Crusaders first hit Jerusalem, they discovered a civilization numerically ahead of theirs—and don't get that pun wrong. An Arab named al Khowarazimi in 825 AD was one of the first to work out arithmetic rules of addition, subtraction, multiplication and division. The name of al Khowarazimi gave us the word algorithm.[6] Another Arab, Omar Khayyam, went further and formulated concepts of the triangle, and how to figure out squares, cubes, and other powers of higher mathematics, before Salahadin and King Richard the Lionheart jousted in the Holy Land.

The Merchants of Venice were the first to be enlightened by this new numbering system from the East, as they saw visiting Arab traders making their rapid calculations. As the natural gateway between Western Europe and the Byzantine and Ottoman empires to the East, Venice was well placed to make a fortune trading—and it did. The first regular institution in the world resembling a modern bank opened there in 1127. In 1494

6. Bernstein, *Against the Gods,* 33–34.

Luca Pacioli published his majestic volume, the 'Summa de arithmetica, geometria, proportioni et proportionalita' which contained the 'Particulars of Reckonings and Writings' in Venice, introducing double entry book-keeping. Numbers were well on the way to being monetized.

You'll recall from the previous chapter that after fighting each other for eight hundred years, both the Ottoman Empire and Western empires backed off from fighting each other. It was too expensive, and either side was roughly equal in power. The West had reclaimed back Spain, while the Ottomans eventually took Constantinople, also known as Byzantium. By the time Western powers returned with military intent in World War 1, Middle Eastern states were minnows compared to Western ones.

How did the West draw ahead?

It happened via numbers, legally turned into money, machinery and logistics. Debates over the way the West pulled away from the rest of the world have been going on for a couple of centuries, since it began to be noticed back then. Traditional theories were based around the nineteenth century Industrial Revolution, but experts tell us it started earlier.

Angus Maddison, an Emeritus Professor in Economic Growth and Development, said the story began around 1000 AD, but it wasn't until about 1600 AD that the West started to draw ahead of others, including the Middle East. Maddison summarized the five main factors for the West drawing ahead as;

- Trade in Europe and legal property rights, which favored entrepreneurship and risk, but required accounting skills.

- Printed books, and the spread of academies of science.

- Christianity enforcing monogamy. Familial inheritance by birth broke down loyalty to tribe or clan, promoting individualism and accumulation of wealth.

- Maritime technology enabling new worlds to be conquered and merchants to make money offshore.

- Emergence of Nation States trading with each other. This 'benign fragmentation' stimulated innovation and competition.[7]

Don't underestimate the fourth point. The British government handsomely rewarded John Harrison for inventing the marine chronometer in 1773 because it enabled the English to know where they were. Latitude was

7. Maddison, "West and the Rest," 76–78.

easy. Just look where the sun rises, and you've got a fair idea of how far north you are. Longitude was the tough nut to crack because it's not sun related, and the earth is always turning.

This magnificent extension of man, this measuring of the earth, was crucial for England to create the world's most far flung empire. The Captain of a trading ship knew where he could set sail, confident of plotting his progress. Merchants gained confidence investing in foreign ventures, as they would know approximately when the ship would return home. Longitude is another niche story of the magic of counting.

Josiah Wedgewood adopted Double Entry accounting in 1772 and discovered the difference between fixed and variable costs, assisting him to build his huge prosperous company. Bookkeeping became a crucial element in the commercial benefits of mass production, and cost accounting was born. The great railway investment boom in Britain in the nineteenth century was only enabled by the collective pooling of funds for a 10 percent dividend return. Bookkeeping and decimal moved from merchants to manufacturing, fueling the industrial revolution.

Then the French aristocrats stepped in with their great penchant for gambling. That genius Pascal was employed by wealthy men to work out odds of winning at the table. Card players began calculating how many times an Ace came up in the pack, no matter how often you shuffled it. Pascal and later experts worked on probability theory—because it paid.

Prior to working out the chances of a dice rolling, the disorderly nature of life was put down to the capriciousness of the Gods. The same deities who organized the night and day sky into an extremely orderly rhythm seemed to take delight in working the opposite among mankind. Disease, flood, war, death, and famine were interpreted as the will of God. Or Allah.

Pioneers such as John Gaunt started to change that. Gaunt worked with births and deaths from Parish records in 1660s statistical work. He mapped out the probability of someone living to a certain age, an act so common today that it is no longer the breakthrough it was then. Theorists such as the great Bernoulli family, publishing their famous mathematical work, 'The Art of Conjecture' in 1705, contributed to the growing body of knowledge about numbers, and its increasing fusion with money. The great master of economics, Keynes himself, wrote his 'Treatise on Probability' in 1921. Probability theory certainly impacts lending as banks calculate the chances of loans going bad. Interest rates are hiked or lowered depending on risk. Thus it was that probability theory became financial mainstream, eroding the concept of the whimsical or punishing God.

In the West.

Today one can easily find probability theory does not go down well in Islam. Using the terms 'probability theory Islam' I clicked on the first result in the organic search list, and discovered an Islamic expert answering a question of an inquirer, replying; "Probability are only predicting outcome on paper but the real and final outcome will be according to what ALLAH wills."[8]

Sometimes Google's two hundred complicated 'algorithms' of search don't return the best answer first. Knowing that 42.3 percent of us will click on the first result, I persevered further down and came up with an enlightening article from some Saudi bankers entitled Decision under Uncertainty.

> In Islamic culture, uncertainty is strongly linked to causes. Once we face an uncertain decision problem, we usually think that one shall perform the cause and leave the final result to the will of Allah, the Almighty. This inherent behavior is well established in Islamic principles, with the saying of the Prophet, peace be upon him, regarding the Arabian's camel: "Tie it and entrust" is frequently cited. This rule is compatible with the types of risk mentioned above. The cause, tying the camel, addresses controllable risk, while entrust (twakkul) addresses uncontrollable risk.[9]

I love the way they quote from a scripture or holy person, to back up a modern finance principle. Don't be amazed that you can take a saying about camels and build it into a mortgage application.

Issues with probability theory extend further, into the medical realm. A university paper appeared even further down the Google page, qualms evident in its title;

> ISLAMIC PERSPECTIVES IN THE TEACHING OF PROBABIL-
> ITY TO MEDICAL STUDENTS
> The paper explains how probability concepts can be taught to Muslim students using concepts and examples from the Islamic perspective.
> The concepts and applications of probability are difficult to teach to medical students because they appear very abstract with

8. "Teaching Probability Theory," para. 2.

9. Kuzelewska and Kloza, "Challenges of modern democracy," 130.

no apparent direct relationship with the students' socio–cultural and intellectual background.[10]

In May 2013 the Western world was treated to a celebrity medical decision based on probability theory when Angelina Jolie had a double mastectomy performed. Medics calculated she had an 87 percent risk of developing breast cancer, so she had hers surgically removed. Her choice was heralded as heroic. It would be interesting to see how Muslim medical students think their way around that, especially if Middle Eastern medical testing and procedures publish percentages among their own populations.

Back to usury.

Charging interest was forbidden to clerics from 314 AD, and forbidden for laymen in 1179. Luther condemned it in the sixteenth century, but Calvin, whose influence in Switzerland cannot be understated, and some progressive Catholic thinkers such as Antoine, argued that charging interest did not constitute usury. They felt that as long as it represented the real difference between the value of present and future sums of money, interest was not mere extortion. The Catholic Church still forbids usury—meaning extortionate charges—providing penalties in Canon Law, but this does not mean that all interest–taking is wicked. It took until the nineteenth century for the Roman Catholic Church to decide formally that interest was not in itself a sin. That's some eight hundred years since decimal numbering was introduced into Europe.

Fundamentally church rulings got swamped. Banks emerged, charging interest for money. The decline of church prohibitions may well correlate inversely with the rise of banking theory. The very word usury underwent a change. Usurious changed from merely charging interest, to charging excessive interest. We divide the world morally into those who charge fair interest versus those who charge unfair interest.

The decimalization of money, or perhaps the monetization of decimal, took a long time to conquer currency itself, and fittingly it was the English that held out the longest in the world they gave their language to. In an article entitled, 'The day Britain lost its soul: How decimalization signaled the demise of a proudly independent nation,' Prime Minister Edward Heath was remembered. In 1971, 'obsessed with modernising Britain,' he announced the end of twelve pennies to the shilling and other anachronisms.[11]

10. Kasule, "Islamic Perspectives in the teaching of Probability to Medical Students," 1.

11. "The day Britain lost its soul," para. 16.

They were the last amongst decent sized European nations to do so. In 1789 only the Russian currency was decimal, but the French went that way after all those heads rolled. The nostalgic article laments the loss of yet another peculiarly British institution, lauding their foul weather as an asset, as they do at such moments.

And so, by the end of the twentieth century, without really being aware of it, one could posit the whole world had succumbed to a universal language. It is not English, or French, nor is it Mandarin Chinese, even though more speak that than any other tongue. That language is decimal, and it only has ten symbols.

This is a good point to revisit the technique theory of Ellul. Decimal's infiltration into our minds is one way to grasp the totality of how our thinking has changed. Everything is both measurable, and comparable with decimal, from the area of land we own, to the portion of elderly in our society, to how the price of a McDonalds hamburger compares between Paris and Singapore.

It is impossible to remove these powers from our thinking. If we were able to however, we would not be able to compare our wealth, or land ownership, or literacy levels, or even the percentage of our community that believes in one faith rather than another. And as such, these would not be criteria by which we could judge nations, peoples or individuals on. We cannot undo this way of thinking.

The other side of the coin, if you turn one over, informs us about legal matters. Generally cash has an image symbolizing the law on the side opposite the one with a number on it.

Western law permitted the development of a legal company that could outlive its owners. Islamic law did not. Islamic jurisprudence required the business to be sold off, even if only one of the joint owners died. This worked amongst a nomadic people who valued cash and cows, but not land. Dividing up coins and cattle between the heirs of the deceased was straightforward. In a socially responsible move, Islamic law spread it around vulnerable members of the family too, including women.

Unfortunately however, little incentive existed to build large companies. By definition, the more partners there were, the more likely it was that one might pass away. By the time the Ottomans realized this in the nineteenth century, the economic horse had bolted in favor of the West.

Huge conglomerates in Europe mass produced goods made by artisans in Turkey, and the mass produced ones were cheaper. As the Turkish poet Ziya Pasa said in the nineteenth century;

> I passed through the lands of the infidels, I saw cities and mansions;
> I wandered in the realm of Islam, I saw nothing but ruins.[12]

The West went a step further with decimal and legalized numeric shareholdings. That enabled the firm to last beyond the death of any partners, and for shareholders to sell out, or accrue more shares. Creating the limited liability company was a brilliant stroke because one individual, or a board of directors, could make decisions for the entire group.

Basically Adam Smith got his way. He theorized that all of society would move ahead economically if individuals followed their own individualistic pecuniary drive. Without anyone intending to work for the social good, Smith maintained selfish competition worked out for the betterment of all.

Islam preferred a communalist approach rather than an individualist one. While communalist it was also personalist, in that Islamic law encouraged trade between partners who knew each other.[13] It intended to protect both parties by making everything in a deal transparent to both buyer and seller. An individualist, on the other hand, has no problem outfoxing the buyer or the seller to their advantage.

Trust was important in Islamic commercial connections, but it tended to close off the number of outlets anyone had. In other words, the Islamic system didn't foster expansive growth as mentioned before. But then it wasn't developed for GDP numbers. Now of course many Muslim commercial enterprises never operated along theoretically beneficial Islamic lines. Corruption of all sorts entered their ranks, spoiling well intentioned ideas.

Over the past several hundred years, Smith has basically been proven correct. Western law depersonalized commercial transactions, which allowed the development of huge corporations with immense wealth. And lots of it did trickle down to the poor. Those poor became middle class and bought Westinghouse dishwashers and Ford Mustangs. Commercial trading infringements were handled by an evolving legal system which recognized non–personal commercial entities.

12. "Lost glory of Ottomans," para. 2.
13. Kuran, "Islamic Commercial Crisis," 417–424.

To cut a long story short, both ended up with current day problems: Islam couldn't generate the wealth the West could; the West has unlearnt how to share it around. Western nations in 2015 have the greatest inequality of wealth ever known inside their own borders. Small wonder that modern Islamic economists criticize the Western model.

Furthermore in the last forty years Western firms discovered lots of poor people in other nations, and began shifting work over to them because they cost less to hire. They invaded the Third World playing the financial game their way under the term globalization.

FROM MATTRESS TO BANK

The first Islamic banking theorist Wikipedia knows of wrote a book only in 1942. Did Islam not have banks before then? Of course they did. Perhaps not banks as we know them, but financial transactions certainly occurred. I have seen them at work personally in a Third World context. The Mandingo people moved down over the nineteenth and twentieth century's from their homeland in Mali to several West African nations including Liberia. 99 percent of Mandingos are Muslims. I sold my Land Rover to a Mandingo diamond miner with wives in three different countries. He would interrupt negotiations to get his prayer mat out and face Mecca.

As immigrants, Liberian Mandingos did not own much land in Liberia, yet they were the wealthiest tribe by a country mile. They were detested by the Gio and Mano tribes in Nimba County, where I lived in 1979. Despite their tribe representing only 9 percent of the community, they ran nearly 40 percent of commercial businesses[14]. Their colorfully dressed women bought fruit and vegetables in rural markets and trucked them down in vehicles driven by their young men to the coastal cities where they sold them at a profit. It was well known, and logical, that the Mano and Gio wanted to get into this trade because they, after all, were the growers of the produce, being farming landowners.

Indeed the Mano and Gio knew how the Mandingo financed their young into trucking on a cooperative basis. Occasionally a Mano village would pool their money, aiming at buying a truck between themselves. The outcome was legend in those days—the fund–holder would run away with the money, never to be seen again. Mano were great farmers, but financial cooperation was too much for them.

14. Hasselmann, *Liberia*, 172–187.

The Mandingos meanwhile went on to build bigger homes, and invest in diesel driven electric generators via which they sold power to Mano villages. They peacefully operated diamond mines, which I visited, failing to identify gems from gravel to their amusement, long before the era of blood diamonds. Many took overseas holidays to Paris, all from the middle of Third World West Africa. I never found out whether they walked into an office of the Bank of Liberia. I was continually astonished however, by the serious roll of American dollars that some of them could extract from a pocket. They had a cash economy.

Clearly the Mandingos knew how to hold their own commercially, but you couldn't pick up a bank brochure, or email their customer services representative. They were a community of families, bound together by tribal and religious affiliation, conducting financial affairs successfully without modern accoutrements. Would you and I have recognized their 'bank' as we trudged around a Liberian village? More to the point of the twenty–first century, would we recognize a modern Islamic bank?

There are many incidents in the history of numbers and finance to help us see what may have happened. Three significant events took place in 1492 in Spain. Columbus discovered America, that's what we all remember, but at the time, that wasn't headline news. Bigger than that was the expulsion of the last Muslims from Spain, the end of the only successful Crusade in history, as Spain was now a 'Christian' nation. In an even more astounding move, considering the Spanish had been fighting the Moors, not their Semitic cousins, the Spanish monarchy kicked all the Jews out.

Gone were the Court Jews with their market and economic knowledge. In what helps explain a once convivial relationship, the Spanish Jews were welcomed into the Ottoman Empire. Sultan Bayazid II gladly accepted their wealth and expertise, commenting that, "They tell me that Ferdinand of Spain is a wise man but he is a fool. For he takes his treasure and sends it all to me."[15]

Those Jews were able to undertake the same role they always had, enabling Muslims to avoid the sordid matters of charging interest, while Spain had to find ways to do it themselves. While the Bank of England began operations in Britain in 1694, it was not until 1856 that the Ottoman bank finally opened, carrying out the functions of a central bank, or reserve bank, as many nations term that institution. Even so, over 95 percent of its shareholders were English and French.

15. "Israel and Turkey," para. 4.

In other words, by the time modern Muslim nations encountered Europeans again around the time of World War 1, those Westerners were powerful, wealthy, astute businessmen, and investors, with economies capable of producing battleships and aeroplanes. Salahadin had gotten rid of the Crusaders eight hundred years previously, but now they were back. In spades.

To paint a simplistic picture, Omar Khayyam and his ilk had spent their time working out elaborate algebraic and triangle theories; Islamic legal systems weren't conducive to industrial growth; the West turned their mathematical energy to money, streamlining the law to assist economic growth.

Perhaps jockeying for position after the fall of the Ottoman Empire in World War 1 and the disappointment that the British didn't do much that Lawrence of Arabia hoped they might, Islamic scholars realized they had to take on that new world. They certainly tried in Turkey, adopting the first constitution separating mosque and state under Kemal Ataturk in the 1920s, that whiskey drinking founder of modern Turkey. As late as 1924, the Ottoman bank was finally taken over by Turks themselves, ejecting the British and French who had humiliated them in the war to end all wars.

In 1942 the first known treatise on Islamic banking was written. Small wonder perhaps, less than forty years later, our Liberian Mandingo friends still ran their bank from their mattress. In 1972, only seven years before my Mandingo experience, the first Islamic bank in the world was set up, and these have since proliferated to over three hundred institutions worldwide. In 2011, banks running according to Islamic banking principles controlled about 2 percent of total global assets. They have a high penetration in the MENA region, especially in Iran and Saudi Arabia. Not unexpectedly perhaps, Islamic banking has a 55 percent share of the total banking sector in Iran, and 13 percent in Saudi Arabia. That figure does fall to 3 percent in Turkey, although Malaysia is a rising star with some 8 percent of their banking sector classed as Islamic.

How do these banks operate? One arrangement is called Murabahah. Instead of lending the buyer money to purchase an item, a bank might buy the item itself from the seller, and re-sell it to the buyer at a profit, while allowing the buyer to pay the bank in installments. However, the bank's profit cannot be made explicit.

How do they work out the installments the buyer should make? One wonders whether they have a spreadsheet on the side with some mathematical interest calculations inside it—but I don't know—and it looks like the Islamic bank isn't going to tell me.

Muhammad Saleem, former president and CEO of Park Avenue Bank in New York, does though. He not only dismisses the founding premise of Sharia and Islamic Banking, but says, "Islamic banks do not practise what they preach: they all charge interest, but disguised in Islamic garb. Thus they engage in deceptive and dishonest banking practices."[16]

So I can't quite see the brochure layout here, and my Western thinking leads me to speculate that the Baron/Jew combination and Islamic banks both employed the same method. Perhaps they pluck a positive figure out of the air, or simply add a sliding amount to the original sum. Reflecting back to the manner in which percentages are embedded in our Western brains, there's a high probability (there's that word again!) others come to the same conclusion. In other words, while Islamic banking may well be logical, they might have trouble persuading Westerners due to the cultural mindset we conceded to decimal and banking long ago.

However we might sit here paternally classing this as an anachronism that will disappear as they swing to the logic of the Western marketplace, but apparently these Islamic institutions run quite well. They have good statistics on things that are important to banks, which includes not losing money, and remaining in business. Their only problem is lack of profitability, and here is where the game changes. The Western world experienced a banking meltdown in 2008 financed by greed, and driven by probability theory gone AWOL. How could Merrill Lynch, AIG and Citigroup have screwed up their risk numbers?

Many citizens of the free world saw Obama's bailout package go to pay bank employee bonuses. That didn't go down well with a populace baying for blood over real estate losses. A few years later, our Western banks are creaming it again to the chagrin of this still seething citizenry.

Now, imagine if those citizens could change the whole thrust of non-personalized commercial law and hold bank Presidents and consultants personally culpable for those losses, as Islamic law intended? Take that thought further and consider a banking system that didn't see profit as its primary objective. Rather, it was safe, stayed in business, and wasn't known for excessive employee bailouts. It could catch on, especially when the home owner discovers the bank shares in his losses. I mean, even the Vatican has put forward the idea that, "banks should look at the rules of

16. Fatah, *Chasing a Mirage*, 261.

Islamic finance to restore confidence amongst their clients at a time of global economic crisis."[17]

Mentioning the Vatican and banking in the same sentence sounds like a Dan Brown novel. Ever since the body of Roberto Calvi, 'God's banker,' was found hanging under London Bridge in 1982, controversy has surrounded the Vatican, who were the main shareholder in Calvi's bank. The Vatican have scrambled—no, wrong word, scrambled conveys too much haste for the Vatican—struggled to shrug off the scandal ever since. It's only taken thirty years, and a new Pope who sides with the poor, to promise to publish an annual report and become more transparent in its dealings by developing a bank website.

Other denominations find themselves mired in the same public relations bog, and now issue statements distancing themselves from whatever moral category the media has set for the Vatican. The Church of England has billions of pounds invested too, and in April 2013 decried those bank executive bonuses that the public has moaned about since 2008. Through their arm called the Ethical Investment Advisory Group (EIAG) the Church complained in May 2013 that Barclays, with whom they have several of those billions lodged, "has repeatedly let down society."[18]

One suspects these Christian denominations, two of the largest on the planet, feel awkward over their involvement in a banking system that has lost the moral confidence of much of the Western world. It's easy to get cynical when one mentions church finance, as if it is an oxymoronic term, considering Jesus himself drove the moneychangers from the temple. However, I've seen a lot of volunteer and underpaid work go into holding these edifices up, and I mean both the historic cathedrals we all still wonder at, as well as the immense church infrastructures of schools, old people's homes, and hospitals. We may well think the EIAGs start in 1994 was a bit late off the mark for a 450 year old institution, but better late than never.

On the other hand the EIAG may well avoid tobacco or armaments investments, but one wonders whether that is particularly earth shaking in a globe infested with news reporters. Perhaps they regret ever sanctioning the charging of interest, and losing that high ground all those hundreds of years ago. We can only speculate.

17. "Vatican Says Islamic Finance May Help," para. 1.
18. "Barclays has 'repeatedly let down society,'" para. 1.

Should Muslims drum up an ad campaign based around this moral unease? Can they progress Islamic banking in this ethical opportunity Wall Street presented them with?

Are you kidding?

Western banking advertising budgets seem as endless as ever, with entire bank refits taking place across entire countries when the branding agency slope the logo letters to indicate more speed, or some other trivial tweak costing millions is white-boarded as a great idea. They would drown any such attempt to thwart their dominance. The first TV spot in their campaign against Islamic finance would be the reminder that if your real estate increases in value, the Islamic bank shares that with you too. I can visualize the advert already, the jaw of the client dropping before it fades away to that new logo.

Now, more of us than Cat Stevens know Islam as a brand carries some connotations working against it in the marketing arena, which might help explain why the original growth in Islamic banking is waning. It's a confusing picture, especially when one reads that the HSBC bank, a global player, shrunk its Islamic retail banking from nine countries to three in 2012—yet A. T. Kearney quote Islamic asset growth is at 20 percent per annum.

A T Kearney think like bankers of course, and they're probably right in their comment that, "Competing against conventional banks means attracting customers who place less importance on Sharia compliance in their financial dealings, and more importance on competitive products and efficient services vis-a-vis the banking market at large."[19]

After all, ethical investment has been around a long time in the West, but most people aren't aware of it. The Quakers have been silently doing it since the nineteenth century, avoiding putting money into armament manufacture long ago.

In January 2014, a major Muslim owned bank dropped the Islamic word from its name. The Dubai-based Noor Islamic Bank changed its name to Noor Bank. This rebranding tactic was part of the banks' plans to expand.[20]

If a Western bank offered Islamic type financing minus the brand word Islam, it would be interesting to see the outcome. This is an unfinished journey as politicians, the real estate industry, media, and the share market, all still worship at the holy grail of GDP growth, which is of course

---

19. "Future of Islamic Banking," para. 12.
20. "What's in a name? Islamic banking rebrands," para. 2.

related to the sins of spending and borrowing. Still, Islamic banking has penetrated the American heartland, the University bank of Michigan being a great example. Bringing up www.university-bank.com in mid 2014 I found a menu link to Islamic banking. That page then claimed it was 'The lowest cost provider in the industry.'

If I was that alien visitor from outer space, hoping to borrow money to buy a home on planet Earth, but unaware of the differences between Christianity and Islam, I might find it hard to choose between the University bank of Michigan, and another American bank down the street. I would do my due diligence using this system called the Internet, and discover websites that both have menus across the top and photographs in the right hand column. I would see logos, and rollover graphics both assuring me they were the best in their industry. And the safest. And the least cost. And the friendliest.

Especially the friendliest. Western banks today almost remind me of modern hip churches: free coffee, welcomed at the door, brochures to take away, comfortable seating, serious emphasis on individual needs, name tags—I could go on.

As usual, it is unlikely I would read the fine print, but I would be welcome to visit either of these banks. Indeed there are possibly menu buttons to press to arrange an appointment on both websites, and there is certainly a 'Contact us' at the foot of every page. In other words, while I may not have been able to describe how the Mandingo village bank operated, I'm now at the point where I can hardly tell the digital financial institutional outcomes of Christendom and Islam apart.

Of course I'm not from outer space.

I can't really appreciate just how similar these financial offerings are, despite their portrayal to that alien engineered and compressed into a virtual mono-theme.

Why? It's because I've been conditioned to note the slight differences. So instead of marveling how all these monetary and numeric challenges have come close to making them twins, I instead wonder at my own cultural reaction. I nitpick out a menu button entitled 'fatwa,' a word the press has conditioned Westerners to think is a death threat.

This is small time stuff compared to the underground arsenal of financial weaponry the US now possesses.

The United States has constructed a financial neutron bomb. For the past 12 years an elite cell at the US Treasury has been sharpening the tools of economic warfare, designing ways to bring almost any country to its knees without firing a shot.[21]

These tools can be wielded against whomever they like, including nations such as Iran. In 2014 Juan Zarate, a Treasury and White House official who helped spearhead policy after 9/11, claimed that, "It's like a new kind or war, a creeping financial insurgency, intended to constrict our enemies financial lifeblood, unprecedented in its reach and effectiveness. The new geo–economic game may be more efficient and subtle than past geo–political competitions, but it is no less ruthless and destructive."[22]

Even the past President of Iran, Ahmadinejad, declared, "A hidden war is under way, on a very far reaching global scale. This is a kind of war in which the enemy assumes it can defeat the Iranian nation."[23]

After several years of financial pressure however, Iran was back at the negotiating table over their nuclear program. The Americans are not fools. They know the power of CNN in bringing war imagery into the living room. A financial war–ground does not yield photographs of bloodstained bodies.

Zarate claims that, "The documents found in Osama Bin Laden's compound in Abbottabad, Pakistan, reflect a terrorist leader and movement in search of new sources of money. Al Qaeda admitted that it has been choked financially."[24]

Since this financial world extends its hidden tentacles everywhere, entrapment scenarios abound elsewhere too. In June 2014, BNP Paribas, the largest bank in France, pleaded guilty to banned transactions with Sudan, Iran and Cuba. The crime was a real life detective story, begun twenty years ago when a grieving father sued a New York bank for funding activities in Gaza that led to his daughter's death. Linking together renamed bank accounts with personal tip–offs, the trail was eventually proven. BNP Paribas had to pay more than $8.9 billion in damages.[25]

$8.9 billion.

---

21. "US financial showdown," para. 1.
22. Ibid., para. 3.
23. Ibid., para. 11.
24. Zarate, "*Conflict by other means,*" 87.
25. "BNP to Pay Almost $9 Billion," title.

That could bankrupt some small nations. International financial law, (which we earlier thought might be an extension of man), makes anyone worldwide culpable in wars linked to money.

WHEN THINGS DON'T ADD UP

David Boyle, author of the aptly named 'The Tyranny of Numbers' makes this point;

> Every time we are exposed to the media, there is a positive flood of statistics controlling and interpreting the world, developing each truth, simplifying each problem. We take our collective pulse 24 hours a day with the use of statistics. We understand life that way, though some how the more figures we use, the more the great truths seem to slip through our fingers. Despite all that numerical control, we feel as ignorant of the answers to the big questions as ever.[26]

Our faith in numbers is boundless. We count everything including the number of camels or houses we own, and dollars in the bank. Yet invalid numbers bounce around the world every day. In 1992, I was asked up to the top floor of the IBM Singapore building to overview their forecast of sales in a particular sector. It only took one look at the figures, and I knew they wrong. How could this be, the forecasters asked. The population of New Zealand was then similar to that of Singapore, and IBM sales to that sector in New Zealand had more years on the ground than in Singapore. I explained the divergence in numbers. The executives paused, looked back and forth, then thanked me for attending. I went back downstairs.

Two days later one of them sought me out. He said they all agreed with my reasoning, and that I was probably right. However they were too far through the planning procedure, so unfortunately they would have to submit the figures they had anyway.

Imagine that this guesswork occurs within every large corporation in the world. A Bank of America executive in Singapore reckoned they would be lucky if they got their numbers right 60 percent of the time. Imagine the mess of data in every governmental, national education, or health administration department. Imagine the politically motivated numbers search, and the budget surpluses that every governmental party promises. Apply

26. Boyle, "Tyranny of Numbers," para. 5–6.

such planning realities as IBM employed that day, the then largest global company selling computational equipment to assist businesses and governments to add things up, and we might have an idea about why not many predictions around numbers eventuate.

Even accountants can have trouble. Gleeson–White refers to two divergent accounting opinions on a firm in Australia. Since the reports were so far apart, the firm hired a third reputable accounting group to assess both the reports. The third accounting organization could find fault with neither, even though the reports were poles apart. Gleeson–White points out that, "'Accounting is never held to account.'"[27]

Nevertheless the world is collecting and calculating more numbers than ever now that Big Data is arriving. Among others, IBM now snap up data analysts, as they are aware of the 140,000 to 190,000 shortfall of workers with deep analytical expertise. Professor Brynjolfsson, an economist at Massachusetts Institute of Technology, gave his opinion;

> In business, economics and other fields, Professor Brynjolfsson says, decisions will increasingly be based on data and analysis rather than on experience and intuition. "We can start being a lot more scientific," he observes.[28]

Will Big Data be able to link together IBM product lifecycles, market demand, factory production, component shortages, shipping delays, interest on borrowings, and advertising schedules, with their planners sudden absence due to his father's death in London, and general work overload in his department, yet come out with a better market segment figure than they managed in 1992?

Yes, says Professor Brynjolfsson. He's proven it. 5 to 6 percent better in fact across 179 companies.[29]

Never argue numbers with a data analyst. By definition you'll lose.

One more time, let me reiterate that we may scoff at the thought that such ill use of data lies at the feet of decimal as a media. That is not the issue. The issue is that decimal opened the door, and metaphorically speaking, in flew that 'devil to darken the spirit and confine man in the bonds of Hell ' that Augustine warned us about.

27. Gleeson–White, *Double Entry*, 215.

28. "Age of Big Data," para. 15.

29. Ibid., para. 19.

It has certainly enabled us to move a long way from the North American Sioux Indians who scoffed at the idea that men could own land. They saw it as foolish as trying to own the air, (which is also up for grabs in parts of our globe, now that it can be measured.) The measurement of land is enmeshed with banking. It is the asset banks hedge themselves against when loaning the householder money.

In poorer parts of our world economic transformations are taking place based on land ownership, a point raised by Maddison earlier. By giving shanty town dwellers title to the land they squat on, many poor people are provided with an asset they can borrow against. This frees them from exorbitant money lender interest rates and enables them to work with authorized banks offering much lower fees.

This is undeniably a good idea in the short term. Loans at prevailing interest rates enable these poor people to start small sewing, cleaning, food or other businesses, and break out of the poverty cycle. It is not a permanent solution though. The longer term process of land accumulation and growing inequality also begins in that shanty town community. This is what acclaimed economist Thomas Piketty referred to when he said money itself has a "vocation."[30] History always demonstrates that money left alone accumulates in the hands of the wealthy.

THE COUNTING OF TIME

Decimal had less of an impact on time as it has always been measured by the seasons and the heavens. Even so, the ancients did not perceive of it like we do. Time itself has modified by men. Jews originally had a flexible view of time. Their word 'olam' in the Hebrew Bible was translated into 'forever' in English, while olam actually means an indefinite period of time, or even the view to the horizon. Given that the horizon is mixed up with time, distance, and the turning of the earth, the Jews had linked time and space together—as Albert Einstein did several millennia later. Olam can be quite short, as used in the book of Jonah. Jonah was in the belly of the whale for three days and nights,[31] yet calls out to God that he was down there 'forever'[32] (In English). In a cultural hangover we often use forever carelessly as in, "it took forever to get there."

30. Piketty, *Capital*, 85.
31. Jonah 1:17
32. Jonah 2:6

Sura 103 from the Qu'ran is often quoted to illustrate how Muslims should view time;

- By time, Indeed, mankind is in loss, Except for those who have believed and done righteous deeds and advised each other to truth and advised each other to patience.[33]

This connects time with purpose, as one commentator claims;

> No matter how lazy, inefficient, unproductive, mediocre or powerless we may be as individuals or as a community—as long as we live and die as Muslims—our life will not be a complete waste of time.
>
> Conversely, no matter how busy, productive, efficient, successful and powerful non–Muslims may appear to be in this world—as long as they die rejecting Islam—none of their work is accepted.[34]

That might upset non–Muslims, but Christians teach similar precepts if the best selling title, 'The Purpose Driven Life' by Pastor Rick Warren,[35] is anything to go by. Let's simply take both definitions as alternative views to time being something neutral, out of our control, that is driven by watches and TV schedules. Remember too, that both religions think we live in a present reality whose future is already decided by a victory yet to be seen.

Year numbering as Westerners understand it started in 532 AD, and not at Bethlehem. It was back fitted by Dionysius Exiguus to start with the birth of Jesus—only he got it wrong by four or so years. It was only in 664 AD that Britain officially chose a calendar. Delegates from Rome and the local Celtic Church debated before King Oswy which Christian denomination the Angles should choose. Rome won, but it wasn't based on theological arguments. They won because they could tell when Easter fell.

Imagine that. The whole nation went Catholic because they could tell the date. Not the time. You didn't arrange to meet your friend at a cafe on Tuesday at 10 AM because there was no cafe. Not much 10 AM happened either, and Tuesday was a reasonably new concept too. Only in 1752 did the English switch to the Gregorian time we use today, deleting eleven days from the old Julian calendar, and beginning the year on January 1st rather than March 25th.

33. Sura 103:1–3

34. "The Concept of Time in the Qur'an," para. 4.

35. Warren, *The Purpose Driven Life*

Muslims have their own calendar, starting in the Western year 622 AD, which was when Muhammad emigrated from Mecca to Medina in Arabia. It has 354 or 355 days, running from our Western November to October. We're not about to drill into lunar cycles here or go further than saying the Iranians have a different system from other Muslim–majority nations. The Western year of 2014 is equivalent to the Muslim year of 1435.

Now of course men knew the approximate length of a year in antiquity, and understood lunar months, but there were no wristwatches. The first clock with a dial resembling a modern one only appeared in 1386 in Wells Cathedral. However, then, and for the foreseeable future, Bristol is ten minutes behind London if you use a sundial. Exact time is different one inch east or west because the earth is continually rotating. Clocks around Britain showed these minor precise variances until the 1840s when British Rail figured out they couldn't have the 8 o'clock express leaving at different times around the nation because they'd be asking for a train collision.

National time is therefore a manmade construction, only linked partially to nature, and certainly not to the habits of cows who can't seem to comprehend daylight saving when they arrive at the milking shed. In all of Britain, only Bristol was stubborn, retaining two minute hands on their clock over the old corn exchange to this day. One shows Bristol exact time, and the other national British time. In other words, time itself was shaped by national and technical needs, especially railways in that era, which Lenin saw as the pinnacle of capitalist production. We're some distance removed by now from indefinite or purposeful time.

It gets worse.

As legendary historian A. J. P. Taylor pointed out in the very title to his 1969 book, 'War by Timetable,'[36] the pre World War 1 powers developed sophisticated mobilization plans to hurry their troops to the battle front before the enemy did. It was an early version of the Mutual Assured Destruction (MAD) theory of nuclear powers in the 1960s and 70s. 'Time' did not allow them to sit down and talk over the assassination of an obscure Serbian archduke in 1914. This marvelous extension of man—the clock—forced nations to declare war on each other. And all those trains full of troops rolled on schedule disgorging eager soldiers at their national borders in 1914 where they proceeded to slaughter each other by the million—with the blessing of the church as we shall see. Nevertheless this nature of time

---

36. Taylor, *War by Timetable*

being the same as the national clock is embedded so deeply in us, we can't think outside that parameter.

Since Einstein, this measuring of time is coming under question. We hear of strange concepts like string theory and alternative universes. In some kind of rebellion against the very concept of time, the leftist government of Bolivia flipped the clock on their Congress building around to run counter clockwise in 2014. The Foreign Minister argued it was not backwards, but rather the fact it is in the Southern Hemisphere. He picked a bad analogy, comparing the swirl of time to water running down the plughole. That's sure to attract cartoonists. The President of Congress was a shade better calling it, "a clear expression of the decolonisation of the people."[37]

That is just politicizing the media, but the point is that in the future, who knows what we might think of the fixed linear time our society has lived by in the past seven hundred years? Our time traveling alien has been useful occasionally in this very book, and we're seeing enough movies such as 'The Time Traveler's Wife' and 'Interstellar.' At the moment it is still all science fiction. However they didn't build that Large Hadron Collider with the help of 10,000 scientists in Switzerland to work on stuff like the deep structure of space and time for a movie though.

Our own memories don't always obey the clock faithfully either;

> . . . our memories are highly selective, and the rendering of memories potentially tells us more about the rememberer's present, his or her desire and denial, than about the actual past events. This is particularly true for cultural memories because they involve intentional fashioning to a greater extent than do individual memories.[38]

She is telling us that we choose how we view our past. This affects all of us. None of us are innocent. We must simply acknowledge again that we don't observe the boundaries between mythology and reality. Nobody can do anything about it anyway, because none of us know everything. Gossip, movies, relatives, community, habit, birthplace, and location influence our view of the past, the present, and the future. So much memory of even recent events is sorted under the heading of mythology that it's pointless trying to convince people otherwise. So to suggest that Islam and Christianity are undergoing re-mythologization is not an insult although some might think so. It happens to all organizations and religions. We all look

37. "Bolivia: Politicians Reverse Time," para. 1.
38. Erll et al., *Media and Cultural Memory,* 333.

back and selectively forget or remember our own personal past, and our collective memories add up to our cultural memory—which tends to override the clock.

6

PROBLEMS WITH SEX

SNOWBOARDING FOR JESUS IN IRAN

SOMETIME IN LATE 2012 five Western, twenty–something year olds, traveled to the Shemshak ski resort in Iran. Four men and one woman—and she couldn't snowboard. They were all Christians, testing a dangerous concept—how to evangelize a Muslim nation. This particular one was embroiled in controversy and suffering severe economic sanctions for their governments desire to become a nuclear power.

Somehow, despite these hardships, rich Iranians took holidays enjoying stints on the slopes. After all, Shemshak is less than fifty kilometers from central Tehran. If this sounds like an Islamic sports media mimic of Boulder, Colorado, then you're onto it. Hardly expecting to find tourists there, our team set about skiing the slopes for five weeks. If this is evangelism, no wonder many adventure seeking, spiritually inclined, Western young, join the para–church organizations behind such missions. This one, which shall remain nameless, did not expect their five to set up a tent or microphone and begin preaching the gospel. That may have worked in the Liberian forest, but definitely wouldn't in Iran.

These young ones were there to look after each other, enjoy skiing, and perhaps meet and mingle with the locals. None were American, because the rumor was such would be chaperoned by officials during their stay. If not a word of their Christian faith passed their lips, their trip would not have been viewed as a failure. What a story line for their own kids one day.

Only the girl fell and broke her leg on the beginner slopes in the first week. Full of pluck, she insisted on being stationed in the resort cafe during the day, so the males could hit the down–hills. The boys returned frequently to check on her. And the locals noticed. To insert yet another pun, this was the icebreaker. Eventually a family invited all five down to their house for dinner one evening. Once seated around the table, the father informed the Westerners his family was Christian, laying a Bible in front of them. The five were led to believe this was an admission that could earn that family the death penalty.

The team was astonished, as they had not uttered any forbidden religious words. The father explained he sensed their faith from their conduct of looking after their wounded female companion. After dinner they watched Sky television. Their host laughed and explained again. Many Iranians purchase Sky TV receivers despite admonitions not to view footage created by the Great Satan. Once a year the police come round, fine them for owning such a device, or accept a bribe, confiscate it, and leave for another year. The family obtain a replacement receiver, fully in the knowledge that it only has a life of twelve months.

Of course, the Christian kids loved being told by their hosts, "you're different from the others." This is music to the ears of a young spiritual snowboarder from New Zealand's Southern Alps or Whistler resort in Canada. It gives meaning to their sojourn there, an assurance they later tell their mentors about, that they "touched lives."

Back at their lodge after the dinner, the Western boys confessed, with laughter, something else had taken place on the slopes while their female compatriot languished in the cafe. Beautiful young Iranian women skiers and snowboarders, replete with makeup, swirling hair flowing freely, and trim fitting ski suits, were constantly onto the boys. It was a single man's paradise. They could have enjoyed several dalliances apiece, daily. Young Western men who snowboard may well boast about their prowess with women, but some truth emerges when they compare the ease or difficulty of conquest between different resorts. If this story results in a surge of tourist numbers to snow resorts in Iran, the writer disavows any such intent.

In this particular scenario none of those Christian boys was about to blow their spiritually motivated quest by being found in bed with an Iranian girl by their fellows—or more critically by anyone from this particular regime. So their discussion was a frank Generation Y eye opener about girls, Islam, and what the TV doesn't tell you.

There's more, as the boys witnessed, their spokesperson expressing it in the wistful idealism of a young Christian out to change the world. As the Iranian girls prepared to return home after their holiday, they donned all the correct scarves, chadors and headgear, giving broad hints about what their return to normal life meant. It's a common scene actually, enacted out in reverse when airliners leave Saudi airspace, as many expatriate oilmen can tell you doing the monthly London reporting run. Women clad head to toe in Muslim modesty retire in turns with a carry bag to the airplane restrooms. Emerging later, they have been transformed into vivacious, lipstick and makeover adorned, tight jean wearing, socialites, on a shopping jaunt to Harrods.

This is a good place to mention that I heard the snowboarder story at the start of my research into what we shall term Islamic feminism and I was thrown. I didn't know what to make of it, or how to position it. Only much later did it make sense. But let's not rush ahead.

Do Islamic feminist movements exist? That's an easy answer—yes, they do, but I don't think they meant to encourage young Islamic women to flirt with Western boys. Did the Western feminist movement intend that? Yes, I think so—but not the Western Christian feminist movement, although that is intertwined with its secular cousin.

And before we're sidetracked too far, can feminism be described as an extension of men? McLuhan used the word men to include masculine and feminine. Yes, whole genres of humor surround this phraseology, as in Christians shouldn't sing 'hymns' any more in church. They shouldn't even sing 'hers.' A truly enlightened congregation will have an 'ours' book. It could easily be argued that releasing all that feminine energy, brains, logic and more onto the planet has extended males whether they wanted it or not.

On a more serious note, and for the sake of brevity, I think we could accept that gender equal education is a media layer leading to greater participation by women in all areas of life. The media point of including feminism in this book is that sexual conduct is deeply woven into both faiths. Our approach is to see how feminism and associated sexual controversies have impacted them.

Those wealthy Iranian girls were not raised by fools obedient to the changing whims of mullahs. They will be aware of Western feminist movements through their Internet searches, and their illegal Sky TV satellite dishes. Indeed they may be more aware of the West than Islamic feminism might want. American Idol, Facebook exposure, and cousins studying in London, all add up to a confusion of ideas. Anyway, we are hardly able to support it with surveyed responses. I'm not about to run around the slopes above Tehran with a clipboard: 'Why did you want to bed those Western boys? Tick any or all of the boxes.'

A CONFUSION OF FEMINISTS

Time for some history. The very term 'feminist' surfaced in the late 1800s in France. 'Feminism' can mean the ideal wife who finds freedom busying herself around the home, raising children, and waiting for her husband's return. A vast array of literature, websites, conference speakers and videos occupy this position. Take Martha Stewart for example, who created an empire in print and TV about cooking, parties, and the wonderful way of American life. Is she a feminist? MS Magazine didn't think so in 2004. "Let's make it clear at the start: Martha Stewart has never been a feminist icon. While we may like her K–Mart paints or appreciate some of her suggestions for décor, she's never made the short list for Ms. Woman of the Year. It doesn't mean we don't consider her a feminist—we have no idea what Ms. Stewart calls herself—it's just that domestic perfection hasn't been one of our top priorities."[1]

MS Magazine are telling us their definition of feminist in that paragraph, and it doesn't appear to include household goddess. The more politically oriented feminist camp might not like Martha because her image props up women's dependency on men. Those recipes and parties cost money, and guess who's paying—hubby. A free woman would be earning her own keep.

Perhaps an Islamic mimic to Martha is the idea that the head to toe chador covering worn by many women in the Middle East is not a sign of bondage—it is a veil of protection. It permits women to be invisible, and therefore gives them freedom to move anywhere. This is not an uncommon concept. It does raise a question—protection from what? Why does a woman need protecting when she ventures out on the street?

The term 'feminism' was not created by Islam or the church. Mimicry has occurred ever since however. Muslims would claim the prophet's

---

1. "An Open Letter from Ms. in Support of Martha Stewart," para. 5.

daughter Fatimah was the first feminist, and Christians would claim Mary of Magdalene was. Even though she probably wasn't a prostitute, as accused in the Middle Ages, it could be liberating for Mary to be that today.

Jews can go further back and claim Miriam, the sister of Moses, was the original musical activist. She led that female tambourine playing dance team inspiring the negro slave spiritual song, 'O Mary, don't you weep, don't you mourn.' Later on she stood up against both her younger brother, who she watched over as a baby in the bull-rushes, and God himself.[2] What greater claim to feminine politics than that? Modern Christian feminist theologians have taken the name of Miriam, or Maryam, translated it into the Judaic–Aramaic name, and connected a string of Mary's together right through the Bible, including the most revered of course—the mother of Jesus. That's quite some progress since the seven Ecumenical Councils between 325 AD and 787 AD. When they invented the Trinity, a word not found in the Bible, it was decidedly masculine. The Trinity is composed of Father, Son, and Holy Spirit.

Muslims quote the prophet who evidently frequently said about his beloved daughter, according to Sunni sources; "Allah, The Most High; is pleased when Fatimah is pleased. He is angered; whenever Fatimah is angered!"[3] Mary is also accorded special status in the Qu'ran, so we even have overlap with the Bible.

Fast forward through those long centuries of military Christianity, and Joan of Arc deserves a mention. Appearing in the early 1400s, she clutched a sword inspired from on high, but, far worse than that, she dressed like a man. It all goes to illustrate how a tempestuous young girl brought up in Burgundy, three hundred years after Pope Urban's speech, was still under the influence of a militaristic faith. Combine admirable sassiness with a sword wielding cultural memory, and you get that young girl winning battles, and flying into a rage against her bosses. It was all too much, and before the age of twenty she was burned at the stake, but not for carrying any weapons. Oh no, that's the thinking of our age. Her fatal crime was donning those pants. Clearly those influence channels have changed. I can't imagine a twenty–first century Christian feminist with an AK47 wearing a camouflage suit, but I can easily see one snowboarding for Jesus—in ski trousers.

2. Numbers 12:1–8

3. "Fatima (A.S.) The Radiant," para. 5.

Rushing past this incomplete history of early Christian feminism, we arrive at the years between 1907 and 1914 when the Original Catholic Encyclopedia was published in the USA, designed to give its readers; "full and authoritative information on the entire cycle of Catholic interests, action and doctrine."[4] Online to this day, the Encyclopedia still contains a summary of women which sets the general tone; "The female sex is in some respects inferior to the male sex, both as regards body and soul."[5]

The term hermeneutics crops up in this area of Biblical study, which means 'concerning interpretation, especially of the Bible or literary texts,' and can mean, 'Historically situated.' You might be forgiven for classing this under active remembering.

As late as 1958 progressive Christians struggled to accommodate women in church services. The highly regarded G.H. Lang, who wrote over twenty books in the mid twentieth century, grappled with the topic. In a book first published in 1928, his chapter, 'The Public Ministry of Women,' extends to some thirty pages, a telling sign in itself. Lang attempted what we might term is a hermeneutic reality to explain why those restrictive verses are in the Bible;

> Moreover, the persons who mostly formed the first churches were not educated, disciplined Westerners, to whom routine and decorum (not to say deadness), especially in public worship, have become second nature and seem wholly proper. On the contrary, they were Orientals, Greeks, Latins; nervous, restless, emotional people, even as today; impulsive, vivacious, talkative; to whom routine was irksome and dullness intolerable.[6]

And later in the same chapter;

> There is not the least question that among such excitable, undisciplined people as are in view the obnoxious, irreverent habit of chattering or gossiping was and is common.[7]

Hence, we derive from Lang, Paul wouldn't let them speak because those Easterners were an impolite crowd. Lang was clever enough to neither confirm nor deny the role of women in churches between 1928 and 1958,

---

4. "Catholic Encyclopedia," para. 1.

5. Ibid., para. 6.

6. Lang, *Churches of God*, 117–147.

7. Ibid., 117–147.

but devoting a whole chapter to it indicates it was becoming contentious. I suggest his book would be classified in the Orientalist category today, but it is nevertheless still sold on Amazon.

Honestly though, it's not particularly illuminating to show the church condemned feminism. Today's Westerners practically expect that of Christianity. We've all seen enough episodes of Downton Abbey. Suffice to say the women's liberation movement started outside the mainstream denominations by the likes of Emily Pankhurst during the same era the Catholic Encyclopedia was published.

Opponents to women's suffrage were never going to win that battle, and like so many others, we look back in amazement that there were even skirmishes. The fight has been taken into practically every avenue of politics, and recruitment adverts show confident young women leading corporate boardroom discussions. Women's sport is expanding, something I can personally testify to, having seen the rise of competitive women's surfing from occasional contests to a worldwide program backed up by retail brands, magazines, and movies.

In Protestantism, that brief (in historical terms) discussion about women participating in church, is nearly forgotten now. Minority denominations such as the Open Brethren, (a great name that could be rejuvenated by a branding agency in this open world), went through a typical transition. As late as the 1970s, Open Brethren ladies silently wore hats in church, with New Testament backing;

- For if a woman does not cover her head, let her also have her hair cut off; but if it is disgraceful for a woman to have her hair cut off or her head shaved, let her cover her head.[8]

- The women are to keep silent in the churches; for they are not permitted to speak, but are to subject themselves, just as the Law also says.[9]

- But I do not allow a woman to teach or exercise authority over a man, but to remain quiet.[10]

The sea of hat–free, talking women, in Open Brethren services is not even mentioned today. Women priest and pastors abound in many denominations, although significantly not yet in the Catholic or Orthodox folds. The Protestant ones speak freely from pulpits, and from the congregation in

8. 1 Corinthians 11:6

9. 1 Corinthians 14:34

10. 1 Timothy 2:12

those institutions that encouraged that sort of behavior from males. Global televangelists such as Joyce Meyer teach via books, TV shows, and let's not forget the microphone in front of vast crowds. How could this happen? Was there any rationale supplied, or was the habit of suppressing women passively forgotten?

We find late twentieth and early twenty–first century teachers are well past blaming Orientals. They tell us we've misunderstood the New Testament. Those verses didn't actually mean what earlier eras thought they did. Christians have been wrong for the past 2000 years. Or 1700 years, as the early church is much in vogue again today. Some creative active remembering was required.

An example comes from the www.christianfeminism.wordpress.com website. The writer looks at that Bible verse above in 1 Timothy, but this time from the New King James Version (NKJV) instead of the New American Standard Bible (NASB) we've been quoting from;

- And I do not permit a woman to teach or to have authority over a man, but to be in silence.[11]

We learn that the Greek word for silence—Hesuchios—has been misinterpreted. The writer tells us; "Traditionalists normally translate this word as "silence" (at least in passages concerning women), but the word in all other places is translated as peacefulness, peaceable, or quietness. The word does not carry the meaning of literal silence or absence of speech, but of an atmosphere or presence in which learning should take place."[12]

Conveniently, in this Internet driven world, the author linked the word 'silence' to an online Greek lexicon, which confirmed Hesuchios means 'quiet' or 'tranquil.' The article concluded that, "None of these verses are about silence, as in the literal absence of speech, but a tranquil quietness or peaceable presence/environment. This fits the context much better than a literal silence, since Paul just rebuked the men in the congregation for praying while angry or quarreling."[13]

It seems like a good argument, but that is not our point in this media study. The main question to ask is why did it take two thousand years for this understanding to be revealed? Is it purely coincident that a powerful rethinking of the role of women was sweeping the earth well prior to this article posted on July 4, 2008?

11. 1 Timothy 2:12 (NKJV)

12. "Mistranslation of Timothy," para. 1.

13. Ibid., para. 2.

It's not a 100 percent shift in any case, even in Protestantism. Other Christian writers disagree, proving that Paul really did mean women to keep silent. The novice, such as myself, can get lost in the technical maze of opinions and interpretations. Those opposing the feminist interpretation allege the liberals are simply finding a meaning that coincides with a feminist definition of freedom, and back fit that onto scripture. Feminist supporters however will undoubtedly claim that opponents have their head in the sand and can't see the bigger picture of the Bible. Both sides will accuse the other of taking the verse out of context.

Larger, and more historic denominations, meaning the Roman Catholic and Orthodox communities, turn to church tradition to back up their rejection of women priesthood. Females weren't allowed in those positions for the past two millennia, and fundamentally, they're not about to start now. Protestants dislike church history as a rationale, so their feminists can always quote St. Paul from the New Testament, sticking to their sola scriptura stance;

- There is neither Jew nor Greek, there is neither slave nor free man, there is neither male nor female; for you are all one in Christ Jesus.[14]

Conversely some liberal wings downplay the Biblical admonitions against women, saying it was a cultural element of the times, and not relevant today. Such would point to Old Testament laws commanding women's hands to be cut off if they touch a man in the wrong place,[15] or death for adultery.[16] Since those laws have been discarded, so too must churches allow women to lead in church. This is the historical setting or hermeneutical argument.

The above is a brief foray into Christian feminist circles. Whatever the debates, the plain facts are that women's freedom has blossomed in many denominations. Nobody could hold back the tide of public sentiment in the West, least of all the church. While the Catholics and Orthodox have some historic cultural issues, one could bet that history itself is against them. It's only a matter of time. Roman Catholicism has attempted to hold their stance against chemical birth control, yet it is claimed up to 98 percent of American Catholic women practice it.[17]

Any parallels among Muslims?

14. Galatians 3:28
15. Deuteronomy 25:11
16. Leviticus 20:10
17. "In the contraception furor," para. 5.

As mentioned already, we have an expanding Islamic feminist movement in the Middle East. Some say it started in 1995 when Benazir Bhutto addressed the Fourth World Conference on Women in Beijing;

> As the first woman ever elected to head an Islamic nation, I feel a special responsibility towards women's issues and towards all women. And as a Muslim woman, I feel a special responsibility to counter the propaganda of a handful that Islam gives women a second class status. This is not true. Today the Muslim world boasts three women Prime Ministers, elected by male and female voters on our abilities as people, as persons, not as women. Our election has destroyed the myth built by social taboo that a woman's place is in the house that it is shameful or dishonourable or socially unacceptable for a Muslim woman to work.
>
> Muslim women have a special responsibility to help distinguish between Islamic teachings and social taboos spun by the traditions of a patriarchal society. In distinguishing between Islamic teachings and social taboos, we must remember that Islam forbids injustice; Injustice against people, against nations and against the women.[18]

Bhutto represented one of only three nations to recognize the Taliban government of Afghanistan, which surely did not agree with her analysis of Muslim women. However, perhaps she opened the door for other Muslim women to go public.

Azar Nafisi[19] gave a differing view of Islamic feminism from an insider's female viewpoint in Iran;

> At the start of the twentieth century, the age of marriage in Iran—nine, according to sharia laws (the prophet married a nine year old girl)—was changed to thirteen and then later to eighteen. . . . By the time my daughter was born (after the 1979 Islamic Revolution), the laws had regressed to what they had been before my grandmother's time. . . . The age of marriage was lowered to nine—eight and a half lunar years, we were told; adultery and prostitution were to be punished by stoning to death; and women, under law, were considered to have half the worth of men. Sharia law replaced the existing system of jurisprudence and became the norm.

---

18. "Address by Mohtarma Benazir Bhutto," para. 9.

19. Azar Nafisi is an Iranian writer and professor of English literature. She left Iran in 1997 and became an American citizen in 2008.

Our society was far more advanced than its new rulers, and women, regardless of their religious and ideological beliefs, had come out into the streets to protest the new laws. They had tasted power and were not about to give it up without a fight. It was then that the myth of Islamic feminism—a contradictory notion—attempting to reconcile the concept of women's rights with the tenets of Islam—took root. It enabled the rulers to have their cake and eat it too: they could claim to be progressive and Islamic, while modern women were denounced as Westernized, decadent and disloyal.[20]

Even so, let's peer through some of the doors Benazir Bhutto may have opened.

Microfinance is an area where women shine, worldwide. By arranging small loans, such as to buy a sewing machine, microfinance seeks to lift people from exorbitant interest rate charges of moneylenders, and out of poverty. Roshaneh Zafar started the Kashf microfinance organization in 1996 in Pakistan on only $4,000. All of Kashf's borrowers are female. By 2012, Kashf had made loans to over 2,000,000 women, making it the fastest growing microfinance institution in the country. Zafar insists that Pakistan's Islamic conservatism is not an impediment to Kashf's growth. Rather it is "Pakistan's patriarchal culture that limits women's participation in activities outside the home,"[21] quotes Coleman, who interviewed Zafar.

Coleman also met Dr Amina Wadud, an American who converted to Islam in the 1970s. She controversially led prayers publicly in New York city before a mixed group, obtaining censure from protesters including a sign reading, "May Allah's Curse be Upon Amina Wadud."[22] Sounds like a tough lady. She began a lifelong study of the Qu'ran following some initial doubts after her conversion to the faith. Coleman says, "Soon enough, her meticulous research convinced her that much of what has been used to justify the mistreatment of women under Islam is actually misinterpretation of the Qu'ran."[23]

Wadud is not alone. Other Islamic feminists think the same. Fatima Mernissi from Morocco learnt from her mother that male superiority was nonsense. "Allah made us all equal,"[24] she often told her daughter. Eventu-

20. Nafisi, *Reading Lolita,* 261–262.

21. Coleman, *Paradise,* location 662.

22. Ibid., location 988.

23. Ibid., location 1002.

24. Ibid., location 1042.

ally this led Mernissi to investigate the truth of a well known hadith, or saying of the prophet, told her by a schoolteacher; "Those who entrust their affairs to a woman will never know prosperity."[25]

While very few Muslims question anything in the Qu'ran, the second tier hadith can come under scrutiny as we found with the beautiful Zaynab whom Muhammad married. Mernissi found this particular saying was remembered some twenty five years after the passing of Muhammad, and the person who claimed to have heard the prophet had been accused of lying in other instances, making him unreliable. Accused, please note, not a proven liar.

Interesting. It turns out this hadith was accepted by an authority named Bukhari. If he of all people approved it, that is usually a seal of authenticity. Another hadith by Bukhari reads;

> Allah's Apostle once said to a group of women: 'I have not seen any one more deficient in intelligence and religion than you. A cautious, sensible man could be led astray by some of you.' The women asked: 'O Allah's Apostle, what is deficient in our intelligence and religion?' He said: 'Is not the evidence of two women equal to the witness of one man?' They replied in the affirmative. He said: 'This is the deficiency of your intelligence.'[26]

By the time we move to the incontestable Qu'ran itself, we can read the following verses;

- Men are in charge of women by (right of) what Allah has given one over the other and what they spend (for maintenance) from their wealth. So righteous women are devoutly obedient, guarding in (the husband's) absence what Allah would have them guard. But those (wives) from whom you fear arrogance—(first) advise them; (then if they persist), forsake them in bed; and (finally), strike them.[27]

- And due to the wives is similar to what is expected of them, according to what is reasonable. But the men have a degree over them (in responsibility and authority).[28]

---

25. Ibid., location 1066.
26. Sahih Bukhari, "Volume 1, Book 6, Number 301," para. 1.
27. Sura 4:34
28. Sura 2:228

Wadud is able to re-frame these for us by de-constructing verses. Up comes 'complex hermeneutic totality' and 'historically situated' text. Now then, don't start counting mimicries.

Wadud takes Sura 2:228, the verse above. Actually, she takes it apart. That's what de-constructing means;

- And [(the rights) due to the women are similar to (the rights) against them, (or responsibilities they owe) with regard to] the ma'ruf, and men have a degree [darajah] above them (feminine plural).

The Arabic term ma'ruf has been translated as 'kindness,' or 'fairness' as in our first translation. This is too limited for Amina Wadud. To her it means something "well known," "obvious" or "conventionally accepted." In other words, "the basis for equitable treatment is conventionally agreed upon in society."[29]

Convention is a relative term, not an absolute one. Wadud has managed to turn this verse, so often used by people to prove the anti-feminist nature of the Qu'ran, into a theme of the times it was written in. Hermeneutics again.

It takes a while to simply grasp what Wadud actually means. Or that people would exhaustively comb through Arabic word translations in order to pick out a different meaning, and present it as a fresh understanding, given feminism has been with us for over 100 years now. But they do. Just as our Christian feminists did earlier. To the non-believer such examination of holy texts is incredible. It might seem like counting angels on a pinhead again, but this process is very important in both faiths. It is active remembering at its best.

Although slightly oblique to feminism, the most humorous recent re-interpretation was attempted by Christoph Luxenberg. Various references to virgins in paradise are promised to males in the Qu'ran[30] and the hadiths.[31] Luxenberg attempted to tell us the word virgins had been mistranslated, and it actually meant 'white raisins.'[32] It has been pointed out that white raisins do not have large beautiful eyes, nor are they devoted to their husbands, as the Qu'ran passage promises.

We might ask whether some re-mythologizing is going on here, or simply a desire to see what they want to see in the holy scripts. The answer

29. Wadud, Qu'ran and Woman, 68–69.

30. Sura 56:12–37

31. "72 Virgins Hadith Narrations," section 2.

32. "New Theories of the Koran," para. 4.

is that it doesn't matter. We have a fair idea what the outcome will be—the liberation and participation of women.

Further work is being done by the www.wluml.org site (which stands for Women Living Under Muslim Laws). Founded in 1984, it has branches in both the West and Asian nations including Pakistan. They claim; "Women Living Under Muslim Laws is an international solidarity network that provides information, support and a collective space for women whose lives are shaped, conditioned or governed by laws and customs said to derive from Islam."[33] After spending time on Qu'ranic interpretations between 1990 and 2004, they have moved on to projects including;

- The Global Campaign to Stop Killing and Stoning Women! (2007—present)

- The International Coalition on Women Human Rights Defenders (2005—present)

Are they well known? The phrase "women living under muslim laws" in quote marks to force searching the full phrase, gathered over 100,000 hits from Google. I couldn't resist trying "women living under christian laws" and received just one back from a site parodying Islam, asking whether such a counterpart website exists.

However freedom for women never occurs in the way that the church or the mosque or the website wants. If you open the feminist door, all kinds of angels, goddesses, witches, and jinns, fly in. Hence our Iranian snowboarding girls. The Iranian feminist movement probably didn't mean to create those racy downhill beauties. Neither, I suspect, did they call for Islamic women's fashion shows, as was headlined by The Economist;

> Designers are profiting from Muslim women's desire to look good
> The Islamic revival of the 1970s, and then a shared sense of persecution in the aftermath of the September 11th attacks, led many Muslim women to wear their hearts on their sleeves, says Reina Lewis, an academic at the London College of Fashion and editor of "Modest Fashion: Styling Bodies, Mediating Faith." Many say that Islamic dress is better suited than their country's traditional garb to modern life. "The hijab helps women be treated for their minds, not their looks," says Aziza Al-Yousef, a Saudi professor.[34]

33. "About WLUML," para. 1.

34. "Hijab couture," para. 2.

Is this doublespeak? If they wanted to be appreciated, "for their minds, not their looks," surely a chess competition would be better.

However this is nothing compared to the Christian fashion industry which boasts its own website, www.christianfashionweek.com. From an idea in 2010, CFW has now run an event yearly since 2013. In 2014 they expanded to run over an entire week, and they have a day of prayer for success. CFW has sister sites such as Model4Jesus, which is purportedly a Christian ministry but is still not at the most comedic end of the spectrum. Christian Jazzercise was invented in the 1990s, with slogans such as 'firm believer.' I even saw one promotion quoting the Gospel of John;

- He must increase, but I must decrease.[35]

Clothing company www.yahwear.com ran for a few years, the URL being a play on the name Yahweh, sometimes assigned to the Christian and Jewish God. Thankfully it has fallen through, perhaps a sign that you can't take commerce too far into the faith. Jesus' most violent act was to drive the moneychangers from the temple when all said and done.

I digress somewhat, but we might return to mimicry. Why are Christianity and Islam even in the fashion arena, surely one of the most ego driven, God forsaken industries in the world? Are they mimicking each other or the globe in general? Don't tell me, it's rhetorical.

THE CLOSET

Cracks are appearing in the Christian wall against homosexuality. In July 2013 Pope Francis famously quipped, "If a person is gay and seeks God and has good will, who am I to judge him?"[36] Blog sites around the world welcomed his news, although in late September 2013 he excommunicated a Melbourne priest for supporting women's ordination and gay marriage. It's not easy running the world's largest denomination, so no wonder mixed signals emerge.

Many so called Christian nations support homosexuality, including 60 percent of Americans, 76 percent of the British, and 88 percent of the Spanish in 2013. These three nations still have over 50 percent of their population ticking the census Christian box. So let's not examine how the

---

35. John 3:30

36. "If a person is gay and seeks God," para. 2.

church used to decry homosexuals since that is now yesteryear. Instead we'll dive into the emerging pro–gay Christian movement.

It is divided into what I term militant and gentle sectors. I discovered this purely by chance. I was in the home of some gay, Christian, male, friends, on my quest to understand their world. By chance I plucked a book from their shelf on homosexual theologies. It happened to be written by one James Alison. Alison is a gay Catholic writer, who addresses the issue gently to, "people of whatever background negotiating the world of faith in the time of the collapsing closet."[37] His writing was sensitive, and I read several of his works, including a theological argument on how to read the Bible. Our Bible today is presented in chapters and verses, but it wasn't written that way by Paul and the Apostles. Remember that versification of the Bible took place in the twelfth century as an aid to finding your way around the scriptures.

Here are the key anti–homosexual verses in the New Testament, from Romans Chapter 1:27–32, with verse numbers deliberately inserted.

- 27 and in the same way also the men abandoned the natural function of the woman and burned in their desire toward one another, men with men committing indecent acts and receiving in their own persons the due penalty of their error. 28 And just as they did not see fit to acknowledge God any longer, God gave them over to a depraved mind, to do those things which are not proper, 29 being filled with all unrighteousness, wickedness, greed, evil; full of envy, murder, strife, deceit, malice; they are gossips, 30 slanderers, haters of God, insolent, arrogant, boastful, inventors of evil, disobedient to parents, 31 without understanding, untrustworthy, unloving, unmerciful; 32 and although they know the ordinance of God, that those who practice such things are worthy of death, they not only do the same, but also give hearty approval to those who practice them.

It appears to condemn the practice. Here is the very next verse, in the next chapter, Romans 2:1.

- 1 Therefore you have no excuse, everyone of you who passes judgment, for in that which you judge another, you condemn yourself; for you who judge practice the same things.

Alison explains that not only does the chapter break represent a twelfth century insert, but the word 'Therefore' in the first verse of chapter

---

37. "Faith beyond Resentment," para. 2.

2 indicates it is referring to a previous section. And the implication of 'Therefore' is that the reader is committing the very same sins outlined in Chapter 1. Since most readers weren't homosexual, the earlier verses need to be reviewed as to their real intent. It is a thought provoking argument.

Just hold that there. If Alison is right, and Christians have misinterpreted the lesson from Paul because of a chapter insertion, that is serious. It's laying the responsibility for anti–homosexual messages at the door of those twelfth century people who aimed to enhance the Bible by making chapter divisions. Perhaps they meant to do that in this particular case, I don't know. It does make one wonder whether other intentions of Biblical texts have been disturbed by chapter and verse contexts.

By chance again, on another day, I plucked a different author from the bookshelf of my friends. This time it had a militant homosexual theme, blaming the heterosexual world for all the indignities the gay community suffers. Its blasé predictability had me tossing it back into their shelf, and I focused on Alison instead.

My reaction may well be typical of many. Faced with an issue we claim we want to explore, sometimes we're really looking for evidence that it's wrong. We will do cursory research, find a supporting author, then move on, able to assure others we looked into it. None of us are immune from this. Beware the writer who claims he or she is completely neutral. Alison headed me off at the pass because he understood how I might begin.

More cursory research uncovered the traditional Islamic response to homosexuality, the crime that can cost you your life in many Muslim–majority nations. www.islamawareness.net tells us "Homosexuality is not allowed in Islam. There are various verses in Qu'ran where Allah clearly says about Homosexuality."[38]

- And [We had sent] Lot when he said to his people, "Do you commit such immorality as no one has preceded you with from among the worlds? Indeed, you approach men with desire, instead of women. Rather, you are a transgressing people."[39]

- Do you approach males among the worlds and leave what your Lord has created for you as mates? But you are a people transgressing.[40]

---

38. "Islamic view about Homosexuality," para. 1.

39. Sura 7:80–81

40. Sura 26:165–166

Pew Research published a global tolerance survey of homosexuality in 2013. Among the least tolerant nations surveyed was Pakistan, where only 2 percent of those surveyed said society should accept homosexuality.[41] As of 2014, Iran had no compunction in prosecuting, and frequently executing, homosexuals.[42] Wikiislam claimed 678 gay and trans-gendered men were killed in Iraq in ten years starting in 2004.[43]

A slightly deeper search uncovered support for Muslim homosexuals. One such site is www.imaan.org.uk, an LGBTQI (Lesbian, Gay, Bisexual, Transgender, Queer or Questioning, and Intersex) Support Group in Britain. Right at the top of their FAQ we find;

Q: What does the Qur'an say about Homosexuality: Isn't it a sin?

A: The Qur'an says little about homosexuality and many claims are made about the content of the Qur'an that do not necessarily stand scrutiny.

We have prepared a FAQ Document that discusses the subject.

Down came the PDF and it went straight into the Qu'ran as I expected it would. On the first page it referred to the same Qu'ranic verse mentioned by the anti-homosexual site above. Here is the paragraph, verbatim;

> There is no term, technically, for homosexuality. Certain words in some passages refer to certain acts, and these are open to interpretation.
>
> Fahisha (7:80, 27:54) Lewdness, indecency, gross.
>
> Khabaidh (21:74) Improper
>
> Sayyi'aat (11:78) Evil
>
> Certain sura refer to fahisha, and this has long believed to refer to homosexuality. For example, sura 7:80: 'And Lut, when he said to his people, 'Do ye approach an abomination which no one in all the world ever anticipated you in?'[44]

This pro-homosexuality PDF ran to ten pages, and based on my previous judgment, I placed it in the gentle category. I now had, side by side, unconscious mimicry. Both religions condemn homosexuality, and both have growing movements within them rejecting that view.

---

41. "Global Acceptance of Homosexuality," map.
42. "Experts Predict: Iran Will Remain Deadly," para. 1–7.
43. "Persecution of Homosexuals (Iraq)," para. 4.
44. "Quran FAQ," 2.

The LGBTQI journey has the potential to split Christianity. Richer Western nations support the movement, but poorer Third World ones do not. Unfortunately wealthy ones have money, whereas impoverished ones have expanding congregations. In theory neither can do without the other, but that's not a factor to consider. In particular the Anglican Communion (which is the global name for their denomination) is under threat.[45]

Close behind them are others. On the same day many Christian marchers opposed homosexual marriage, The General Assembly of the Presbyterian Church (U.S.A.) voted on June 19th, 2014 to change the definition of marriage from "a man and a woman" to "two people," and to allow ministers to perform same sex marriages in states where it is legal.[46]

The same trend, in embryonic form, might surface in the Islamic world. It is not yet at the stage of potentially splitting the faith along East—West lines, but the pressure is on from the non–Muslim Western community. Muslim intellectuals might speak against it, but news reporters and politicians won't let it go. A leading Dane gave us an insight to this public sentiment. Quite a crowd turned up to the opening of the first mosque in Denmark, which only happened in 2014. Lars Aslan Rasmussen, a local Social Democrat, and a supporter of the mosque, nevertheless questioned the claim of the Danish Islamic Council to speak for a Danish–Muslim identity. "But what is more important is that there should be new ideas in Islam and you will have imams who accept homosexuals. It will come, but this mosque is not representing something new and that is a shame."[47]

The homosexuality issue will not be solved on technical details, such as whether the Bible or the Qu'ran disapproves it or not. It is a hearts and minds agenda. Changes in marital law are very public, so reporting is mandatory. It is also inevitable that organizations like Amnesty International will continue telling the World about Middle Eastern executions of homosexuals. In other words, this is one arena where religious leaders will be forced eventually to make public statements. Given the public relations cocoons around them, we can safely assume any such words will postdate the actual social trend.

And yet Christianity will survive. It's been through worse if you remember Popes once sent armies to the Middle East. Islam will too. Despite

---

45. See "Archbishop Justin Welby: 'There is a possibility that we will not hold together.'"

46. "PC (USA) leaders issue pastoral letter," para. 3.

47. "Denmark's first mosque," para. 22.

an increasing number of couples co–habiting in Iran, rather than marrying, the faith will endure. The Ayatollah Khamenei wanted to; "show no mercy in clamping down on cohabitation."[48] A betting man might think he'll lose that battle. Equally so, Western Muslim homosexual movements may, one day, spread to the MENA region.

GENDER AGENDAS

All this above research was enabled using media including books, the Internet, statistics, and global surveys. I still didn't have my head around the Iranian snowboarder girls though. I'd seen a fairly predictable array of outcomes in either religion—the 'already free' women cooking, or 'free wearing a veil' concept, the 'evil men subverting scripture' claim, and a sprinkle of 'rediscovering' meanings from the holy texts.

Step one to sorting out the snowboarder girls happened when I saw the next statistics on pornography, and I began to grasp their deceptive nature. Statistics that is, or rather the answers people give to questions on sex. Google Trends (www.google.com/trends/) has received scholarly attention since at least 2012. Google Trends provides a time series index of the volume of queries users enter into Google and can be viewed in a given geographic area. Some satirists used Google Trends to geo–position the use of homosexual search terms. Despite 98 percent of Pakistanis disapproving of homosexuality according to Pew,[49] Google Trends ranked Pakistan the highest in the world for using various homosexual search words in the years from 2004 to 2014. In descending order the top six nations were Pakistan, Ethiopia, Sri Lanka, Tanzania, Libya, Sudan, and Saint Helena of all places. This is virtually an inverse report to the Pew one. Anyone can examine Google trends to see their colorful world maps with deepening colors showing national rankings.

Google trends
homosexual searches

It's that wicked Internet again, reaching into everyone's private predilections, adding them together by nation, and presenting them to the world—and all automatically, without the single verbal asking of a question. Perhaps that's what the Muslim jokester in chapter one really meant when he said, "The difference between us

48. "Can Iran 'control' its cohabiting couples?" para. 9.
49. "Global Acceptance of Homosexuality," map.

is that we pray in public and have sex in private. You Westerners pray in private and have sex in public."

All sorts of motivations to both believe or deny the Google search statistics could emerge—if they ever reach mainstream reporting, that is. Is there a hidden mother lode of sexual deviancy/freedom stories waiting to be discovered in the Muslim world by CNN? Why doesn't Pew Research incorporate the Google Trends figures into its reports?

One only has to recall our snowboarder story to grasp difficulties in obtaining real answers. Remember that science itself is a media, and the very act of investigating at a conscious level interferes with the real answer. That's termed the Heisenberg principle, which ascribes the uncertainty in the measurable quantities to the jolt–like disturbance triggered by observing it. It'd be a jolt–like disturbance to quiz those Iranian snowboarder girls on the slopes, and they would reply no to any questions about flirting. Is the same principle at play between the conscious answers given to Pew surveys in Pakistan, as compared to the surreptitious technique of Google trends?

Of course it is. Any teenager can confirm that. Coincidentally there are moves to restrict Google's data collection. One wonders about motivations, but we're not here to confirm or deny iniquity.

NOT DUMB VILLAGE LASSES

Step two in my enlightenment took place upon seeing two entirely different events involving women. In May 2014, the Islamist Boko Haram group captured world attention by kidnapping three hundred girls in northern Nigeria, and later parading the frightened youngsters in hijabs declaring their conversion to Islam.

With stunning simultaneous timing, and much less publicity, a Facebook site was launched in Iran called My Stealthy Freedom.[50] It portrayed Iranian women without the hijab, mostly in remote beautiful places. Within a week of its launch the site had received 130,000 likes, mostly from Iranian men and women. The incongruity of African girls being 'freed' by Boko Haram, with the photographs of young Iranian women feeling, "a brief moment of peace in the air my body has the right to enjoy," has been interpreted as a political statement—as if the Boko Haram one wasn't.

Both the events were statements about the uses of media, but the Iranian one also demonstrated statistics (130,000 Facebook likes) outside

50. "My Stealthy Freedom Community."

the traditional arena of surveys. However, the latter demonstrated personal choice. These Iranian women were not the dumb village lasses Boko Haram wanted in their world.

As for Europe, it is now replete with urbane Muslim women.

> Young Muslim women are often forced to lead double lives in Europe. They have sex in public restrooms and stuff mobile phones in their bras to hide their secret existences from strict families. They are often forbidden from visiting gynecologists or receiving sex ed. In the worst cases, they undergo hymen reconstruction surgery, have late-term abortions or even commit suicide. Gulay, 22, lives in Berlin, wears tight jeans, low-cut blouses and has long hair that she doesn't keep covered. Gulay is thinking about how best to sum up her dilemma. She nervously stirs her tea before launching into a litany of complaints. "The boys can screw around as much as they want, but if a girl does it she can expect to be shot," she says. "That's just sick." She first had sex five years ago, and it completely changed her life. Since then, she has been deathly afraid of being branded by her family as a dishonorable girl—or, worse yet, punished and cast out.[51]

The Iranian snowboarder girls were making sense now. They probably had conversations behind the scenes like this one recorded by Nafisi in Tehran about university students listening to an Islamic morality lecture;

> On one side he had written, in large white letters, MUSLIM GIRL, and drawn a vertical line in the middle of the board. On the other sides, in large pink letters, he wrote CHRISTIAN GIRL. He then asked the class if they knew the difference between the two. One was a virgin, he said at last, after an uncomfortable silence, white and pure, keeping herself for her husband and her husband only. Her power came from her modesty. The other, well, there was not much to say about her except that she was not a virgin. To Yassi's surprise, the two girls behind her, both active members of the Muslim Students' Association, had started to giggle, whispering, "No wonder more and more Muslim girls are converting to Christianity."[52]

This is not Joan of Arc speaking. These are the voices of educated, cheeky young women, the type you'd meet on any campus. Only they were

51. "Forbidden Love: Taboos and Fear among Muslim Girls," para. 1–5.

52. Nafisi, *Reading Lolita*, 30.

in Tehran, coping with what Tehran served up. Various parties might conjecture that they had been contaminated by Western morals, but they certainly sound intelligent. I might conjecture that such stories are not what Benazir Bhutto or Amina Wadud or the other iconic Islamic feminists were calling for. I might conjecture they wanted young women teaching school, doing charity work, or furthering their political career. I don't believe either intended to turn Islamic girlhood into flirtatious beauties in mountain outfits.

Then again, neither do serious Christian feminists encourage young girls to display their faith on the catwalk, or be a witness to Christ via a half clothed front cover shot on Vogue magazine. In the long run, feminine freedoms won't turn out all peaches and cream in the Middle East. But it is probably inevitable.

ABERRATIONS

Unfortunately, one might even say, very unfortunately, putting up barriers for young men and women to meet each other freely in Islamic society has a widespread downside. One look at the global prevalence of consanguinity (marriage between near relatives) shows a concentration in the MENA region. Indeed the prophet Muhammad himself married Zaynab, his first cousin, and so the practice is openly encouraged by Muslim commentators; "We hope that you can see that there is no basis for disputing the issue of a Muslim marrying his first cousin. It is established by the Qur'ân, the Sunnah, the practice of the Companions including the Rightly Guided Caliphs, and the consensus of the Muslim Ummah."[53] Consanguinity is widespread among Western Muslims too. One study found 55 percent of Pakistani women in Britain were wedded to their first cousins.[54]

Cousin marriage worldwide

The genetic evidence against inbreeding is well established, as it leads to various disorders, and higher mortality rates.[55] As one might expect, it is a delicate topic, and is not restricted to only Muslim peoples. Hindu marriages in India often follow the same trend. Nevertheless how does

53. "Marriage between first cousins," para. 10.

54. Darr and Modell, "Frequency of consanguineous marriage, 186.

55. See "Genetic disorders."

the Muslim community, which prides itself on laws and regulations in the family sphere, handle this in the light of scientific evidence against the practice? One paper blamed it on earlier practices in the MENA region, predating Islam;

> A hadith is cited: "marry from afar (not nearby relatives) so that the offspring is not weakened." The second Caliph Omar is reported to have given this advice to (Bane–Saeeb tribe), because of offspring weakness in that tribe ("strange hadith" –Abu–Maleka). In fact the custom of consanguinity has nothing to do with Islam entirely as many criticizers believe; it is just a time–honored tradition.[56]

It seems strange that such a core practice could survive fourteen centuries of Islamic law. However that reasoning is nothing compared to a 2013 lecture given to Canadian youth, which wondered why all this "propaganda" about the dangers of cousin marriage had appeared in recent years. The author managed to dig up a couple of medics who believed there was nothing wrong with it. They also pinned the blame on Western powers seeking to break down the family unit and replace it with a more state centric social model.[57]

Lastly, Muslims face a pedophile challenge, just as the Catholics do. In mid 2014 the Pope was quoted as conceding that 2 percent of priests are pedophiles, or 8,000 in total.[58] It has taken many, many, news reports to get a pontiff to this point. We can be sure the Roman Catholics would have wanted to solve this problem behind closed doors, which of course no longer exist in the information drenched Western world.

Islam has yet to cope with pedophilia or sex with children, on the front page. The Internet swirls with opinions about it though. Muslims have a particular challenge in that Muhammad himself married a nine year old girl. The Islamic writings don't try and cover up the fact she was playing with her toys when Muhammad came for her. Instead they revel in the day he arrived. The best summary I have read on the current status of this historical event was an abstract by Kecia Ali entitled, 'I was a girl of nine';

> Many (Muslims) refused to accept the evidence presented for Aisha's age at the time of marriage, even though it was taken from Sahih Bukhari, the most authoritative Sunni hadith collection. The radically different responses received by these Muslim questioners

56. Abdalla and Zaher, "Consanguineous Marriages," 5.

57. "Cousin Marriages," para. 22–24.

58. "Pope says about two percent of priests are pedophiles," para. 1.

asking about age differences in marriage suggest that many Muslims are caught between uncritical acceptance of their inherited tradition and the fear that any critical stance toward that tradition will be a capitulation to, as one author puts it, "the enemies of Islam."[59]

Considering a Human Rights report noted in 2013, that; "there are troubling reports that Iranian parliament's legal affairs committee is pushing to lower the legal age of marriage for girls back to 9 years of age"[60] it places Muslims today in a quandary.

How easy is it to become an enemy of Islam?

59. Ali, "I was a girl of nine," 1.
60. "Early and Forced Marriages in the Islamic Republic of Iran," 1.

7

THE VILLAGE AND THE GLOBE

READING THE JUNGLE

At twenty-six years of age, with a liberal arts degree and three years of teaching human geography under my belt, I taught school in the West African bush. I had a Land Rover parked outside my multi-room, electric powered, plaster covered house and a fridge that worked on kerosene. I was a champagne socialist.

One day I persuaded a secondary school pupil named Sam, who was the same age as me probably, to help retrieve some cane I had found growing in the forest. I was captivated by the idea I could make eco-friendly lounge furniture from this natural, organic, provision of the jungle. He reluctantly followed me to the clearing where I proudly pointed out the cluster of tall straight saplings. Groaning more than inwardly, he debated with me, then took over the project.

With single slashes from his omnipresent machete, he leveled a dozen or so lengths. Selecting what seemed to me a random tree, he cut around a narrow branch and pulled a meter of bark off. Using two or three of these as ropes, he lashed the cane bunch together. Weaving his hand through a certain grass, he quickly fashioned a turban and placed it on his head. Stooping, he swung the bound cluster of cane up, balanced it on his cranium, and we walked home. I was astounded at his oneness with nature, his effortless use of jungle items to solve a problem.

He could 'read' the forest. It informed him, telling him the passage of a green mamba snake through the upper canopy from the warning chatter of the squirrels. These skills were commonplace amongst his peers, and he could not understand my praise of them, saying it was merely bush stuff.

A fortnight later I was bouncing through the gloriously thick forest of Liberia along a pot holed road in my Land Rover with Sam. And he asked me to teach him to drive. In a second I saw it all—my liberal distrust of the fruits of capitalism, environmental destruction, community decline, and Western values, meant nothing to Sam. To him I could 'read' the Western world. I was informed by it. The world he imagined I came from was so rich, powerful, glossy, and attractive, it was impossible for him to resist—as impossible as it was for me to tell him not to mimic it.

Fifteen years later I had another epiphany, this time in an Asian nation that had caught up to the West. A delightful, elderly Singaporean lady was telling me the shock she experienced when she first visited Britain, the country that once owned her island state. "I saw a white man sweeping the street!" she chuckled. "Of course I knew they had to do that, but I'd never seen one."

It's difficult for Westerners to really, deeply, feel how denizens of those other worlds, the Third one, or the South one, or the Poor one, whatever you call it, feel when they move to the West. I sometimes think the only parallel would be to have our alien drop by in his UFO on an afternoon jaunt from Alpha Centauri.

As his saucer hovers motionlessly above the ground, he is talking to us. "Oh, two or three minutes of your time to get here I guess, I'm not sure. I was busy looking at the interplanetary relay race, you know those new solo cars are quite fast, fifty times the speed of light I'm told. No, you'd hate those multi level transportable condo units, I'm told they're a little chilly after a month on Saturn, although the visuals are great from Mars. What language are you speaking, I'm sorry, let's just take this pill, ah, now I understand you. What a strange way of communicating, so loud, how do your thought wave transfer mechanisms work. Must go, I've just had an alert there's a supernova explosion worth watching on the other side of the Milky way."

Off he flies, down some black hole inter–stellar highway, with education, wealth, and technology, beyond our dreams. And we can't follow.

How would we feel if we managed to creep in their back door?

Actually researchers know. They've looked at how immigrants from poor nations settle in when they move to the West. They cluster with their own kind, and implement a version of their home planet on new soil. Their male children are allowed more freedom than their girls, and they reminisce about how good life was on the old world, while sending money back to relatives who can't make it over.

They keep their pride. You can see that by the way they emphasize their culture, religion, clothing, morals, and food. They came as underdogs, as people needing the money or education or safety that the West supplies. And dammit, they're not going to become like one of those powerful, rich, knowledgeable ones they are forced to work long menial hours for.

I watched an elderly Muslim man on crutches, waiting for the pedestrian crossing, on his way back home from the huge two storey mosque that seems to permanently have cars and people in its grounds. Inside the mosque, he may well be a leading personage, a man of influence. Outside it, on the road, hobbling home alone, he looked absolutely out of place, a caricature for people to come to their own conclusions about. He was the alien now, snatched from his poverty stricken planet and placed here amidst rich, powerful, different people whose gaze averts if he returns any stares.

The neighborhood houses a cluster of halal meat butchers, garish second hand shops, and a video store specializing in movies Westerners wouldn't hire. Other portly males in flowing clothes, all with those long beards and the little caps, were chatting along the street.

Over the road from the mosque, literally a stone's throw away, stands another religious building representing another immigrant community. Auckland, New Zealand, is the Polynesian capital of the world, meaning more of those South Pacific Islanders live there than anywhere else. They love churches.

Unlike the Islamic 1400 year heritage, Samoa has only had 200 years of Christian influence. It transformed Samoan society however. Visitors to their islands are struck by the frequency and stature of their churches. Every small village has one or two, and they are always the largest buildings. Despite this proliferation, signs of construction of new ones are common. Sunday in Samoa finds all the women in white, and the men in black, heading down to church. Taxis are difficult to summon, and the islands virtually go to sleep.

Thousands of Samoans left, and still leave, their benign, warm, islands, to find work in New Zealand. They brought a religious culture with them which still forms the basis of their community. So their shops selling flowers and fruit mingle amongst the halal butcher and the video stores. Perhaps neither the Islamic nor the Samoan communities want the word mimicry applied here. During the formation of their respective religious cultures, they most likely didn't know the other existed. I am sure that senior Islamic men and Samoan elders cleaning toilets and roads for the Council find more satisfaction officiating at kava ceremonies or mosque prayers, and if I was in their shoes, so would I.

Perhaps they rub shoulders with each other, nodding as acquaintances, one turning left and the other right on their respective religious days. Research didn't need to go far to find a dualist mentality in both communities. These parallels are not deliberate. The Islamic community did not read the research on the Samoan scenario and conclude, aha!—that's how we'll settle in. Choosing the same street was cute though.

One significant difference is demonstrated in the fact that both www. ex–muslim.org.uk and www.ex–christian.org are sited in Western nations. The ex–Muslim site would be illegal in many Muslim-majority nations today. Malaysia is deemed a progressive Muslim regime. If you try to leave Islam though, the clerics have worked their way around the confusing freedom of religion laws, and you might be put into a rehab center. That's right. In their logic, considering exiting the faith can be seen as a mental illness. Six months counseling should see you right. That's better than the death sentence that Bukhari quoted from the prophet; "I would have killed them according to the statement of Allah's Apostle, 'Whoever changed his Islamic religion, then kill him.'"[1]

So despite admonitions in the Qu'ran that there is "no compulsion in religion,"[2] in practice severe social severance, sometimes death threats, and occasionally death, is a widespread outcome of exiting Islam in Western nations. Some Western Muslims concede this is a problem. Britain's ex–Muslim site began in 2007 and promises to help apostates who depart Islam. It lists an expanding worldwide network of ex–Muslim affiliates in Austria, France, Germany, Iran, Morocco, New Zealand, North America, Pakistan, Scandinavia and Turkey.

The Pakistani website operates from outside the country; my Internet browser warned me the Iranian one was a hazard to my computer; Morocco claims to be the first site within a Muslim nation, (created in 2013) but it runs off Facebook; and Turkey is constitutionally bound to allow freedom

1. Sahih Bukhari, "Volume 9, Book 84, Number 57," para. 5.
2. Sura 2:256

of religion, so they formed an atheistic society in April, 2014—no website as yet.

While social pressure may keep you in the church, that is lessening by the day in the West. Declines in church attendance are a well known fact. Most leavers simply drift away. However, again, not so in the Samoan community. A tight social bond of an immigrant people is paralleled two hundred meters away from the mosque on that Auckland street.

Is Globalization an extension of man? Perhaps it is better defined as an outcome of many factors including international monetization, the emergence of the global labor market, and of course mass travel. Christianity and Islam are indeed global religions, but then so are all the others, even the minority Bahai. Globalization goes a long way back, to Rome actually. The Roman Empire built new cities, moved people to and fro disrupting their lives, and incidentally, thereby laid the groundwork for the spread of Christianity. Romans could post a letter from Rome to Alexandria in Egypt, and if the winds were right, it could arrive in eleven days. That's still a relatively quick time in 2015 via surface mail.

Gone are the days when the forces of Islam matched those of Christendom. Gone are the days that the West feared Europe would be defeated by vast Moorish armies. Today global events involving the two religions are both peaceful and military. In a strange quirk of fate, millions of Muslims have emigrated to nations outside the realm of Islam. For about 50 or 60 years, Muslims have left their Middle Eastern homelands and moved permanently to the West—to earn more money and live more stable lives.

A much smaller niche of Westerners live in the Middle East organizing oil production or building ridiculously high skyscrapers for the princes who own those oil fields. Whereas Westerners seem to be able to settle into South East Asian communities and mix with locals, very few fraternize with Middle Eastern communities. Most pull out of Saudi, Dubai, or UAE, when they have bankrolled themselves. That is the experience of many expatriates who have lived in both regions.

Let's not ignore people movements within the Third World itself. As mentioned elsewhere, the Mandingos migrated south from the Sahel into the forested nations of West Africa, bringing their Islam with them. A very different Islam too, without veils for the women. In fact the Mandingo women seemed like the economic engine of their community when I lived amongst them. More to our point though, they were somewhat equals with the local Africans. True, they moved there for work, but not to clean loos.

No, they developed their own businesses, enterprises that local tribes could have organized themselves to their own chagrin.

Perhaps this attitude was behind the Mandingo self confidence. Waiting at the garage near a mosque one day, a crowd emerged. One very black, beautiful Mandingo middle aged lady walked up to me and engaged me in conversation. As that twenty six year old, I had no idea how that could have led to her death in some Muslim–majority nations. I recall the genuine smile from her eyes, and her inner beauty decades after she walked away from that two minute discussion, and her gratitude for my coming to her village to teach young Africans.

We will focus on Muslims moving to the West, the powerful, rich, intimidating West. Those millions of Muslims that emigrated to Europe don't want to return. At least one must assume that given their deliberate strategies to remain, and build their own communities and mosques. Obviously Muslims have moved to other Western nations, but the numbers are stacked mostly in Europe. You can readily find Youtube videos on the Islamization of Europe but not many on the Islamization of Australia or Canada.

COMPARING MEASUREMENTS

One feature of Globalization is mankind's ability and penchant to measure and compare himself across the world. Such surveys are less than one hundred years old, but are now so common we resist mall questionnaires, let alone telephone interviewers. Statistics is definitely an extension of man, allowing him to examine life spans, health, income, food intake, education, and attitudes. Statistics, as a science, began about 1749, according to Wikipedia. Statistics are based around probability theory, which appears to be a four letter word in many Islamic circles, as we discovered earlier.

That's not a good start then, because it hints at iniquity. Muslims aren't alone. Christians, and Jews too, share an Old Testament tale about the evil of statistics.

- Then Satan stood up against Israel and moved David to number Israel.[3]

David went ahead anyway despite advice, and later had to choose between three evils God offered him. It is a fascinating episode with

3. 1 Chronicles 21:1

ramifications rolling through cultures to this day. Thousands of years ago at least one society felt it was immoral for the government to just know of your existence—not even your personal existence, just the fact you were counted. Today we have no qualms about census taking, ages, maladies, education, and all sorts of data being collected about us.

Our problem today is with particular forms of data, and particular collection methods. Western society doesn't want data collected about themselves via the Internet, and they're not very crisp on what they don't want either. A famous founder of the world wide web called for an international Magna Carta in 2014[4] to keep the Internet free from various sins.

My, how times have changed over the past three thousand years.

Anyway, here we are today, collecting global statistics. And wouldn't you know it, the activity is organized by the West. The most prolific gatherer of worldwide religious statistics is Pew Research. They are located in Washington, USA, about as close to the heart of the Great Satan as you can get. I tried, but could not locate, an institute based in the Middle East running indepth global religious surveys. I did discover The Middle East Media Research Institute (MEMRI). In their words, MEMRI, ". . . explores the Middle East and South Asia through their media. MEMRI (does) . . . original analysis of political, ideological, intellectual, social, cultural, and religious trends."[5] And they too are based in Washington DC.

Pew Research have conducted surveys on religious tolerance and religious hostilities since 2007.[6] The news is all bad for Muslim–majority nations. There are over two hundred nation states in the world today. Pew list twenty as having the worst religious restrictions. Fourteen are Muslim–majority nations, mostly from the MENA region. Islam's Far Eastern outposts, Malaysia and Indonesia, are also included.

Government restrictions on religion

The MENA region has the highest religious hostility index of 4.4. The next highest is Asia–Pacific with 2.2, dropping away to the Americas at 0.4. Pews rationale includes examining politics and law. For example, Egypt permits residents to convert to Islam, but not to leave. That is illegal. Pew attempt to be as objective as possible, and have lots of scientific credentials. The reader is invited to examine reports at www.pewresearch.org.

4. "An online Magna Carta," para. 1.

5. "MEMRI," para. 1.

6. "Key findings about growing religious hostilities," line 1.

Pew data is freely available to anyone. See their global map on Government restrictions on religion here.

Who are the victims of these religious hostilities? Christians consistently suffer more hostility in more nations than any other religion.[7] Islam is second. A quarter of the Middle East was Christian in 1914. Today it is less than 5 percent, and the new term Christianophobia has been raised about the plight of believers in the MENA region. Now that we know how to run our own surveys on Google, I searched on the single words in Google in February 2015;

- Islamophobia—About 4,380,000 results.

- Christianophobia—About 63,500 results.

This is a rough measure of how often the word appears in statements, websites, and public media at that time. It is not a measure of whether the issue is worse or not. Don't value Google searches above what they reveal. They measure noise, not rights or wrongs.

Google isn't the only alternative to Pew Research. In another survey, conducted annually by Transparency International, the global coalition against corruption, other unfortunate statistics emerge. In 2013 eight out of the ten most corrupt nations on earth were Muslim–majority nations.[8]

Pew also run surveys measuring how people in the MENA region feel about the religious freedoms of others in their midst. In their 2013 report, Pew say this about the inhabitants of Muslim majority nations; "In 31 of the 38 countries where the question was asked, majorities of Muslims say people of other faiths can practice their religion very freely."[9]

To summarize then, the MENA nations have the highest religious hostility index, yet if you ask their own people, they think everyone is free to practice their particular religion, including Christians. This disparity might help us understand the Islamophobia word. Perhaps Muslims are unaware their own nations repress other religious beliefs, and cry foul when it seems to happen to them.

It turns out there are plenty of Muslims who think the Islamophobia word is misused. Tarek Fatah, a Muslim originally from Pakistan but now living in Canada, felt so strongly he wrote a book about it. A group of Muslims in Canada including leading figures from the Canadian Arab

7. "Religious Hostilities Reach Six-Year High." para. 36.

8. See "Corruption by country."

9. "Key findings about growing religious hostilities," section 2, subsection 5.

Federation, the Muslim Canadian Congress, PEN Canada, University of Toronto, University of Calgary, and York University, submitted an article to The Toronto Star which included the following;

> A curtain of fear has descended on the intelligentsia of the West, including Canada. The fear of being misunderstood as Islamo-phobic has sealed their lips, dried their pens and locked their keyboards. Canada's writers, politicians and media have imposed a frightening censorship on themselves, refusing to speak their minds, thus ensuring that the only voices being heard are that of the Muslim extremists and the racist right.[10]

A former UK Salafi sister told about her experiences in the movement, which is part of the Sunni sect; "Salafis were told to shout 'Islamophobia' if the Police ever tried to investigate any of their 'community affairs,' I was told this was a tried and tested tactic that always worked."[11]

TEXTS FROM THE WEST

My next stop on the globalization trail was to understand how Western Muslims think about their worlds. I say their worlds because they live in two; one is their location in a Western nation, and the other is what they identify themselves as. Many Muslims think of themselves as Muslims first, then their nationality second.[12] That's what dualist means. Obviously some Muslims were wary about the Islamophobia word, so there was no single body of thought.

Let's remember that religious leaders need to be cautious in a world sending their words instantly around the globe. Both Christianity and Is-lam have their no-go topic zones, and these are made much clearer today by readership statistics and reviews. Neither Pope Urban nor the Caliph Umar had to contend with such extensions of men long ago. But today, stepping outside the accepted window of opinion can quickly be identified, and equally rapidly, destroy your following.

An example of this occurred in 2011 with the publication of, 'Love Wins: A Book about Heaven, Hell, and the Fate of Every Person Who Ever Lived.' The author, Rob Bell, was a rising star in the U.S.A., with followings

10. Fatah, *Chasing aMirage*, 316.
11. *"Salafi exploitation,"* para. 3.
12. "How Muslims See Themselves," para. 1–2.

around the Western world. Bell even got on Time Magazine's top 100 most influential people list in 2011.[13] His book relayed a message very close to Universalism, which is still that sticky topic in Christianity despite all the websites talking about it. Bell intimated nobody goes to hell, although without specifically stating it.

It was close enough though. Following the book's release, Bell fell from favor with mainstream Protestantism, summed up neatly by a tweet from respected evangelical pastor John Piper; "Farewell Rob Bell."[14] His Time 100 listing provided no cushion to the fall. Several pastors in New Zealand warned their flocks against the dangers of Universalism, accompanied by many more in larger nations. Bell spoke outside the window of acceptable discussion that his following permitted. Although these windows change over time, that's only acknowledged in hindsight, and as of 2011, Universal Reconciliation was still too close to the core.

There are many spectrums within Islam including writers who do not want to risk their mainstream readership, and others who make a reputation out of castigating their faith. Outsider views are interesting to outsiders, but their views may be ignored inside the religious camp. We're entering a video driven world too, so I read many books by Western Muslims and watched lots of videos, before settling on three titles and one movie as a short representation of opinions. And finally, remember it's important to pick up what is not said as well as what is. Our titles are;

- Umosqued. It's a one hour documentary movie about the current state of mosques in the United States. Many mosque leaders and attendees are interviewed.[15]

- The Future of Religion: Traditions in Transition, Edited by Kathleen Mulhern. In 2012. This is a collection of many authors writing about many religions.

- Western Muslims and the Future of Islam, by Tariq Ramadan, in 2008. We've already learnt this Swiss born academic keeps opinions to himself.

- The Trouble with Islam Today: A Muslim's Call for Reform in Her Faith, by Irshad Manji. Manji has no problem questioning anything within Islam, resulting in her book being banned from Malaysia.

13. See "2011 Time 100."

14. "Mark Driscoll Responds to Rob Bell Controversy on Hell," para. 15.

15. "Unmosqued."

Some qualms were apparent in the Unmosqued movie, but they somewhat mimic the squabbles in any suburban church. One lovely old lady went on about how they erected a wall in her mosque, cutting off women from communal prayer. It reminded me of the complaints of elderly parishioners about noisy toddlers in the play space at the rear, matched by retorts from young mums who feel they shouldn't be excluded from sitting in services with their offspring.

Made in 2013, the website told me it was based on research by Dr. Ihsan Bagby entitled, The Mosque Studies. Dr. Bagby comes to an interesting conclusion; "The mosques of America are healthy and growing, but mosques are still in the initial stage of development and many deficiencies are visible. Overall Muslims should be proud of the accomplishments in this pioneering phase of mosque development in America. Future prospects also seem extremely bright."[16]

However the film doesn't illustrate this. Person after person tells stories about how male oriented the mosques are, how attendance is declining, and how Imams are always appealing for more funds. Of course it was heart rending to hear that old lady weep about when the wall was put up, and how she hadn't returned to the mosque. On a positive note, a team of young people got together and planned a successful takeover of their ancient mosque board of governors. All in all, the film is worth watching, but again, what is not said is very interesting. Not a single word is spoken about global violence in the name of Islam. This topic does not appear to exist in conversations in American mosques about their problems.

Mulhern's collection was a compilation from several religions. The first article in the Islam section had an off putting title: 'Twenty First Century Islam: A Lived, Dynamic And Nurturing Religion.'[17] Nothing new there. It repeats what we already know—that militants have misunderstood the Qu'ran about Jihad, and that it is really spiritual warfare, not with AK47s. It gets to the point that Muslims should accept they're not going to get Islamic government in the West; ". . . the future of Islam as a lived, dynamic, and nurturing religion for the 21st century hinges on the liberal world–view gaining ground among Muslims. I am cautiously optimistic that this will happen because that is the more historically credible and morally compelling alternative . . ."[18]

16. Bagby, "American Mosque 2011," 26.

17. Mulhern et al., *Future of Religion*, location 2941.

18. Ibid., location 2988.

She clearly believes in the re–mythologizing of Islam. To suggest it is a more 'historically credible and morally compelling alternative ' was a great phrase in 2012. It wasn't so believable in 2014 and 2015 considering the IS backed up their every beheading and slaughter from historical sources.

The easiest article to read in Mulhern's book was entitled 'Big Tent Citizen Islam.' The author, Eboo Patel, compares an integrated model with 'civil war Islam,' which everyone hopes to avoid, and 'bubble Islam,' the protective cocoons where old men cluster, lament the morals on TV, and worry that the kids won't come to mosque.

> Citizen Islam encourages Muslims to vote, join the PTA, lead volunteer projects, join interfaith coalitions, run for office, do the whole Toquevillian American participatory thing.
>
> Big Tent Citizen Islam has slowly but surely become the domi-nant trend in American Muslim life over the past twenty years.
>
> So welcome to the American scene. Big Tent Citizen Islam. Please stand alongside your cousins, Big Tent Citizen Christian-ity and Big Tent Citizen Judaism; both of them know what you have been through. Congratulations on becoming an American religion.[19]

I love the terminology, and admire his rosy eyed summary, but Amer-ican religion is at the shopping mall. Just as cathedrals were at the centers of medieval villages, tying the community together that gathered there, so shopping malls now attract more Westerners than any other communal activity. The other American religions Patel lists are harmless affairs, with rock bands, glitter and other trivia, but pale in comparison to the faithful supporting the retail economy.

Ramadan betrayed a hint of reflection in his book on Western Mus-lims, as in this paragraph, deliberately selected for its scarcity:

> Muslims may feel safer in the West, as far as the free exercise of their religion is concerned, than in some so–called Muslim coun-tries. This analysis could lead us to conclude, on the basis of the criteria of safety and security, that the description dar al–islam is applicable to almost all Western countries, while it can hardly be given to the great majority of actual Muslim countries, whose population is 60, 70, 80, or even 95 percent Muslim.[20]

---

19. Ibid., location 3125–3148.
20. Ramadan, *Western Muslims*, 67.

But that's it. Mostly Ramadan is like this;

> The intellectual revolution we are referring to here is extremely demanding, as we shall see in part II: it compels us, from within, as free citizens in societies under the rule of law, to strengthen our faith and to use our intelligence to find solutions and alternatives to the problems of our societies—to move from integration to contribution, from adaptation to reform and transformation.[21]
>
> "the way of faithfulness" is a way that leads toward more justice, and civic and political involvement in a society of whatever kind must move in the same direction.[22]

That's an intriguing claim considering he admits Muslim–majority nations are unsafe. He knows there is no successful Muslim case study to refer to. He does not have an Islamic proof story to demonstrate more justice. Many Westerners also know this, and fear that Muslim 'civic and political involvement' in their society will result in 'transformation' of their own nations to parallel actual Muslim–majority states, not the theoretical ones Ramadan conjures up.

I personally agree with a lot of Ramadan's perspectives on the declining morality of the West, its trivia, its noise, its materialism, and all the other things grumpy old men like he and I complain about. But that's just showing our age. To suggest however that every problem needs an indepth brainstorming session with the local ulama, and the issuing of a fatwa, is not an imaginative leap forward, but it will gain acceptance amongst his readership.

Not once does Ramadan mention anything along the lines of the surveys of Pew or Transparency International. Not once does he mention the trouble Christians have building churches in the Middle East. Not once does he mention that the Muslim–majority nations tend to be grouped at the foot of the religious tolerance ladder.

How could such a leading spokesman leave all these items out, especially when writing a book for Muslims living in the West? The plain answer is he can't risk being labeled an enemy of Islam. This in fact has happened to him at least once. Ramadan tells what happened when he opposed the death penalty in Pakistan. "I have been criticized. I have been just put outside the realm of Islam. For example in Mauritius, the mufti of Mauritius

---

21. Ibid., 56.
22. Ibid., 165.

was saying, "Tariq Ramadan is kafir murtad." If you know Arabic, kafir— "infidel"—in the way he was using it, murtad—"he is an apostate."[23]

Ramadan has very little room to maneuver. Neither can Pope Francis let us know his real thoughts on homosexuality. He might even be called an enemy of Christianity. In our mediatized world, he and Ramadan can only issue tidbits.

To see how appalling life was in Britain for the folks Ramadan had to be concerned about, I Googled 'Muslim support agencies in Britain.' Their extent is astounding. Community groups, University courses, self created support groups, political messages of support, and more, adorn any search list gathered by Google. The dangers of Islamophobia are trumpeted left, right and center by political and community groups of all persuasions in Britain. With very little work, I found the following list of positive white papers, reports and books on Islam in Britain;

- Mosques & Youth Engagement, Guidelines & Toolkit

- Contextualising Islam in Britain, Part II

- Muslim Women and Shari'ah Councils—Transcending the Boundaries of Community and Law

- Young Muslims, Pedagogy and Islam: Contexts and Concepts

- At Home In Europe: Muslims in London

- Minority legal orders in the UK: Minorities, pluralism and the law

- Islam and the English Enlightenment, 1670–1840

- Wandering Lonely in a Crowd—Reflections on the Muslim Condition in the West

- Young British Muslims and Relationships

- 7/7 Muslim Perspectives

- Meeting the needs of Muslim women—A directory of mosques in England

- Sport, Muslim Identities and Cultures in the UK: Case studies of Leicester and Birmingham

- You Can't Put Me in a Box—Super-diversity and the end of identity politics in Britain

- Islamophobia and Anti–Muslim Hate Crime: a London Case Study

23. "Conversation With Tariq Ramadan," para. 136.

One starts to appreciate Ramadan's comment. After all, Britain did have a thousand year learning curve with colonialism, so perhaps they are finding that making smartphone apps is better than making war. Towards the end of that thousand years they finally realized that healing and reconciliation were good ideas, especially in the decades following Bloody Sunday in 1972 in Northern Ireland. Conway put the challenge neatly in that context; "Unwilling to view the Northern Ireland state or the regime that coordinated it as legitimate, Catholics defined their identity in opposition to the identity of Protestants thus creating a social world of two opposing identity categories of 'us' and 'them'"[24] If we think about 'us' and 'them' in today's context, we might have a clue why all those papers above were written, and those helpful agencies exist.

I next Googled for 'Christian support agencies in the Middle East.' That list turned out to be a combination of two different agendas; firstly those Western bodies drawing attention to the plight of oppressed Christians in the Middle East; secondly offshore headquartered aid organizations present in the Middle East on World Vision like tasks. In other words, there don't seem to be any organizations of Middle Eastern origin set up to support minority Christian groups in those Muslim–majority states.

Most Muslims in Britain emigrated from Pakistan. Is it reasonable to compare Pakistan's work with its Christian minority to British work with its Muslim minority? I started to think that gets you nowhere until I read Irshad Manji.

Irshad Manji rips into Muslims around the world. She's visited Israel, and finds it okay. She brings up the Banu Qurayza beheadings, the first time I found a modern Muslim remembering that episode rather than trying to forget it. If the conservative Ramadan gets called an apostate, Manji is a serial offender judging by Internet searches. It's not surprising as Manji goes right for what she thinks is the jugular—Muslim lack of introspection; "For all our denunciations of Islam's fringe sickness, Muslims studiously avoided addressing the paralyzing sickliness of the entire religion—the untouchability of mainstream Islam."[25]

Her solution is; "Not j–i–h–a–d, but i–j–t–i–h–a–d"[26] Simply put, Ijtihad is self reflection. Muslims claim that is part of their religion, although she felt the gates closed on independent thought in the twelfth century, and

---

24. Conway, "Active Remembering," 15.

25. Manji, *The Trouble with Islam Today*, 49.

26. Ibid., 50.

Muftis took over patrolling the truth.[27] Manji relishes in exposing ironies such as;

> Why do the Saudis outlaw Christian activity on their soil while financing a Center for Muslim–Christian Understanding in Washington, D.C.? Who, exactly, needs this "understanding"? What lessons from the center have the Saudis applied at home?[28]

She is definitely outside the window of influencing Muslims. She is not a lone voice. Mona Eltahawy, an Egyptian journalist based in New York, inflames fellow Muslims with her opinions, sparking a response entitled; "Dear Mona Eltahawy, You Do Not Represent us"[29] which blamed gender inequality on that perennial whipping boy—colonialism.

Amazon does more than sell us these books—it indicates who reads them. Ramadan's intellectual tome is read by fewer people, but the two biggest review marks, out of 12 in total, are four and five stars (at the top). Manji is read more and received 261 reviews. Her reviews are clustered at both ends of the spectrum—one star and five stars. Manji is read by Muslim and non–Muslim Westerners—and possibly by Ramadan behind closed doors. People love her or hate her. She polarizes opinion, whereas Ramadan would never risk that.

No balanced, middle point of view, exists in this debate. All sides use the same sources, constantly use the word 'truth,' and quote different verses from the Qu'ran and the hadiths. For example another book, 'The Truth about Islam and Jihad' sets about proving, convincingly so too, that Islam has always been militant. Written by an American and an ex–Muslim, it lists verse after verse condoning violence in the Qu'ran.

From the other side comes 'Their Jihad, not my Jihad.' Written by a Canadian Muslim who emigrated from Pakistan, the reader is drawn into the devastation the writer feels over the way violent militants have "hijacked"[30] her religion. She passionately tells us, convincingly so also, how she spends "valuable time and energy informing non–Muslims about the true interpretation of jihad (moral, intellectual and spiritual striving) and that violence and suicide are forbidden in Islam."[31]

27. Ibid., 144.
28. Ibid., 181.
29. "Dear Mona Eltahawy," line 1.
30. Raza, *Their Jihad*, 15.
31. Ibid., 38.

THE BISHOP, THE MULLAH, AND THE SMARTPHONE

The authors of 'The Truth about Islam and Jihad' fear for the future, hinting hopefully that a wonderful Islamic leader will bring Muslims out of their chaos.[32] Hopefully also, they grasp how carefully such a leader must tread, and the narrow window of influence they would have. The Canadian Muslim lady weeps because her heart is torn, but she does appreciate that Western immigration agencies do have a challenge at the airport gate, and compliments their overall courtesy whenever they quiz her.

Both subconsciously refer to the re–mythologization occurring in Islam, without using the term. The first book claims; "This belief about militant jihad held near unanimity until modern times."[33] On a return visit to Pakistan, the second author is amazed at the violent turn the whole nation seems to have taken while she lived in Canada.[34] She finds common cause with Ramadan that Islam has taken a wrong turn in Muslim–majority nations, and being a peaceful Muslim in the West is much happier.

The main point is that both want the same thing—a non–violent faith. One side cannot admit they ignore events from their past, while the other cannot see that telling them that has no effect.

DEFINING ENEMIES

We are probably all guilty of reading books and watching documentaries that agree with us. Amazon and Youtube track our purchases and viewing to suggest new reading and videos based on what we are already consuming. So we can't expect a technological solution to any biases we have. It might be nice to imagine an intuitive system could be built that eventually said, "Woah, you've read enough from that sector, we need to supply you with knowledge from another viewpoint."

I'm dreaming. Neither Amazon nor Youtube have tick boxes with that option.

Unfortunately each side of an opinion can be led further along their respective spectrums until they reach the point where the other is deemed as wicked. All those layers of media and mythology have a role to play in this too. The first thing to grasp are those comparisons we referred to earlier. Even within a nation. Residents of Arkansas used to joke, "thank God

32. Ankerberg and Caner, *Truth about Islam*, 60.

33. Ibid., 24.

34. Raza, *Their Jihad*, 34–37.

for Missouri" as their own state often ended up ranked forty ninth out of the fifty United States of America.

'Down the bottom of the ladder' is a common phrase now, but it wasn't in an international sense four hundred years ago. Neither people nor nations knew much more than size of armies and weapons of their opponents (always the first media to get noticed, remember). Now we know how long they live, what they earn, and how much that Big Mac costs in their nation.

This rather obvious point frequently gets left out of the discussion. If you live in a poverty stricken nation, you probably know that, whereas you didn't long ago. Even if you're not fully aware of the numbers proving it, you've seen it on television. Even if, like the poor residents of Calcutta, India, you watch TV through the window of a nearby shop, you'll think your city looks grimy compared to the ones paraded on that screen, including during the adverts.

Globalization changed the value we place on information as happened to my school boy friend Sam. Forest or local knowledge has been bested by digital media, television and newspaper. The world outside our local horizons has been exposed to all of us. And, unlike Sam's forebears in the jungle, most of it is information we cannot act on. Worse than that, most of the information we receive is unpleasant.

All Westerners and most Middle Easterners receive a deluge of particles of information, news about a train crash, bad weather, or a rock stars divorce. Hundreds of bits of information, mixed with about three thousand brand visuals, are showered upon us daily. There is no coherence to all this, and since most news highlights things that went wrong, we tend to think we are in a world falling apart. No news is delivered on the tens of thousands of trains that arrived safely, just the one that was derailed.

This plethora of data is like a painting of a million dots, with many blank spaces, that is paraded in front of us. We cannot see a coherent picture, just a bewildering array of colors. News reporting being what it is, it cannot connect these dots together as it has to move on and show us fresh ones.

We even joke about what is revealed to us, and our lack of power to do anything; "In our house I make all the important decisions, like how the US should reorganize healthcare, or when the IMF should call in loans to Argentina. My wife does all the unimportant stuff like who we are visiting on the weekend, and where we're going on holiday."

These factors lay us open to propaganda, according to Ellul. He used the word as the title to one of his books, the subtitle being 'the formation of men's attitudes.' It was reviewed by Marshal McLuhan, and published in the 1960s, long before the resurgence of militant Islam. We think propaganda belongs back in those evil ages of Nazism or Stalin's communism in the USSR. However propaganda is a bedfellow to ideology, religion and myth. And, according to Ellul; "propaganda aims less at modifying personal opinions than at leading people into action."[35]

The propagandist provides us with an answer, a reason behind all we see, an explanation of the canvas. Communism excelled in this area. A good communist could explain everything. I once heard how the architecture of modern houses, with multiple bedrooms, was simply a capitalist outcome, illustrating the individualization of society, whereby we all had to have our own unique space. One assumes communists would have designed dwellings where we all slept together as in the Middle Ages, and everyone was then content, nestled in alongside sweating, snoring others.

It's only a little over 150 years since we started to receive news from far away. There is the old tale how the telegraph company trumpeted their aim to connect Texas to Maine, and Thoreau's comment in 1854 that, . . . "Maine and Texas, it may be, have nothing important to communicate."[36]

At best, in that earlier era, news from far away was interesting, but mainly irrelevant apart from those smoke signals warning of danger. Rich Londoners had horsemen waiting in Plymouth for ships from the Orient so they could have news about India raced to them, but that only occurred at that end of the social scale. Mostly it was sad to hear of warfare or farming ruin in another nation, but mostly there was little we could do about it. More than that, it was not connected to us. Similarly, if we suffered financial disaster, that was not something we generally blamed on a country far away.

Globalization changed all that. Now we learn of distant tragedies all the time. International guilt and blame are bound up with this news, and to a degree, this has truth in it. The global money system affects everyone when it coughs. This cycle of guilt and blame is daily foisted on a population of ordinary people that can do nothing of themselves about it. The poor learn that someone else, far away, is responsible for their poverty, and the rich hear it's their fault. Some of the rich believe it too, which is why

35. Ellul, *Propaganda*, 207.
36. Thoreau, *Walden*, 43.

more international empathy can be found in those populations. This, too, is measured. Western citizens feel more guilt for misery far away.[37]

In fact both demographics watch much the same events, from much the same media channels, and feel much the same impotence to alter the situation—middle class Westerners feel powerless to change injustice, and so do poverty stricken Middle Eastern denizens.

Whether we are Pakistani, Samoan, American, French, or Malaysian—CNN, BBC and Al-Jazeera channel the same stuff at us. There is much more commonality than societies had prior to say, 1500AD. Not only that, but it is delivered via a commonality of media. Given that 'the medium is the message' we all hear and see and follow the same information via newspaper, TV, radio or the Internet.

That is way, way, less than the multiplicity of local communications before the digital age. Just think of the information signals provided by mother nature that we no longer know how to interpret: squirrels chattering in the jungle, moss on trees, flower budding patterns, geese flying north, and supple bark for ropes. These were usable signals for communities and individuals.

A Lakota Sioux Indian named Lone Dog recorded a calendar that tells us about an earlier period of information. He drew a single picture on the same buffalo robe for each year, illustrating the main annual incident. The Time Life book on it tells us; "The span of time runs from 1800 to 1871, the major period of white invasion. Yet the white man plays almost no direct part in this pictorial history. Lone Dog's winters include seven references to trade with the white man and four references to epidemics of such white man's diseases as measles and smallpox. Surprisingly there is no indication of battles with the white invaders, yet there are 24 symbols referring to intertribal conflicts."[38]

During that era, the American Civil war, purportedly involving the entire USA, ran its course. It's not listed on the robe. This is an example of a people immune from global news or propaganda. They were still concerned with their own challenges and lives, and certainly not impacted by CNN. Their news was mostly taken up with local, real events that you could act on, like being careful when visiting the trading post because you might fall ill.

---

37. "The Great Divide: How Westerners and Muslims View Each Other," page 2, para. 3–6.

38. Korn, *Old West*, 20.

It's not a wider intake channel today—it's narrower. Very few of us today could understand the rich and wide range of content conveyed through natural or cultural information channels. They're just tourist attractions now. Real news today, proper information, comes packaged in printed or digital media channels, and they implicitly tell us we are helpless to fend off these global problems.

In a single word, we have been mediatized. We no longer know how to think outside a media driven world.

Now that today's media are in place, the propagandist has all the elements he needs to mobilize a crowd into action. That is his challenge. He needs something to work with though. If the propagandist can connect aim, passion and energy, then he has a crowd he can direct. He is not interested in getting the crowd thinking, just action.

Let's introduce Ellul's two types of propaganda. He wrote about Agitation propaganda and Integration propaganda; "The former leads men from mere restatement to rebellion; the latter aims at making them adjust themselves to desired patterns."[39]

Ellul used the example of propaganda during the years France clashed with Algeria, a French colony in the post World War 2 era. On the one hand the Front de Libération Nationale used agitation propaganda along the lines of, "You are unhappy, so rise and slay your master and tomorrow you will be free."

A French government response (not actual, but representative) was one of integration propaganda. "We will help you, work with you, and in the end all your problems will be solved."[40]

Of course the first message had more appeal.

Ho Chi Minh used agitation propaganda to motivate North Vietnam to drive the Americans out during the Vietnam war. He persuaded his people of the tyranny of American imperialism, which had an element of truth in it. Meanwhile the Americans were trying to persuade the Vietnamese that communism would put them in chains, which also had an element of truth in it. In the early 1970s the Americans didn't grasp that the communist economic system wasn't going to produce wealth, so their integration propaganda was along the lines of political freedom. It was a complex argument posed by foreigners with big guns, so it never caught

39. Ellul, *Propaganda*, vi.
40. Ibid., 79.

on with a suspicious North Vietnamese mind set who had been overrun by external powers for centuries.

Ho Chi Minh won the hearts and minds battle, leading perhaps four million of his countrymen to their deaths. America left, and Vietnam was rewarded with twenty five years of poverty before they realized that communism was not going to feed their teeming millions. Eventually they changed their minds about Uncle Sam, and Kentucky Fried Chicken and McDonalds have outlets there today.

Agitation propaganda requires a clean division of right and wrong. Whether we like it or not, even the apparently morally correct sides divide wicked from righteous. It's easy pointing at propaganda case studies within Nazism. It's not straightforward acknowledging the so called good guys practice it too. I saw it with my own eyes during the 1981 anti South African Springbok tour protests in New Zealand. The anti tour movement strongly felt that allowing a South African rugby team to tour New Zealand tacitly supported the then Apartheid regime of South Africa. They organized protests throughout the country. I listened to a debate raging one day in the Victoria University of Wellington cafe as to whether the anti–tour movement should apologize for some violent acts by some of its members. Eventually an exasperated speaker rose to the microphone. "No outrages have been committed by the anti tour movement. All outrages have been committed by the police."

And that was the end of the discussion. The students marched out, inspired by their own righteousness, to act against the wicked forces of the state. Do not misinterpret this episode to mean that the writer supported the South African Apartheid regime. Such a conclusion is what the propagandist indeed wants. He does not want thought or reflection about events, he wants action. This activity is also known as scapegoating, or assigning any guilt away from the core group.

None of this is to say that the actors in either agitation or integration propaganda exercises are not well intentioned. New Zealand sent personnel to Afghanistan to build schools and infrastructure as part of the coalition from 2002 to 2014 to rebuild the nation. Although they sometimes ended up hunting insurgents, New Zealand's main aim was humanitarian, and they pointed with pride at the roads and schools and education achieved. Islamist agitation propagandists simply interpreted that as a veneer, disguising the real intent of the West, which is to dominate and destroy Islam.

Persuasive arguments from a powerful party tend not to be believed. Listeners think they must have an agenda, and to an extent they do. However passionate arguments from under–gunned voices also have agendas. They just sound better coming from an underdog. Today, in the West by and large, integration propaganda works. Forty years ago there were plenty of people against the system in all Western nations. 1970s youth watched films like 'Easy Rider' or the groundbreaking surfing movie, 'Morning of the Earth' portray happy go lucky, freedom loving, dope taking, motor cyclists, riding Hogs across the US of A, and marijuana smoking surfers living hippy lives in vacant houses near the coast. Anyone who was anyone attended Woodstock, a music festival in 1969 blatantly promoting hallucinogenic and sexual freedoms.

That would never do today. Now we work with at–risk youth, getting them off the drugs portrayed in those films, and trying to stop teenage pregnancies. We implore them instead to make a difference to society by attending a corporate sponsored surfing contest, or getting on a list of 100 leading young activists.

Another example is rising city house prices in much of the Western world. There is very little angry dissent by today's youth about this. They do not protest on the streets. Instead they are taken in by banking adverts, real estate persuasion, financial experts and vague government promises to redress the problem. Inequality of this nature in the past led urban dwellers to take to the barricades, and break into the homes of the rich.

This is not to say that getting youth off drugs is not a good move. Of course it is. It is actually a good example of how government and corporations have successfully moved us away from those sixties freedom movements by focusing on their obvious flaws. Aging hippies and surfers wonder what happened to their dreams of growing vegetables near the beach, making wooden surfboards, and installing solar powered hot water. They can't figure out why modern surfers are busy smartphone app developers, rushing down in their shiny new Jeeps for a few lunchtime waves. Explain integration propaganda to them however, and they nod sagely, fingers trembling as they look around for another joint.

They can easily look at finance too, and the bondage of people to huge mortgage debts unknown in the 1960s. We might think those chains of debt are immoral, but we don't need to wonder why it slips under the radar. Integration propaganda integrates people into society when all is said and done. Having a huge debt on your house ties you into the social contract, and keeps you loyal to the system. Many other examples emerge along the spectrum of propaganda. The worst place to sit on that spectrum is where we think only the people at the other end are subject to propaganda, and we're not.

To summarize then, information as we understand it today, which is the packaged printed and digital stuff, is a prerequisite for widespread global propaganda to emerge. Compare that to local awareness about when to plant your crops. Such self sufficient societies have no need for propaganda, and to a certain degree can resist it. Break down their self sufficiency, overload them with worldwide information, and you have cleared the slate for propaganda. It then comes at them from various angles, depending on different contexts.

How does this fit in with religion?

We can find it by observations of time separated mimicry. If we compare Christianity during World War 1 with some Muslim–majority populations today, we find some interesting similarities.

The Church of England was still on the side of the battalions in World War 1, as it had by and large been since at least the Crusades. They swung virtually completely behind the war effort. Bishop Arthur Winnington–Ingram of London was one of the most outspoken and patriotic proponents of the war and head of its most prominent diocese. He claimed to have added ten thousand men to the armed services with his sermons and other recruiting.

Fielden showed that initially the church did not vilify the enemy, until the threat to the English way of life by German civilization was underway;

> Propaganda became an important tool during the war and one in which the Church was a willing participant. The pastors and their leaders became both participants in and "victims" of propaganda. Most Anglican ministers found it hard to believe that the civilized Germans could be responsible for the atrocities claimed in the initial stories. However, the burning of Louvain and especially the university library there, the publication of the Bryce report, and finally the sinking of the Lusitania all were decisive in changing their minds. Once their faith in German civilization had been breached, nearly every atrocity story in circulation was believed and transmitted by the pastors to their flocks. In fact, the religious press spent the entire conflict extolling the virtues of giving

"without stint, and without flinching, the blood of his sons to the national cause."[41]

We know that young men lied about their age to join that war, and millions flocked willingly to European battlefields from all over the world. Early twentieth century communications, media, and propaganda, were good enough to summon men from all four corners of the globe to die in muddy trenches. Metaphorically, Maine now had plenty to tell Texas.

Not only that—military commanders had the power to order men to their certain deaths. They would climb out of their trenches and run towards machine gun fire that was absolutely bound to kill them. It seems incredible now that millions of soldiers firstly went to war, then that many of them obeyed those suicidal orders. But they did. None of these strategies would work today in the West. To my knowledge, not a single Western church blesses soldiers promising them a stained glass window like the one in Tenby if they are slain in the current War on Terror.

This form of Propaganda was able to run its course during that war. The propagandists had an aim—fight and win the war. They had a passionate argument that linked church, sacrifice and nation together. And they had a receptive population. Lots of other media elements were there as well including those clocks and train timetables that had to be obeyed. Don't ignore the naval race as Germany tried to mimic British sea–power, nor the mythology of the nobility of battle.

One small challenge existed—the enemy had the same religion as the English. That required some points of differentiation. Of all media, literary criticism (termed higher criticism then) was dragged out of the cupboard. The Germans were painted as the worst enemies of all, the ones seeking to subvert Christianity from within.[42]

So when the church reached that stage, they were able to use the most absurd arguments to persuade men to action—'the virtues of giving "without stint, and without flinching, the blood of his sons to the national cause."—and millions believed, obeyed, and died, on both sides.

Here is Ellul on the outcome of successful propaganda;

> Everywhere we find people who have blind confidence in a political party, a general, a movie star, a country, or a cause, and who will not tolerate the slightest challenge to that god. Everywhere we meet people who, because they are filled with the consciousness of

41. Fielden, "Church of England," 40.
42. Ibid., 30–33.

Higher Interests they must serve unto death, are no longer capable of making the simplest moral or intellectual distinctions or of engaging in the most elementary reasoning.[43]

As we relayed earlier, provision of information began to alter after World War 1. Communication media began recording the carnage and the death toll wrought by new weaponry. The churches support of military engagement withered after that. Seventy years later—a short period in religious terms—the church had mostly shrugged off its thousand year folly of supporting armies, and began to rediscover its roots in non-violence.

And so to some Islamic parallels.

Ellul gave an opinion about the use of propaganda in this setting in the 1960s;

> In an Arab country colonized by whites, in view of the Islamic ideology that has developed hatred for Christians, a perfect predisposition to nationalist Arab and anti-colonialist propaganda will exist. The propagandist will use that ideology directly, regardless of its content. He can become an ardent protagonist of Islam without believing in the least in its religious doctrine.[44]

It is not uncommon to see a violent crowd demonstration in Pakistan or Iraq or Libya or Egypt, either destroying a church or burning the US flag or an effigy of a President. It happens immediately after a reported incident far away. Without either proof or investigation into the story, a crowd explodes onto the street. Action occurs, purportedly due to an outrage committed on the other side of the world.

Islamic ideology has become highly usable by political bodies in many Muslim–majority nations. The media pieces are all in place. Muslim–majority nations are aware they are poor apart from an oil rich elite; statistics and TV does that. Much self sufficient information has been marginalized, and they are connected into international media. The rich world is displayed daily to them, reminding them of their inferior status, and their inability to alter it.[45]

---

43. Ellul, *Propaganda,* 273.

44. Ibid., 198.

45. This very point has been examined by an economist. Carvalho built a convincing argument that; ". . .the contemporary Islamic revival is based upon two forms of relative deprivation—envy and unfulfilled aspirations." See Carvalho, "A Theory of the Islamic Revival," 1.

Various accusations including the impact of colonialism, global businesses, and environmental destruction have been laid at the door of the West. These are not enough to hit the go button though. A highly passionate mantra is needed. The action clause is that the West is an enemy of Islam. This brings people out on the street. 'Enemy of Islam' is the neatest, simplest passion available in Muslim–majority nations and it provides a moral rationale for their predicaments. Rights and wrongs are neatly sorted out. It is usable by propagandists against anyone, including other Muslims. Here is an example published in 2014 recalling events in Iraq shortly after the fall of Saddam Hussein in 2003. Note that this is not after a dozen years of war there. It occurred just after Saddam fell, when the locals were joyfully pulling down his statues;

> An American arms dump had just exploded in a residential suburb. Nearby houses that had withstood weeks of allied bombardment were obliterated. Families were wiped out. But what was striking was how quickly public anger was channelled. Within an hour there was a "spontaneous" demonstration of Iraqis—hundreds, perhaps thousands, strong—already with printed placards and leaflets blaming the Americans for deliberately endangering the lives of Iraqis. I went along. I marched with them, interviewed them for television. One man told me, in fluent English, that "the United States of America is the enemy of Islam, it is written so in the Holy Qu'ran."[46]

To say that the word America does not appear in the Qu'ran is too simplistic. This man would have been told it is there, or shown a verse intimating it.

In September 2014 the Islamic State published some of the most abhorrent video footage ever aired, as they beheaded prisoners online. A masked IS militant, dressed in black, cut the throat of an American journalist captured some months earlier after intoning;

> "I'm back, Obama, and I'm back because of your arrogant foreign policy towards the Islamic State. . . despite our serious warnings. We take this opportunity to warn those governments that enter this evil alliance of America against the Islamic State to back off and leave our people alone."[47]

46. "Faceless men," para. 11.
47. "Islamic State 'beheads US hostage," para. 17–18.

How could this executioner completely ignore atrocities his side committed, and blame others in such a self righteous tone while slitting the throat of a journalist? Answer: he had been propagandized not to reflect on his activities, but to act for a higher interest.

The same process of propaganda works fighting internal as well as external foes. After many years of investigation, the Iran Tribunal in The Hague published findings concerning the approximately 20,000 political prisoners who were slain during the purges of the Ayatollah Khomeini in the 1980s;

> In the 1980s the Islamic Republic of Iran went about arresting, imprisoning and executing thousands upon thousands of Iranian citizens because their beliefs and political engagements conflicted with the regime, the judges wrote. The religious fervour of these crimes makes them even more shocking: for instance, a womans rape was frequently the last act that preceded her execution in Iran, as under the Sharia law guidelines, the execution of a virgin female is non–permissible.[48]

Competing forces of agitation and integration propaganda were demonstrated in Ohio in October 2014. From a town ironically called Dublin, a name synonymous with Christian sectarian strife and a history of agitation propaganda, US Muslims asked their government for help; ". . . parents and community leaders are expressing growing fears that their youths may succumb to the Islamic State's savvy social media appeal to join its fight on battlefields in Iraq and Syria."[49]

The New York Times was likely referring to the online IS Dabiq magazine, which anyone in the world can download. This was the agitation propaganda segment, and the community recognized it as such. They then blamed the government for not doing enough. Perhaps they don't yet grasp that the US government knows it will be blamed for everything wrong in the world, yet is continually dragged into scenarios in the belief it can fix them. Omar Saqr, the young cultural center's youth coordinator, said; "Our relationship has to be built on trust, but the U.S. government hasn't given us very many reasons to build up that trust."[50]

---

48. "Iran's Srebrenica: How Ayatollah Khomeini sanctioned the deaths of 20,000," para. 5.

49. "U.S. Is Trying to Counter ISIS' Efforts," para. 1.

50. Ibid., para. 4.

This was despite the fact the FBI and the Department of Homeland Security had attempted to forge ties with community leaders. However, like any government departments, they had both blundered in their efforts. The departments acknowledged this. Bureaucracy hasn't changed in the past three thousand years;

- If you see oppression of the poor and denial of justice and righteousness in the province, do not be shocked at the sight; for one official watches over another official, and there are higher officials over them.[51]

The nation's top homeland security official told the NY Times; "We can't allow youth to fall prey to ISIL's ideology. We need to provide them an alternative to rechannel their hopes and rechannel their passions."[52]

We can see a glimmering of integration propaganda in his words, but the departments were still on a learning curve—they had an infiltration strategy. They wanted local community groups to help them ferret out would be jihadists. A comment by the National Network for Arab American Communities was understandable; "I don't know how we can have a partnership with the same government that spies on you."[53]

The US government had forgotten how to conduct successful integration propaganda efforts. As we learnt earlier, Muslims did not move to America or France or Britain or New Zealand to fight infidels—they went there to find work, buy a house, and raise happy children. Only they couldn't find good work. Many ended up cleaning toilets, or unemployed, especially so amongst the testosterone laden youthful demographic.

Two generations have passed since the South East Asian domino theory which was thought to usher communism into Australia after stepping nation by nation down from impoverished Communist China. After that awful war in Vietnam, the West changed tack and ensured people got work in the next domino to fall to communism, which was Malaysia. It's a simple formula, and classic integration propaganda—people will trade an AK47 for a job.

Perhaps the Department of Homeland Security will try this one day, but history says it takes a while to figure out an effective integration propaganda platform. There are a lot more pieces to organize on the chess board than an agitation propagandist needs. And unfortunately, economic

51. Ecclesiastes 5:8
52. "U.S. Is Trying to Counter ISIS' Efforts," para. 18.
53. Ibid., para. 32.

circumstances are against them. Would that the world emerges from a recession caused by bankers.

Use of the wartime camera has evolved over time. The violent Islamist movements exploit this same media device that undermined Christian wartime support, to further their militant cause. They don't own CNN, but they crave attention and supply their own video footage. Proof of their very existence relies on the news corporations. Are they not students of history? Do they not wonder whether those same media devices will eventually be their demise? There are many views on this, especially since we are dealing with our recall of war which has historically been very mythological as we have seen.

It's tempting to think that well thought logical analyses was applied before the IS showed videos beheading reporters in 2014. It seems incredibly stupid that the IS would video those hundreds of soldiers they shot after they had surrendered. Perhaps they're just dumb boys with guns, cameras and Internet connections. The camera was rare in World War 1 and Youtube didn't exist. Now they're both available to anyone. Then again, as in Dublin, Ohio, maybe the videos will strike a chord with young men who want to solve world problems with firearms. We don't know, and that is the whole point. A wide array of opinions on the causes and outcomes of these various extensions of man are aired all the time. And only time will reveal what happens.

No one knew how the evolution of graphical media in combination with the Internet would change the rules. Whilst some claimed that there was a photo that ended the Vietnam war, a thousand stills and videos of worse barbarity than that one are uploaded to the Internet daily today. A single photo means nothing any more. The Israeli Prime Minister probably felt Gaza was gaining the upper hand during their mid 2014 mutual rocket firing on each other when he said; "We're using missile defense to protect our civilians, and they're using their civilians to protect their missiles."[54] He was hinting at the publicity gains of Hamas when all that footage emerged of schools and innocents being bombed. Nobody can prove the truth or falsity of this statement, but there is no denying who won the media war in their 2014 round of violence if the numbers of protest marchers supporting Gaza were added up.

Photographs of beheadings have been available for 80 years. I have an old history series periodical showing the actual sword swinging as a

---

54. "Huckabee: America keeps world guessing," para. 3.

Chinese warlord dispenses 'justice' on the street in the 1930s. That photo did not halt the warlord nature of pre World War 2 China, nor did it result in protest marches in London. It could not because other extensions of men were not present, among them the speed and ungovernable nature of image transfer, and the concept of the global community. There was no United Nations or NATO available to pass condemnations or provide a multinational peace keeping force.

So the US walked into Iraq in 2003, at best to dislodge a tyrant. Youtube did not exist until 2005, nor its many covert competitors that you might view atrocities on if you search long enough. The US used 'shock and awe,' a spectacular display of military force strategy that came out of the National Defense University of the USA. Designed to paralyze the opposition rapidly, it seemed to do just that.

It was more successful than June 1916, when General Haig ordered a million and a half shells flung from 1,537 guns at the German trenches over the course of a week. This largest military engagement fought since the beginning of history resulted in 60,000 British deaths on the first day. They swarmed out of their trenches to attack what should have been a demoralized enemy after that bombardment. No one imagined the Germans could have built such deep dugouts, or just how quickly they could get their machine guns mounted once the bombardment stopped.

Based on those numbers the US in Iraq were well ahead, losing far less men in twelve years than Britain did in a day. However, both campaigns suffered from that lack of imagination. No one imagined that the tyrant was not the issue in 2003 Iraq. In fact there are so many opinions about what the real problem is that the world didn't really know what to do about the IS problem in 2015 Iraq apart from bombing them too. All we do know is everyone, from the US to Al Qaeda to the Islamic State know and recognize that half of any war in the MENA region is now a media battle for hearts and minds.

It is that way because it can be that way. Anyone can upload the most grisly movie. Somehow it is not possible to stop that on the Internet. Al Qaeda had learnt as early as 2007 how to swirl around within 4000 different websites to confuse detectors, and quintupled their annual video output from sixteen in 2005 to ninety in 2007. Either Youtube or the idea of Internet as TV was a godsend to them.

We have another incredible thing to imagine then. Imagine if we had told General Haig that one day men would take movies of the shelling and the soldiers perishing on barbed wire and show them to the world about one hour after it had happened—and that neither the army nor any government in the world could stop that happening. Would General Haig have been promoted to Field Marshall, as he was, seven months after his campaign, if such videos had been distributed then?

In complete recognition of the current battlefield for hearts and minds, the US State Department released its own video in September 2014[55] showing the same gruesome acts committed by IS with US text additions. Phrases encouraged viewers to come to Iraq so they could learn new skills like blowing up mosques. It almost looked like IS made it. However it was a deliberate parody, a subtlety some viewers didn't get. It was a State Department attempt to get to the at-risk hearts and minds in America, showing the pointlessness of IS. It was attempting to show realities beneath the agitation claim to, 'rise, slay their masters, and then they will be free.'

Who knows whether these or any other messages in this turbulent age of many media will be effective? The point of this whole book is that we will not know the outcomes until later. We're probably no further ahead than General Haig, possibly behind due to the multiple extensions of men we've constructed since. And it might not stop soon because Islam faces two problems that Christianity has been moved on from with less effort.

Firstly, Islam still condones the rights of Muslims to defend themselves. Even top Islamic scholars insist Muslims have the right to fight back if attacked. It's all there in the Qu'ran,[56] which is unfortunately useful for the propagandist arsenal of the militant Islamists. Thirteen hundred years ago, it was simpler to define who was attacking you: they were closer, within sword or spear range. In today's complex world of drones launched from afar, of international peace keeping forces, of soldiers shooting insurgents in between building schools in Afghanistan, those boundaries are very blurry.

That Islamic edict was interpreted by one young man in London in 2013 as permission to kill any militia that had served in the Middle East. It was taken by Osama bin Laden as the divine right to fly hijacked jet planes into the World Trade Centre in New York. So, as much as Muslims living anywhere are concerned, they are in a bind. Even Western Muslims defend that right to resist, but the modern playing field makes it hard to differentiate between resistance, retribution, and revenge.

55. "See brutal anti-ISIS video," line 1.

56. Sura 2:178–179

Secondly, formal Islam still clings to the theory that it runs both political and spiritual sides of life. Pure Islam wants to govern nations. It is a religion of laws when all said and done. Christianity used to be like that too, but the church was pulled away from running nations.

Will integration propaganda win the overall day? Maybe. We can see more evidence of change beyond Mr Cameron's claim that violence has no place in Islam. Since 2002, Pew Research have reported a; "Much diminished support for suicide bombing."[57]

Statistics show a gradual drop in the approval of suicide bombing since surveys began. Some of these stats are still high, as in the Palestinian territories where suicide bombing support dropped from 70 percent to 62 percent between 2007 and 2013. Some nations seem to have no pattern, such as Turkey which jumps around between 3 percent and the 16 percent support it returned to in 2013. Pakistan saw the most identifiable trend, support falling rather evenly from 33 percent in 2002 to 3 percent in 2013.[58]

So, at both local and central government level, volunteer agency, and even commercial sector, there are widespread integration initiatives along Ellul's lines of, "We will help you, work with you, and in the end all your problems will be solved."

The same information comes through the same channels to everyone. At the top of the ladder, governments call on vast resources of expertise to advise the best moves they should make as they juggle political, social and financial data. Western governments have little interest in religion beyond lip service, but they are concerned with social harmony. It is in their interests to promote both a peaceful Islam and a peaceful Christianity.

Are the emerging mythologies of Western peaceful Islam in the interests of a burgeoning Muslim population now entering its second and third generation in Britain? The only answer possible is yes. The deeper question is whether it will be seen to be in the interests of that demographic, by that very demographic. It might be touch and go with our hiphop friend, Manifest ONE.

What about Christianity?

Christianity is more easily able to rediscover peaceful roots from its early days. Some may be offended by this claim, but one of its founders

---

57. "Muslim Publics Share Concerns about Extremist Groups. Much Diminished Support for Suicide Bombing," line 1.

58. Ibid., para. 10–16.

did advise people to love their enemies, whereas the founder of the other religion advised followers to defend themselves against enemies. We all accept that Christians didn't do what they were asked for centuries. Nobody is denying that. But it's an easier path back if a founder recommended it.

Christianity is in a different bind due to that rediscovery however—irrelevance. As it has discarded regime support, regimes have discarded church roles in guiding political leaders. Since Christianity by and large no longer supports territorial expansion, or the maintenance of nations based on armies and navies, it has been dropped from the West's political arsenal.

Remember we live in a so called post–Christian era. People interpret this as a decline in belief, but perhaps it's not. Perhaps post–Christian really means that world powers have discarded it as a viable pawn to use in their global chess games. In other words, its beliefs and ideologies have become unusable politically. As such it has been reduced to private belief, rock band churches, and prosperity doctrines.

Of course there are still Christians acting covertly to shift Western governments towards military aggression. But the party is over for Western right wing Christian political parties. If they contain the name, like the Christian Democratic Union of Germany (CDU) founded in the late 1940s, it's an historic anachronism. Despite being in power since 2005, it was only in 2012 that the CDU's leader, Angela Merkel, stated publicly she was a Christian. New political parties in the West with the word Christian in them don't succeed. Many Christians are embarrassed by them in fact.

Pew confirmed this in September 2014.

> Nearly three–quarters of the public (72%) now thinks religion is losing influence in American life, up 5 percentage points from 2010 to the highest level in Pew Research polling over the past decade.[59]

True, this is mixed because the traditional denominations want to see more political involvement, whereas those with no religion want to see less—but non–religionists are gaining numbers at the expense of denominational loyalty. Perhaps if those same Christians were aware that Western Muslims are less supportive of Sharia than they used to be, they wouldn't complain so much.

Ellul summed it in his style of language fifty years ago;

---

59. "Public Sees Religion's Influence Waning," para. 1.

> Christians are caught in a psycho–sociological mechanism that
> conditions them to certain practices, despite their attachment to
> other ideas. Those ideas remain pure ideology because they are
> not being taken over by propaganda; and they are not taken over
> because they are not usable. In this fashion, such an ideology loses
> its reality and becomes an abstraction. It loses all effectiveness in
> relation to other ideologies being used by propaganda.[60]

Even Hitler had his own way of phrasing this according to Albert
Speer, Hitler's Minister of Armaments and War Production, who wrote a
memoir of his World War 2 experiences while serving a twenty year prison
sentence imposed by the Nuremberg tribunal. Speer quoted Hitler as often
saying something like;

> "You see, it's been our misfortune to have the wrong religion. Why
> didn't we have the religion of the Japanese, who regard sacrifice for
> the Fatherland as the highest good? The Mohammedan religion
> too would have been much more compatible to us than Christi-
> anity. Why did it have to be Christianity with its meekness and
> flabbiness?"[61]

So Eboo Patel, a well meaning young man undoubtedly, who is the
founder of Interfaith Youth Care, and a member of President Obama's
Advisory Council of the White House of Faith–based and Neighborhood
Partnerships, can be understood when he welcomes Big Tent Citizen Islam. He, and officialdom in the USA to the highest level, want Islam in the
modern religious camp that is out of the war theater, and into the zone that
votes. He is to be applauded for this.

And if he is right, Islam in America will be neutered, just like Christianity is undergoing, shorn of political clout, set to music and social work.
These are of course the safest and best outcomes anyone could hope for. A
refusal to bear the sword, and acts of helping the poor, are the best existen-
tial choices any person can make in today's world.

Just like Christianity though, the corollary is that Muslims will end up
ignoring other issues of our time, such as housing, health–care inequality,
the international money circuit, and our continuing focus on fossil fuels.
Their political efforts will be expended on modern democracy, which is the
celebration of personalities and fine differences that attempt to cover up

---

60. Ellul, *Propaganda*, 201.

61. Speer, *Inside the Third Reich*, 96.

that vast machine termed 'the system' that President Obama found impervious to the vote.

Integration propaganda at its best.

8

THE CITY

CHUGGING BACK INTO PORT at the natural world heritage site in Ha Long bay, Vietnam, I struck up a conversation with a fellow tourist. It turned out this Canadian had been advising Hanoi on sewage as his home city had links with the council there. He had been mentoring a lady in Hanoi for years.

"One lady," I prodded.

"Oh, yeah," he affirmed. "She's pretty smart though."

"I mean there is one lady managing the sewage system in Hanoi?" I wanted to get my point across.

His head shook with bewildering acknowledgment. "I know, I know. Ten million people. They don't know where to start, that's their main problem. You see, all decision making was centrally organized. Now they have to think local."

My mind started to boggle. "Gee," I mused out loud, "how do you start charging ten million poor Vietnamese people taxes so the city government can build a sewage system?"

"Exactly."

"Hang on, are you telling me there is no sewage system there now?" I asked.

"No, they do have one," he replied, "but it's small and antiquated. The city is growing perhaps ten percent a year. Another million per annum."

Good grief. The population of Auckland is added every year. Imagine trying to persuade first world Aucklanders to pay for an entirely new city-wide sewage system, let alone the citizens of Hanoi.

"You think that's a problem?" the Canadian prompted. "What about water? Hanoi loses a fifth of the water it pipes in. They say Ho Chi Minh City loses a quarter. It's siphoned off or it leaks through faulty pipes. Imagine if they try and introduce taxes for using water? How many more people will tap illegally into a city pipe rather than pay?"

Good grief again.

Less than one week later we walked the streets of central Hanoi on Christmas Eve. This purportedly communist nation is singular for having thrown out three superpowers—China, France, and the USA. On a wide sweeping boulevard, the mortal remains of their hero Ho Chi Minh are still guarded night and day by soldiers in white parading around a giant Soviet–grey mausoleum.

Near the old town center stands the St. Josephs Roman Catholic cathedral, and would do any European city proud with its stained glass windows, including a Crusader like knight, and the stations of the cross. The area draws upwards of one million Vietnamese in on Christmas Eve. Finally, tourists feel safe crossing streets, because they are so clogged with cheery scooter riders that walkers can weave comfortably through the stalled, happy throng.

If you follow the crowd, it will lead you to the cathedral, with its annual display of the angels and the manger and the mother and the child. Walk up three flights of stairs and secure an outdoor balcony table at the protective rail of Marilyn's restaurant, and you are in for an evening of wonder, provide you slowly pay your way through the entrees, the mains, the dessert, and the coffee.

Not a hint of drunken behavior is apparent from the huge crowds who all attempt to find a square meter or two later near the city lake to lay an evening picnic rug down. Despite the fact we probably looked like Americans to the North Vietnamese, they waved happily and returned any greeting or wisecrack with laughter.

The cesspool. The cathedral. The crowd. All part of the city.

Christianity is ambivalent about the city. Ellul wrote a heralded work entitled "The Meaning of the City" pointing out a rather obvious myth. Cain, the first murderer in the Bible, is credited with building the first city.[1] That might have been problematic considering he was only the third human being, and an outcast at that. After God confronts him over the slaying of his brother Abel, Cain realizes he has lost the protection of God. So he builds his own security—a city.[2]

Ellul also alerts to us to something that seldom gets mentioned about cities; "the city is one of the rare invariables of civilization, considered both geographically and historically."[3] The city is not blamed on colonialism, capitalism, socialism or television. Worthy versions are desired by all nations without demur, such that we could agree with Ellul that, "the city is man's greatest work."[4]

Other Christians love their cities, especially those appointed Bishops or Archbishops over parishes or ecclesiastical land. Ellul recognizes this creation of man finally gets accepted by God however, and by the time we get to the other end of the Bible, God has provided man with a new city. It's a holy one called the new Jerusalem,[5] the very city held in reverence by Muslims, Christians and Jews.

Muslims don't seem to have this ambivalence and our Google search results return an interesting pair of numbers;

- "the city in Islam" About 216,000 results

- "the city in Christianity" About 107,000 results

Today many Muslim writers laud the Islamic city, actively remembering the words of their famous philosopher, Ibn Khaldun;

> "Furthermore, towns and cities with their monuments, vast constructions, and large buildings, are set up for the masses and not for the few. Therefore, united effort and much co-operation are needed for them. They are not among the things that are necessary matters of general concern to human beings, in the sense that all human beings desire them or feel compelled to have them. As a matter of fact, a(human beings) must be forced and driven to (build cities). The stick of royal authority is what compels them, or they may be stimulated by promise of reward and compensation. (Such reward) amounts to so large a sum that only royal authority and a dynasty can pay for it. Thus, dynasties and royal authority

1. Genesis 4:17
2. Genesis 4:15
3. Ellul, *Meaning of the City*, 150.
4. Ibid., 154.
5. Revelation 21:2

are absolutely necessary for the building of cities and the planning of towns.

Then, when the town has been built and is all finished, as the builder saw fit and as the climatic and geographical conditions required, the life of the dynasty is the life of the town."[6]

Mind you, Khaldun also distrusted the seductive force of an easier urban life, warning that a harsh desert existence is better for mankind.

THE CESSPOOL

The city is both the worst and the best of mankind's achievements and is continually evolving. From ancient times we have the wicked city, the eternal city, the city of joy, and the city of water. Modern cities take on mantras like Auckland, New Zealand has, with the largest marina in the southern hemisphere bolstering its claim to be the city of sails.

In reality, none of these used to be cities by modern standards. Jerusalem had a population of about 40,000 during Jesus' time, and Mecca was possibly only 10,000 strong when Muhammad returned. There had only ever been one super-city in Europe and the Middle East housing almost a million people, and that was Rome. And yes, Rome had a sewage system, which you could link to if you were wealthy enough. In his Natural History, Pliny remarks that of all Rome built, the sewers were; "the most noteworthy things of all."[7] Without going into details why, by the time a city reaches a million, it needs a sewage system. Trust me on this claim.

Not that life was all peachy once the sewers were built. Householders had to hand carry waste water to a 'manhole.' An easy alternative was to pitch it straight out of a third storey window onto the street below in the hope it would find its own way by gravity thereafter. Poems were written about the risk of venturing into the street without first looking up.

Do not laugh. When the Singaporeans began to be shifted from villages to high-rises in the 1960s, the hazard of the falling TV set was frequent. It took tropical denizens, whose natural environment decayed organic rubbish quickly, some time to realize that tossing an old washing machine off your fifth storey balcony didn't remove your problem—and possibly created a worse one.

---

6. Ibn Khaldun, *Muqaddimah*, section 2:235.

7. "Sanitation," section 2, para. 4.

So Rome got by with an inadequate system compared with today. Viewed from our hindsight, ancient Rome would be a disease ridden, stinking warren, of temporary houses interspersed with the odd stone building. Most residences were not built from rock. Only the rich could afford to erect those villas we see in movies like 'Gladiator.' Yet Rome sucked up taxation money from the provinces like a vacuum cleaner.

Since 1900 the motorcar, electricity, the railways, and new building technology, dwarf any previous layers in large cities. The modern city bears no comparison with Rome, whose million residents disappeared with its empire, or indeed London, the second European one to reach a million a long time later—in 1750 AD. London was a cesspool at that stage. Today, that twenty million strong megalopolis is cleaner than ever, and fish swim again in the Thames river.

How could all this happen? How could cities balloon beyond any historic sizing? And how can they be operated effectively? Religions have attempted to shape cities, right from Cain's time, and religions have also been shaped by them. We're going to look at one aspect only, and that is whether Islam, this religion conceived in the desert, but planted in a small town, has answers about running the sewage system of a megalopolis.

We begin with taxation. Taxation is an extension of man from long ago, that is continually worked on. As the second guarantee after death, of course taxation is mentioned in the Bible and the Qu'ran. The medieval church grew rich from its taxation revenues, enabling them to build all those stone cathedrals that lasted much longer than the third storey tenement buildings with splash marks on their walls. Small wonder that Henry VIII wanted to expropriate them from Rome as part of his Protestant reformation, only to waste it on unsuccessful military expeditions.

Monarchs spent a lot of tax revenues on war, and that tactic can yield dividends—if you win. Don't forget that people were learning to count in the Middle Ages with the spread of decimal taught to them in church sponsored schools. We know that sixteenth and seventeenth century gentry put much effort into educating their sons, and with that learning it's reasonable to suggest that English society saw through the Kings wasteful use of money. One thing is certain—they rebelled against it in the early seventeenth century, and Charles I could not get the cash he wanted from Parliament, so he ruled without them for a while. The ensuing civil war tore English families asunder with all sorts of groupings under religious banners fighting each other or moving to North America in search of a

New World. Squabbles about money and the divine right of kings were eventually won by Parliament in the Glorious revolution of 1688, which installed the earliest form of the powerless English monarchs that now grace celebrity magazines. However, once they were in power, Parliament found it was one thing to protest about taxes, and it was another to run a country.

Hello. Welcome to democracy. To say tax burdens didn't decrease is an understatement.

Professor Voth illustrated how England just got better at taxing her own people. Spain, on the other hand, who were the prime world superpower around 1550, didn't need to get good at internal revenue deductions because much of their finance came from the silver mines they found after they dislodged that Inca king.[8]

When a silver mine ran out, or some ships didn't get past Sir Francis Drake's pirate fleet, the income stream proved lumpy as they say in the tax revenue trade. When all the mines ran out, the lumps turned into huge holes. Unfortunately Spain let time pass by without learning how to efficiently tax their own subjects, and they never got a steady income stream going before it mattered. This is not the only reason Spain fell down the super power list only 100 years after they led the world, but it's a significant one. English tax takes climbed and climbed, which meant they could spend more on important things like battleships, which in turn led to waging successful wars.

Voth also makes the strong argument that higher taxes are positively linked with higher overall income. Although that sounds contradictory at first blush, it's not. It's not hard to imagine that a rational economic government builds infrastructure like railways, docks, power stations and the like because industry improves and you enter a positive revenue cycle.

So, incrementally over the years, the English government learnt how to implement effective taxation, a prime example being taxing the Scots. One government minister, after the Act of Union with Scotland of 1707, had a valid point when he said that, "some method should be taken to make Scotland pay the taxes, but could any ministry hit upon that method?"[9] Somehow the English cracked that supreme challenge of tapping into that rawest of Scottish nerves, which is the wallet. Gradually the denizens of the Western world realized they had to pay central government taxes, and following that, city corporation levies. In the middle of this, power had shifted

8. Voth, "Debt, Default and Empire," film.
9. Ibid., film.

not only from king to state, but the church lost its foothold too. In 1802 Jefferson used the phrase 'separation of church and state' for the first time, because, in hindsight, it had happened. This was a far cry from the Holy Roman Empire, which by its very name strongly hints it was a territory ruled by God, or at least by his earthly representatives in the Latin city.

It had taken a long time to happen. Christianity entered its political power phase around 330 AD with Constantine, and it lasted another 1300 to 1400 years. Coincidentally Islam has been in a political power phase for about 1300 to 1400 years as well, but that is certainly not a deliberate mimic. Islam has always claimed it is a unitary religio/political force. To this day many Muslims believe the mosque cannot be separated from the state, which ultimately means they refer to the Qu'ran and the Hadiths for guidance on taxation.

That's an interesting position because if you want to run a nation today, including maintaining sewage systems and roads, building schools, installing high speed broadband lines, and keeping public zoos running in an eco-friendly manner, then it's fair to ask if Muslim tax policy is up to the task. Either central government or your city council pays for that as Hanoi well knows. In 2004 New York City told its residents it was spending between $17 and $24 billion on maintaining and upgrading its sewage system. They are expensive beasts to operate.

Muslims do not come empty handed to this challenge. Lots of Westerners will agree wholeheartedly with our first quote attributed to the prophet. "the tax collector will not enter paradise."[10]

Despite that comment purportedly from Muhammad, the Qu'ran itself outlines a number of taxes that Muslims have implemented over the centuries. Let's get the bad news ones, in terms of non-Muslims, over with first;

- And know that anything you obtain of war booty—then indeed, for Allah is one fifth of it and for the Messenger and for his near relatives and the orphans, the needy, and the stranded traveler, if you have believed in Allah and in that which We sent down to Our Servant on the day of criterion—the day when the two armies met. And Allah , over all things, is competent.[11]

10. Zalloom, *Funds in The Khilafah State*, 91.

11. Sura 8:41

Actually, the Spanish kings also took one fifth of the proceeds from their silver mines. They were too busy doing other things to organize all that pillage themselves, and those shipping, labor, and contractors fees, all add up.

Revenue from war booty is fine—until you start losing. Then the rate of return takes a serious dip. Rolling empires forward on the basis of successful conquest has been attempted several times since Alexander the Great built his enormous land holdings before he turned thirty. He died before his newly liberated subjects had time to complain about the lack of good latrines between Greece and India, so we will never know the full extent of the infrastructural improvements he may have had in mind. The same problem struck our old friends in the Ottoman Empire. Following their defeat at the battle of Lepanto in 1571, the enraged Sultan built a new fleet within six months. But it never sailed due to mounting debts. To simplify the issue, imagine you no longer have territorial ambitions, but you still want to run a strictly Islamic economy. Strike that 20 percent of revenue from booty off.

As part of the re–mythologization going on though, we are now finding that the phrase 'war booty' (or khums in Arabic) in Sura 8:41 is wrong. This sura can evidently be re–translated into English, replacing 'war booty' with 'acquire' as follows;

- Know that whatever of a thing you acquire, a fifth is for Allah, for the Messenger, for the near relative, and the orphans, the needy and the wayfarer.[12]

The author of this idea claims there are six other meanings of 'acquire' apart from 'spoils of war.' He warns the danger is; "thus confining the obligation of khums to the spoils of war only. This interpretation is based on an ignorance of the Arabic language."[13] That's a handy concept to justify that fifth back into the coffers.

Next is the infamous Jizya tax, mentioned way back to the Persians in the eighth century as an option to converting to Islam. Jizya is a payment by non–Muslims for the protection offered them by their Muslim rulers. Here's the Qu'ranic injunction;

- Fight those who do not believe in Allah or in the Last Day and who do not consider unlawful what Allah and His Messenger have made

---

12. "Khums: 20%, an Islamic tax," slide 8.

13. Ibid., slide 9.

unlawful and who do not adopt the religion of truth from those who were given the Scripture—fight until they give the jizyah willingly while they are humbled.[14]

There was some logic to jizya, in that you couldn't expect non–Muslims to help fighting infidels, since they themselves were vanquished infidels. Jizya tax rates often exceeded 20 percent, sometimes up to 80 percent, and were a great cash–flow for the Moghuls, the Muslim rulers of India. Their subjects were overwhelming non–Muslim, and had to pay. For some reason the Indians didn't like this tax and rebelled in 1679. Despite protests and riots the Moghuls crushed the dissenters.

Jizya is not so acceptable on grounds of religious discrimination today, and would be tough to push past human rights lawyers although it was still charged illegally in Egypt in 2013.[15] So it too, gets stripped out of the peaceful Islamic economist's modern taxation scheme.

Kharaj, or land tax, used to be an option, apart from one major sticking point today—we're talking about urban areas here, not farming communities. Back when the kharaj was the main source of state revenue, the economy was agrarian.

All is not lost however, because one of the five pillars of Islam is Zakat, or giving to the poor. This 2.5 percent is incumbent upon all Muslims to pay. Dedicated Muslims believe that the true Islamic man would naturally pay zakat, which would make Islamic society the most just on the planet. Christians might claim the same thing, and after all their 10 percent tithe is four times bigger than the Zakat. If we all gave something, willingly, and the aid agencies didn't have those serious internal costs, then yes, the world would definitely be a better place.

The Zakat concept has received a boost from an interesting Western source though—Thomas Piketty began to transform global thinking in his book, 'Capital in the Twenty-First Century.' He proposed a global tax based on capital assets as well as income. Simply put, it would be a tax on wealth. Given that people get rich through accumulating capital assets, not income, economists think he has a point. Zakat is a wealth tax. It didn't originally differentiate between income and capital assets. Many problems exist in finding out how much the rich own because they split it up and store it around the world. Piketty proposes an international global tax to get

14. Sura 9:29
15. "Egypt Christians Killed for Not Paying 'Jizya' Tax," line 1.

around this, and here he is aligned with theories of the worldwide Islamic economy which would be instituted with the global Caliphate.

This would only work however if it was compulsory because we already have evidence of how many Muslims and Christians voluntarily pay their Zakat or tithe. The Barna Group informs us that only 12 percent of born again Christians in the USA voluntarily pay their Christian tithe.[16] Singapore instituted a government department that accepts voluntary Zakat from Muslims.[17] Since Singapore loves publishing numbers, average contributions from Muslim households can be calculated, and it works out around 0.11 percent, a far cry from 2.5 percent.

It didn't used to be voluntary with Christians, and with compulsory always come evasion. Unschooled European peasants proved remarkably clever at outwitting church taxmen. French farmers mixed non–titheable with titheable crops to confuse the collector when he came, or to prove the former were the majority crop, therefore the tax was not valid in that field.[18]

Whereas the legal tithe disappeared with the French monarchy after a thousand years, compulsory Zakat was introduced into Malaysia as recently as 1955. Unwilling to pay since the surveyed villagers claimed never to have seen a dollar returned to the poor of their community, they termed the tax the zakat raja, insinuating it went into the Sultan's palace. Techniques of evasion were practiced resulting in only 11 percent of small farmers paying Zakat in the 1977 to 1979 seasons.[19]

Scott makes the obvious point about these two scenarios, vastly distant from each other in both time and space; "The resistance of the French peasantry to the Catholic tithe, until its abolition shortly after the Revolution, bears a striking family resemblance to Malay evasion of the zakat raja."[20]

Perhaps 88 to 89 percent of Christians and Muslims are not yet perfected. It's all a question of theoretical balance according to Weiss; "It would be the responsibility of the Islamic state to care for the social welfare of all people, whereas the primary role of the Islamic norms is to make the

16. "American Donor Trends," para. 13.

17. "Zakat Calculator," title.

18. Scott, "Resistance without Protest," 444–447.

19. Ibid., 429.

20. Ibid., 437.

individual member of Islamic society, homo islamicus, socially responsible and altruistic."[21]

He's almost saying if enough Muslim teaching was applied, that percentage of willing givers would be much higher. It's somewhat parallel to Karl Marx. He told us that a communist government was but an interim step. Once we were all safely ensconced on collective farms sharing our Skoda vans, we would lose any desire for the latest BMW, and the state would be superfluous. It would wither away. He and Lenin both acknowledged there would be some pain getting there, but the outcome would vastly repay any inconveniences imposed during the journey. Be that as it may, our internationally politically acceptable, non–compulsory, Islamic state today, would have to survive on a tax rate of 2.5 percent that only 12 percent of its flawed citizens paid.

To return to the bottom layer of the city, I am of the opinion that sewage is the least attractive social improvement you can put on the volunteer list. Protesters wanting to change the world don't march with placards asking for assistance in maintaining the sewage system of Lahore, Pakistan, where the pipes have not been upgraded since independence in 1947. (That's sixty seven years. Actually some Roman pipes lasted one thousand five hundred years, so all is not lost yet.)

Based on the New York City costs, and the relative population of either city, an upgrade and maintenance program for Lahore will cost $2000 from every one of its five million residents. Who will persuade those five million, whose average annual income is about $1200, that they all need to pay this to the Lahore City Corporation so their toilets will continue to flush? In fact the; "entire city's sewage is discharged, untreated, into River Ravi."[22] This is the challenge our seasoned Canadian could not answer about Hanoi. If we are to learn anything from the British, who installed the Lahore system when they ran the place, it is that it takes a long, long, long time before you get all those people paying taxes for something as mundane, yet as necessary. Position this in the context of Islamic taxation;

> The Muslim ruler was caught in a dilemma—to increase taxes and face the possibility of a revolt or to stick to the ideal and face a financial crisis. This dilemma provided Ibn Khaldun with his theory of the rise and fall of states as well as Ernst Gellner (following Ibn Khaldun) with his notion of the 'permanent Islamic revolution':

21. Weiss et al., *Social Welfare in Muslim Societies,* 10.

22. "On providing sewage," para. 3.

"But what would happen . . . if some authoritative cleric, having with some show of plausibility denounced the impiety and immorality of the ruler, thereby also provided a banner, a focus, a measure of unitary leadership for the wolves? What if he went into the wilderness to ponder the corruption of the time, and there encountered, not only God, but also some armed tribesmen, who responded to his message? This ever–latent possibility hangs over the political order, and is perhaps the Islamic form of permanent revolution."[23]

Another parallel, communist strategy, comes to mind, this time behind Mao tse tung's Cultural Revolution in China in the 1960s. Following the early enthusiasm of the communist takeover in 1949, romance with his glorious future waned. Mao tried to rev it back up with his form of permanent revolution. This unleashed forces leading to the greatest death toll the world has ever known outside war. Somewhere between 30 and 60 million Chinese perished.

Do not construe these Islamic taxation scenarios to come out of a superheroine Qaehera comic. After the capture of Constantinople in 1453, the Ottomans experienced a financial boom, as one would expect from victors who pocketed a fifth of the greatest city in the Mediterranean. World realities soon followed as wider links unfolded. International exchange rates turned against the Ottomans fueled by the inflation in Europe following the addition of all that silver from Spanish South America. The Ottomans also started losing battles, and yes, that kissed the 20 percent booty income goodbye. At that point Islamic experts began telling Ottoman rulers that the empire was not flourishing because Muslim rules were not being obeyed.[24]

So if the Islamic taxation system does not work unless you are collecting khums and jizya from conquered peoples, it might not stand up that well to financing mundane sewage systems for a city bloated with believers. Unfortunately this unrealistic thinking afflicts some Muslim commentators to this day. On July 8th 2014, www.khilafah.com reported on Egypt that "The Tyrant Sisi Hikes Fuel Prices to Rob the People." This condemnation came despite they themselves acknowledged a paragraph or so down that "The rise in fuel prices is part of the Egyptian government's efforts to

23. Weiss et al., *Social Welfare in Muslim Societies*, 13.

24. See Stone, *Turkey: A Short History*

trim the budget deficit after decades of economic mismanagement during Mubarak's rule."[25]

Focusing on taxes needed to maintain a sewage system was deliberate. The Roman one existed before either Christianity or Islam. They take on new dimensions of cost and planning in the megacities, and their cost cannot be calculated on the basis of a rule derived from either Qu'ranic sources or the Sunna or the Hadith. To put it bluntly they cost a certain amount which has to be funded somehow or the town stinks.

Kuran makes several pertinent observations when aligning Islamic law against the requirements of a legal system. He examines factors such as Government accountability, equal access to Justice and the political process, efficiency, clear laws, stable laws, and protection of fundamental rights. He points out that;

> A modern training in Islamic law does not provide the skills to evaluate policies involving the money supply, the global trading system, food safety, or building codes, to name a few of the issues that governments address.[26]
>
> Because zakat revenue was meant to finance all expenditures of the Islamic state, except those met through booty, the fixity of the rates capped individual tax obligations. This fixity also limited the states economic reach.[27]

Worse than Hanoi's scenario, a technically proper Islamic city could not contemplate fixing the sewers with costs, such as we have discovered, via taxation of its citizens. Since all those other extensions of man layered into the modern millionaire cities of the globe require more money to operate than the Qu'ran allocates, we reach a glaring question mark—is Islamic taxation theory adequate?

Before you answer, remember that Islamic law, including tax levies, is also called Sharia.

Everyone knows the Sharia word. Intelligent Westerners joke about the days when they might be discussing Sharia law. Intelligent Muslims believe it is the answer to world problems. Militant Muslims enforce it. Peaceful rulers such as the Sultan of Brunei institute it, with its penalties of limb severing and stoning. Celebrities boycotted his Beverly Hills hotel where an international women's freedom conference was due to be held in 2014. And

25. "The Tyrant Sisi," line 1.

26. Kuran, "Rule of Law," 12.

27. Ibid., 23.

the hotel manager complained that such behavior would affect the income of the many cleaners and menial laboring workers employed there.

Every university in Muslim–majority nations teaches Islamic law and jurisprudence. If you took law out of Islam, the religion would be severely gutted. Not terminally however, because Islam thrives in nations that don't allow it to practice its laws. As we saw in the previous chapter, even conservative Muslims reluctantly agree that in this current era, the West is a safer place than societies attempting to implement Islamic law. This conundrum, caused by layer upon layer of those extensions of men, is opening up a shift in Islam, evident among Muslims living in Western nations. In other words, Sharia is a contentious issue. Given that church and state were separated quite some time ago, small wonder that attempts to fuse mosque and law in the West might run into a few hurdles.

Now, some parallels can be found with different laws pertaining to different cultures living under the same flag. For example in Australia, Aboriginals have an option to undergo penalties from their customary background, such as getting speared through the calf of their leg. The Australian Law Reform Commission states; ".. the fact that the defendant has been subjected to some traditional punishment under Aboriginal customary laws is relevant in sentencing, especially where the local community is thereby reconciled."[28]

In our ethnographically and anthropologically aware world, many nations attempt to listen to the needs of their first peoples, or wandering groups, or displaced tribes. All in all, cultural awareness is a positive extension of man. Even among the Aboriginals though, unanimity of opinion does not exist. Bess Price, an Aboriginal woman, sums it up like this; "It is not somehow more acceptable to be raped, abused and murdered when the one doing it to you has the same colour skin."[29]

Introducing Sharia to the West is a bit more problematic. You can't claim native rights.

Despite this it's not difficult to find a global champion of Sharia. Abul Ala Maududi, a Pakistani scholar last century and recipient of the King Faisal International Award for Islamic services in 1979, had this to say;

> That if an Islamic society consciously resolves not to accept the Sharia, and decides to enact its own constitution and laws or borrow them from any other source in disregard of the Sharia, such

28. "Aboriginal Customary Laws," section 507.
29. Price, "We need to change our law," para. 7.

a society breaks its contract with God and forfeits its right to be called Islamic.[30]

I don't think he looked through the city sewage regulations before making this claim. Maududi went further, agreeing with the boys who run www.khilafah.com;

> Islam wishes to destroy all states and governments anywhere on the face of the earth which are opposed to the ideology and pro-gramme of Islam, regardless of the country or the nation which rules it. The purpose of Islam is to set up a state on the basis of its own ideology and programme, regardless of which nation assumes the role of the standard-bearer of Islam or the rule of which nation is undermined in the process of the establishment of an ideological Islamic State. Islam requires the earth—not just a portion, but the whole planet, because the entire mankind should benefit from the ideology and welfare programme. Towards this end, Islam wishes to press into service all forces which can bring about a revolution and a composite term for the use of all these forces is 'Jihad.' The objective of the Islamic 'jihād' is to eliminate the rule of an un-Islamic system and establish in its stead an Is-lamic system of state rule.[31]

His desire to see an Islamic state rule everywhere must include the governing of Australian Aboriginals, despite the fact Muhammad had no Arabic word for boomerang. Maududi is regarded as a modern Muslim revivalist and a father of political Islam. He said those words on the eve of World War 2, and six years prior to the formation of the United Na-tions. Not unexpectedly, his words, and others similar to him, raise fears in the Western world. Westerners, it would seem, are not so easily persuaded that mankind could 'benefit from the ideology and welfare programme' of Islam.

So this is a good time to outline a spat between several parties over the introduction of Sharia law into Canada for Canadian Muslims. Muster-ing considerable support, the Canadian Islamic Congress, the Council for American–Islamic Relations, the Islamic Society of North America and the Islamic Circle of North America all threw their combined weight behind a proposal to introduce Sharia law to the state of Ontario in 2003 as family law for Muslim residents. Buttressed by some Western celebrities, fighting

30. Maududi, *Islamic Law*, 13–14.
31. Maududi, *Jihad in Islam*, 6.

for minority rights, and a few Leninists of all people, they very nearly pushed it through.

These organizations hadn't accounted for Muslim opposition however. The Muslim Canadian Congress along with various feminist organizations wrote to every newspaper under the Canadian sun alerting readers to the direct contravention to the UN Declaration of Human Rights that Sharia entailed. Accordingly the pro–Sharia body retorted that those who opposed Sharia were; "non–religious Muslims who had no right to tell religious people what to do."[32]

Tarek Fatah goes into some depth demonstrating to an outsider, that in fact Sharia is a derived concept. It doesn't come out of the Qu'ran at all. An example is the Sharia laws on rape. The relevant Qu'ran verses are:

- And those who accuse chaste women and then do not produce four witnesses—lash them with eighty lashes and do not accept from them testimony ever after.[33]

- Why did they (who slandered) not produce for it four witnesses? And when they do not produce the witnesses, then it is they, in the sight of Allah , who are the liars.[34]

It's quite hard finding four witnesses to any sex attack. Rape tends to occur behind closed doors. FrontPageMagazine.com summarizes the Sharia contradiction;

> Because such "proofs" are almost impossible to obtain and because circumstantial evidence is not accepted, a rape cannot be proved as rape in a Sharia court. Instead, "sex outside marriage" is proved for the woman by her complaint or physical scars or torn cloths or pregnancy etc. Then the law of "Punishment for Sex Outside Marriage" i.e. stoning to death for married adulterers and flogging and exile for unmarried adulterers are applied to the rape–victims.[35]

In other words, just as there is a long history of Sharia law, there is a growing rejection of it from the Muslim community itself—especially in the West. Fatah, a Canadian Muslim, not an Islamophobic white farmer, claims that; "With Canada as a model of multiculturalism and pluralism, the Islamists would have forced this option on European countries such as

32. Fatah, *Chasing a Mirage,* 246.

33. Sura 24:2

34. Sura 24:13

35. "How Sharia Law Punishes Raped Women," para. 23.

Britain and the Scandinavian nations, where there is still a well–meaning naivety in dealing with Islamists (unlike among the German and French).”[36]

Fatah is not alone. Tawfik Hamid, an Egyptian Muslim writer, says in his book, 'Observations on Radicalized Islam'; “Examining Sharia law carefully reveals many important facts that cast doubts as to whether it is part of Islam.”[37] And he then spends a whole chapter explaining why it's not.

Okay, we might expect this from the National Front or other right wing organizations, but not from Muslim writers. It appears the USA might be following Ontario's lead. As of August 2013, seven US states have banned Sharia law. It's not just North America either. A British survey was reported under the headline; “Poll reveals 40 percent of Muslims want sharia law in UK.”[38] Why didn't the headline read 'Poll reveals 60 percent of Muslims don't want sharia law in UK'?

This will take a long, long time to filter through to Muslim–majority nations. I am sure any parallels drawn between paying city sewage system taxes and sharia law will be scorned. However, I applaud Narendra Modi, elected to be Prime Minister of India in 2014, for aiming to give hundreds of millions of his fellow citizens clean loos rather than get dragged into interviews over past religious slights.

There is good news though, which is the revival of Zakat. Every year, somewhere between US$200 billion and $1 trillion are spent in “mandatory” alms and voluntary charity across the Muslim world, Islamic financial analysts estimate. At the low end of the estimate, this is fifteen times more than global humanitarian aid contributions in 2011.[39]

If that's impressive, there's more. For every reference to jizya you might scour through Google Scholar for, there are ten times as many listing Zakat. A Malaysian writer in 2012 tells us a further link;

> History proves that zakat is an effective tool to alleviate poverty as during the period of Umar bin Al Khattab and Umar bin Abdul Aziz poverty is completely eliminated. However, with the fall of Islamic Empire and the increasing European influence during the colonialism period, Zakat Institutions have lost their glory. Therefore, the objective of this paper is to provide a conceptual study on the roles of zakat in alleviating poverty especially in Malaysia by

---

36. Fatah, *Chasing a Mirage*, 241.
37. Hamid, “Understanding Radical Islam,” 26.
38. “Poll reveals 40pc of Muslims want sharia law in UK,” title.
39. “Analysis: A faith-based aid revolution,” para. 1.

examining both theory and practical aspects. It is also suggested that the effectiveness of Zakat Institutions may improve by collaborating with other institutions such as Microfinance Institutions.[40]

Try and get past the claim that poverty was completely eliminated under Umar, that rightly guided Caliph, and the obligatory reference to the evils of Europeans and colonialism. And they haven't read Scott's piece on Zakat dodgers.[41] Focus instead on the practical suggestion of collaborating with microfinance in alleviating poverty. Microfinance is already strong in Muslim–majority Bangladesh, exemplified by the Grameen bank. Although Grameen charge interest on their small loans, let's also ignore that iniquity. Significantly the writer recommends blending the concept of Zakat with microfinance, which might be a good idea. We should view the fading of Jizya and Khums, and the rise of Zakat as evidence that Islam is moving in a peaceful direction. In fact, both Muslims and Christians are being nudged towards the social sector—the very space they excel in. This is exactly what Eboo Patel meant when he welcomed Big Tent Citizen Islam to the space where Big Tent Citizen Christianity was already pitched.

THE CATHEDRAL

Cathedrals have a safer future in England than they did three hundred and fifty years ago. Following a century of Protestant making started by Henry VIII, the monarch–free Parliament of 1649 voted to abolish them. Since Jesus himself predicted the destruction of the awesome stone building known as the Temple of Jerusalem, it's no surprise that quite a few Christians have always wondered how the fad of building these immense, expensive places ever caught on. We've now discovered how they were financed, with all those tax collectors out in the fields extracting grain from recalcitrant French peasants for nigh on a thousand years.

It was one thing to build them, another to decide to get rid of them, and yet another to actually do it. "The Church of England has cathedrals not because anyone decided to have them, but because no–one successfully decided not to have them."[42] The buildings survived, and were voted back

---

40. Nadzri, "Zakat and Poverty Alleviation," 1.

41. See Scott, "Resistance without Protest,"

42. Rowe, "Roles of the Cathedral," 30.

into favor with the return of Charles II to the throne in 1660. And here they are today, surviving generation after generation of post–church society.

In fact they proliferated around the globe, often built by nations with fading beliefs. One could get cynical, laying the blame with colonial powers seeking to subjugate natives, but that doesn't explain the million turning up in post–France Hanoi. There is no single answer, and the reasons why they were constructed in New Zealand, including their cardboard one, probably differ from how several ended up in Vietnam. France was always more post–Christian than England, or post–Catholic actually, yet its cathedrals flourish too. As for Germany, we are told the finishing of theirs in Cologne in 1880 was a nation unifying exercise, since modern Germany only came into existence in 1870. It had taken 632 years from its start in 1248, but was completed according to the original plan.

British committees and commissions have grappled with the future of the cathedral for hundreds of years. Some of their earlier decisions were rather sensible, especially after discovering the habits of some absentee clergy. The last Earl of Bridgewater resided in Paris off the incomes from Durham Cathedral from 1780 until his death in 1829.[43] Questions still vex them today, if the introduction to 'Spiritual Capital: The Present and Future of English Cathedrals,' tells us anything; The objective of this project was "to enable cathedrals and those who run and work in them to understand better the function they fulfill in society, thereby equipping them to identify and respond faithfully and fruitfully to mission opportunities."[44] So they're still not sure what their purpose is. Or, to paraphrase Postman, does the technology of cathedrals mean they have an agenda of their own?

Recalling the shaping of Christianity by the Hagia Sophia Church itself, perhaps the very nature of English cathedrals determines what must be done. Most of those British commissioners had lofty aims using the language of their times. The Grubb report is no different, devoting a whole chapter to 'Emergent spiritualities' but is concerned they have enough funds to run on. The very heading 'Spiritual Capital' gives us this broad hint.

Faced with the misdemeanors of the last Earl of Bridgewater, Lord Henley's report in 1832 was more matter of fact, at least wanting staff to be present and accounted for, then to celebrate services. Since then, adaptations and experiments have been made. You can't turn them into shopping

43. Ibid., 42.

44. Grubb Institute, "Spiritual Capital," 10.

malls, although they tried that in the cloister of St Paul's long ago. However, you can add the cathedral store off to the side where you can generally get a coffee along with a poster or a CD. Cathedrals have not proved themselves useful as educational institutions. We only see teaching residues in the stained glass window comics. Nobody is about to extract all the military monuments, and lay Lord Nelson elsewhere. Who can the head of John the Baptist be returned to?

However they are good at music, and portraying history. And increasingly since the 1960s, visitors have flocked in to take photographs, or feel moved. It doesn't matter how you cut the mustard then, you will need cassocked priests wandering around as though they are busy preparing for the next service. If they're good multi-taskers, they will respond to the old man who sits in the back row weeping over the death of his wife, which still does happen amidst the two million who pour through St. Paul's each year.

Therefore the cathedral is a worthy legacy. Church history is displayed, warts and all, and cannot be modified by a political pamphlet, or a Hollywood movie. Those two million know they are viewing the output of a violent past as there is no attempt to hide it. It cannot be concealed. Even if the church wanted to, they could not. All those memories are displayed in stone, fulfilling a Bible verse;

- Be sure that your sin will find you out.[45]

Since these things are researched, we do know that many, many visitors find their tour through all the pomp, paraphernalia and princes, spiritually refreshing and uplifting. Is this cultural memory at its best now? And, perhaps realizing their new role, Amiens cathedral at least, in mid 2013, had large pictorial boards openly displaying the checkered history of the church in a time line. Walking around the extensive charts, I noticed the Crusades were included. No effort was made to hide any past iniquities. If people are critical of the churches role in that turbulent era, Amiens certainly doesn't attempt any active forgetting. Given my earlier concern about public awareness of the past, I'm prepared to claim it may be the first time many visitors have ever looked at such a historical presentation.

What is the challenge for the church? It turns out to be somewhat parallel to the permanent revolution challenge faced in Islam. In the middle of this muddling through that the English are good at, the comments of Dean Bennett seem to sum up the religious dilemma linking us back to the

---

45. Numbers 32:23

Muslim quandary about Sharia taxes. In response to yet another Cathedral report in 1927, Bennett wrote in 1928;

> Most of us, clergy and laity alike, have in religious matters either the prophetic or the priestly type of mind. The prophetic type of mind is adventurous, sees visions, and takes risks; the priestly type is cautious, conservative, consistent. My hope is that in any Permanent Commission appointed soon, the prophetic type of mind will predominate and that, after a period of experiment and readjustment, the prophet will, in a measure, make room for the priest.[46]

Another P word lurks behind priests and prophets. I say in the background because it can be a pathway a priest or prophet takes, that both these archetypes may be tempted by—propaganda. The priest is in danger of being swallowed by the system, advising his flock, "we will help you, work with you, and in the end all your problems will be solved." The prophet may have visions of grandeur, and instruct his followers to "slay their masters, and then they will be free." I speak metaphorically.

Since the 1960s, another category of cathedral visitor has flourished which would upset any ideas that Bennett had about things settling down. 'Gawpers' were one of four visitor categories identified in Lincoln Cathedral in 1992, the others being, 'Cultured despisers,' 'Prayer–makers,' and 'True believers.'[47] Those tourist Gawpers are the best opportunities for the buildings to make a spiritual impact on because they come in open. Just like Cat Stevens, they might stumble in at an opportune moment, and sense something that leads to a life changing event. Small wonder then that cathedrals welcome in a mixture of backpackers, the poor, the dispossessed, and bus tours from Arkansas. And it doesn't seem to matter how old the buildings are. Even the new cardboard cathedral in Christchurch, New Zealand, draws overseas and local tourists.

Perhaps it is fitting in an age that measures everything, that we can change buildings focused on one day a week to six, or seven. I say seven because some even throw open their welcoming doors to the visitor dollar on Sunday. And wait until you experience the sound and light shows illuminating the outer walls of French cathedrals during summer evenings. Amazing gadgetry transforms the beige of Amiens to a brilliant array of colors, brightening every face and shawl of every saint or disciple chiseled

46. Bennett, *On Cathedrals in the Meantime*, 6.
47. Francis et al. "Understanding Cathedral Visitors," 4.

into the edifice. Or witness the animated history of builders scuttling up and down the uneven twin towers of Chartres. If your wife persuades you to overnight in either town, then financial planners in their city departments will congratulate themselves for their investment in installing those automated marvels.

Amiens by day and night

All of this is the legacy that is handed on to an enthusiastic young vicar out to the change the world. Our alien should have visited these stone time capsules known as cathedrals or temples or mosques as soon as he arrived. They would have shown him the background to so much of life on earth. From the engravings on the walls of Angkor Wat to the World War 1 soldier in stained glass in Tenby, they would have informed him. And this is the resource the church can provide to help those young vicars in their lofty aim—crowds of people come in to St Paul's all the time, and once they're inside, who knows, you might be able to help one life at a time.

Only a few such qualms about function or legacy are evident from Islamic voices yet. Islam Question and Answer General Supervisor, Shaykh Muhammad Saalih al-Munajjid easily replied to;

> When does a place become a mosque?
> A masjid or mosque is a place which is prepared for the purpose of offering the five daily prayers on a permanent basis and is devoted for that purpose.[48]

And this indeed was one of the primary purposes of a medieval cathedral, and why they started tolling bells to alert the faithful around 450 AD. Some Western Muslims are having second thoughts, evidenced by a study in Britain entitled, The Role of the Mosque in Britain.[49] A significant heading in the article, 'Time to re-think the role of our Mosques,' tells us moves are afoot. When we examine what ought to be done, most of it is marketing again, advising a friendly welcome at the door, and even refreshing the air in the main room if men have been sleeping there. According to our Google search method, "mosque tourism" has half as many hits as "cathedral tourism," so perhaps a light is dawning for Muslims too.

Numbers are certainly in their favor. The famous Blue Mosque in Istanbul, completed in 1616 to rival the Hagia Sophia down the road, receives

---

48. "When does a place become a mosque," para. 1.

49. Maqsood, Role of the Mosque in Britain, title.

five million visitors a year, compared to St Paul's paltry two million. Recalling that Islam doesn't like imagery, don't expect to find funerary within the Blue Mosque, or indeed the flags of battalions or artwork. Mosques do not exist to display history, checkered or otherwise.

Fortunately in today's world you can visit the most famous sites via the Internet. High tech wizardry is available to compare the buildings of the faiths from your living room. Walk through the Blue Mosque,[50] then compare it with Westminster Abbey,[51] and you'll see the British penchant for embedding paraphernalia of power from their past.

Despite that daily rhythm of prayer, bell ringing, and choir practice, in the Middle Ages, we could safely say attendance is better than ever during the week if we worked out the mathematics for St Paul's. Tourists don't tend to mingle into an actual service though, as we did in Salisbury cathedral for the 4:30 evensong on a Sunday afternoon. In fact the congregation was only the same number as the glorious choir and we were encouraged to sit among them in the very center of the structure while visitors continued their stroll around us. It's all part of the multi-tasking encouragement I referred to above, and that Muslims are now being advised about.

Go to a megalopolis and the city central parish church is even more anachronistic as it has no parishioners. Only about ten thousand people actually live in the central district known as the City of London, but hundreds of thousands commute daily to work. 27 percent of visitors to English cathedrals are from out of town.

Travel has done more than reinvent cathedrals—it has moved into the pilgrimage business too. It is said that Mecca spends all year preparing for, and recovering from, the Haj. That obligatory trip by Muslims is fraught with outbreaks of tuberculosis and other hazardous diseases, as well as accommodation and flight challenges. An infrastructure providing basic human needs underlies any pilgrimage. Indeed solving pilgrim problems was a prime factor in that speech by Pope Urban in 1095. He was tired of Arab bandits holding up European travelers to Jerusalem. The Knight Templars grew out of a bodyguard strategy to keep pilgrims to the sacred city safe. In a request of unbelievable irony, some nasty incidents between Australian

---

50. Found here in early 2015. http://www.3dmekanlar.com/en/blue-mosque.html

51. Found here in early 2015. http://www.sphericalimages.com/virtual-tours/bbc-westminster-abbey

and American Muslims in 2013 were recalled. Hoping this would not happen again, several newspapers could not resist telling the world;

US Muslims ask John Kerry for protection on Mecca pilgrimage

U.S. Muslims on the hajj "need to know that the State Department has their backs," (the Muslim spokesperson) said.[52]

Had a journalist been at the Vatican around 1090 AD, they may have received a letter from Christian pilgrims to Jerusalem wanting to know that 'the Pope has their backs.' Urban II certainly took more action than the US did.

Apparently Christianity has lots more pilgrimage opportunities besides Jerusalem. The walk of St James along several hundred kilometers of northern Spain only saw 690 pilgrims undertake it in 1985. By 2010 numbers had swelled to over 200,000. The church didn't get a chance to prove it was a resurgence of belief, or perhaps even a reaction against all those media we talk about in this book. No, it was co-opted by the ever creative tourism business, and is viewed as a growth sector by that community.

Standing outside Chartres, which is still only 40,000 strong, viewing the cathedral on its knoll dominating the hinterland, it's still possible to imagine an earlier world before large cities. Time was rung by the only bell in town, and it would be heard in that silence prior to electricity and the automobile. Chartres might have survived on well water and outdoor latrines, but the super-city could never have.

London got there in 1750, and 200 years later, by 1950, there were 83 millionaire cities. 57 years after that, by 2007, the total had risen to 468. Many exceed ten million people. The rise of the super-city is only due to the rise of the technical class capable of running them. If you want to imagine Rome or Angkor Wat or Baghdad or Beijing, which were all ancient megacities, think of food distribution without refrigerated trucks. All that meat, corn, or rice, had to be brought in by oxen, horse or human. It's hard to picture.

Comparisons are available in the Economist's annual Most Livable City list.[53] It is not kind to Muslim–majority nations, with five out of the ten worst listed belonging to that group. Of the top ten, only two European ones are present. The other eight are shared by new countries—Australia, Canada and New Zealand. These ex-British colonies all have the advantage

52. "US Muslims ask John Kerry for protection," para. 7.
53. See "The best places to live."

of starting with somewhat clean slates, and a remnant of native trees. They mimicked the finer points the English learnt over the centuries about their own large cities, and inherited a mindset on how to build good cathedrals.

Criteria for climbing the ladder of the Most Livable City list includes Stability, Healthcare, Culture & Environment, Education, and Infrastructure, If you're searching for cathedrals or mosques, you need to dig into Culture & Environment, and there you will find Social or religious restrictions and Cultural availability listed along with other categories such as Food and drink, and Consumer goods and services. This is exactly as it should be from an organization who names itself after economics. We would expect that Culture & Environment should include the shopping mall because far more locals attend those than cathedrals. The locus of the city fathers has moved from plugging away at your stone church for two hundred years to the financial fine tuning of city corporations with highly paid executives. Belief and doggedness were supplanted by spreadsheets. There is no turning back.

Cities are an evolving project, with rankings and envy freely available from numerous tourist brochures as well. Being endlessly tweaked for financial performance, the capital value and rental prices of city land often rise to the absurd. At its height in the early 1990s, Tokyo was worth three times the entire land value of the USA. One hundred year mortgages were not uncommon. 'I may not pay the house off, but you will, my son.'

All this means the rental cost of that high priced central city store is charged to its customers. No wonder those shoes cost so much. We all know the Internet is poised to change that. Internet mail order from large out of town warehouses, or indeed from overseas, is threatening to close those shops. Value Added Taxes paid over the counter may be avoided with an international purchase. Offshore shoe vendors often back their sales up with a money back return, so it's a no risk decision for the consumer. It all adds up to a sorry outlook for several sectors of brick and mortar retail.

We've already seen what can happen when an industrial sector fails a city. The center of Detroit is being turned back to farmland after decades of automobile factory decline emptied offices there. Will the Internet blight our city centers? How much of the Anglican churches retirement scheme funds are sunk into central city buildings—that will not be rented by smartphone app developers? The de–centralization possible due to the information economy has not yet started to impact central city real estate. However the busiest store on the Champs Elysees in Paris is not jewelry or fashion, but a discount pastry outlet catering to the backpacker crowd. A Damocles sword hangs over High Street, and the buildings they occupy which are owned by the investment and banking communities.

Those stone cathedrals may outlast them all.

THE CROWD

Crowds and movement are inseparable from religion. One million gather in central Hanoi on Christmas Eve. Three million travel across the world in the Haj pilgrimage to Mecca. Twenty million Shia Muslims converge on Karbala, Iraq, to remember Hussein Ali, grandson of the prophet. More than thirty million Hindus gather to bathe in a sacred river for Kumbh Mela. Pope Francis clearly has pulling power, mustering six million for the Catholic mass in the Philippines in 2015.

Crowds swarm over the oceans seeking new lands, which they have always done, sometimes spectacularly so as with the Polynesian migration across the Pacific Ocean. Somehow they navigated thousands of miles to beach at an unpopulated place they called Aotearoa, or land of the long white cloud. Several hundred years later another migration of pale skinned people arrived, sometimes leading the earlier settlers to rename their place as the land of the wrong white crowd.

Rather than plan for rough seas today, crowds from the MENA region worry about a rough arrival through refugee camps in Europe and Australia. Perhaps if they arrived in seaworthy vessels, they may well be turned back. As always, they departed hoping for a new life, but as always, they took their cultural memories along. While it was intolerable enough for the Mayflower crowd to risk their lives leaving Europe, it never occurred to them not to set up communities of faith modeling those that had driven them out. And so it is today. If it is so bad in the MENA region, some Westerners might wonder, why don't Muslims drop their beliefs if they start again in a new world. This reasonably logical deduction is very rarely arrived at. So they pine for their homeland, just as the Israelites did in that potentially mythical exodus, longing to return from the desert to the leeks and garlics of Egypt.[54] Urban myth in New Zealand says it takes two or three return trips before English migrants really settle in. They need to experience the weather they left again, and find the same old men propping up bar stools in their Bristol pub are telling the same old jokes.

54. Numbers 11:5

Then there are those significant individuals who leave crowds behind. Abraham departed from his homeland, never to return, breeding several generations of wanderers. Hundreds, then thousands of years passed, before their descendants had finally morphed into the Jews, the Christians, and the Muslims. Crowds become tribes, then nations, then sometimes tribes again, even in England; "What seems to us obvious—that Britain is an island nation, with a distinct identity, whose language, culture and politico–legal system distinguish it from its continental neighbors—would have been incomprehensible to the subjects of Henry II (Monarch 1154–1189)."[55]

England was part of western Christendom, a crowd extending from the Atlantic seaboard to the Carpathians and the Danube basin, beyond which lay Byzantine Christianity, Islam, or heathendom. Christendom's ideological center was Rome, from where the Pope exercised a very real influence over temporal affairs. This European crowd dissolved into a series of nation states over a long violent history that is ongoing if one included Ukraine within Europe in 2015. Long after that process of cutting church influence away from state, the very term Christendom has become unfashionable, and is now declared "dead."[56]

At least violence did not attend the possible triumph of the tribal crowd when Scotland voted not to leave England in September 2014 but there is no enduring settlement to their boundaries. Similar referendums may take place in Spain, one of the oldest extant nations in the world. Hong Kong still wants the freedoms they tasted under Britain, and native tribes are slowly clawing back lands and governance in Australia and New Zealand. Of course the United Nations supports the very concept of stable boundaries, since that is its underlying charter, but that has never occurred historically. We seethe over the face of the earth.

At a macro level, the crowd of a whole nation is compared with that of others. Pecking orders of envy and contempt exist, disguised by labels like 'National pride.' Numbering enables us to list these crowds in order of wealth, health, suicide rates, and even happiness, as we just saw in the Most Livable City list. There is almost nothing we don't know about crowds, and yet their behavior is quite often a mystery. If commerce knew the right formula for selling products to a crowd, we could safely say the globes marketing budget would be slashed in two, based on their own admission that only 50 percent of advertising works, but they're not sure which half.

55. Wilson, *Plantagenets*, 1.

56. See, for example, Cashin, "Christendom is dead."

Crowd behavior is labeled under other terms such as population demographics or dynamics. A nation, which is a politically defined crowd, wants to know how many babies will be born next year, how many of us will die, and where we will live. Crowd rules, known as legal systems, are tinkered with. Some of these, such as the forbidding of charging interest, or the ban on bikinis at Bondi Beach, are forgotten but not repealed, sometimes lying inert for decades before a clown rediscovers them.

The most common numerical concept to examine crowds at both national and regional level is the population pyramid. This wonderful chart can explain almost anything. In poor countries, there is a very wide base of babies born, then it slopes up evenly like a triangle to the few very old that make it that far. That's why it's called a pyramid. Since families in poverty know some of their children will perish when young, they accordingly bear more. The pyramid for a developed nation is not a triangle. It's more like a bottle, with almost straight sides, curving in at the top. Most babies survive until about 60 years of age, then deaths occur evenly from then on. Correspondingly families in the developed nations learn, or choose to have, only one or two babies each. Naturally enough, the internet kindly provides us with instant access to every nation's population pyramid.

Population pyramid
Mali

It has been shown that the transition from regular to bottle shaped pyramid corresponds with urbanization. Look at the population of Mali in 2015 for example. Lots of babies die young. When people move to cities, their living conditions improve. Kids in a city family are expensive. They can't herd goats or harvest corn because your back garden doesn't permit that, nor do city regulations. Children become a hobby, not a necessity.

Population pyramid
Norway

Thing is, when people first shift to the city, on average, they don't understand those dynamics. It takes two generations before families grasp this. Two generations after migrating to Birmingham, England, or Tours, France, the average Muslim family will be down to 2.4 children or thereabouts. Their demographic profile will look much more like this population pyramid of Norway with less children. Meanwhile the Muslim family will have four kids. If you take the four per Muslim family and project it forward, it doesn't take too many years to overtake a resident European population that breeds two or less per household. This is the Islamization fear of the right wing because after Muslims achieve parity, the scare mongers think they're going to vote in Sharia law and start chopping hands off. Except, as we've just seen, not all Muslims will vote that way. And neither will their numbers expand that high, at least not through births alone after that second generation.

Urbanization occurs in the Middle East as well. People move to cities for the same reasons they did in the West in the early twentieth century—to find paying jobs. Agriculture used to employ most American workers only 100 years ago. Now less than 2 percent farm that immense nation. Most people work in the services sector. Much the same population movement is occurring in the so called Third World. Apparently, in 2014, the earth's entire urban population outnumbered the rural for the first time. This means that those increasing numbers in South Asia will start to slow down. In fact it took one year longer for the globe to move from 6 billion to 7 billion than it did to go from 5 to 6 billion. Work out the percentages and mathematics for yourself. There is a reasonable chance the earth may level out at around 9 billion people, all going well.

Unfortunately as the Middle Eastern millionaire cities expand, job creation within them doesn't grow at the same rate. Currently the Middle East has at least 25 million unemployed young men. Chances are they are urbanized. Chances are many of those 25 million watch television. Who knows how many see billboard adverts with beautiful people scampering along beaches they'll never sit on, or driving cars they'll never sit in, or reminders they'll never get their decaying teeth fixed. Many have a rudimentary grasp at the least that their culture, their religion, their economy, and their future, are blighted, and well behind any nation of the world that flies drones across their territory. These 25 million unemployed are a reservoir of discontent that the militant Islamist units can tap into. It's much harder persuading Muslim yuppies into strapping on a bomb. And if the population pyramid straightens out into the bottle, there are more older people with wives, and less testosterone driven, crazy youth

There is also a calculated end to all that oil lying under the land owned by Muslim–majority crowds. It is not endless in supply, especially as we burn through over 32 billion barrels every year. Peak oil is either here or approaching soon. Already we imagine a future of electric cars populating our roads. Add this to the crowd trends, and the terse summary by one writer might have a point; "Islam has one generation in which to establish a global theocracy before hitting a demographic barrier. Islam has enough young men to fight a war during the next 30 years. The Muslim world has generated only two great surpluses, namely people and oil. By the middle of the century both of these will have begun to dwindle."[57]

This is the sort of future gazing possible if you play around with numbers. It's logical, and huge in its scope. It makes sense because we know that arming crowds of warriors is expensive, which is the point of mentioning the oil. However, we need to remind ourselves that most futurist predictions don't come true.

Lots of micro changes occur in crowds, again illustrated via the population pyramid. The national pyramid differs markedly from specific regional ones. A sun–belt tourist town has a completely different age structure than a university city. Modern cities have driven Christians in different directions, and driven is the operative word. That extension of man, the motor car, wrecked the local community church. No longer did you walk there, summoned by the cathedral bells. If you wanted to go, you drove. If you didn't like the Vicar, you could find one closer to your heart—further away. Almost every penchant known to man is available in a church somewhere. All you need is Googlemaps to find it, and that generally comes with your smartphone.

Early teens in a Chartres Cathedral service arise one by one, taking turns uttering their vows before returning to the clucking parents and nuns who will see them disappear to Paris in a few years. Old members gather in St Florentin for choir practice, that forgotten town with the stained–glassed windowed cathedral in Burgundy. Hip young surfers, gyrating to rock music, crowd out a popular seaside resort church. Young inner city professional couples find there is less for them to do when they have children, and wander off to a city fringe family gathering with an up–market crèche. When posed with my question about what will happen when his current crop of old ladies dies off, one vicar responded, "A new bunch of old ladies will have arrived."

In the West, that city picture is now mixed with the influx of the Muslim crowd. Religious diversity and change in Vienna, Austria, has been pedantically observed over the last forty years, right down to suburban composition and age demographics.[58] One gets the feeling from reading their material that we are observing two time capsules in the same era—one

57. "Demographics of Radical Islam," para. 2, 14.
58. "Past, present and future religious prospects in Vienna," line 1.

is a wealthy ageing sector with fewer young and decaying belief, whereas the other is only beginning to discover how costly kids are but attend mosque. The point of their study, and indeed of this whole crowd section is that it will continue to alter, and indeed already is if we look elsewhere.

From Britain we hear repeated comments about the young Muslim population there. They are in transition, and a growing number were born there. According to demographers, they have that mix of families producing between 2.4 and 4 kids each. California has the largest number of mosques of any state in the USA, but then it has the largest number of most things in America. One mosque tells us; "The age groups range from infants to elders with the majority of the community members ranging from 40 to 60 years old."[59] Declines in both church and mosque attendance have been recorded in the Netherlands, so we have definite mimicry there. In fact the decline is sharper among Muslims. Monthly mosque attendance by Muslims in Holland shrank from 47 percent in 1998 to 35 percent in 2008. The percentage of Catholics who regularly visit services, dropped from 31 percent to 23 percent.[60]

At first glance this looks like the profile of a Western church, mostly clustered in the older age bracket. Significantly it hints that one of the strongest movements in Western Christendom may be infecting the Muslim community—the rise of the Nones. None is the box on the form that more Westerners tick each census year. In Canada the Nones rose from 10 percent in 1985 to 25 percent in 2014.[61] They are a diverse group, spanning militant atheists, freelance spiritualists, onetime Catholics, non–observant Jews, secular Muslims, and others. Don't assume all Nones have become atheists. Not so. Evidence is beginning to build that the unaffiliated are not necessarily unreligious. This is known as believing without belonging.

Behind these statistics lie an enormous number of personal decisions. Church Pastors tend to think that people who leave got hurt at church somehow. This is not backed up by Pew, whose surveys present an amorphous answer—the majority just drifted away.[62] And remember that many Christians are not disturbed by this trend anyway. Some welcome the decline of the institutional church as a good sign that it ought to be powerless. As Jesus was powerless, they argue, and chose the role of a servant, so

59. "FAQ," para. 12.
60. "Muslim Statistics," section 9, para. 2–3.
61. "Canada's Changing Religious Landscape," para. 4.
62. "Faith in Flux," para. 12.

should Christians be who claim to follow him. They have no problem with the death of Christendom.

Unbelievably perhaps to Westerners, the lowest mosque attendance rate in the MENA region is in Iran. While 99 percent of the population claim to be Muslims, less than 30 percent attend mosque once a week. The Economist produced a special report detailing the decline in attendance, and the rise of the mall crowd, entitled 'The Revolution is Over.'[63] Bangladesh, Egypt, Indonesia and Pakistan have attendance rates more commensurate with the number of believers, but then they haven't formally been an Islamic State or Islamic Republic for a long time, if ever.

As if to validate all those numbers we've just looked at, in recent years the crowd has become wise, largely stemming from the title to Surowiecki's best seller, The Wisdom of Crowds. This is counter to religious history. Moses was sorely tested by the rebellious crowd of Israelites he led around the desert for forty years in the Bible book of Exodus. Muhammad could not make headway initially with the Meccan crowd and left for several years. Jesus himself did not trust the crowds, and was proved correct when they switched from welcoming him back to Jerusalem to demanding his crucifixion within days.

Surowiecki cleverly shows us many magic crowd skills. If you average out all the guesses of the weight of a bull at a rural exhibition, chances are you get an accurate answer. Work out the median from estimates of sweets in a jar by a crowd, and you get near the actual number too. Jarvis tells us we need to trust the public,[64] especially when it comes to Internet feedback. Both authors produce numerous stories backed up by numerical data, as indeed I have throughout this book too.

And therein lies a significant difference from the days of the founders of our faiths—neither Jesus, nor Paul, nor Muhammad, nor Moses, computed crowd statistics into sagacity. They had pre–decimal wisdom. Nowhere in either the Bible or the Qu'ran will you find an argument for wisdom backed by averages or percentages. This is not to dismiss Surowiecki or Jarvis. Rather it is to marvel again how our thinking has been so imbued with decimal that it has even permeated our definitions of wisdom, and somehow bestowed it on the mob. To his credit Surowiecki agrees, (in

63. "Revolution is over," title.
64. Jarvis, *What Would Google Do*, 83.

his own style[65]), with this verse from Ecclesiastes that wisdom or success cannot always be calculated;

- I again saw under the sun that the race is not to the swift and the battle is not to the warriors, and neither is bread to the wise nor wealth to the discerning nor favor to men of ability; for time and chance overtake them all.[66]

Both Islamic and Christian crowds have been reshaped by the political extensions of man. A prime example is the changing nature of what Christians call missions. Spanish missions to the New World were based around two drives—education, and conversion to the faith. Protestants eventually caught onto the vision of international conversion missions too, culminating in the great 1950s Crusades worldwide by Billy Graham. Somewhere between the 1600s and the 1950s, the first mission of education was taken over by the state.

The church was the great educator for centuries in Europe. Gradually the state took over, and today we are mainly surrounded by state run schools. Not completely though. All those seventeenth century gentry sons were educated in church backed establishments, and their presence is still felt. Private church schools exist aplenty, especially those run by the two major denominations in the West, the Roman Catholics and the Anglicans. Those church schools have to meet government standards of education, and teach a core of state prescribed curricula.

In plain language, the law pushed Christianity out of its control over education. Incidentally, some may agree with Peter Drucker that despite this takeover by the state, or perhaps because of it, education is doing no better than it did under the church.[67] We won't go there. The law intervened to control many areas of social work the church was engaged with, including old people's homes, charities, and care of the poor. Western legal statutes covering health, registration, accounting and taxation now shape Christian endeavors.

The Social sector, or the third sector, (after the private and public sectors) of a modern Western economy is often huge. It varies by nation, and obviously the USA with the largest population of any Western nation, tops the list. France is not good at it apparently, but Britain is, so there are

---

65. Surowiecki, *Wisdom of Crowds*, 219.

66. Ecclesiastes 9:11

67. Drucker, "Age of Social Transformation," 18–21.

cultural elements in this matrix. It is estimated that the volunteer sector in the USA would cost $150 billion annually if the services were invoiced. What proportion of the volunteer sector is still church affiliated, church sponsored, or in fact just church run? Look around you.

Don't imagine Muslim–majority nations are without a volunteer sector either. Pakistan was estimated to have over 260,000 people employed in the Not for Profit sector, which includes schools, hospitals, advocacies, housing and welfare. The sector was worth $130 million at the time of the 2002 survey.

The second major legal change affecting church mission is the ban on proselytizing, or seeking converts in the international arena. From about 1860 to 1960, Protestants in particular had a heyday setting up worldwide evangelical organizations. Indeed a common cry was that the whole world must be evangelized before the second coming of Christ can happen. While still a relatively widespread idea, voices are quieter because many countries will not let an overt evangelical mission into their country any more.

It's probably obvious that group of nations denying entry will include the Muslim–majority countries, but there are many others as well. The church has a solution to this challenge. Para–church groups arrange Christian professionals who will help poorer nations with technical, medical, banking, water purification, well digging, farming and other expertise. Or they go snowboarding in Iran. While they're over in the Third World, their lives are meant to be a witness, or an evangelical message in themselves.

Loosely speaking then, Christianity has been pushed, managed, or willingly gone into, the social sector, and away from evangelism. Most of us endorse their humanitarian aid work, and their ilk are probably the best parts of the Christian brand. This is not uniform by any means, and startup preaching type churches will always be starting up somewhere. However we will not see the likes of a Billy Graham preaching to 200 million people again, or for a long time anyway.

CONFUSION

Big Data intimates it might be able to link those dots that we've previously had trouble with. It could possibly solve a problem that afflicted London in the early 1990s. A colleague of mine told me about the expense every year of the different work parties that dug up the sewer along the kerb near your house, and filled it over—to be followed by the power line crew, who dug again then filled it over—and the phone line team who came the following week. Simply coordinating them to a single dig was estimated to save London $200,000,000 annually.

Everyone has a tale ranging from the purchase of new commuter trains that won't fit through existing tunnels, to buildings designed not to fall down during earthquakes—but do, to the zero sum gain of new motorways that encourage urban sprawl. In the middle of this are local political machinations of competing city corporations, and council elections for people the residents don't know—so they choose those at the top of the list. Managing the city produces mythologies left, right and center in any political spectrum. Auckland, New Zealand, has a real chance at being voted the most livable city in the world by 2020, a myth sustained by motivating TV adverts aimed at tourists. Yet the entire Auckland crowd complains about the traffic. The North–Western motorway is referred to as the car–park.

Peter Kageyama, co–founder of the Creative Cities Summit, found creative ways to extract a relative city–love index from Google, and he asks what people love about their particular city. It's not parking spaces, or how many square meters of shopping mall exist; "What do we love about cities? These tend to be smaller, intimate connections we make with places. It might be a favorite park, a corner cafe, a place where you walk your dog, a favorite tree, a street festival or a restaurant."[68]

Kageyama is closer to the "soul of the city," a phrase that returned about 31,600,000 results from Google in September 2014, more than seven times as many as "most livable city." He has a point. Will we feel we live in a better city than our cousin because ours has 18.2 square meters of park per person, whereas his has only 17.6? In any case we tend to go to the same park rather than sequentially visit the several hundred green spaces available in most large cities.

Despite the nightmare of numbers encountered in running an urban center, they may not be the most important factor in the Gross National Happiness (GNH) index, founded by Bhutan. The GNH list is no mimic of the most livable city list, and many Muslim–majority nations including Bangladesh, Indonesia, Pakistan, Algeria, Jordan, Palestine, Iraq, Kyrgyzstan, Tajikistan, Uzbekistan, Saudi Arabia, Yemen, Iran, Azerbaijan, Libya, Malaysia, Egypt, Sudan, and Turkmenistan, were happier than the USA in 2012. But only Bangladesh, Indonesia, Pakistan, Algeria, and Jordan were

---

68. Kageyama, *For the Love of Cities*, 56.

happier than New Zealand so it won't pay to generalize about Western grimness.[69]

But when we return to the cathedral, Big Data might not uncover the linkages. Considering France hardly left Vietnam on good terms after taxing it and crushing uprisings during its years as a colony, it might be difficult for the number crunchers to determine why those million crowd into Hanoi on Christmas eve to celebrate the religion the French imported. Subtler links might evade those knowledge specialists. Ho Chi Minh studied in France in the early 1920s. It was there that his eyes were opened to a Socialist future, by French men enamored with the new world of equality promised by the USSR, a utopia that later failed to deliver Big Macs.

Layers of media and myths, ranging from newspapers to politics to history to libraries to internationalization, lecture halls, train journeys, language institutes, and dozens more contributed to ongoing outcomes. At the end of these a pointless war was fought with the Americans after the French left. The yellow arches of McDonalds now adorn the streets of a nation that found communism couldn't feed its people after all, but is still run by a communist party. And now harmony reigns each Christmas around a cathedral standing in the same city as a prison of war tourist attraction still running under the name, 'Hanoi Hilton.'

It's not alone. In the other French colony we've referred to stands another cathedral, renovated in 2010 after years of neglect. Yes, even though Algeria is 99 percent Muslim and also fought a bitter war filled with propaganda against France, Our Lady of Africa Cathedral has been restored to its prior Mediterranean styled beauty in Algiers. Hundreds of Muslims, a few local Christians, along with Ugandan students studying medicine went to the re-opening. In this building, one whose function we cannot pinpoint any more in a post-church or perhaps a post-state crowd, harmony prevailed as Christians and Muslims united there. Perhaps the advertising magnates are right after all—at best we only know 50 percent about why things happen. And nothing remains the same. Life is not like taking a snapshot—it is more like dropping into a movie that's already started—and you'll leave soon, without knowing the ending, because there isn't one.

---

69. See "GNH Index."

9

THE THIRD HALF OF YOUR BRAIN

RELIGIOUS BRAND MIMICRY

The headline on the blog read, Christianity: A brand in crisis. It went on to quote an author, Anna Rice on her Facebook page;

> "For those who care, and I understand if you don't: Today I quit being a Christian. I'm out. I remain committed to Christ as always but not to being "Christian" or to being part of Christianity. It's simply impossible for me to "belong" to this quarrelsome, hostile, disputatious, and deservedly infamous group. For ten years, I've tried. I've failed. I'm an outsider. My conscience will allow nothing else.
>
> In the name of Christ, I refuse to be anti–gay. I refuse to be anti–feminist. I refuse to be anti–artificial birth control. I refuse to be anti–Democrat. I refuse to be anti–secular humanism. I refuse to be anti–science. I refuse to be anti–life. In the name of Christ, I quit Christianity and being Christian. Amen."[1]

The complaints of Anna Rice are commonplace, echoed in book titles like 'Saving Jesus from the Church'[2] by Robin Meyers—who is a church Pastor. Even though moves in Christianity abound supporting gay people,

---

1. "Christianity, a brand in crisis," para. 1–2.

2. Meyers, *Saving Jesus*

feminists, birth control, and science, she is not alone. I am reliably informed there are Christian Democrats too.

Remember however, we are not seeking to rebut her issues or explain how difficult it is to alter the sailing manifesto of the ship called Christianity. We are interested in the journey of two religions into the digital age, and clearly Facebook gave her the opportunity to say this, and she had followers, and it got quoted elsewhere, including the above blog article on branding.

Christianity and Islam are global brands whether they want it or not. Books such as 'Brand Jesus: Christianity in a Consumer Age' by Tyler Wigg Stevenson obviously recognize this. If many life coaches had their way, we would all be walking brands, displaying ourselves to the world, aided by our smartphones and social media posts. Westerners encounter 3000 brand signals a day, and all those logos have altered our thinking. We have no time to inquire, so we pigeon hole. No organization can opt out because it's not the self image that matters here—it's the customer, the outsider, and the competitor, who defines your brand. They're the ones who talk about you, or worse than that, are silent.

How do you tell what the world is saying about your brand? You already know our crude answer, the one that measures Internet noise. None of the following numbers can be classed under the wisdom of crowds—they are merely crowd totals. Complainants could indeed find many reasons why our Google method is wrong, such as the fact it ignores any full stops between the words. The end of one sentence and the beginning of another count, as for example with . . .Islamic. Terrorism . . . Nevertheless all those discrepancies are evenly spread, so it averages out, and Google is the widest spread, automatic method, of finding numbers without clipboards. Anyone can, and many do, use this simple system.

Google search phrase results of major world religions in January 2015 were;

- "Islamic terrorism" About 602,000 results

- "Hindu terrorism" About 72,400 results

- "Christian terrorism" About 48,800 results

- "Buddhist terrorism" About 5,980 results

We've covered other topics here, not all of which are easily definable, but two are;
- "Christian music" About 10,400,000 results

- "Islamic music" About 351,000 results
- "Christian feminism" About 39,600 results
- "Islamic feminism" About 140,000 results

Multinationals began to discover the power of online branding in 2005 when Dell computers didn't respond to a customer complaint. Jeff Jarvis received the PC he had ordered, but it had faults. After pursuing Dell customer service unsuccessfully, Jarvis, in his words, began "unwittingly unleashing a blog storm around the computer company." He did this on his blog under the headline: "Dell sucks."

Why 'Dell sucks?' In his words again, he: "learned some time ago that you can search Google for any brand, followed by the word "sucks," to find out just how much ill will is attached."[3]

To save you the effort, in January 2015, the results from Google for each phrase in quotes were as follows;

- "Christianity sucks" About 4,380 results.
- "Islam sucks" About 27,400 results.

Jarvis's blog went viral, and Dell's fiscal third quarter profit fell 28 percent. In a frank explanation of the power of Internet media, Jarvis added; "This is a story of customer relations in the new age—an age when, to quote blogger and Cluetrain Manifesto co-author Doc Searls, "'consumer' is an industrial-age word, a broadcast-age word. It implies that we are all tied to our chairs, head back, eating 'content' and crapping cash." Now consumers don't just consume. We spit back. We have our own printing presses."[4]

Neither Christianity nor Islam are clones of Dell, but the same printing presses sit in nearly everyone's room, or hand now, with the smartphone. The Roman Catholics and Anglicans are slightly closer to the Dell model as they each have a CEO. No such worldwide influential commanders figure in Islam. Customers of each faith tend to be much, much, much, more loyal to their brand than Dell users. Apple has a more successful hearts and minds strategy than Dell, but they're still way, way, way, behind Islam and Christianity. Islam will not suffer a 28 percent loss of following due to the atrocities in 2014 and 2015 under its brand name. Christianity is losing people, but not because they were fighting wars in 2015. The ship called Christianity has been producing lifeboats for five hundred years enabling

3. "My Dell hell," para. 2.
4. Ibid., para. 6.

passengers to sail off in a myriad of directions, some to oblivion, others to join different vessels. Many don't like being counted under existing flags.

Christians appear relatively unscathed in the terror stakes, although the violent Central African Lord's Resistance Army claims space on their turf. Mind you, the LRA does not upload videos of any atrocities it commits. Neither does it appear 'sticky' to the Christian brand. One might say religious branding is unfair. That's probably what Dell thought too.

Modern Christianity overwhelming appears the winner in music, but this is not a contest. We have not measured the number of good works done by either faith, and will not list the top ten religious charities because numerous bloggers do that to drive readership to their sites, and it would be problematic using our simple method of detecting volume. And Islamic music registers interest, whether the mullahs want it or not.

There's plenty of chatter regarding feminism in the Muslim world, which is a good result for the faith to have. Is it mimicry, or pressures from various extensions of man? Who cares? It's the outcome that matters, and those signs are encouraging.

That's the good news.

The bad news is that it's now unstoppable. These printing presses churn out material that is inappropriate or a poor way to draw attention. Such disparaging remarks by mainstream press are irrelevant. The printing presses churn because they can. Bloggers, Facebook users, and ordinary citizens, have opinions. And, by definition, since they use keyboards, they also have rudimentary skills of reading, writing, and possibly thinking.

Christianity has had a longer time to come to terms with media. A New York Times report in June 2014 said it all:

> U.S. Bishops Seek to Match Vatican in Shifting Tone.
> They are rethinking what kinds of houses they live in, and what kinds of cars they drive. They are wondering whether, in anticipation of the 2016 presidential election, they need to rewrite their advice to parishioners to make sure that poverty, and not just abortion, is discussed as a high–priority issue. And they are trying to get better about returning phone calls, reaching out to the disenchanted and the disenfranchised, and showing up at events.[5]

You can almost hear the back room Catholic research team talking over the trend stats, and mass emailing recommendations to priests.

No, I've changed my mind. Better to do that quietly. Leaks, you know.

5. "U.S. Bishops Seek to Match Vatican," para. 1.

In one way it's amazing that you would have to tell a Roman Catholic priest they should get better at returning customer dissatisfaction phone calls, and arriving at public relations events. Have those back room boys been doing some Search Engine Optimization (SEO) to figure out the most common customer inquiry terms? Did they read the Facebook stats, and now want to mimic the popularity of the boss? Good grief, did they need to go back to their original charter to discover they were meant to be looking after the poor?

What is Islam doing?

Unfortunately, lacking a global head, or a branding agency, there is currently no strategy at all to handle the stress caused by these extensions of men. Faced with a news media that daily reports violence, Muslims, and many Westerners too, have tactically defended Islam with the tools they've had available, which fall into the memory and mythology matrix.

Omid Safi, an academic teaching in the US, had this illuminating claim; "Yet Muhammad bashing is not a new phenomenon. The last decades of the twentieth century and the beginning of the twenty–first have seen both the continuation of the old polemics against Muhammad and the deployment of new ones. One thousand years ago, the polemics were about violence, sex and heresy. Today the polemics are still primarily about violence, sex and heresy. One cannot help but wonder at how unoriginal these polemics have been over the course of the last thousand years."[6]

It seems incredible that a religious spokesman, equivalent to a leading manager in commerce, would tell us they have ignored the same complaints about their brand for a thousand years. He is wrong though. In the next section on memory, we shall see an example of Islam subliminally reworking itself through the process of active forgetting—with the participation of management.

However, while religions seek adulation, they also thrive on opposition. Here we strike the very yin and yang of either faith. Both claim to be directed by God, and not by any number of Facebook likes. Fiercely faithful adherents have perished throughout history rather than submit to political power, let alone pandering to an adoring public. There is no point criticizing adherents of either faith, as demonstrated by Safi's claim. It's not quite water off a duck's back, but it's close. The best you'll hear in reply is 'let us solve our own problems.'

6. Safi, *A biography—Memories of Muhammad,* 6.

Signs are emerging that Muslims realize they have to cope with a media savvy world though. The Muslim Council of Britain polished up their website to portray a better image using the services of a company called rebrandme.co.uk. The Cordoba Foundation is a British Islamic think tank whose website photographs do not include a single image of old men in glasses with those long grey beards. It's much smarter. It's full of professional snapshots of board room meetings, and purposeful, business suited men hurrying out to catch their international flights to an important conference. They also supply;

> Working with the media: A guide for Muslim groups
> The Media Guide is designed to help individuals and local groups better meet their media and communications needs. It introduces the media, outlines how journalists operate and offers practical advice for spearheading a proactive public relations (PR) strategy. The Guide is written for local Muslim groups and Mosques who are unfamiliar with working and dealing with the media.[7]

Having said that, some attempts at re–mythologization are far too obvious;

> "Islamic group beheads journalist," one of the American newspapers said in big, bold print. Others similarly described the tragedy of James Foley, the journalist murdered by members of the Islamic State in Iraq and Syria. It was days before another innocent reporter, Steven Sotloff, would suffer the same barbarism.
> Darshini Kanda, a journalist who works for Kuala Lumpur-based Malaysiakini, an independent online newspaper, was appalled and confused.
> "Why didn't they just say terrorist group?" she asked me later as she reflected on her travels throughout the U.S. "Nearly every Muslim country has condemned what they do as un–Islamic."[8]

This blatant crack at active forgetting didn't work. Every blog reply in the first nine hours ridiculed the idea. A sample blogger response was;

> umm. . .maybe its a part of islam, just like the crusades were a part of the catholic church during the middle ages. just because its ugly and you don't like it doesnt mean its not a part of your religion. ISIS is doing what they are in the name of Islam (regardless if its your interpretation of islam or not) and they are recruiting from

7. "Working with the media," para. 1.
8. "ISIS, U.S. Media and The Muslim World," para. 2.

your communities. So instead of being in denial maybe accept that there is something going wrong in your communities. "Accepting a problem is the first step to recovery"—AA.[9]

The AA (Alcoholics Anonymous) advice will not be taken. At the end of 2014 no global Muslim leaders had admitted there might be something wrong with their faith. We know the reasons they can't. Eventually too much bad news does impact even the most hard core voters though. Christians have been learning how to get out ahead of the story occasionally, and shuffling to public opinion polls. Muslims have been trying to weather their storms by ignoring them. Declining mosque attendance figures in the Netherlands could be a wake-up call, but the question remains—who do you wake up?

Ayatollah Khamenei must be aware of the softening of Western Muslim trends since he claimed in 2014 that; "The American Islam, despite its Islamic appearance and label, is in compliance with despotism and Zionism, yields to the supremacy of arrogant powers and entirely serves the goals of despotism and the US."[10] That was a serious rebuke for Western Muslims from a world leader, but one that obviously recognized the nature of branding given his use of the phrase 'appearance and label.' If anything, his comments betray the stress the religion is under. Sectors of Islam vocally criticize each other regularly. Western Muslims castigate the militants. The militants taunt them back, challenging them to put their faith on the front line. Western Muslims squabble with each other in court over Sharia. If there is no monolithic nature to Islam, there is certainly no agreement on what true Islam is.

An email advertising a conference floated by me the other day, with the headline, 'Christendom is dead!' I was urged to listen to a group of speakers tell me about the new Christianity. One needs to be careful however, because the new one is usually a glossy version covering up an old message. Much the same is happening in Islam. Wonderfully graphical websites show young, smiling, head-geared Muslim women with punch-lines like 'Do you believe in freedom? So did Muhammad.'

Is this all a mimic of the hard to pigeon hole feminist movements? Are the happy domestic goddess housewife and the smiling hijab clad girl truly free? They tell us they are as they scamper down the fashion accessory aisles. Scratch deep enough through these new covers and you will

9. Ibid., comments.

10. "Leader urges vigilance," para. 2.

still find vast fields of exclusionist beliefs. Many of those racy clerics and affable televangelists from either faith still tell the same old story about who is going to heaven and who to hell. It just looks better with a multimedia background, boom boxes, or a well designed website. However, instead of hanging those who question their faith, Christians now welcome debates over issues such as the infallibility of their texts and founders of their faith, believe it or not. That's a long way past that last blasphemy execution in 1697.

These topics are still non-negotiable in Islam. Many Muslims are still focused on rote learning if an advert for a Deputy Imam school teacher in New Zealand was characteristic. The job criteria could have been written a thousand years ago; "The minimum qualification required is to be a Hafiz of Quraan (person who has memorised the full Quraan).[11]

However, just to show that Islam is not this monolithic entity, the very next day New Zealand Iraqis marched for peace in Auckland. A confident young Muslim woman (in headgear, but face uncovered) told the TV cameraman that Iraq was for all people of all religions. It was an excellent attempt to get out in front of the story. Their placards warned off foreign intervention in Iraq, which a cynic might say would support the ruthless IS strategy. But I prefer to believe they just didn't think that part through.

Following the IS beheading of James Foley several weeks later, at least one mosque opened its doors to the New Zealand public. Welcoming them in for what looked like delicious cuisine, the spokesman explained how they were Muslim New Zealanders and wanted to show the nation what true Islam was like. Hundreds from other nationalities and faiths arrived in support, indicating that those violent excesses elsewhere may not be enough to derail the re-mythologization going on.

Two points sprang out at me, the first of which was, yes, this was happening in New Zealand, a tiny Western outpost in the South Pacific, as far from international angst as one could get. Yet the occasional Muslim is barred from leaving the country, and a mosque manager was beaten up by members of his congregation. We must be seeing global issues at work if they have emerged in this end of the earth.

Secondly, most of the nation, including that mosque culinary team, have little idea about the militant start of Islam, nor about that Ottoman ambassadors aggressive chat with Jefferson in 1786.[12] And that doesn't

11. "Classifieds," advert.

12. "American Commissioners," para. 6.

matter. It doesn't matter which of the rhyming words of true or new you choose, the outcome will hopefully be the same. The main point was that, in a nation as far away from Iraq as you can get, Muslims immigrants were not in hiding, hoping it would all go away; the Islamophobia word wasn't aired in the news report; and local support vastly outweighed the odd redneck.

Of course there are mishaps on all sides. While it's always acceptable to criticize American blunders, much humbler efforts have difficulty lining everything up too. At the height of the 2014 IS beheadings, one young Muslim wrote to New Zealand's premiere current affairs TV show asking for the opportunity to portray peaceful Islam. His offer was warmly accepted and an eager team arrived to film proceedings at his mosque. In front of the nation, some mosque elders cornered their young advocate asking him what these women were doing inside without head coverings. He tried to shrug it off when fronting the camera again, but the episode illustrated how sectors of the Islamic community were completely unaware of brand imaging, even in a time of crisis. It was also a street level case study of how difficult it is to get all the chess pieces in order on the board. And the larger the scenario, the trickier it is.

The Economist in July 2014 got very close to saying there were problems with Islam as they reflected on the IS surge; "Islam, or at least modern reinterpretations of it, is at the core of some of the Arabs' deep troubles. The faith's claim, promoted by many of its leading lights, to combine spiritual and earthly authority, with no separation of mosque and state, has stunted the development of independent political institutions."[13] Considering the still wide global support among Muslims for sharia law, which is the fusion of mosque and state, the article was careful to mention; "And this violent perversion of Islam has spread to places as distant as northern Nigeria and northern England."

They are to be applauded for saying 'perversion of Islam.' No leading publication in the Western world should risk becoming an 'enemy of Islam.' Their tenuous channel to those 1.7 billion people would be turned off.

The Economist was not alone. Even leaders of Muslim–majority nations understood the quandary Tariq Ramadan is in, one being Egyptian President Abdul Fattah al–Sisi. When asked his thoughts about leading his nation by Time Magazine on October 6th, 2014, he replied;

> On the role of Islam: I simply represent moderate Islam. I'm concerned about the challenges of poverty and ignorance in the

13. "Tragedy of the Arabs," para. 5.

Muslim world. I can't be against Islam—I consider myself a devout Muslim—but the reality poses a challenge.[14]

He too, knew what he could not say. The standard response of Islamic commentators was still silence in 2014, which we have termed active forgetting. Or they claimed the IS were not Sharia compliant, despite the fact it was led by a man with a Ph.D in Islamic Studies. That is unlikely to persuade the outsider and the competitor, although it's readily swallowed by most existing customers. The other two categories will see it as an argument like, 'my Sharia is better than yours.' Like the Dell consumer, Westerners have trouble picking differences between models, especially when they all have the same logo on them.

Although the Sharia concept was being discredited by the IS and Boko Haram, and losing ground amongst Western Muslims, it will be a long time before Islam drops the link between mosque and state. Well, it did take Christianity a long, long, time to separate church and state too. Muslims can survive without Sharia if Tarek Fatah, the Canadian Muslim opposing it, is an example. Let's not forget only 40 percent of UK Muslims want Sharia law. Not so in the Middle East. Most residents still want it. That's the clipboard answer anyway.

The commercial sector has another angle on branding of religions. They drill further and define brand segments. Starting in the 1950s, segmentation has become mainstream in commerce as companies seek to understand their customers by categorizing them. Eventually it crept into the church. Many Christian based organizations besides churches have segmented their market, especially faced with falling attendance. We saw some of this earlier from Lincoln Cathedral. Tearfund developed their own model of the British population with four categories remarkably similar to Lincoln's;

- Regular churchgoers (Lincoln 'True believers')

- Fringe churchgoers, attend Christmas carols, christening and funerals (Lincoln 'Prayer–makers')

- Unchurched—never attended, don't know anything about Christianity. (Lincoln 'Gawpers')

14. "After the Revolution," para. 10.

- Dechurched—once attended, and drifted off or got turned off. (Lincoln 'Cultured despisers')[15]

Each segment requires a different marketing strategy if vicars are interested in increasing the size of the first slice. This type of analysis is useful to organizations marketing to the church community, which is huge—and accessible. Get the Pastor on side, and a door opens to hundreds, perhaps thousands of potential clients. Christian bookstores now acknowledge the emerging dechurched market, which is part of that rising census crowd called the Nones. Some chains look for stories of Christians pulling out of church and staying out.

As late as 2010, Ogilvy & Mather claimed they were the first to segment the Islamic market. Their Muslim matrix is illuminating;

- The Traditionalists

  - The connected—'religion connects me' (27 percent)

  - The centred—'religion centres me' (23 percent)

  - The immaculate—'religion purifies me' (11 percent)

- The Futurists

  - The synthesizers—'religion individuates me' (6 percent)

  - The movers—' religion enables me' (6 percent)

  - The identifiers—' religion identifies me' (27 percent)[16]

Ogilvy Noor (their Islamic focused team) claim the obvious mistakes Westerners make about Muslims are; "Stereotyping, insensitivity, over-simplification, causing many marketers to stumble, inadvertently offend, fail to cross borders, or fail to resonate."[17] They tell marketers to aim at the Futurists. That's where the money is. These are the fashion conscious hijab clad girls, and the young men arriving at the mosque in an Audi. Ogilvy Noor have even analyzed which market sectors, such as Food products, Haircare, and Travel, require high Sharia compliance.

Ogilvy Noor plainly tell us how unforgiving they are, which is a huge admission from an organization dedicated to selling them things; "once they feel wronged, Muslim consumers find it extremely difficult to forgive

---

15. Ashworth et al., "Churchgoing in the U.K.," 4–7.

16. "Brands, Islam and the new Muslim Consumer," 18.

17. Ibid., 9.

and even harder to forget. . . . When faced with a brand that has offended Muslims, almost 99% of consumers said that they would stop using it, 65% doing so even if the available alternatives were not as good. To make matters even more alarming, a full 83% feel it is their responsibility to inform all their friends and family of what they know of the brand's behavior."[18] That compares with generic industry averages of 89 percent who will switch brands after a bad experience. Evidently an average dissatisfied customer will tell between nine and fifteen people. Ogilvy Noor warn us American Muslims will tell all their friends and family.

Ogilvy Noor encourage businesses that the American Muslim community has $170 billion to spend. Be good to them, and they flock in—upset them, and they tell everyone. Their research is being heard, and Ogilvy Noor cite positive case studies in the US marketplace. This is classic integration propaganda. Companies seeking to do business with the Muslim demographic will be paid if they listen to them. And that definitely integrates them into the American consumer model.

Research such as Ogilvy's will have a far wider impact than the urbane arguments of modern Islamic political theorists, who critique each other's writings rather than do customer impact studies. As the Dell experience illustrated, commerce has one huge advantage over religion after all—if they don't listen to their flocks, they fail. The mere existence of brand segmentation in Christianity demonstrates a late take up of this lesson.

Islam has cherished what they perceive as another advantage for a long time, and that is difficulty of exit. The downsides to leaving Islam are serious, or at best somewhat comic as we learnt earlier from Malaysia. Ogilvy did not factor ex–Muslims into their model as that would currently be anathema to all the other segments. Yet their numbers are growing in the West as we have seen in mosque attendance numbers, and the rise of the ex–muslim Internet world.

We will know when this is acknowledged within Islam by the appearance of a new segment, mimicking one already in both the Tearfund and Lincoln segments—the 'cultured despisers' or the dechurched. The Unmosqued movie[19] is the first step in this direction, but it won't get Ogilvy approval yet. It took Christianity centuries to get to the point where leaving the faith was easy.

18. "A little empathy goes a long way," 10–11.
19. www.unmosquedfilm.com

Another comparison appears in the Google noise rankings that we've alluded to now and then, particularly when dealing with distributing wealth.

- "Islamic equality" About 10,100 results
- "Christian equality" About 8,340 results

Perhaps it indicates that early message of slowing down, of sharing the cattle and the cows around, has not been entirely lost under the other messy outcomes of militancy, LGBTQI rights, corruption, and aging sewage systems in the Muslim world. Zakat is a great concept to revive the Islamic brand, especially as it is an all encompassing wealth tax designed to counter inequality, which is an emerging global discussion. It is a small statement that Islam can speak messages in a language the West understands. Unfortunately, it's difficult to raise Zakat seriously when bombs go off every day in the MENA region, and here we get back to the global outrage Islam is able to muster. Muslims don't march under banners demanding a worldwide wealth tax. They rally against cartoons of Muhammad. Imagine if they could channel their collective energy to the former rather than the latter.

Nothing remains the same though. Egypt's President Sisi was emboldened by the global disgust at the Charlie Hebdo massacre of seventeen Parisians in January 2015 to call; "for a "revolution" in Islam to reform interpretations of the faith entrenched for hundreds of years, which he said have made the Muslim world a source of "destruction" and pitted it against the rest of the world."[20] He too, is pitted against the one thousand year old Al–Azhar University in Cairo which is also seeking change, but is; "wary of addressing deeper and more controversial issues."[21]

Some might have breathed a sigh of relief at Sisi's comments—at last a Muslim leader brave enough to criticize Islam. It's not quite as simple as that in a branded world where political messaging is distrusted though. US and UK leaders may continue to tell us Islamist terrorists are not Muslims. We can expect no more as; "The political class is obsessed with reputation management as a means to advance a political agenda and to win elections."[22] Westerners know this, hence the low percentage of believers in politicians. Accusing Islam itself was still beyond the pale at the start of 2015. Time spent learning such political skills may preclude understand-

20. "From Egypt's leader," para. 1.

21. Ibid., para. 3.

22. Marland, "What is a political brand," page 2.

ing the complexities of the situation, explaining how Archbishop Williams encountered that ignorance when he visited the British Parliament.[23]

Internal pressure may cause Western leaders to abandon their view however. The New York Times stated the case when it reported that; "Mr. Obama's verbal tactics have become a target for a growing chorus of critics who believe the evasive language is a sign that he is failing to look squarely at the threat from militant Islam."[24] In response, a former top counterterrorism official commented; "Our allies against ISIS in the region are out there every day saying, 'This is not Islam.' We don't want to undermine them. Any good it would do to trumpet 'Islamic radicalism' would be overwhelmed by the damage it would do to those relationships."[25]

Neither will Sisi, a politician, be believed in his own nation. His words can be reshaped by militant Islamists to show he has abandoned the true path, and become an enemy of Islam. Sensing this, the liberal wing of Egypt clarified matters ahead of that story; "What the president meant is that we need a contemporary reading for religious texts to deal with our contemporary reality," said Affifi, who is secretary general of the Islamic Research Center.[26] In other words, expect some creative active remembering and forgetting.

Which brings us to why this section is referenced to the mimicry view: the reason is that in a frantic, brand clogged world, most of the non-religious don't have the time or energy to differentiate between faiths or investigate what is going on. Too much tongue in cheek political maneuvering exhausts an already weary Western public worried about their jobs and their children. This very book listed more similarities between Islam and Christianity in the first chapter than the average Westerner could probably think up on the spot. Since Cat Stevens didn't even know Muslims believed in God, we can safely assume many outside these faiths can't differentiate either. Perhaps they could before the world was mediatized. Perhaps there was a time when people thought about religion rather than learn spirituality from Lord of the Rings movies.

Branding is hardly compatible with reflection and consideration, which ought to be functions of faith. Google's top search result in February

23. "When foreign policy was closer to heaven," para. 5.
24. "Faulted for Avoiding 'Islamic' Labels," para 3.
25. "Ibid.," para 20.
26. Ibid., para. 10.

2015 told me that your brand; "tells them what they can expect from your products and services, and it differentiates your offering from your competitors."[27] Unfortunately, overloaded with all that information in the world today, we all make rapid branding decisions, especially about 'products and services' we are only marginally interested in. Our alien couldn't tell much difference between the faiths because his visits were fleeting. As modern media and myths work on our memories, more and more of us may end up like him. We may look across at the half of mankind represented by Islam and Christianity, only to comment, 'all religions are the same.'

MORE MEMORY THAN EVER

At the start of this book we introduced some concepts about memory. We have one more to add to that from the Cultural Memory school—the net/fabric imagery.[28] A tight fabric allows little through it, whereas a lot slips through a net. We might think of our net/fabric as the core strands of a faith. We each capture different items, which makes us individuals. Our social identity is a tapestry of collective and personal experiences.

Sometimes an idea we don't like gets stuck in our net, and becomes annoying. We wish we had never come across it, but we can't discard it. More than that, we want others to forget it too. That might help explain Ogilvy Noor's finding that Muslims; "find it extremely difficult to forgive and even harder to forget."[29]

We're learning not to hurt the feelings of those who act this way. Back in 2002, Tom Clancy could tell Time Magazine that; "anti–Catholicism is the last respectable prejudice. You can't hate black people anymore, of course, and you can't hate homosexuals anymore, but you can hate all the Catholics you want."[30] That's changing. In India, Pakistan, and Bangladesh, legal charges can be laid if people hurt your religious feelings.[31] Even the US Embassy in Egypt issued a statement condemning "the continuing efforts by misguided individuals to hurt the religious feelings of Muslims."[32]

27. "The Basics of Branding," para. 2.

28. Erll et al., *Media and Cultural Memory*, 85–96.

29. "A little empathy goes a long way," 10–11.

30. "10 Questions for Tom Clancy," para. 5.

31. "Pakistan police register blasphemy case." para. 3.

32. "U.S. Embassy Condemns Those Who 'Hurt the Religious Feelings," para. 2.

Of course fundamentalist Christians could claim their feelings got hurt when the literary critics told them Jesus didn't actually say John 3:16. They haven't had their day in Western courts, so they may not entirely empathize with Muslims. However, they also haven't left their home nation to settle permanently into a wealthier, more powerful culture than the West provides. Leaving your home Muslim–majority nation challenges both religious feelings and social identity. Cultural memory comes from, and is reinforced by, the flow of daily life around us, our families, friends, and familiar religious symbols. Threaten those, and you might feel like a young Iranian girl who Nafisi quotes;

> "The worst fear you can have is losing your faith. Because then you're not accepted by anyone—not by those who consider themselves secular or by people of your own faith. It's terrible. Mahshid and I have been talking about that, about how ever since we could remember, our religion has defined every single action we've taken. If one day I lose my faith, it will be like dying and having to start new again in a world without guarantees."[33]

Kamala, the superheroine Muslim girl in New Jersey, struggles with her identity. No wonder. Her traditional storehouse of cultural memories got rattled when her family moved to the Great Satan and found it was the Big Apple. Qahera, the Egyptian hijab wearing heroine, gets angry. Is something stuck in her net? One Muslims poignant moment was caught while the café siege was still going in central Sydney, Australia, in which an Islamic gunman died along with two hostages in late 2014.

> The spark was this post on Facebook by Rachael Jacobs, who said she'd seen a woman she presumed was Muslim silently removing her hijab while sitting next to her on the train: "I ran after her at the train station. I said 'put it back on. I'll walk with u.' She started to cry and hugged me for about a minute—then walked off alone."[34]

Her grief was captured in that chance meeting, her questioning of a long lineage that had been her cultural rock. And another woman saw her anguish and reached out to her. This book seems to have been full of women expressing their peaceful version of their faith, usually painfully.

To one extent or another, these deep memory traumas have happened to millions of Muslims who moved to the West. Usama Hasan is a cleric and

33. Nafisi, *Reading Lolita*, 327.
34. "Sydney café," para. 2.

former jihadi, and part of an 'intellectual conversation' on radicalization in Britain. He later revealed the stresses to the social identity of many young Muslims in the West;

> "Throughout the 80s and 90s there was a huge resurgence in Muslim identity amongst my generation," he says. "We were caught often between two worlds—the world of our parents and home communities, usually from Pakistan or Bangladesh or India or the Arab world who were devout traditional Muslims. "We were living and being brought up in an increasingly secular post–religious Western British environment. And that had caused an identity crisis. Many of our generation decided to solve this identity crisis by firmly adopting political Islam and becoming not only devout Muslims but highly politicised Muslims and connecting with that resurgence of political Islam around the world."[35]

This stress to the cultural net is a worry to Western governments. Basically, it can be the start of a path to violence and terrorism. Blend the concept of the cultural memory net in with the propaganda matrix, and you have a trail to move the young along. In the worst cases, from 2011 to 2015, they wanted to go to Afghanistan or Syria to fight the enemies of Islam—who mostly turned out to be fellow Muslims. Chance meetings with the wrong people can result in the wrong choices being made. Very few become terror merchants despite cultural net stress—but it does happen on a case by case basis.

Researchers are beginning to understand the connections that lead a young Western Muslim into becoming a terrorist, rather than joining the Big Tent Islam of Eboo Patel. Security analysts have reasonable grounds for saying that the more a Western Muslim male youth is involved only with Islamic groups, as compared with mixing in a combination of Islamic organizations and secular ones, the more likely they are to end up down a terrorist path. Young Western Muslims do not simply walk into a terror recruitment cell, saying "Hello, I'm here." There is a path through Muslim–only groups.[36]

And naturally, Western governments, that huge extension of men, cannot ignore that research. They fear they may lose their seats of power if an explosion in a subway occurred. And that personal type data, by private individual, is increasingly becoming available. And news media know it is.

35. "Babar Ahmad," para. 17.
36. Al Raffie, "Social Identity Theory," 74–89.

And stories like that sell—which are read by humans right groups—who have valid complaints. So Britain decided it would buck the EU rulings and allow telephone monitoring to ensure Jihadis can't get out of the UK, if only to ensure they didn't come back worse than ever. France began pondering the same move. The protesters emerged.

The new capacity of stored memory is shaping those rules. Thanks to the digital world, the globe now stores more data than ever before, in excess of one zettabyte in 2010, and probably two zettabytes by 2014. Data storage is increasing that fast. A zettabyte is one thousand billion gigabytes. One zettabyte is equivalent to 140 GB of data for every human inhabitant on earth. The world may well be producing 40 zettabytes a year by 2020.

We increasingly have the capacity to remember nearly everything then. Up until our era, forgetting was far and away the major outcome. Most events, prices, divorces, deaths, births, fires, earthquakes etc, were passively forgotten. From now on that category is shrinking. We are filmed on smartphone snaps or shopping mall surveillance videos, and recorded in school, medical, or legal records. It is astonishing what is added to the knowledge base compared to twenty years back. Don't even try and con-template how little was known one thousand years ago. As Britain enacted

Danish jihadist movie

its new rules, a 29 minute documentary movie was pub-lished following the journey of a Danish criminal to Syria on his Jihadist journey.[37] Real life and real death footage of the anti–hero fighting alongside militia is in-cluded. Horrific tales from victim's families are related, and a dulcet recording of Al–Awlaki is heard assuring recruits that before the first drop of their blood hits the ground, they will be in paradise.

Our point is not so much the morality of all this, as the fact such knowledge can be trapped. It is amazing to be at this transition in history from lack of knowledge to so, so, much of it. It's almost as though we don't need to use our personal memory to recall anything, if devices such as Google Glass remind us of our best friend's names. Except, again, it's not amazing. It's ho hum, because we are surrounded by it. We are mediatized.

Many of us know the quote, "when all is known, all is forgiven." Now we're getting closer to religion. Christians and Muslims have long played with the concept that God knows everything. God is the master of both remembering and forgetting. God knows our innermost thoughts, and

37. "On the frontline in Syria," film.

since he alone is in possession of that data, he can make the best judgment about us, at the appointed time. Most of us rationalize that we did our best. Surely God will forgive us. This is immensely significant amongst adherents. And both religions talk about this, while also proffering some bad outcomes depending on which of those multiple theologies you imbibe. Some commentators make an analogy between the data we humans are collecting, as we attempt to catch up with the knowledge God already has. Will we end up forgiving our fellows because we know everything about them? We know a thousand times more about the circumstances surrounding any international controversy these days than we did a thousand years ago. Are we a thousand times better at forgiveness?

With caution, let's introduce a fourth memory—cellular memory. This is an old field in religious terms, but it might be on the threshold of scientific acceptability. Various individuals receiving heart transplants have been tracked, with interesting outcomes. A foundry worker developed a taste for classical music, later discovering his donor loved it. A girl received a heart transplant from someone who was murdered. Piecing together her later flashbacks and unexpected recalls, the police were able to identify the killer of her donor.[38]

Perhaps this field of inquiry will become mainstream one day. Then again it may simply be a reformat of ancient knowledge. Some of the breathing exercises recommended by modern specialists have been practiced by Orthodox Christian monks for over a thousand years as they tried to align heart and mind. Go to the public arena however, and it's already there. The concept of 'decisions of the heart' is no longer franchised by religion. It has plenty of currency elsewhere, given the phrase 'hearts and minds' has been popularized. People no longer say "I'm paid to do XYZ." They tell us they "are passionate about XYZ."

Meanwhile, remember we have not talked about processing this data—just about the fact it is there. When we move to the forgetting or deleting of this memory, we're in processing mode. Decision mode if you like. Gathering data is now easy. Deleting it requires thought. It joins our category of active forgetting. The EU has enacted "the right to be forgotten," to remove memory foot prints although it's not to the degree of allowing individuals to photoshop their lives. Basically it comes down to who decides to delete memory. The USSR showed us how with printed encyclopedias. Early responsibility for forgetting data in 2014 was thrown back to Google

38. "Memory transference in organ transplant recipients, " para. 6–7.

and Facebook, as they are termed Data controllers. Intriguing choice, considering those two are data collectors too.

One obvious danger is that the wrong people, such as the Mafia, will want to be forgotten. Discussion is afoot on how to program data warehouses to forget things similar to the way human memories fade. Maybe they will let memories age, or see how many access attempts are made to revive the data, that sort of thing. Google has young brains working in a field called Moral Artificial Intelligence (AI). I wonder if they can help.

How will this major shift impact our religions who have invested so much in active remembering and quite a lot in active forgetting? That is a very good question. The first thing we can say, looking back, is that active forgetting does not have a reputable past. It tended to be selective, and the sins of those enacting it have been found out. Nevertheless researchers have started investigating how businesses forget, which yields insights we could compare with religions. At least one definition of Knowledge Active Forgetting (KAF) has emerged; "the process in which an organization tries to deal with its old and obsolete knowledge in order to reduce its possibly negative impacts and to ensure the achievement of organizational goals in a conscious way."[39]

The article listed five methods of KAF in business;

- Simply be aware which knowledge is obsolete or harmful. Choose not to go there.

- Stop using outdated knowledge by edict.

- Stop developing outdated knowledge.

- Old knowledge will be pushed out by new. Unconscious abandonment.

- Wipe out old knowledge. The Soviet Encyclopedia again.

Each point conjures up ideas about what either religion does or does not do. Indeed, one of the business managers interviewed gave an illuminating statement about some entrenched ideas; "In fact it is not operationally possible for us to throw them away."[40]

Where was the world in 2015, nearly fourteen hundred years after the memory of the Banu Qurayza beheadings? Our case study, occasionally referred to throughout this book, was relevant in the light of actual beheadings in Iraq and Algeria, and planned ones in Australia. A memory

39. Niri et al., "Let's Learn Unlearning," 606.
40. Ibid., 611.

shift started with an article in 1976 entitled 'New light on the story of Banu Qurayza and the Jews of Medina'[41] by Wael N. Arafat, rejecting the tale. For the first time someone challenged the beheadings actually happened. It took a while to get traction in the academic world though. As late as 1983 an esteemed biography, praised by Muslim expert Shaykh Hamza Yusuf, who told us women could lead prayer from the front of the mosque, still had Muhammad in the thick of the Banu Qurayza plot.[42]

Omid Safi pointed out the real problem with the Banu Qurayza incident in 2009; "If Muhammad had consented to this harsh treatment, his consent would have carried the weight of precedence for later Muslims."[43] He is correct. It certainly would. It would legitimize beheading of captives by Muslims. Both the Islamic jurisprudence experts referred to earlier knew that and developed legal frameworks incorporating the practice. Safi doesn't mention those two; "Had there been a massacre of Jews carried out with the tacit approval of Muhammad, we would expect to find ample references to it in the early legal tradition—which we do not."[44] One wonders how Safi does not recall the legal opinions of al-Shafi'i and al-Mawardi, those early Muslim jurists who mulled over the incident, or others Kister refers to.[45] Then we reach Safi's logical conclusion; "This has led some of the leading scholars of early Islam, such as Wael N. Arafat, to conclude that this episode represents an early fabrication."[46]

Safi is not alone in rejecting the story of the massacre. After that slow start in 1976, the story is widespread today. Dozens, if not hundreds, of websites, all quote Arafat, who ends up blaming the episode on the Jews anyway. It doesn't take much to see that Muslims cannot accept the story. It was not immoral a thousand years ago to slaughter foes who had surrendered—it is now. Therefore the story of Muhammad, this perfect man, requires modification.

So finally, after a thousand years of ignoring external feedback, we see change under way, and it is via memory tools. Safi, a leading Muslim in his own right, declares this himself, although he certainly doesn't mean it in the sense we are referring to here; ". . . if our aim is to develop an understanding

41. Arafat, "New Light on the story of Banu Qurayza," 100–107.

42. Lings, *Muhammad*, 232.

43. Safi, *Memories of Muhammad*, 139.

44. Ibid., 139.

45. Kister, "Massacre of the Banu Qurayza," 61–96.

46. Safi, *Memories of Muhammad*, 139.

of the significance and centrality of Muhammad for Muslims, then we have to step in and out of his life narratives and look at how Muslims have remembered and interpreted these significant episodes."[47]

Active remembering is also going on of course. For centuries, on the day of Ashura, which is the tenth day of the Mourning of Muharram, many Islamic Shi'a devotees do violence to themselves, and 20 million visit Hussein's grave. Westerners are shocked by photos of blood drenched men slashing themselves as a sign of solidarity with the killing of this grandson of Muhammad.

In a book purportedly written to explain to Westerners that Islam is a peaceful, merciful religion, Safi nevertheless exhorts Muslims to actively remember what makes Shi'ites separate from the majority Sunni belief; "Much of Shi'ism is about memory and commemoration—about the need to remember those who came before, how they lived, and how they died. The ethos of Shi'ism is about more than sentimental remembrance: it is about the cosmic urge to not forget—to not forget Hussein, to not forget the possibility of rising up, and to not forget the possibility of living a heroic life."[48]

Actively remembering sectarian divisions is an unhelpful memory aid to a religious brand image. The major divisions of Christianity into Roman Catholic, Orthodox, and Protestant, occurred respectively one thousand and then five hundred years ago. They are also actively remembered and analyzed by outsiders and critics, and by the major denominations themselves, although patch up work is under way. As we mentioned in the first paragraph in this book, Protestants, who endlessly trumpet unity despite their 35,000 denominations, will celebrate their separation from Rome in 2017. Given this example, one wonders whether Islamic leaders will ever stop advising their clientele to remember Hussein. Masking this event with phrases like 'rising up' and 'heroic life' which can easily be understood in a negative sense, are hardly helpful to their logo.

We have a memory problem with the worldwide growth of knowledge—it has been accompanied by easy global access to it. Anyone can ask Google questions such as "how do I change a car tyre?" In my experience most people aren't yet aware of that. When people pose a technical question I'm unsure of, I ask if they've queried Google. Most hadn't thought of that by 2015. This will change.

47. Safi, *Memories of Muhammad*, 37.
48. Safi, *Memories of Muhammad*, 220.

However, besides storing endless references to the Banu Qurayza incident, this global access is also allowing peaceful ends of the religious spectrum to find each other. Global knowledge availability has seen both universalism, that theology taught by four out of the six Christian theological schools for the first few hundred years of the faith,[49] and interest in the Gospel of Thomas, spring back to new life.

Actually it's wider than that. Using the extension of man known as law, those Constantinian clerics began creating church theologies. Now another extension—the Internet—allows anyone to question them all, retrieve others from the cupboard, and even invent new theories. And no burning stake awaits you. All this is part of the current state of Christianity. There is no globally accepted theology any more. Constantine's bishops attempted to get the boat sailing in one direction, and they mostly succeeded. Sailors are now running around building lifeboats from the infrastructure of that old ship, and launching out on their own. Replacement timber does arrive from elsewhere, but it takes much, much longer to rebuild that old huge boat, and keep it going, than it does to throw together a lifeboat and leave the mother vessel.

Same with Islam. The world wide web is full of sites written by Muslims exploring ideas that were forbidden, including universalism, LGBTQI awareness, and the questioning of Sharia law. Old men with long grey beards and glasses writing fatwas cannot suppress this. The Internet memory is too big, and too connected. And if this is so, will we see Muslims pulling timber from the hull of Islam and building new lifeboats?

We already are. We've seen that repeatedly throughout our entire voyage.

These two faiths are the globes premiere historic examples in the memory sector. Eventually both will have opinions on what to forget, although in reality, they've always exercised that choice. Probably Christianity will be first to offer stances as the church loves being involved in current issues. Islam has other challenges for the next few decades at least, but eventually we will see a Muslim view of all that knowledge. If Boko Haram had their way they would burn it up just like that library in Alexandria in 640 AD. Peaceful Muslims will need to persuade the West that knowledge opposed to their faith is still legitimate.

Let's not forget those old stone buildings either, and the memories contained in their very architecture. Their recall of past good and evil are

49. Herzog and Schaff, *New Encyclopedia of Religious Knowledge*, volume 12, page 96.

displayed to millions every day, although not many dwell on that as they hurry to avoid the queues. The clergy may puzzle over what to do with them, but in an era that blends past with present like the 2014 movie Interstellar did so effectively, the cathedrals retain and display memories outside the scope of church strategy plans.

Hopefully the West is resilient enough to encourage Muslims such as Raheel Raza who is doing a sterling job educating church people, and anyone else who will listen to her in Canada, about the peaceful version of Islam.[50] She is to be applauded, as is Malala, who survived a bullet from the Taliban and received a Nobel Peace prize despite being castigated by the management team governing 150,000 schools in her home nation as being; "against the Constitution and Islamic ideology of Pakistan."[51]

Opposition to the peaceful version of Islam will continue from elsewhere too. The Banu Qurayza incident will be recalled by parties attempting to prove Islam is violent, and the likes of the Islamic State will use the incident as the juridical proof to behead reporters. All this threatens the fragile place occupied by the Razas and Malalas of this world, which is a pity. Why on earth would anyone want to extract an admission from these peace mongers about an eminently forgettable incident in Islamic history, and threaten their good work? The Islamic terror merchants would like nothing more than have Western leaders confirm that beheading was approved by Muhammad. They would parade the admission in front of their non–militant brethren, taunting them.

This is the conundrum we face. We know too much. It's too easily findable and provable. Perhaps it's better in the long run for the Banu Qurayza story to slip quietly away into mythology. Perhaps that's what God might do. Perhaps we can alter the phrase 'right to be forgotten,' to 'right thing to be forgotten.' The Bible gives us a clue about appropriate active forgetting, somehow including Westerners and Easterners in the matrix;

- As far as the east is from the west, so far has He (God) removed our transgressions from us . . . For He Himself knows our frame; He is mindful that we are but dust.[52]

Of course, we cannot be God. Any decisions over such historical events cannot be made by men formed from dust. All we can do is acknowledge that none of us have reached the position of, "when all is known, all is

50. Raza, *Their Jihad*, 27–33.

51. "Malala Yousafzai, Nobel Laureate," para. 3.

52. Psalm 103:12–14

forgiven." However, we can take the lead from Rachael Jacobs, who felt the pain of the unknown Muslim lady in Sydney, and simply said to her, "I'll walk with you."

DISRUPTION, THE CHILD OF MEDIA

'Disruptive by Design' was the 2015 mantra of Oakley,[53] a world leader in sunglasses. They pride themselves on disruption, their website movie leading us to believe they are providing us with a new and improved future. Disruption has moved from problem school–child to promise of a better world.

Is this a new mythology?

No, it's a business strategy. Eric Hippeau, Managing Director at the New York–based Lerer Hippeau Venture, said; "We're looking for big disruptive ideas, that can have a very large impact creating a new market or changing the face of an existing market."[54]

Firstly let's define disruption as he means it. I doubt his venture firm would give two seconds thought to the idea mentioned earlier that Amazon and Youtube could have a reflective plugin that realized you were consuming too much knowledge from one side of a debate, and that your thinking needed disrupting. Oh no, disruption does not mean challenging any deeply held mindsets we might have. That might hurt our feelings. Disruption means toppling a business that has deep pockets. Disruption employs new extensions of man to produce and sell things cheaper than mainstream commerce is currently able to.

The surfboard industry was once dominated by artisans but has been severely disrupted. Even until recent years, a large percentage were hand crafted in small factories dotted around the coast, selling to local board riders. Several careful hours of skilled labor went into each and every board, contributing to a production cost of X. Demand was growing worldwide, so for cost and future potential, it was, as they say in the disruption trade, low hanging fruit. South Korean and Chinese firms with a global outlook easily saw how to mechanize production and reduce costs to half or even quarter of X.

Before long these items hit the countries that buy them, like Australia. In 2006 one long time surfboard maker saw the writing on the wall,

53. "Disruptive by design," title.

54. "The dos and don'ts of pitching for business investment," para. 35.

and later commented; "I went, 'Mate, if this is what's going to come out of China, our industry's stuffed.' In the next 10 years, there will be a few factories around but they will be few and far between."[55]

That's disruption. Industries are targeted from anywhere in the world. Location or skill are not issues. Even 'buy local' mantras falter in the face of 50 or 60 percent price differentials.

Let's race through a brief history of disruption in the information technology industry.

The sector was disruptive from the start, erasing the jobs of clerks who added things up. We'll dodge past lots of their iniquities and pick up the trail at the typewriter. This extension of men led to the computer keyboard. The QWERTY layout was designed to slow users down in case the mechanical typewriter jammed. The golf–ball typewriter didn't jam, but by then QWERTY was there to stay, backed up by courses teaching us how to get faster on it.

In fact the typewriter bypassed many Westerners who never learnt how to use one, which is interesting in itself. Despite the fact it was present in Western society for one hundred years, most people didn't learn ten finger typing. It takes a long time for these skills to filter down and finally arrive in a national educational system. Even then, typing was designated to girl's classes, since boys were destined to instruct them what to type.

Compare that to the printed book. Over many centuries both genders, eventually, learnt how to cope with hand writing and with books. Even what was left of South American native society after that last Inca king had several hundred years to learn how a book worked. Don't think that the cover, the table of contents, page numbering, and the index are all naturally intuitive. It's only the passing of multiple generations of learning that lead us to assume that.

Before many learnt to type, that paper was replaced by a screen in front of them. And that screen used to be hooked to the PC it sat on, but now it's not. It's linked to something in the cloud. And you better learn how to get on the cloud, which browser to install, and how to crank up either a blog site, a Facebook page, or an advert embedded free website. No wonder older people shake their head, as they do many times when I talk about technology, and ask, "how do you keep up?"

---

55. "Paradise Lost for Aussie Surfboard Makers," para. 22.

Steve Krug tells a lot about our real challenge in his book, Don't make me think.[56] You may be tempted to believe he is talking about trivia on the Internet, but he's not. He's referring to the difficulty people face because they don't know how to read a webpage. It's so new, in general, that no standard pattern of engagement has emerged, as it has with the hard–copy book. Metaphorically speaking, they spend their time grappling with the framework—the modern versions of the book cover, table of contents, and the index. Unfortunately, in its brief history, the webpage is already moving from being PC based to mobile device and PC based—which provides users with at least two different patterns of engagement with the same site.

One ramification is this—so much effort goes into the framework of the content that not much is left for the quality of the content itself. That's what Krug means. He pleads with web developers to make their framework understandable. So they make them pictorial to help us out, and focus on that part rather than crisp text. The most highly graphical, marvelously intuitive, video and audio embedded sites imaginable, can be full of junk content. Or quarter full. Spelling mistakes galore sit neatly amidst glorious graphics. This apparently doesn't matter because people skim, and anyway, more than 50 percent of web content is now video based.

In other words I'm wrong—the image content is fine, that's just poor text I'm complaining about. A web developer, whose business depends on selling websites, remarked to me that it is better to create the text content for a reading age of a twelve year old. To assist such readers, graphics experts encourage us to use imagery to convey concepts. So it's a value judgment. Western educationalists tell us our kids are smarter than ever. When it comes to creating visual imagery, they are quite right. We do not have the space to adequately offer a response here, so I'll simply quote Ellul from his aptly titled 'The Humiliation of the Word'; "Experience tends to show that a person who thinks by images becomes less and less capable of thinking by reasoning, and vice versa. The intellectual process based on images is contradictory to the intellectual process of reasoning that is related to the word."[57]

Enter the smartphone, and whether by coincidence or design, we see the pace of disruption increase markedly. The smartphone is layered on at least three contributing media—the personal computer, the Internet, and cellular phone coverage.

---

56. Krug, *Don't make me think*, title.

57. Ellul, *Humiliation*, 214.

Computers weren't always personal, a business scenario that cost the market leader in the 1980s its position. IBM was six times larger than its nearest competitor in 1981, yet nearly went out of business ten years later. Making such huge profits on mainframes, they were annoyed with the personal computer market, until finally giving a small team twelve months to build one in 1981. That team needed two vital items that IBM could not extract from its own vast laboratories—a chip suited to such a device, and an operating system. Intel and Microsoft submitted successful tenders for those two items, and both were clever enough to retain some autonomy outside of IBM. They grew large enough to survive on their own in the PC industry, and disruption hit the largest computer supplier in the world. IBM was left with a shell of a business when the industry went personal.

Those PCs started to invade the consumer marketplace, and many Western Dads managed to get the household purchase past Mum who said, "we don't need one." Dad showed her the brochure proving there was a free encyclopedia on board, which Microsoft had cunningly installed to outfox her. "The kids need it for homework," he said. Once it got back home, the games went on. Never mind that the free digital one knocked out Encyclopedia Britannica, the largest and most famous of them all. Their demise is used as a case study of how the Internet disrupted the encyclopedia business sector. Many folks weren't taken by this ploy however. Some budget conscious Mums won those arguments. For a few years they could get by until the schools themselves became enamored by discount deals from Microsoft and Apple. As computers entered the classroom, the family did need one, and wants moved to needs.

In the mid 1990s, it was obvious the Internet was emerging in a major way, the next big thing, as they said. It posited a future problem for Microsoft who had banked their strategy on a world of personal computers storing data at home or at work, not in some nebulous cloud. They couldn't see that at the time, thinking they were safe by giving away Internet Explorer, their web browser. Well, the tactic worked with Encarta, the digital encyclopedia they gifted, then dumped when the cost of printing CDs exceeded looking up that disruptive Wikipedia.

Microsoft also put Hotmail up free of charge, and an interesting statistic started to get noticed. People began talking about how long it took products to reach 50 million users. It took 37 years for radio to reach 50 million listeners, 13 years for television to reach 50 million viewers and 4 years for the Internet to reach 50 million subscribers. It only took Hotmail 18 months.

Put this in perspective. Although we learnt earlier it only took 20 years for the microphone to penetrate the mosque, (or disrupt the airwaves), we don't know how long it took to reach 50 million books in the Muslim world. We do know that it must have taken longer than 200 years in the Ottoman Empire because they banned printing for all those centuries.[58]

So when, in 2015, people say they don't need a smartphone, they're still right—but far fewer tell me. The uptake on new devices is much faster. Accumulating all that media, or technique, or whatever you call it, over all those millennia, has brought us to the way the globe now accepts the next big, or even small thing, without question. In fact we queue up for it. In religious terms this is a total reverse from that evil day when King David merely counted how many lived in Israel, or the Ottomans forbade industrial printing.

For the first time in history, the globe welcomes disruption.

Smartphones and tablets fit into this world that is increasingly open to taking on new media without any idea about its impact. Those Islamic scholars may have been wrong about the printed book, but at least they thought about it and had opinions. At the beginning of this book we related how Don Fabun suggested forty years ago that we ought to slow down. He must have been an Ottoman mullah in a previous life. In 1985 Postman told us; "Twenty years ago, the question, Does television shape culture or merely reflect it? held considerable interest for many scholars and social critics. The question has largely disappeared as television became our culture."[59]

National education curricula has not raised that question today in regards to the digital world. It too, has jumped on the bandwagon, proving to us that kids will use these things. Besides, they're becoming cheaper than purchasing multiple books. That's a good Third World argument as hard copy books are expensive. So the players with foresight, such as Google, think the Third World, the populous world albeit the poor world, including the Middle East world, is the real volume market. Statistics seem to be proving them correct. For all its wonder, the personal computer was mainly a first world device. The smartphone is already showing a more even

---

58. In 2014 the 50 million record stood at 35 days, achieved by the smartphone app, Angry Birds. More than 500 man years of trivia were consumed every day in 2014 playing Angry Birds.

59. Postman, *Amusing ourselves to death*, 79.

distribution across the globe. One 2015 headline told us something about the most populous Muslim nation on earth; "Facebook Users in Indonesia Have Highest Mobile Usage Rate Worldwide."[60]

And very quickly too. As the 50 million user theory would suggest, the uptake is faster, even in our religions. In mid 2013 an Islamic smartphone was released by renowned preacher and scholar Dr. Zakir Naik who guided the Islamic Research Foundation (IRF). Dr Naik built up the Peace TV Channel which beamed out to 200 million people. "People will be able to experience the difference, as communicating through technology will make life easy and convenient par excellence while fostering an intimate relationship with the Creator."[61]

How different is that claim from the fatwas that were introduced by those Ottoman advisors in the sixteenth century to fend off the book? In 2013, this renowned preacher welcomed this new media because it would assist religion. Demand immediately ramped up in Saudi Arabia to order the device online. The phone has; "over 80 hours of Naik's videos, 50 Islamic applications, hundreds of Islamic wallpaper and 200 Islamic ringtones, the phone contains numerous books on Islam and comparative religion written by Naik, apart from other Islamic programs."[62]

Muslims are not alone. In 2010 Faith Communities Today published a colorful PDF, with text boxes and graphics resembling a website, entitled Virtually Religious: Technology and Internet Use in American Congregations. Among their conclusions were;

- Judicious use of tech and social media can make congregational activities more congruent with the everyday lives of members.

- Properly employed, technology can make members' daily lives outside of the worship service richer with religious meaning.

- Strategic use of technology can further enhance the number and depth of ties between members thus solidifying the connections between members and leaders.[63]

It's practically a mimic of the peace mobile's claim.

Remember we talked about that experiment to swap a new industrial/economic layer into Muslim–majority nations one hundred years ago? And

60. "Facebook Users in Indonesia," line 1.

61. "Islamic smartphone," para. 9.

62. Ibid., para. 8.

63. Thumma, "Virtually Religious," 9.

how other layers pulled at it stressfully? These new technology layers of computers, Internet and mobile devices are sliding into those same societies, following close behind different perspectives on money, genders, transport, and international law, and this time not from the top like an economic plan. These devices, concepts and ideas come in from all directions because ordinary people want them and international travel, satellite television, and the Internet, have made national borders very porous when it comes to knowledge. Just as Christianity has taken them all on and is turning into an entertainment brand, similar outcomes might await Islam. No Muslim, even at government level, can hold music and feminism back. Or to put it more bluntly, no Muslim–majority nation can put a hold on disruption even though that was once the core strength of Islam.

Oblivious to any social impact it might have, the business model of digital tries to cash in, using this new society as its plaything. The digital world is the perfect way to make money, and the buzzword is disruption. Professionals roam Linkedin with titles like 'Disruption Specialist.' You do not need a warehouse, a distribution system, shipping manifestos, packing boxes, or even employees, if you want to sell a digital product. It is a low cost option to break into if you have the skill. Once you've created the software, it costs you nothing to make another copy—you have that perfect business that earns money with no cost of replication.

Hundreds of thousands of people try making and selling digital items. Millions if you include Amazon ebook authors. The early 1990s was the best time to sell software, as it was early days. While there was not much trade on the Internet to the public, the same rules applied to product packaging. You only needed to copy your software program onto a diskette or a portable hard drive. These would change hands for millions of dollars at the high end of the market. As developers realized the money to be made, they flooded into the trade. The market soon shifted from one driven by need to one of oversupply. E–commerce on the Internet opened the doors for any kid to hawk his program across the globe. The earth started to fill up with software applications in search of a need. And much of the time the business need didn't exist. Sitting in his room, the kid simply imagined it did.

To draw disruption and our ever bulging digital memory together, we've actually combined both throughout this book as a research tool. Google Trends, among others, collects all that data about people's secret habits in Pakistan, and elsewhere—without clipboards. Not only that, but those search algorithms (remember where that word came from, by the way), avoid the Heisenberg effect of disturbing the environment one is examining. And it doesn't cost anything. Will this burgeoning mountain of data disrupt the traditional research sector? Will we find thousands of investigators, whose livelihood depends on the sale of their skill, protesting that the digital version is inferior? Or will Lerer Hippeau Venture throw some capital to a startup firm that finds whatever is required from those zettabytes in the sky?[64]

By now you might be wondering if it's worth revisiting the Microsoft CEO's quote and our religious version of it. To remind you, he said; "our industry does not respect tradition —it only respects innovation." And we mooted; "religion does not respect innovation —it only respects tradition." One of our religions traditionally forbade innovation. The term bid'ah in early Islamic thought meant opposition to innovation. Abd Allah ibn Umar said; "Every innovation is misguidance, even if the people see it as something good."[65] Active remembering is altering that interpretation to allow inclusion of things purportedly outside religion. Modernist interpretations simplify it to down to judging whether something is for or against Islam. The Ayatollah Khamenei told the world that Facebook was only forbidden if it caused; "corruption, lies and falsehoods, fear of committing a sin or led to strengthening the enemies of Islam."[66]

Then he launched his own Facebook site in 2012. He couldn't hold it back even though it was outlawed in Iran, the nation he rules. What else can he do in a world that welcomes disruption? Behind the scenes, like Tariq Ramadan, he may have other views, but publicly he cannot condemn another secular layer sliding into the society he cherishes. He must be aware that you can't introduce such layers with impunity as though they have no effect, but his own people are voting with their satellite TV dishes and illegal Internet searches.

So we were wrong—both religions embrace innovation now. One has been buffeted by it more than the other, and is wide open to it. The other is tearing itself away from historic formulas against it. Leaders in both faiths are probably aware that digital innovation is embedded with social disruption. Neither can do anything about that.

64. Don't worry, it's unlikely to impact Pew Research. Like those Qu'ran copyists long ago in Muslim Istanbul, there is no 'glaring problem' of cost—Pew data is free of charge.

65. "Bid'ah," section 1.2, para. 2.

66. "Iran's supreme leader Ayatollah Ali Khamenei launches Facebook page," para. 6.

We've come a long way tracking disruption in this book, beginning with the fall of the Roman Empire. Islamic conquests disrupted the Mediterranean trade routes in the 700sAD, but it led to a stronger northern Europe from whence sprang Western civilization, although the Ayatollahs don't grace it with that term. That Mediterranean disruption rippled into northern Europe for a long time, including the so called Dark Ages of anarchy. However that anarchy gradually began to sort itself out as local lords realized the kings needed them, and vice versa. Loyalty was sworn to the monarch, but not without a price—the lord wanted security over lands and tenure. Over centuries of in-fighting, intrigue and double cross, this trade-off led to the feudal system. The feudal knights forced King John's signature to the Magna Carta in 1215 as part of that long journey, and legal ownership of land slowly became a reality. Eventually even the lower classes felt they had a stake in society and the 1832 reform bill allowed some of them to vote in England. The pace quickened and the rights of everyman, and everywoman, were recognized in the twentieth century after a long hard struggle for democracy.

Today, the Englishman can own his house, if it hasn't been priced out of his reach, and the Prime Minister or the Queen must knock before entering. These rights are taken for granted in the West, but their roots are buried in a disruptive phase of history that dislodged the authority of Rome by turning the Mediterranean Sea into a Muslim lake, and reducing Europe to barbarism. The torturous route led to what is termed civil society, in which most citizens accept the authority of the state as it supports their freedoms and legal rights. Most citizens obey laws, partly out of fear of consequences, but mainly because their own good is synchronized with the good of the state. Perhaps this is integration propaganda, but among the options available for looking after oneself rather than one's neighbor, it's currently the best choice around. It's certainly envied by the half of Arab youth that would prefer to live in the West.

Commentators observe that civil society failed to develop in the Ottoman Empire, that Middle Eastern superpower that lasted so long. The powerful Sultans didn't need the cooperation of lords in the same manner that weakened European kings did. Accordingly, legal rights for the common man didn't gradually evolve either, and now we are witnessing a faster version of that process, and one attended with similar anarchy that gave birth to Western European privileges.

The point is that disruption has several faces. It is historically intriguing that it eventually saved Western society after the bulwarks to Constantinople were finally overcome in 1453. As part of the grand ebb and flow of civilizations, Islam unleashed disruptive forces that humbled it centuries later. They were all unexpected outcomes, and we're staring down the barrel of another if the worst scenario of the digital revolution occurs. This new technological wave; "puts 47% of employment in America at high risk of being automated away over the next decade or two."[67] With all the will in the world, can the US government create enough jobs to fill that pending gap? Will they find work for the unemployed Muslim youth in Dublin, Ohio, to deter them from joining a Jihad in Syria? Pew Research informed us in October 2014 that citizens of the developed world are pessimistic about that. In the main they feel their children will be worse off than them, and inequality will rise.[68]

We also hear the rosy eyed visions of the future from the digital business community, boasting how we won't need to move in order to visit Istanbul. We can do that today in fact. Those entrepreneurs fail to tell us how the job market will expand while they eagerly talk about lower service delivery costs enjoyed as digitization replaces labor. Their only answer to the job question is education, but let's cross surfboard shaping off their needed skills list. And if the poor record in teaching boys to type is anything to go by, how can we expect education to keep up with even faster changes? Do they think everyone will now stay young, and in fifty years time we won't have older people asking, "how do you keep up?"

Do those technology industry leaders think they themselves are immune from disruption?—no they don't, if you recall the Microsoft CEOs comment—but his solution is more disruption. The three most valuable firms on the planet, Apple, Microsoft, and Google, were all younger than fifty years in 2015. They know they have to plunder their own customer base before anyone else does. Yes, we have all heard Luddite fears before, and labor saving machines have been smashed from time to time in history. However even the White House must be worried this time since they also published a condensed version of Race Against the Machine on their website. This initiative by MIT concedes we have; "An Economy That's Not Putting People Back to Work."[69] The most illuminating chart shows that the

67. "Onrushing Wave," para. 9.
68. "Emerging and Developing Economies," para. 1.
69. "Race Against the Machine," 2.

growth in economic productivity is not matched by an expansion of jobs for the first time in recent history. Then again, it's always possible that the technology priests endorsing disruption might be correct as they encourage us to 'work with them, and in the end, all our problems will be solved.'

Let's conclude by returning to our religions and our initial observation of the global outrage Islam is able to muster. In a mixed up, barely coherent manner, their anger includes huge questions about the disruptive world. True, they've contributed to it from their beginnings. And they don't articulate it very well, which is a pity. Westerners are no more enemies of Islam than most Muslims are terrorists.

Race against the machine

Would that both crowds could agree they're worried about the same problems.

THE SMARTPHONE

So we come to this device which is a symbol of all we have seen. Our old friend, The Economist, says a lot of it for us;

> They have become the fastest-selling gadgets in history, outstripping the growth of the simple mobile phones that preceded them. They outsell personal computers four to one. Today about half the adult population owns a smartphone; by 2020, 80% will. Smartphones have also penetrated every aspect of daily life. The average American is buried in one for over two hours every day. Asked which media they would miss most, British teenagers pick mobile devices over TV sets, PCs and games consoles. Nearly 80% of smartphone-owners check messages, news or other services within 15 minutes of getting up. About 10% admit to having used the gadget during sex.

> The bedroom is just the beginning. Smartphones are more than a convenient route online, rather as cars are more than engines on wheels and clocks are not merely a means to count the hours. Much as the car and the clock did in their time, so today the smartphone is poised to enrich lives, reshape entire industries and

transform societies—and in ways that Snapchatting teenagers can-not begin to imagine.[70]

Way up the fastest rankings of the 50 million acceptance level, it dis-rupts conversations with our consent. Used judiciously, a terror merchant can trigger annihilation via a remote IED (Improvised Explosive Device), an outcome not intended by Google or Apple. It has far more digital mem-ory and processing power than a whole bank used in the 1980s for less than 0.5 percent of the cost.

Its social prominence can be plotted via the population pyramid—re-search confirms youth love placing their phones on cafe tables, while old ladies store them in handbags. This might indicate the difference between a digital native and a digital immigrant because the former accept disruption overrides a personal conversation.[71] We are told to turn them off in ca-thedrals, lest they disturb worship amidst the din of tourists. Smartphones contain Bibles and Qu'rans, and someone knows the location of the reader. You can already swap money around in bank accounts, and buy items by touching them with your smartphone. Transferring data between phones using Near Field Communications (NFC) is preferred over Bluetooth as the process "offers stronger joint experiences."[72] Touching the phones together in NFC is a visual, collaborative exercise, after all.

Examine genders and the pink handset case appears, while the ac-cessory battery–as–cover keeps those surfer boys in contact on their long road trips. That wave seeking community has come a long way from their deserted houses on 1970s beaches. Samsung was the major global sponsor of the premiere contest circuit in 2014 and 2015, playing soft music during the ad breaks while a father guided his eight year old daughter to shore on her first small rides.

The smartphone is an example of polymedia, (which is not a branding agency run by a macaw). Polymedia recognizes we use multiple digital plat-forms, and that we easily forget where we learnt something. Chat rooms, texting, music, Facebook, phone calls and more, all coalesce in this device. Layer upon layer. Surrounding it is the PC, the tablet, the camera, and the smart TV.

Soon to arrive is the 'Internet of things,' already boasting the acronym IoT. An illuminating video by Corning was uploaded onto youtube in 2011.

70. "Planet of the phones," para. 2–3.

71. "Smartphones and (smart) people," 10–11.

72. Ibid., 4.

Viewed over 24 million times by 2015, it portrays a possible future of the IoT as emails appear on the bathroom mirror. Grandma pops up on the kitchen table, and is slid across to the kids when they rush in for a breakfast byte. Many people thought it was an advert, and tried to order what they thought was a home system.

Corning glass future

Connected scenarios are underway already however. The toilet of the future has actually been around for twenty years, sifting through human output at home and sending data to your doctor. It might take off when connected to your Internet driven fridge though, comparing your digestive input to your waste, and making conclusions about your waist. Perhaps a drone with drug remedies will be automatically dispatched to your home—if you take out the premium option on your healthcare plan. Certainly a predetermined warning level will flash on your smartphone advising you to eat an apple while you read your Apple.

Some British software guru has already hacked into one of those refrigerators, persuading it to send 30 thousand spam emails. Evidently the modern car has about 200 computers installed in it already. Most are hackable, and we don't know which small processor controls what in our autos. Even heart pacemaker machines, implanted in human bodies, might be vulnerable. Such realities don't bother the inventors or the branding agencies who can't wait for the IoT to provide us with a new and better future, assured by the security promises of the international framework known as the Cloud Control Matrix (CCM).

Add in the rapidly expanding memory and accessibility of the cloud, and we already give much away. Far from an age that would burn you if you destroyed a holy text, then recanted and wanted you to buy a printed one, digital information is now infinitely reproducible at zero cost. That Hindu god contemplating nothingness has morphed into another in the sky that has everything for nothing.

It all adds up to the frenetic, freemium model. Given the competition, yet attraction of digital as a business, most of the apps in the world are free until they can get a wide footprint of users, and a reason can be established for users to purchase the premium version. That conversion rate is low though, around 1–2 percent of users. In some cases, the makers never plan a premium version. They give the app away for other reasons, including impressing a corporation with their work and getting a good job, or selling ad space to third parties at the foot of the app.

This freemium strategy doesn't even fool rats any longer in New Zealand. Conservation authorities tell us rodent pests have learnt to turn their nose up at free poisoned food dropped from helicopters. Nowadays they have to 'train' them with drops of healthy pellets. The rats first taste them sparingly, looking around to see if any of their kind keel over like a professional food taster at ancient Caesar's table. It is only after a few harmless drops that rodent confidence builds and the premium version is downloaded. This is not to suggest ad-free apps are poisonous, but it goes a way to explaining that adoption percentage.

The age of free is upon us as never before. It has been termed a truism that all digital products tend to a lowering, and even a disappearing of cost. Take data storage. In 1987, IBM marketed the 3380 disk drive, which was 1.5 meters high, and stood alongside mainframe computers behind locked doors in banks. The 3380 had 3 gigabytes of storage space. That was massive at the time. It cost US$100,000. In 2014 you could get 5 gigabytes of storage for nothing. Anyone in the world could. Sign up to Dropbox and it's yours for zero cost. This is a major game changer from previous millennia. Nothing was gifted in previous eras. You even had to bribe the executioner to sharpen his axe before you knelt at the block.

So we've got something to add to the challenges facing Islam and Christianity—they are embracing an inexpensive device for youth which supplies endless, personalized, envy. I'm sure there are bishops and mullahs who fret that the smartphone distributes iniquity without monetary cost—but they keep their opinions to themselves so as not to disturb their personal brand. It will be more ubiquitous than any previous digital device due to the cost, portability, global accessibility, and universal acceptance. It is already a desirable social object.

Any young Muslim girl in Mali, Uzbekistan, Kenya or Egypt who has a smartphone and some data access, can download free apps. They can look at Western photos of scantily clad young girls flirting with their boyfriends as they climb out of shiny new eco-friendly cars. Whatever the chador defending Islamic feminists think, or Qahera the comic book queen might yell at us, we don't know whether Senegalese Muslim teenage girls will despise those Western lasses or be jealous. We do know Malian girls in the middle of the Sahara desert downloaded tunes because the Islamist lads who briefly held Timbuktu in 2013 went around cleaning out such sin.

We've also come a long way from a world prior to decimal, newspapers, printed books, telegraph, and iPads. Conversation was better in AD 1000 than it is now. People lived in the same community for the whole of their lives in the main. It didn't pay to create enemies through crude speech. Adults like to imagine children were more obedient, but ancient Greek comments fretting about youth might dispel that myth, so we won't go that far.

They used a communications medium affectionately called F2F today—face to face, or friend to friend. F2F is the best multimedia extension of man ever invented. It did take tens of thousands of years for upright apes to learn how to converse after all. Nuances, body language, and social give and take, are all incorporated in this two way mediation allowing instant repair, or midstream retreat from misunderstandings or signs of dissent. The cycle of feedback is almost instantaneous between practiced pairs and groups. Moreover the players in an F2F transaction have invested in it, sometimes deeply when an envoy flies across the globe for a discussion, rather than sending an email asking another national leader to join a bombing raid.

F2F got hit in the 1960s and 1970s when Westerners stopped playing tennis with their neighbors and started watching television. By 2002 it had worsened as researchers found; "that the more time people spend using the Internet, the more they lose contact with their social environment."[73] Twelve years later Time magazine made sense when they noted; "Over the past decade, humanity hasn't just adopted Facebook; we've fallen on it like starving people who have been waiting for it our entire lives, as if it were the last missing piece of our social infrastructure as a species."[74]

We know intuitively, and from research, how the absence of the recipient correlates negatively with polite conversation. It's easy to gossip behind people's backs. It's also easier to send an email than talk a hard issue through. Hundreds of millions of emails are sent every day, of which at least tens of millions create offense or misunderstandings.

Blogging is worse, and the appropriate word troll has crept into online use. These are "people who sow discord on the Internet in the form of comments, starting arguments or upsetting people, off–topic messages or deliberately provoking readers into an emotional response." Nearly 30

73. Nie and Erbring, "Internet and Society," 275.

74. "Inside Facebook's plan," 42.

percent of US Internet users have posted something malicious online to people they don't know.[75]

Texts are instant emails. Text is the favorite form of communication amongst Western youth. They prefer it to phoning. In fact many never use their smartphone as a phone—it's for Social Media and texting. Text bullying is a topic on talk–back shows and in schools. How long does it take to repair a misunderstanding in an email, a text, or a social media post?

While those mullahs who delayed the printing press are long gone, a brief, almost parallel influence, started two years after Don Fabun's dream of an International Council for Technological Review. The Office of Technology Assessment ran in the USA from 1972 until it was disbanded in 1995. Perhaps it didn't manage to foster the debates it would have liked to, but it was a start. In 2014, a young man aged thirty wanted his product in every home, and his thought process, or lack of it, was recorded by Time Magazine when he visited a remote village in India to open a school computer center;

> "I actually don't read most of the coverage about Facebook," Zuckerberg says. "I try to learn from getting input from people who use our services directly more than from pundits. But yeah, I've heard the general critique. Whenever any technology or innovation comes along and it changes the nature of something, there are always people who lament the change and wish to go back to the previous time. But, I mean, I think that it's so clearly positive for people in terms of their ability to stay connected to folks."
>
> One might argue that somebody who shapes the social lives of a billion people and counting ought to have a more finely wrought sense of human nature, a deeper appreciation for what is lost when a new technology becomes part of our lives as well as what is gained. That would certainly be nice, but like the nervous and insecure, people with finely wrought sensibilities rarely build companies like Facebook.[76]

Zuckerberg is unlikely to visit Norfolk Island, a dot of two thousand people in the South Pacific who still recycle glass bottles. They also collectively decided against the cellphone, perhaps only something a small, aware, self reliant community, freer from integration propaganda than the rest of us, would do. Alas, they are ruled by Australia, who overturned the

75. "How Online Trolling Victims Respond," para. 1.
76. "Inside Facebook's plan," 42.

decision after five years on the grounds of economic growth. This is an interesting rationale for an island less than seven kilometers long, but tells us a lot about village choices in a global world. Nor has Zuckerberg probably read Neil Postman, who seemed to prophesy Facebook over twenty years ago, when he asked; "Will the computer raise egocentrism to the status of a virtue?"[77]

Samsung, the world's largest smartphone supplier, used the phrase 'personal companion' to promote their successful 2013 model, the S4. Personal companion might be an appropriate term. Walking home past the cafe where bronzed chatty young surfers had their Samsungs carelessly lying on their table, I passed a young shop girl on her break, crouched in the sun outside her store, intent on her small screen, fingers flying.

She was connected to someone somewhere, although not in an F2F conversation. Writing letters was also a relationship enhancing exercise long ago, although days or weeks passed between deliveries. It's all much quicker now, but that isn't really the point of the Samsung mantra. The phone is a personal companion, the ultimate version of mediatization, where the device itself has a relationship with you.

We may scoff at the personal piece but there is truth to it. We've been assaulted by mass media for generations now, but the same newspaper and the same TV channels went one way out to us all. Our location and our personal tastes are now recorded by GPS and our search habits on Google. Not only can we answer back to the media sent at us, our personal companion delivers our version of the world to us, the one we have been looking at. Such data is as useful for marketers as it is for governments tracking would be terrorists, although the latter are learning to be careful with their Facebook posts.

Of course your tastes change over time, quite quickly in fact, because you skim. Clever smartphone app developers produce apps that deliberately have transience. Tinder, launched in 2012, was a dating app with a feature called Moments. Your uploaded image only lasts 24 hours, and is part of a strategy to allow users to form more meaningful relationships.

How oxymoronic. To repeat that—Tinder images vanish so you can form meaningful relationships. That's a huge leap from hard-copy photo albums which are deliberately kept to remind us of the good times we had. The Vine app exploits the same transience by playing uploaded videos only when viewers are looking at them. Swipe down and the next one starts.

---

77. Postman, *Technopoly*, 17.

Undoubtedly statistics behind the scenes track the number of views, and were used to persuade investors how Vine would make money because they achieved the dream of all young geek startups—they got bought out. All of their effort is aimed at the Western youth sector, a demographic notoriously short of money. Perhaps the EU should get Tinder and Vine to help with the stored memory forgetting algorithms.

Samsung upgraded to the S5 in 2014, with the new phrase, 'powering my life.' Any of us could be the young woman shown jogging in the park, then running a board room, and later checking her Samsung watch in a night club with her boyfriend, possibly alerted by a vibration warning her to summon the taxi for her international air flight. Just to show the advertisers addressed other demographics, the surfer boys ended up in the rain, showing us how water resistant the phone was as they called mates while changing into wetsuits by the car, with a brief view of the screen telling us it was going to save power while they were out in the waves.

Ad agencies run by the best psychologists money can buy have undoubtedly tweaked the messages and are able to demonstrate to their client how many Internet or TV views of the adverts took place, and by which market segment, and the percentage shift in buyer behavior they could expect. Wait until Ogilvy get their Islamic model refined, and some sales data to verify their research. It's the same in principle as West African Sam envying my Land Rover, that expensive, but enticing extension of men from the West. Now the enticing extension is inexpensive. Sam's grandchildren won't be able to follow snakes through the upper forest layer, or find bark ropes whenever they need them in the jungle—but they'll know how to play Angry Birds.

If we didn't know the installation statistics by genre, I might have suggested those grandchildren would be able to identify bark ropes and grass turbans through an advanced version of Wikitude, an app that finds things near you. GPS and those huge databases can deliver that information to your smartphone. However we do know the download numbers of this relatively useful app and the trivial one. On Android mobile devices alone, the totals in 2015 were;

- Wikitude—1,000,000 to 5,000,000

- Angry Birds—50,000,000 to 100,000,000

So after all that advertising on how great we will feel owning one, and all the business reasons why it will improve our productivity, and all that guilt about not being more connected to our distant offspring, we're simply going to fritter it away. Squandering time on trivia has been spoken about by many others, so we won't dwell on it. However, those Malian girl's parents would probably have confiscated their phones if they had read the reports from down under. Latrobe University in Melbourne found 70 percent of sexually active teens 'sext' (graphically sexual explicit texts) each other nude pictures via their smartphones. This activity has not resulted in higher rates of teenage pregnancy evidently. Those figures were interpreted by the reporting professor as a practice between sexually active couples, not inactive ones.[78] I wonder how she knows. Perhaps she could show me how to ask those type of clipboard questions and I'll get to snow ski Tehran after all.

Indeed the study found no problems with the activity. It was the TV reporter who showed more surprise than the university professor. A parent interviewed on the street was shocked by the practice, but had to admit he did not know what was on his own daughter's smartphone. Reflecting, he conceded the question was, "a wake up call."

Sherry Turkle enlightened us about teenage daughters. One of the cruelest twists of fate is that the twin tower bombing in 2001 solidified the concept of being connected; "9/11 was a day when they could not be in touch. Classmates had no way to contact their parents. "I was in fourth grade," Julia said. "I didn't have a cell phone then. I needed to talk to my mother.""[79] 9/11 is part of connectivity culture. Cell phones became a symbol of protection. Like the electric lights that are meant to make us feel safe, but give us restless sleep, this new connection promises security, but only until the next text or phone call.

American youngsters, in fact Western youngsters, are growing up in an era of disconnected families. Turkle relays how Julia's mother had been through at least two relationships, and they were now making it without a male figure. Julia constantly tells her mother where she is, when she arrives at school, or at a friend's house. Is there a subliminal link between family breakdowns and the need to be constantly connected?

Who do they turn to, in their connected world? Half the time it may be a fictitious person. Turkle tells the story of Zeke; "(Zeke) created "fake" identities on MySpace. He scanned in pictures from magazines and wrote profiles for imaginary people. Then, he used their identities to begin

78. "Teen sexual health survey," para. 9–11.

79. Turkle, *Alone Together*, 246.

conversations about himself, very critical conversations, and he could see who joined in. This is a way, he says, "to find out if people hate you.""[80]

Turkle introduces Hannah who has a relationship with a boy she's never met. Via an Internet Relay Channel, Hannah met Ian. They have chatted online for years, eventually in a private chat room. They would talk and play scrabble for hours; "Hannah is wistful about Ian. "Even if I feel that I know him, I still don't feel that I know him the same I know someone in real life.""[81]

Eventually Hannah took a break from the chat room. While neither Hannah, nor the author says it, the implicit feeling one gains is that Ian may not actually exist as Ian. His real name could be Roger. Since they chatted for years, and he never tried to extract money, it is probably not a hoax. One end to the fantasy might be the coffee shop meeting where she discovers he is not what she imagined.

Will the smartphone alter religion?

Some outcomes are predictable. Pastors introduce smartphones, twitter, Facebook, blogs, you name it, to their congregations since they have been numbed by disruption. Neither Christianity nor Islam is immune from the sudden adoption mentality. There are Christian apps, just as there are Islamic apps. There are Bibles and there are Qu'rans. These Bibles come with several versions, inbuilt search aids, bookmarks, reading plans, and add-ons. Conveniently they weigh nothing because they're digital.

So parishioners don't need to take a Bible along to a study or a sermon. Not that they ever did, but for a while after they've downloaded the above marvelous free apps they do, just to show the Pastor they're up with the play. When the said parishioners get asked to turn to a section on their smartphone Bible however, the more astute of these Pastors have noticed attention wavers. Simply opening up their device distracts people.

We all know why—while they've been sitting there, two or three of their apps have notified they require an update, their calendar lets them know of a meeting they have early next morning, a Linkedin invitation arrived, or they forgot to charge the battery before they left home. I realize all of this might be additional script for that comedy show that incorporated Luther's Indulgences with Hell Pizza, but it is also a function of the media. A hard-copy book does not require a download update, and does not run out of electric power, and does not, of itself, distract you. The neighbor's

80. Ibid., 241.
81. Ibid., 249.

lawnmower might do that, but not the very device you're hoping to learn from.

Nor does this bode well for the promises of the Islamic Peace Mobile. Given its interrupt driven nature, some mullahs might have trouble agreeing with the maker's assertion that "communicating through technology will make life easy and convenient par excellence while fostering an intimate relationship with the Creator."[82] Nevertheless I am sure these devices will find their way into monastic communities of either faith, and we may one day view Youtube clips by holy men. Perhaps they could teach us how to separate ourselves from a mediatized world, and listen to animals traversing the forest.

Meanwhile the congregations in hip churches tweet messages up to a big screen behind the preacher in full flight showing two way communication exists in his flock. Islamic smartphones can certainly point you at Mecca, and vibrate five times daily at prayer time. I'm sure if a team of unemployed Irish geeks geo–position halal compliant restaurants of the world into an app, they will be able to monetize a deal with the maker of the Peace mobile, and Muslims will tell all their friends and family via Facebook—especially if they're upset.

The integration propaganda of consumption, of a never ending rise in GNP rather than GNH, has triumphed amongst adherents of both faiths, even the one that rejects secularism and other fruits of the West. I follow families sometimes in airports, all dressed in their flowing Arabic garb, the bearded young men fixed on their screens as they walk, with a Grandma shuffling along behind. This fantastically capable machine is purchased by legions of people who don't know how to use them. I seem to be always showing people how to take a photograph, or download an app, amongst the most basic of functions. Yet Samsung and Apple can sell 10 million in less than a month.

I would love to sit alongside one of those Middle Eastern thirty–somethings and show them how to take a panorama shot of the airport lounge. It might open up a conversation, maybe give us a starting block to compare how we might live with these things in our different worlds.

You see, they are here to stay. The world is not getting off the digital bandwagon. It is unstoppable.

The Greeks loved stories like these. Mythology at its best.

---

82. "Islamic smartphone," para. 9.

BIBLIOGRAPHY

"#BBCtrending: The women having a laugh in Turkey." *BBC News*. 2014.

"10 Questions for Tom Clancy." *Time Magazine*. 2002. http://content.time.com

"18th Century Mathematics—Bernoulli Brothers." *The Story of Mathematics*. 2010. http://www.storyofmathematics.com

"72 Virgins Hadith Narrations." *Wikiislam*. 2015. http://wikiislam.net

"A Conversation With Tariq Ramadan." *Pew Research*. 2010. http://www.pewforum.org

"A little empathy goes a long way: How brands can engage the American Muslim consumer." *Ogilvy Noor*. 2010. http://www.ogilvynoor.com

Abdalla, Bowirrat and Armaly Zaher. "Consanguineous Marriages in the Middle East: Nature Versus Nurture." *The Open Complementary Medicine Journal*, 2013, 5, 1–10.

"Aboriginal Customary Laws and Sentencing." *Australian Law Reform Commission*. 2015. http://www.alrc.gov.au

"About Khilafah.com." *Khilafah.com*. 2014. http://www.khilafah.com

"About WLUML." *WLUML*. 2014. http://www.wluml.org

Abushouk, Ahmed Ibrahim. "Globalization and Muslim Identity Challenges and Prospects." *The Muslim World*, July 2006.

"Address by Mohtarma Benazir Bhutto, Prime Minister of Islamic Republic of Pakistan at the Fourth World Conference on Women, Beijing." *United Nations*. 1995. http://www.un.org

"After the Revolution: Sitting Down With Egyptian President Abdul Fattah al-Sisi." 2014. *Time Magazine*. http://time.com

"Ahmad Akkari, Danish Muslim: I was wrong to damn Muhammad cartoons." *The Guardian*. 2013. http://www.theguardian.com

Al Raffie, Dina. "Social Identity Theory for Investigating Islamic Extremism in the Diaspora." *Journal of Strategic Security* 6, no. 4 (2013): 67–91.

Ali, Kecia. "'I was a girl of nine': Online Controversies over the Prophet's Marriage to 'A'ishah." *American Academy of Religion*. November 2004.

Alison, James. *Undergoing God: dispatches from the scene of a break-in*. London: Continuum, 2006.

Allen, Charlotte. "The Wife of Jesus Tale." *The Weekly Standard*. 2014. http://www.weeklystandard.com

Al-Tabari, Muhammad ibn Jarir. *The History of al-Tabari Vol. 8: The Victory of Islam: Muhammad at Medina A.D. 626–630/A.H. 5–8*. Translated by Michael Fishbein. 1997. New York: Suny Press, 1997.

BIBLIOGRAPHY

"American Commissioners to John Jay, 28 March 1786." *Founders Online*. http://founders. archives.gov

"American Donor Trends." *Barna Group*. 2013. https://www.barna.org

"An online Magna Carta: Berners-Lee calls for bill of rights for web." *The Guardian*. 2014. http://www.theguardian.com

"An Open Letter from Ms. in Support of Martha Stewart." *MS. Magazine*. 2004. http:// www.msmagazine.com

"Analysis: A faith-based aid revolution in the Muslim world?" *IRIN: United Nations*. 2012. http://www.irinnews.org

Andersson, Tobias. "Governance and Economics in Early Islamic Historiography: A comparative study of historical narratives of Umar's caliphate in the works of al-Baladhuri and at-Tabari." M.A. Diss., Hogskolan I Gavle, 2013.

Ankerberg, John and Emir Caner. *The Truth about Islam and Jihad*. Oregon: Harvest House, 2009.

"Anti-Sharia Bill Passed In North Carolina Without Governor Pat McCrory's signature." *Huffington Post*. 2013. http://www.huffingtonpost.com

"Appendix A: U.S. Muslims: Beliefs and Practices in a Global Context." *Pew Forum*. 2012. http://www.pewforum.org/

Arafat, Wael N. "New Light on the story of Banu Qurayza and the Jews of Medina." *Journal of the Royal Asiatic Society of Great Britain and Ireland*, 1976. 100–107.

"Archbishop Justin Welby: 'There is a possibility that we will not hold together.'" *Religion News Service*. 2014. http://www.religionnews.com

Ashworth, Jacinta, et al. "Churchgoing in the UK: A research report from Tearfund on church attendance in the UK." *Tearfund*. 2007. http://www.bbc.com

"Attention loss feared as high-tech rewires brain." *San Francisco Chronicle*. 2009. http:// www.sfgate.com

Augustine. *The City of God*. New Advent. http://www.newadvent.org/

"Augustine of Hippo." *Wikiquote*. http://en.wikiquote.org

"Babar Ahmad: The godfather of internet jihad?" *BBC News*. 2014. http://www.bbc.com

Bagby, Ihsan. "The American Mosque 2011, Report Number 2 from the US Mosque Study 2011." *Activities, Administration and Vitality of the American Mosque*. 2012.

Barber, Benjamin. *Jihad vs McWorld*. New York: Ballantine, 1995.

"Barclays has 'repeatedly let down society,' says Church of England." *The Guardian*. 2013. http://www.theguardian.com

Barlas, Asma. "Reviving Islamic Universalism: East/s, West/s, and Coexistence." *Conference on Contemporary Islamic Synthesis, Alexandria, Egypt*, October 4–5, 2003. http://www.asmabarlas.com

"Belgium Islamists call author, Dutch legislator 'apostates.'" *Jerusalem Post*. 2011. http:// www.jpost.com

Bell, Rob. *Love Wins: A Book about Heaven, Hell, and the Fate of Every Person Who Ever Lived*. New York: HarperOne, 2011.

Bennett, F.S.M. *On Cathedrals in the meantime*. London: The Faith Press, 1928.

Bernstein, Peter L. *Against the Gods: The remarkable story of risk*. New York: John Wiley & Sons, 1996.

"Biblical criticism." *Wikipedia*. 2015. http://en.wikipedia.org

"Bid'ah." *Wikipedia*. 2015. http://en.wikipedia.org

"BNP to Pay Almost $9 Billion in U.S. Sanctions Plea Deal." *Bloomberg*. 2014. http://www. bloomberg.com

Bodman, Whitney S. "The Poetics of Iblis: Narrative Theology in the Qu'ran." *Harvard Theological Studies*. 2011. https://catalyst.library.jhu.edu

"Bolivia: Politicians Reverse Time." *New York Times*. 2014. http://www.nytimes.com

Borg, Marcus. *Evolution of the Word: The New Testament in the Order the Books were written*. New York: HarperOne, 2012.

Boyle, David. "The Tyranny of Numbers." *David Boyle*. 2001.http://www.david-boyle.co.uk

Bradshaw, Tom and Bonnie Nichols. "Reading At Risk: A Survey of Literary Reading in America." *Research Division Report #46, 2004. National Endowment for the Arts.* http://arts.gov/

"Brain Power." *IBM Research*. 2014. http://www.research.ibm.com

"Brands, Islam and the new Muslim Consumer." *Ogilvy Noor*. 2010. http://www.ogilvynoor.com

"Can Iran 'control' its cohabiting couples?" *BBC news*. 2014. http://www.bbc.com

"Canada's Changing Religious Landscape." *Pew Research*. 2013. http://www.pewforum.org

Carvalho, Jean-Paul. "A Theory of the Islamic Revival. Department of Economics." University of Oxford, 2009.

Cashin, David. "Christendom is dead." *Columbia International University*. 2005. http://www.ciu.edu

"Cat Stevens." *Aliraqi*. http://www.aliraqi.org

"Christianity, a brand in crisis." *Icon*. 2012. http://www.iconmarketingstrategy.com

"Christianity: A History. A series of personal perspectives." *Channel 4 Television UK*. 2009. http://www.channel4.com

"Classifieds." *NZ Herald*. 2014. http://www.nzherald.co.nz

Cleary, Thomas. *The Essential Koran: The Heart of Islam—An introductory selection of readings from the Koran*. San Fransisco: HarperSanFransisco, 1994.

Coleman, Isobel. *Paradise beneath her feet: How women are transforming the Middle East*. New York: Random Books, 2010. Kindle edition.

"Compassion in Islam." *Daily Theosophy*. 2015. http://www.dailytheosophy.net

"Concern and Support for Iraqi Christians Forced by Militants to Flee Mosul." *New York Times*. 2014. http://www.nytimes.com

Conway, Brian. "Active Remembering, Selective Forgetting, and Collective Identity: The Case of Bloody Sunday." *Identity: An International Journal of Theory and Research*. 2003, 3 (4).

"Corruption by country." *Transparency International*. 2014. http://www.transparency.org

"Countries Ranked by Military Strength (2014)." *Globalfirepower*. 2014. http://www.globalfirepower.com

"Cousin Marriages." *The Muslim Times*. 2013. http://www.themuslimtimes.org

Darr A., and B. Modell. "The Frequency of consanguineous marriage among British Pakistanis." *Journal of Medical Genetics* 1988, 25, 186–190.

"Dear Mona Eltahawy, You Do Not Represent "Us."" *al-monitor*. 2012. http://www.al-monitor.com

"Denmark's first mosque opens amid controversy." *Al Jazeera*. 2014. http://www.aljazeera.com

"Didn't he say music is forbidden?" *Discover The Muslim World*. 2011. http://discoverthemuslimworld.de

"Disruptive by Design." *Oakley*. 2015. http://rx.oakley.com

"Does the Catholic Church still sell indulgences?" *Catholic Answers.* 2015. http://www. catholic.com

Drucker, Peter. "The Age of Social Transformation." *The Atlantic Monthly.* 1995. http:// www.theatlantic.com

"Early and Forced Marriages in the Islamic Republic of Iran." *UN Human Rights.* 2013. http://www.ohchr.org

"Egypt Christians Killed for Not Paying 'Jizya' Tax." *CBN News.* 2013. http://www.cbn. com

"Egypt's new hijab-clad superheroine." *BBC News.* 2013. http://www.bbc.com

Ellul, Jacques. *Propaganda: the formation of men's attitudes.* New York: Vintage, 1973.

———. *The Humiliation of the Word.* Michigan: Eerdmans, 1985.

———. *The Meaning of the City.* Michigan: Eerdmans, 1970.

———. *The Technological Bluff.* Michigan: Eerdmans, 1986.

———. *The Technological Society.* New York: Vintage, 1964

"Emerging and Developing Economies Much More Optimistic than Rich Countries about the future." *Pew Research.* 2014. http://www.pewglobal.org

Erdoes, Richard. *A.D. 1000: Living on the Brink of Apocalypse.* New York: HarperCollins, 1989.

Erll, Astrid, et al. *Media and Cultural Memory.* New York: Walter de Gruyter, 2008.

"Everybody Draw Mohammed Day." *Wikipedia.* 2015. http://en.wikipedia.org

"Experts Predict: Iran Will Remain Deadly." *Iran Human Rights Documentation Center.* 2014. http://www.iranhrdc.org/

Fabun, Don. *Dimensions of Change.* California: Glencoe Press, 1971.

"Facebook Users in Indonesia Have Highest Mobile Usage Rate Worldwide." *Emarketer.* 2015. http://www.emarketer.com

"Faith beyond Resentment: Fragments Catholic and Gay." *James Alison.* 2001. http:// jamesalison.co.uk

"Faith in Flux." *Pew Research.* 2009. http://www.pewforum.org

"FAQ." *Mosque of Muhajireen.* 2014. http://masjidmuhajireen.weebly.com

Fatah, Tarek. *Chasing a Mirage: The tragic Illusion of an Islamic State.* Ontario: John Wiley, 2008.

"Fatima (A.S.) The Radiant." *Imam Reza.* 2015. http://www.imamreza.net

"Faulted for Avoiding 'Islamic' Labels to Describe Terrorism, White House Cites a Strategic Logic." *New York Times.* 2015. http://www.nytimes.com/

Fielden, Kevin Christopher. "The Church of England in the First World War." M.A. Thesis. East Tennessee State University, 2005.

"Film at 9/11 Museum Sets Off Clash Over Reference to Islam." *New York Times.* 2014. http://www.nytimes.com

"For Wall Street's Math Brains, Miscalculations." *Washington Post.* 2007. http://www. washingtonpost.com/

"Forbidden Love: Taboos and Fear among Muslim Girls." *Spiegel Online International.* 2011. http://www.spiegel.de

Francis, Leslie J., et al. "Understanding Cathedral Visitors: Psychological Type and Individual Differences in Experience and Appreciation." 2008. http://www. ingentaconnect.com

Frankopan, Peter. *The First Crusade: The Call from the East.* London: Vintage Books Ltd, 2013.

Friedman, Richard Elliott. *The Bible with Sources Revealed*. New York: HarperSanFransisco, 2003.

———. *Who Wrote the Bible?* New York: HarperSanFransisco, 1989.

"Friedrich Nietzsche Quotes." *Brainyquote*. http://www.brainyquote.com

"From Egypt's leader, an ambitious call for reform in Islam." *Associated Press*. 2015. http://hosted2.ap.org

"Genetic disorders." *Wikipedia*. 2015. http://en.wikipedia.org

Gleeson-White, Jane. *Double Entry: How the Merchants of Venice Created Modern Finance*. New York: W. W. Norton & Company, 2013.

"Global Acceptance of Homosexuality." *PewResearchCenter*. 2013. Map. http://www.pewglobal.org/

"Global Trends and Security in the Muslim World: Dilemmas for U.S. and Regional Policy 2009." *Brookings Institute*. http://www.brookings.edu

"GNH Index." *Gross National Happiness*. 2014. http://www.grossnationalhappiness.com/

"Google CEO Eric Schmidt: 'People Aren't Ready For The Technology Revolution.'" *Huffington Post*. 2010. http://www.huffingtonpost.com

Graves, Dan. "We did not know where we were." *Christian History Institute*. https://www.christianhistoryinstitute.org

"Hadith: "If not for you I would not have created creation."" *As-Sunnah Foundation of America*. 2012. http://sunnah.org

Hamid, Tawfik. "Understanding Radical Islam." *Tawfik Hamid*. 2011. www.tawfikhamid.com

Hasselmann, Karl Heinz. *Liberia: Geographical Mosaics of the Land and the People*. Monrovia: MICAT, 1979.

Hawkings, Stephen, and Leonard Mlodinov. *The Grand Design*. New York: Bantam, 2011.

"Henry David Thoreau Quotes." *Inspirational quotes*. http://www.inspirationalstories.com

Herzog, Johann Jakob and Philip Schaff. *The New Encyclopedia of Religious Knowledge*. South Carolina: Nabu (reprint) 2012.

"Hijab couture." *The Economist*. 2014. http://www.economist.com

Hjarvard, Stig, "The Mediatization of Religion: A Theory of the Media as an Agent of Religious Change." *Paper presented at 5th International Conference on Media, Religion and Culture*, 2006.

———. "The Mediatization of Society: A Theory of the Media as Agents of Social and Cultural Change." *Nordicom Review* 29, 2008.

"How Luther went viral." *The Economist*. 2011. http://www.economist.com

"How Online Trolling Victims Respond to the Haters." *Emarketer*. 2014. http://www.emarketer.com

"How Sharia Law Punishes Raped Women." *Front Page Magazine*. 2008. http://archive.frontpagemag.com

"Huckabee: America keeps world guessing who it stands with." *Fox News*. 2014. http://www.foxnews.com

Ibn Khaldun. *The Muqaddimah*. 1377. Translated by Franz Rosenthal.

"Ibn Khaldun." *Wikipedia*. 2015. http://en.wikipedia.org/

"If a person is gay and seeks God and has good will, who am I to judge him?" *Catholic Herald*. 2013. http://www.catholicherald.co.uk

"III. How Muslims See Themselves and Islam's Role." *Pew Research*. 2008. http://www.pewglobal.org

BIBLIOGRAPHY

"In Britain, School Report Cites Division Over Islam." *New York Times.* 2014. http://www. nytimes.com

"In the contraception furor, the loud voices of a few threaten revolutionary gains of all U.S. women." *Washington Post.* 2012. http://www.washingtonpost.com

"Inside Facebook's plan to wire the world." *Time Magazine.* 2014. http://time.com

"Intercession in the Hereafter." *Islam Question and Answer.* 2014. http://islamqa.info

"Iran Bars Music in Private Schools, May Impose Moral Code for Universities." *Bloomberg.* 2010. http://www.bloomberg.com

"Iran's Srebrenica: How Ayatollah Khomeini sanctioned the deaths of 20,000 'enemies of the state.'" *The Independent.* 2013. http://www.independent.co.uk

"Iran's supreme leader Ayatollah Ali Khamenei launches Facebook page." *Telegraph.* 2012. http://www.telegraph.co.uk

"Iraqi Christians flee after Isis issue Mosul ultimatum." *BBC News.* 2014. http://www.bbc. com

"Iraqis use Firechat messaging app to overcome net block." *BBC News.* 2014. http://www. bbc.com

"Isis militants 'seize Iraq monastery and expel monks.'" *BBC News.* 2014. http://www.bbc. com

"ISIS, U.S. Media and The Muslim World." *Huffington Post.* 2014. http://www. huffingtonpost.com

Islam, Yusuf. "Floating on a Cloud of Mercy." *Belief Net.* 2006. http://www.beliefnet.com/

"Islam in Spain." *Islamcan.* http://www.islamcan.com

"Islamic smartphone ready for launch." *Arab News.* 2013. http://www.arabnews.com

"Islamic State 'beheads US hostage Steven Sotloff.'" *BBC News.* 2014. http://www.bbc.com

"Islamic view about Homosexuality." *Islamawarenss.* 2015. http://www.islamawareness. net

"Islamic view of the Trinity." *Wikipedia.* 2014. http://en.wikipedia.org

"Israel and Turkey: End of an Alliance." *USC Center on Public Diplomacy.* 2010. http:// uscpublicdiplomacy.org

"It's Not Just Newspapers: Circulation Tanks at Al-Qaeda's Magazine, 'Inspire.'" *The Atlantic.* 2012. http://www.theatlantic.com

Jarvis, Jeff. *What Would Google Do?* New York: HarperCollins, 2009.

Jenkins, Philip. *The Lost History of Christianity: The thousand year golden age of the church in the Middle East, Africa and Asia—and how it died.* New York: HarperOne, 2008.

"Jesus Christ Is a Model of Perfect Love." *Catechesis of the Popes.* 2015. https:// catechesisofthepopes.wordpress.com

"Jesus Son Of God Lyrics." *Metrolyrics.* 2015. http://www.metrolyrics.com

"Join the Movement." *Christian Fashion Week.* http://www.christianfashionweek.com/

Jones, Tony. "Pope row in past, PM tells Muslims." *Australia Broadcasting Corporation.* 2006. http://www.abc.net.au

"Just War Theory." *Wikipedia.* 2015. http://en.wikipedia.org

"Jyllands-Posten Muhammad cartoons controversy." *Wikipedia.* 2015. http://en.wikipedia. org

Kageyama, Peter. *For the Love of Cities.* Florida: Creative Cities Productions, 2011.

"Karyn Williams." *Today's Christian Music.* 2015. http://www.todayschristianmusic.com

Kasule, Omar Hasan. "Islamic Perspectives in the teaching of Probability to Medical Students." *Paper presented at 5th National Conference on Medical Sciences,* 4–5 May 1999.

"Key findings about growing religious hostilities around the world." *Pew Research*. 2014. http://www.pewresearch.org

"Khums: 20%, an Islamic tax." *Slideshare*. 2013. http://www.slideshare.net

Kister, M. J. "The Massacre of the Banu Qurayza: A Re-Examination of a Tradition." *Jerusalem Studies in Arabic and Islam 8* (1986): 61–96.

Korn, Jerry. *The Old West: The Indians*. New York: Time Life, 1973.

Krug, Steve. *Don't make me think revisited: A Common Sense Approach to Web and Mobile Usability*. San Fransisco: New Riders, 2014.

Kuran, Timur. "Economic Underdevelopment in the Middle East: The Historical Role of Culture, Institutions, and Religion." *Proparco*. 2007. http://www.proparco.fr

———. "The Islamic Commercial Crisis. Institutional Roots of Economic Underdevelopment in the Middle East." *The Journal of Economic History* Vol. 63, (2003) 414–446.

———."The Rule of Law in Islamic thought and practice: A historical perspective." *World Justice Forum in Vienna*, 2008. http://www.yale.edu

Kuzelewska, Elzbieta, and Dariusz Kloza. "The challenges of modern democracy and European integration." *European Integration and Democracy Series*, Warsaw, 2012.

Lang, G. H. *The Churches of God*. London: Paternoster Press, 1959.

Lankshear, Colin, et al. "Digital literacy and participation in online social networking spaces." *Academia.edu*. http://www.academia.edu

"Leader urges vigilance against 'American Islam,' Zionism." *Alalam*. 2014. http://en.alalam.ir

LeVine, Mark. *Heavy Metal Islam: Rock, Resistance, and the Struggle for the Soul of Islam*. New York: Crown, 2008.

"Light bedrooms 'link to obesity.'" *BBC News*. 2014. http://www.bbc.com

Lings, Martin. *Muhammad: his life based on the earliest sources*. Vermont: Inner Traditions, 1983.

Longhurst, Christopher E. Theology of a Mosque. *LONAARD*. Volume 2, issue 8, March 2012. https://www.academia.edu

"Lost glory of Ottomans." *The Washington Times*. 2001. http://www.washingtontimes.com

"Loudspeakers in Singapore Mosque." *The Straits Times*. 1936. http://eresources.nlb.gov.sg

Lundberg, Niclas. "Smartphones and (smart) people–How smartphones affect personal interactions." Master thesis, Department of informatics, Umea Universitat, 2013.

Maddison, Angus. "The West and the Rest in the World Economy: 1000–2030 Maddisonian and Malthusian interpretations." *World Economics* Vol. 9, No. 4, October–December 2008.

"Majority of Americans Don't Trust Newspapers and Television News." *US News*. 2013. http://www.usnews.com

"Malala Yousafzai, Nobel Laureate, Is Assailed by Schools Group in Pakistan." *New York Times*. 2014. http://www.nytimes.com/

"Man versus myth: does it matter if the Moses story is based on fact?" *The Guardian*. 2014. http://www.theguardian.com

"Manifest ONE." *Muslimhiphop*. 2015. http://www.muslimhiphop.com

Manji, Irshad. *The Trouble with Islam Today: A Muslim's Call for Reform in Her Faith*. New York: St. Martin's Griffin, 2003.

Maqsood, Ruqaiyyah Waris. *The Role of the Mosque in Britain*. London: The Muslim Parliament of Great Britain, 2005.

Marcuse, Herbert. *One Dimensional Man: Studies in the Ideology of Advanced Industrial Society*. London: Routledge & Kegan Paul, 1964.

"Mark Driscoll Responds to Rob Bell Controversy on Hell." *The Christian Post*. 2011. http://www.christianpost.com

Marland, Alex. "What is a political brand?: Justin Trudeau and the theory of political branding." *Canadian Political Science Association*. 2013. http://www.cpsa-acsp.ca

"Marriage between first cousins." *Islamtoday*. 2015. http://en.islamtoday.net

Martin, Henri-Jean. *The History and Power of Writing*. Chicago: University of Chicago Press, 1995.

"Mary, don't you weep." *Wikipedia*. 2015. http://en.wikipedia.org

Maududi, S. Abdul A'la. *Islamic Law and Its Introduction*. Pakistan: Islamic Publications, 1955.

————. *Jihad in Islam*. Beirut: The Holy Koran Publishing House, 1939.

McDonald, Lee, M. *The Formation of the Christian Biblical Canon*. Massachusetts: Hendrickson, 2002.

McLuhan, Marshall. *Understanding Media*. London: Abacus, 1973.

"Mediatization (media)." *Wikipedia*. 2014. http://en.wikipedia.org

"Meet the CEO." *Microsoft News*. 2014. http://news.microsoft.com

"Memory transference in organ transplant recipients." *Journal of New Approaches to Medicine and Health*, Volume 19, Issue 1, 24th April 2011. http://www.namahjournal.com

"MEMRI." *The Middle East Research Association*. 2014. http://www.memri.org/

Meyers, Robin, R. *Saving Jesus from the Church: How to stop Worshiping Christ and following Jesus*. New York: HarperOne, 2009.

"Mighty, Muslim and Leaping Off the Page: Marvel Comics Introducing a Muslim Girl Superhero." *New York Times*. 2013. http://www.nytimes.com

Mir, Mustansir. "The Qur'?n As Literature." *Renaissance, 2000*, Volume 10, No. 5. http://www.islamic-awareness.org

"Muhammad's wives." *Wikipedia*. 2012. http://en.wikipedia.org

Muir, William. *The Life of Mahomet*. London: Smith, Elder and Co, 1861.

Mulhern, Kathleen, et al. *The Future of Religion: Traditions in Transition*. Colorado:Patheos Press, 2012. Kindle edition.

"Musical notation." *Wikipedia*. 2015. http://en.wikipedia.org

"Muslim Americans: Middle Class and Mostly Mainstream." *PewRsearchCenter*. 2007. http://www.pewresearch.org

"Muslim Publics Share Concerns about Extremist Groups. Much Diminished Support for Suicide Bombing." *Pew Research*. 2013. http://www.pewglobal.org

"Muslim Statistics (Mosques)." *Wikiislam*. 2014. http://wikiislam.net

"Muslim views on Suicide Bombing." *Pew Research*. 2013. http://www.pewglobal.org

"Muslim-Western Tensions Persist." *Pew Global*. 2011. http://www.pewglobal.org

"My Dell hell." *The Guardian*. 2005. http://www.theguardian.com

"My Stealthy Freedom Community." *Facebook*. 2015. https://www.facebook.com

Nadzri, Farah Aida Ahmad. "Zakat and Poverty Alleviation: Roles of Zakat Institutions in Malaysia." *International Journal of Arts and Commerce* Vol. 1, 7 December 2012.

Nafisi, Azar. *Reading Lolita in Tehran: A Memoir in Books*. London: Hodder, 2003.

Nasr, Ghali. "The Reasons behind the delay of adopting the early printing in Muslim countries: Brief thoughts." *Academia.edu*. 2012. http://www.academia.edu

Nasr, Seyyed Hossein. "Islam and Music: The Views of The Views of Ruzbahan Baqli, the Patron Saint of Shiraz." *Studies in Comparative Religion*. Vol. 10, No. 1. (Winter, 1976).

Newman, Jay. *Religion vs. Television: Competitors in Cultural Context*. Santa Barbara: Greenwood, 1996.

Nie, Norman H. and Lutz Erbring. "Internet and Society: A Preliminary Report." *IT&SOCIETY*, Vol. 1, Issue 1, Summer 2002.

Niri, M. B, et. al. "Let's Learn Unlearning: how top Managers Conceive and Implement Knowledge Active Forgetting" *Electronic Journal of Knowledge Management* Volume 7 Issue 5 (pp605—614) 2009. www.ejkm com

"On providing sewage." *Express Tribune*. 2012. http://tribune.com.pk

"On the frontline in Syria: the Danish gangster who turned jihadi." *The Guardian*. 2014. Film. http://www.theguardian.com

"Opinions About September 11." *Pew Research*. 2011. http://www.pewglobal.org

"Orientalism." *Oxford Dictionaries*. http://www.oxforddictionaries.com

"Pakistan police register blasphemy case against 'disco mullah.'" *Reuters*. 2014. http://www.reuters.com

"Paradise Lost for Aussie Surfboard Makers Amid China Imports." *Bloomberg*. 2012. http://www.bloomberg.com

"Past, present and future religious prospects in Vienna 1950–2050." *Wirel*. 2015. http://vidwirel.oeaw.ac.at/

"PC (USA) leaders issue pastoral letter to the church on Assembly's marriage actions." *Presbyterian Church (USA)*. 2014. https://www.pcusa.org

Pentcheva, Bissera V. "Hagia Sophia and Multisensory Aesthetics." *Gesta: International Center of Medieval Art*, Vol 50/2, 2011, 93114.

"Persecution of Homosexuals (Iraq)." *Wikiislam*. 2013. http://wikiislam.net/

Piketty, Thomas. *Capital in the Twenty-First Century*. Massachusetts: Harvard University Press, 2014.

Pirenne, Henri. *Mohammed and Charlemagne*. London: George Allen & Unwin, 1937.

"Plato: Quotes." *Goodreads*. https://www.goodreads.com

"Political Correctness on Islam Can Lead to More Killings." *Arab World News*. 2014. http://www.arab-news.biz

"Poll reveals 40pc of Muslims want sharia law in UK." *The Telegraph*. 2006. http://www.telegraph.co.uk

"Pope row in past, PM tells Muslims." *The Australian News*. 2006. http://www.theaustralian.com.au

"Pope says about two percent of priests are pedophiles: paper." *Reuters*. 2014. http://www.reuters.com

Postman, Neil. *Amusing Ourselves to Death: Public Discourse in the Age of Show Business*. New York: Penguin, 1985.

———. *Technopoly: The Surrender of Culture to Technology*. New York: Vintage, 1993.

"Planet of the phones." *The Economist*. 2015. http://www.economist.com

Price, Bess Nungarrayi. "We need to change our law." *Australian Review of Public Affairs*. 2010. http://www.australianreview.net

"Public Sees Religion's Influence Waning." *Pew Research*. 2014. http://www.pewforum.org

"Quran FAQ." *LGBTQI Muslim Support Group*. 2015. http://www.imaan.org.uk

Qureshi, Eamran and Michael A. Sells, et. al. *The New Crusades: Constructing the Muslim Enemy*. New York: Columbia University Press, 2003.

Qureshi, Nabeel. "Should Christians Read the Qur'an?" *Nabeel Qureshi*. 2013. http://blog. nabeelqureshi.com

"Race Against the Machine." *White House*. 2012. http://www.whitehouse.gov

Rahman, Fazlur. "Islamic Modernism: Its Scope, Method and Alternatives." *International Journal of Middle East Studies*, Vol 1, 1970, 317 333. http://www.researchgate.net

"Raising Questions Within Islam After France Shooting." *New York Times*. 2015. http:// www.nytimes.com

Ramadan, Tariq. *Western Muslims and the Future of Islam*. New York: Oxford University Press, 2004.

Raza, Raheel. *Their Jihad. . . not my Jihad: A Muslim Canadian woman speaks out*. Ontario: Basileia Books, 2005.

Reagan, Ronald. "News Conference." *The Ronald Reagan Presidential Foundation & Library*. http://www.reaganfoundation.org

"Religious Hostilities Reach Six-Year High." *Pew Forum*. 2014. http://www.pewforum.org

"Remains of the day: At the 9/11 Museum, history is preserved in memories and debris." *Time Magazine*. May 26, 2014.

"Remarks by the President to the UN General Assembly." *White House*. 2012. http://www. whitehouse.gov

"Remarks on the words "Pope" and "Patriarch" in the Christian religion and on the word "Kohen" used by the Jews." *Islamic Philosophy Online*. http://www.muslimphilosophy. com

"Rethinking Islamic Reform." *The Revival*. 2010. Film. http://www.therevival.co.uk

Reynolds, Gabriel Said, ed. *The Qur'an in its Historical Context*. New York: Routledge, 2008.

"Richard Dawkins: First he was a 'cultural Anglican,' now he's a 'secular Christian.'" *Christian Today*. 2014. http://www.christiantoday.com

Rifkind, Hugo. "This is a poor way to draw attention to intolerance." *The Times*. 2010. http://www.thetimes.co.uk

"Rift Deepens in Britain Over Claims of School Infiltration Plot by Islamic Extremists." *New York Times*. 2014. http://www.nytimes.com

Rose, Fleming. "Why I Published Those Cartoons." *The Washington Post*. 2006. http:// www.washingtonpost.com

Roszak, Theodore. *The Making of a Counter Culture: Reflections on the Technocratic Society and Its Youthful Opposition*. Los Angeles: University of California Press, 1968.

Rowe, Peter Anthony. "The Roles Of The Cathedral in the modern English Church." PhD diss., University of St. Andrews, 2011.

"Sabri brothers "Embodied light."" *Facebook*. 2013. https://www.facebook.com

"Sacred architecture." *Wikipedia*. 2014. http://en.wikipedia.org

Safi, Omid. *A biography-Memories of Muhammad: Why the Prophet Matters*. New York: HarperOne, 2009.

Saheeh International. *The Qur'an: Arabic Text with Corresponding English Meanings*. Translated by Saheeh International, Riyadh: Abulqasim Publishing House, 1997.

Sahih Bukhari. "Volume 1, Book 6, Number 301. Menstrual Periods." *University of Southern California*. http://www.usc.edu

———. "Volume 4, Book 53, Number 386: One-fifth of Booty to the Cause of Allah." *University of Southern California*. http://www.usc.edu

———. "Volume 9, Book 84, Number 57: Dealing with Apostates." *University of Southern California*. http://www.usc.edu

"Sanitation in ancient Rome." *Wikipedia.* 2014. http://en.wikipedia.org

Santayana, George. "Quotes." *Wikiquote.* http://en.wikiquote.org

"Saudi cleric says chatting online is haram; 'the devil would be present when women talk to men.'" *Discussionist.* 2014. http://www.discussionist.com

Saunders. J. J. *Aspects of the Crusades.* Christchurch: Whitcombe and Tombs, 1968.

Scambray, Terry. "Islam: Victors Vanquishing Victims." *New Oxford Review.* 2014. http://www.newoxfordreview.org

Schmandt-Besserat, Denise. "How Writing Came About." *Jstor,* (1982) 16 https://www.mtholyoke.edu

"Scholars Are Quietly Offering New Theories of the Koran." *New York Times.* 2002. http://www.nytimes.com

Schwartz, Stephen. *The Other Islam: Sufism and the Road to Global Harmony.* London: Doubleday, 2008.

Scott, James, C. "Resistance without Protest and Without Organization: Peasant Opposition to the Islamic Zakat and the Christian Tithe." *Comparative Studies in Society and History,* Vol. 29, pp. 417–452. 1987.

"See brutal anti-ISIS video—State Department releases graphic anti-ISIS video— BREAKING NEWS." *Youtube.* 2014. https://www.youtube.com

"Sergey Brin: "We Want Google To Be The Third Half Of Your Brain."" *Business Insider Australia.* 2010. http://www.businessinsider.com.au

"Speech at Council of Clermont, 1095, according to Fulcher of Chartres." *Fordham University: Medieval sourcebook.* http://www.fordham.edu

Speer, Albert. *Inside the Third Reich.* New York: Simon & Schuster, 1997.

Stark, Rodney. *The Rise of Christianity: How the obscure, marginal Jesus movement became the dominant religious force in the Western world in a few centuries.* San Fransisco: HarperSanFransisco, 1997.

"Statement by the President on ISIL." *White House.* 2014. http://www.whitehouse.gov

Stevenson, Tyler Wigg. *Brand Jesus: Christianity in a Consumerist Age.* New York: Seabury, 2007.

Stone, Norman. *Turkey: A short history.* London: Thames & Hudson, 2010.

Storper, Michael and Anthony J. Venables. "Buzz: face-to-face contact and the urban economy." *Journal of Economic Geography* 4, 2004.

Surowiecki, James. *The Wisdom of Crowds.* New York: Random House, 2005.

"Sydney cafe: Australians say to Muslims "I'll ride with you." *BBC News.* 2014. http://www.bbc.com

"Tag Archive." *The Muslim Council of Britain (MCB).* 2014. http://www.mcb.org.uk

"Taqiyya." *Wikipedia.* 2015. http://en.wikipedia.org

Taylor, A.J.P. *War by Timetable: How the First World War Began.* Endeavour Press. 2013 (Originally printed 1969).

"Teaching Probability Theory." *Sunni Forum.* 2013. http://www.sunniforum.com

"Teen sexual health survey launched." *La Trobe University.* 2014. http://www.latrobe.edu.au

"Terror attack will not divide us but makes us stronger." *Daily Mail.* 2013. http://www.dailymail.co.uk

"Text Illustration Search Results for Ali, quotes." *Sermoncentral.* http://www.sermoncentral.com

"The 2011 Time 100." *Time Magazine.* 2012. http://content.time.com

"The Age of Big Data." *New York Times.* 2012. http://www.nytimes.com

"The Arrangement of Verses and Chapters in the Qur'an." *Islam-info.* 2014. http://www.islam-info.ch

"The Basics of Branding." *Entrepreneur.* 2014. http://www.entrepreneur.com

"The best places to live." *The Economist.* 2014. http://www.economist.com

"The Catholic Encyclopedia." *New Advent.* http://www.newadvent.org

"The Concept of Time in the Qur'an." *Productivemuslim.* 2012. http://productivemuslim.com

"The day Britain lost its soul: How decimalization signaled the demise of a proudly independent nation." *MailOnline.* 2011. http://www.dailymail.co.uk

"The Decline of Mohammedanism as a Political Force." *Sacramento Daily Union.* September 5 1878.

"The Demographics of Radical Islam." *Asia Times.* 2005. http://www.atimes.com

"The Doctrine of the Perfect Man (Al-Insan al-Kamil) and its Significance Today." *ISRA International.* 2015. http://www.israinternational.com

"The dos and don'ts of pitching for business investment." *BBC News.* 2014. http://www.bbc.com

"The Faceless men." *BBC News.* 2014. http://www.bbc.com

"The Future of Islamic Banking." *ATKearney.* 2012. https://www.atkearney.com

"The Future Should Belong To Those Who Can Slander The Prophet of Islam." *The Federalist.* 2015. http://thefederalist.com

"The Great Divide: How Westerners and Muslims View Each Other." *Pew Research.* 2006. http://www.pewglobal.org

The Grubb Institute and Theos. "Spiritual Capital: The Present and Future of English Cathedrals. Findings of a Research Project." *Theos.* http://www.theosthinktank.co.uk/

The Holy Qur'an. Translated by Yusuf Ali. 1938. Hertfordshire: Wordsworth Editions, 2001.

"The insect of the future. . . the Robobee." *New Zealand Herald.* 2013. http://www.nzherald.co.nz

"The Jesus Forgery: Josephus Untangled." *Truth Be Known.* 2004. http://www.truthbeknown.com

"The Mistranslation of 1 Timothy 2:11–12." *Christian feminism.* 2008. http://christianfeminism.wordpress.com

"The Muslim who gave up his life for Mosul's Christians." *Vatican Insider.* 2014. http://vaticaninsider.lastampa.it

"The Myth of Inevitability." *Time Magazine.* 2014. http://time.com

The New American Standard Bible. New York: Collins, 1997.

"The Onrushing Wave." *The Economist.* 2014. http://www.economist.com

"The Perfect Man." *Christ in You Ministries.* 1998. http://www.christinyou.net

"The Prophet's Marriage to Zaynab Bint Jahsh." *Islamtoday.* http://en.islamtoday.net

"The Qur'an: English Meanings and Notes." *Saheeh International.* Riyadh: Al-Muntada Alislami Trust, 2001–2011.

"The Revolution is over." *The Economist.* 2014. http://www.economist.com

"The Salafi exploitation of young British Muslim Women." *Al Spitoon.* 2010. http://www.spittoon.org

"The Secret Web: Where Drugs, Porn and Murder Live Online." *Time Magazine.* 2013. http://time.com

"The Summer's Most Unread Book Is. . ." *Wall Street Journal.* 2014. http://online.wsj.com

"The Tragedy of the Arabs." *The Economist.* 2014. http://www.economist.com

"The Tyrant Sisi Hikes Fuel Prices to Rob the People." *Khilafah.com.* 2014. http://www.khilafah.com

"The World's Muslims: Religion, Politics and Society." *Pew Research.* 2013. http://www.pewforum.org

Thoreau, Henry David. *Walden.* An electronic classics series publication. Pennsylvania State University. Originally published 1854.

Thumma, Scott. "Virtually Religious: Technology and Internet Use in American Congregations." *Hartford Institute for Religious Research.* 2010. http://www.hartfordinstitute.org

"Tim Berners-Lee urges government to stop the snooping bill." *The Guardian.* 2012. http://www.theguardian.com

Toffler, Alvin. *Future Shock.* London: Bodley Head, 1970.

Toynbee, Arnold. *A Study of History, Vol. 2: Abridgement of Volumes VII-X.* Oxford: Oxford University Press, 1987.

"Translation of Sahih Bukhari." *University of Southern California.* http://www.usc.edu/

"Tuam babies: Archbishop Diarmuid Martin calls for inquiry." *BBC News.* 2014. http://www.bbc.com

Turkle, Sherry. *Alone Together: Why we expect more from technology and less from each other.* New York: Basic Books, 2011. Kindle edition.

"Twitter Acquires Vine, Launches iOS App For Sharing 6-Second Videos." *Marketing Land.* 2013. http://marketingland.com

"Twitter unblocks 'blasphemous' tweets in Pakistan." *BBC News.* 2014. http://www.bbc.com

"U.S. Bishops Seek to Match Vatican in Shifting Tone." *New York Times.* 2014. http://www.nytimes.com

"U.S. Embassy Condemns Those Who 'Hurt the Religious Feelings of Muslims'" *CNS News.* 2012. http://cnsnews.com

"U.S. Is Trying to Counter ISIS' Efforts to Lure Alienated Young Muslims." *New York Times.* 2014. http://www.nytimes.com

"Unmosqued." *Unmosqued film.* 2013. Film. http://www.unmosquedfilm.com/

"US financial showdown with Russia is more dangerous than it looks, for both sides." *The Telegraph.* 2014. http://www.telegraph.co.uk

"US Muslims ask John Kerry for protection on Mecca pilgrimage." *The Washington Post.* 2014. http://www.washingtonpost.com

Vasiliu, Dana. "The road to the Cathedral. Representations of sacred space in cartography and religious architecture in Medieval England (12th—13th centuries)." Doctorate, University of Bucharest, 2008.

"Vatican rebuffs Muslim outreach: Quran cited as the main obstacle." *A Common Word.* 2007. http://www.acommonword.com

"Vatican Says Islamic Finance May Help Western Banks in Crisis." *Bloomberg.* 2009. http://www.bloomberg.com

Voth, Joachim. "Debt, Default and Empire: State Capacity and Economic Development in England and Spain in the Early Modern Period." *Tawney Lecture,* 2011. Film. http://www.ehs.org.uk

Wadud, Amina. *Qu'ran and Woman. Rereading the Sacred Text from a women's perspective.* New York: Oxford University Press, 1999.

BIBLIOGRAPHY

Waduge, Shenali D. "Mosques and loudspeakers : A Global Issue." *Sri Express*. 2013. http://sriexpress.com

Warren, Rick. *The Purpose Driven Life*. Michigan: Zondervan, 2002.

Weiss, Holger, et al. *Social Welfare in Muslim Societies in Africa*. Stockholm: Elanders Gotab, 2002.

"What Is the Koran?" *The Atlantic*. 1999. http://www.theatlantic.com

"What makes a city Islamic?" *Islamicity*. 2014. http://www.islamicity.com

"What's in a name? Islamic banking rebrands in attempt to go mainstream." *Reuters*. 2014. http://www.reuters.com

"When does a place become a mosque?" *Islam Question and Answer*. 2014. http://islamqa.info/

"When foreign policy was closer to heaven, and hell." *The Economist*. 2014. http://www.economist.com

"Where in the Holy Quran does it say that Music is forbidden?" *Yahoo*. 2007. https://answers.yahoo.com

"Who We Are." *St Paul's Cathedral*. 2015. http://www.stpauls.co.uk

Wilson, Derek. *The Plantagenets: The Kings that made Britain*. London: Quercus, 2011.

"Working with the media: A guide for muslim groups." *The Cordoba Foundation*. 2009. http://www.thecordobafoundation.com

Yousafzai, Malala. *I am Malala: The Girl Who Stood Up for Education and was Shot by the Taliban*. London: Weidenfeld & Nicolson, 2013.

"Zakat Calculator." *Majlis Ugama Islam Singapura*. 2014. http://www.muis.gov.sg

Zalloom, Abdul- Qadeem. *Funds in The Khilafah State*. London: Al- Khilafah, 1988.

Zarate, Juan C. "Conflict by Other Means: The Coming Financial Wars." *Parameters* 43(4) Winter 2013–14.